Essential Texts for Nonprofit and Public Leadership and Management

The Handbook of Nonprofit Governance, by BoardSource

Strategic Planning for Public and Nonprofit Organizations, 3rd edition, by John M. Bryson

The Effective Public Manager, 4th edition, by Steven Cohen et al.

Handbook of Human Resources Management in Government, 3rd edition, by Stephen E. Condrey (Ed.)

The Responsible Administrator, 5th edition, by Terry L. Cooper

Conducting a Successful Capital Campaign, revised and expanded edition, by Kent E. Dove

The Public Relations Handbook for Nonprofits, by Arthur Feinglass

The Jossey-Bass Handbook of Nonprofit Leadership and Management, 3rd edition, by David O. Renz, Robert D. Herman, & Associates (Eds.)

Benchmarking in the Public and Nonprofit Sectors, 2nd edition, by Patricia Keehley et al.

Museum Marketing and Strategy, 2nd edition, by Neil Kotler et al.

The Ethics Challenge in Public Service, 2nd edition, by Carol W. Lewis et al.

Leading Across Boundaries, by Russell M. Linden

Designing and Planning Programs for Nonprofit and Government Organizations, by Edward J. Pawlak

Measuring Performance in Public and Nonprofit Organizations, by Theodore H. Poister

Human Resources Management for Public and Nonprofit Organizations: A Strategic Approach, 3rd edition, by Joan E. Pynes

Understanding and Managing Public Organizations, 4th edition, by Hal G. Rainey

Designing and Conducting Survey Research, 3rd edition, by Louis M. Rea et al.

Fundraising Principles and Practice, by Adrian Sargeant, Jen Shang, & Associates

Making Critical Decisions, by Roberta M. Snow et al.

Handbook of Practical Program Evaluation, 3rd edition, by Joseph S. Wholey, Harry P. Hatry, & Kathryn E. Newcomer (Eds.)

The Instructor's Guide for the third edition of *Achieving Excellence in Fundraising* includes syllabi and supporting materials for semester-long undergraduate and semester-long graduate versions of the course. The Instructor's Guide is available free online. If you would like to download and print a copy of the guide, please visit:

www.wiley.com/college/tempel

For practitioner audiences, a six-unit continuing education format suitable for self-directed study groups seeking an intensive review of fundraising best practices is available from The Fund Raising School at:

www.philanthropy.iupui.edu/TheFundRaisingSchool

The Center on Philanthropy
AT INDIANA UNIVERSITY
INDIANA UNIVERSITY • PURDUE UNIVERSITY • INDIANAPOLIS

The Center on Philanthropy at Indiana University increases the understanding of philanthropy and improves its practice worldwide. The Center on Philanthropy also fosters relationships in the growing field of philanthropic and nonprofit studies. Through research, teaching, professional development and training, and public service and public affairs initiatives, the Center on Philanthropy is increasing knowledge about philanthropy and helping to develop the next generation of nonprofit professionals, scholars, volunteers, and philanthropists.

Founded in 1987, the Center on Philanthropy pioneered the field of Philanthropic Studies, a unique, interdisciplinary approach to studying philanthropy through the lens of the liberal arts that also incorporates the expertise of professional schools, including public affairs, business, law, education, social work, medicine and nursing. Today, more than sixty philanthropic studies faculty members in seventeen disciplines conduct research and teach philanthropy and nonprofit management.

The Center on Philanthropy at Indiana University conducts basic and applied research and seeks to build a closer relationship between research and professional practice in the nonprofit sector. The idea that university research and information on best practices informs and strengthens the work of nonprofit professionals and that the experience of professional practice informs research is one of the core principles that led to the creation of the Center on Philanthropy and remains a hallmark of its work today.

More than fifteen graduate, undergraduate, and doctoral-level academic program options available through the Center on Philanthropy, including online and executive courses, help students to learn both the "how to" and the "why" of nonprofit management and philanthropy. The Center's programs encourage mid-career students and those new to the field to become reflective professionals who understand and consider the cultural, economic, historical, and social context and implications of the work they do and help them enhance their skills through critiquing, teaching, and reinforcing philanthropy's values.

The Fund Raising School, which Hank Rosso moved to Indiana University in 1987 to form the centerpiece for the founding of the Center on Philanthropy, continues today as the premier international, university, and curriculum-based fundraising education program. Since its founding in 1974, The Fund Raising School has taught successful, professional, ethical fundraising, volunteer board leadership, and nonprofit management practices to more than forty thousand people from more than ten thousand organizations on six continents. Experienced fundraising professionals associated with the Center offer multiple sessions of twelve different regularly scheduled courses at The Fund Raising School in Indianapolis and in cities around the nation as well as sponsored courses in locations around the globe.

The Center on Philanthropy at Indiana University is headquartered at Indiana University-Purdue University Indianapolis (IUPUI) and offers programs on the IUPUI and Indiana University Bloomington campuses.

For more information, please visit the Center on Philanthropy's website: www .philanthropy.iupui.edu.

ACHIEVING EXCELLENCE IN FUNDRAISING

THIRD EDITION

Eugene R. Tempel, Timothy L. Seiler,
and Eva E. Aldrich,
Editors

Foreword by Paulette Maehara

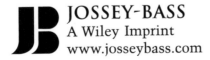

JOSSEY-BASS
A Wiley Imprint
www.josseybass.com

Published by Jossey-Bass
A Wiley Imprint 989 Market Street, San Francisco, CA 94103-1741—www.josseybass.com

Jossey-Bass books and products are available through most bookstores. To contact Jossey-Bass directly
call our Customer Care Department within the U.S. at 800-956-7739, outside the U.S. at 317-572-3986,
or fax 317-572-4002.

Jossey-Bass also publishes its books in a variety of electronic formats. Some content that appears in print
may not be available in electronic books.

Cataloging-in-Publication data on file with the Library of Congress.
    Achieving excellence in fundraising / Eugene R. Tempel, Timothy L. Seiler, and Eva E. Aldrich,
editors; foreword by Paulette Maehara. —3rd ed.
        p.   cm. —(Essential texts for nonprofit and public leadership and management)
    Rev. ed. of: Hank Rosso's Achieving excellence in fund raising / Henry A. Rosso and associates. 2nd ed.
    Includes bibliographical references and index.
        ISBN 978-0-470-55173-8 (hardback)
        1. Fund raising. I. Tempel, Eugene R.   II. Seiler, Timothy L.   III. Aldrich,
Eva E.   IV. Rosso, Henry A. — Hank Rosso's Achieving excellence in fund raising.
    HG177.R67   2010
    658.15'224—dc22
                                                                              2010037986

Printed in the United States of America
THIRD EDITION
HB Printing   10 9 8 7 6 5 4

CONTENTS

LIST OF TABLES, FIGURES, AND EXHIBITS

Tables

Figures

Exhibits

To Mary, Karen, and Mike

FOREWORD

It should be no surprise to anyone that a third edition of *Achieving Excellence in Fundraising* is being published. Times change, the fundraising environment changes, certainly the economy and technology change—but in the end, fundraising success always comes back to the basics, the underpinnings of our profession. And no one was able to convey the essence of fundraising—not just the hows but the whos and whys—quite like Hank Rosso.

Fundraising would look very different today if not for the seminal work of Hank and the many of his followers who are carrying on the traditions today. The impact on the profession is unmatched. Through his teaching, his writing, and his leadership—as well as through the founding of The Fund Raising School—Hank nurtured the professional journeys of thousands of fundraisers. The current professionals who contributed to this volume perpetuate what we've learned—not only how to fundraise but how to inspire our donors, our organizations, and even ourselves. An entire new generation of fundraisers continues to learn through The Fund Raising School that fundraising is more than a job. It's a calling that doesn't just support society but changes society—and for the better.

I imagine Hank would be very pleased with this edition and the authors who have contributed to it, led by Gene Tempel, Tim Seiler, and Eva Aldrich, and supported by the Center on Philanthropy at Indiana University. They have kept the spirit and substance of his teachings while updating the volume, keeping it fresh and relevant to today's changing environment while focusing on the timelessness of the lessons.

If you are new to fundraising or are reading *Achieving Excellence in Fundraising* for the first time, I envy you—it's an extraordinary read that can truly change how you feel about fundraising. If you have read an earlier edition or have been in the profession a while, I encourage you to dive back in. The philosophy of Hank Rosso is truly inspiring, and the authors in this volume make his teachings relevant for today.

Paulette Maehara
President and CEO
Association of Fundraising Professionals

PREFACE

When Henry A. "Hank" Rosso edited the first edition of *Achieving Excellence in Fundraising*, he had achieved a lifelong dream of having fundraising become a serious subject at colleges and universities. He saw a profession more and more dependent on research, education, and training as it developed. In the Foreword to that first edition, Bob Payton predicted that the book would become a classic. This third edition is evidence that this came to pass. It is also a reflection of how farsighted Hank was in his work. Many of the principles that he espoused have been confirmed or modified by research. The longevity of The Fund Raising School, the continuing validity of many of the principles taught there originally, and the modification of others through time by The Fund Raising School are further evidence.

When the Center on Philanthropy at Indiana University supported the publication of the second edition of *Achieving Excellence in Fundraising* a decade ago, it did so out of a commitment to continue the principles and philosophy that Hank Rosso espoused. That edition's Preface mentioned the number of individuals who considered themselves disciples of Rosso. A decade later, there are still, of course, disciples of Rosso. But increasingly there are disciples of The Fund Raising School and the Center on Philanthropy. There are individuals who consider the enhanced work of The Fund Raising School, the academic curricula of the Center on Philanthropy, and the research produced by the Center on Philanthropy as hallmarks of the way they approach their professional development. At the Center on Philanthropy we say that the first task of a nonprofit organization is to survive its founder. The Fund Raising School has proudly done so. We point out that The Fund Raising School has now existed for a longer period of time (twenty-two years) as an integral part of the Center on Philanthropy than it existed (thirteen years) as a separate independent organization. Hank and his wife Dottie founded the School in 1974. Hank served as director until The Fund Raising School became a founding part of the Center on Philanthropy in 1987. He served as an advisor and mentor to all of us until his death in 1999. The current director, Tim Seiler, has been director of The Fund Raising School since 1994, a tenure longer than the original founder's.

This third edition reflects a commitment to the original principles and philosophy that are the hallmark of *Achieving Excellence in Fundraising*. It also reflects the changing environment for philanthropy and fundraising, new developments in the way fundraising work is done, and the increasing understanding and knowledge about philanthropy and fundraising developed by the Center on Philanthropy, other colleges and universities, and research organizations across the United States and around the world.

The authors in this volume have special connections to The Fund Raising School, the Center on Philanthropy, or the Indiana University Foundation where many of the principles and philosophies are put into practice. Some are academics who study the field, some are practitioners who practice the principles espoused in the book, and others are "pracademics" who help bridge the gap between academic work and practice. All are committed to some of the basic philosophies once espoused by Hank and now continued through the work of The Fund Raising School and substantiated, revised, or modified by research at the Center on Philanthropy.

Chiefly, those philosophies hold that the work of philanthropy is about the work of public purposes, and this work rests on the power of the case for support. It reflects the interests and desires of donors to accomplish something beyond themselves. It helps substitute pride for apology in doing fundraising work.

It also focuses on respect for the process of fundraising, respect for the donor, and respect for the individuals being served by the nonprofit organizations we represent. It focuses on the importance of language in conveying that respect. We do not "get" gifts. Hank taught us that fundraising is the work of teaching people the joy of giving. Research substantiates this concept. Never has that been more true than today, with the sophistication of donors, the interests of donors in following their gifts even at smaller levels, and the new generation of philanthropists committed to making things happen. We don't make "the ask," which implies a confrontational situation between volunteers and fundraisers and the donors from whom they seek gifts. We solicit gifts by inviting donors to join us in supporting worthy causes. Although demographics become important to us, especially as we try to understand donors and engage them with organizations based on their own interests, we don't "target" donors, and we don't "move" them toward our desired ends.

Organization of This Book

In this third edition, the editors have endeavored to make the sections of the book more closely correspond with fundraising knowledge domain areas defined by CFRE International while maintaining some of the familiar structure of the prior editions. We hope that this will make the third edition a user-friendly resource for owners of prior editions, those who are using the current volume as a key resource for preparing for the CFRE exam, and instructors of fundraising using this book as a textbook.

The forty-one chapters of this new edition are grouped into eight parts. Part One focuses on fundraising as the art of relationship building and includes some classic chapters—on planning, constituency identification, and case development—that continue to withstand the test of time.

Part Two is about the elements of a total institutional development plan, including the annual fund, major gifts, capital campaigns, and planned giving.

Part Three focuses on contemporary donor dynamics. Chapters in this section not only examine the current context for philanthropy but also focus on understanding donors and their motivations. The role of prospect research is highlighted as one way of learning to understand better the diverse motivations of donor segments such as high-net-worth individuals, women, communities of color, and the different generations.

Part Four concentrates on the art of solicitation and stewardship, examining tactical considerations for effectiveness in utilizing fundraising vehicles such as direct mail, e-mail and social media, special events, telephone solicitation, and personal solicitation. A chapter is also devoted to providing appropriate stewardship to maintain and grow the donor relationship.

Part Five discusses the volunteer role in fundraising, from trustees who provide philanthropic leadership to the volunteers who are there and willing to help, whatever the task. A special feature in this section is a chapter on using social media to engage and inspire volunteers.

Part Six focuses on leadership and management in fundraising and includes such vital topics as the mechanics of building a well-run fundraising program and reflections on the role of the fundraiser as an institutional leader.

Part Seven focuses on ethics and accountability in fundraising, with chapters reflecting fundraisers' needs to honor both the spirit of the law, through adherence to ethical principles, and the letter of the law, through understanding and abiding by legal and regulatory imperatives.

Part Eight concludes the volume with a focus on fundraising as a profession, including a discussion of the importance of credentialing, international perspectives on fundraising, and resources available to fundraisers for learning more about fundraising practice and the profession.

Reflections on the Third Edition

This third edition of *Achieving Excellence in Fundraising* has integrity as a holistic work. Like the two volumes before it, it flows systematically from beginning to end. It is structured to introduce the aspects of a total development program, the internal and external environment for operating the program, and the professional management of the program integrated with a nonprofit organization's other management functions. But each chapter also stands on its own. Those interested in particular areas of fundraising can find access to information related to those areas through the Contents.

This book provides a foundation for practitioners, volunteers, and others involved in the fundraising process. It offers a broad understanding of the process to all who take part in fundraising, as well as a rationale for various initiatives for chief financial officers, program officers, chief executives, and other officers who make organizational decisions related to fundraising.

The first and second editions of *Achieving Excellence in Fundraising* have been used by a range of individuals from college professors teaching courses on development and fundraising to novices in the field looking for a solid foundation, to senior professionals wanting to review a particular aspect of the fundraising programs they manage. Portions of the text, especially Part Six, will be useful to senior professionals who are interested in effective management of the entire development program and planning organizational renewal activities. Volunteers and board members will find Part Five of particular interest. Institutional colleagues will find Chapter Thirty-One on budgeting particularly helpful in understanding how the fundraising process works. Part Four on the art of solicitation will be especially useful for rising development officers.

When we edited the second edition, we recognized the work of our colleague Kent Dove who is recently retired from the Indiana University Foundation. He has published a series of books on fundraising with Jossey-Bass, known as the Dove Series. Tim Seiler had also just initiated a series of workbooks for Jossey-Bass to help practitioners apply principles of The Fund Raising School to their organizations. More recently, our colleague on the philanthropic studies faculty at the Center on Philanthropy, Andrea Walton, along with Marybeth Gasman of the University of Pennsylvania, published a book on fundraising entitled *Philanthropy, Volunteerism, and Fundraising in Higher Education*, which won the 2009 John Grenzebach Award for Outstanding Published Scholarship from the Council for Advancement and Support of Education (CASE). All these works and others can be woven together with *Achieving Excellence in Fundraising* to help round out the professional knowledge needed in today's sophisticated fundraising environment.

We have great hope that the next decade will see continued interest in fundraising and better understanding of practice and donor behavior, and will help contribute to more effective and more efficient fundraising organizations in support of continued development of philanthropy in the United States and around the world.

ACKNOWLEDGMENTS

The third edition of *Achieving Excellence in Fundraising* would not have been possible without the first two volumes. Deep acknowledgment for this edition goes to Hank Rosso, who founded The Fund Raising School and in 1991 accepted the challenge to share his knowledge and experience with a larger audience by editing the first edition. Acknowledgment goes also to The Fund Raising School itself, which has grown and developed from the day when Hank Rosso transferred it to Indiana University to establish the Center on Philanthropy in 1987 to the current time. We, the editors, also owe deep gratitude to the Center on Philanthropy itself for the role it played in sponsoring the second edition and for the role it has played in the development of philanthropic studies as a field, the research dedicated to philanthropy and fundraising through the years, and the contributions it has made to the development of The Fund Raising School, the Women's Philanthropy Institute, the Lake Institute for Faith and Giving, and baccalaureate, master's, and doctoral level programs at Indiana University. These assets all helped to shape the third edition of *Achieving Excellence in Fundraising*.

Next, we thank Hank's widow, Dottie Rosso, one of the founders of The Fund Raising School, for her continued engagement with The Fund Raising School and the Center on Philanthropy. Her encouragement for the continuation of Hank's legacy and her affirmation of the programs The Fund Raising School and the Center on Philanthropy have developed to fulfill Hank's vision for the study of philanthropy and fundraising, have been a source of support to all.

Thanks to the authors who have not only contributed to this book but have also contributed to the ongoing development of knowledge and training through The Fund Raising School and to the application of principles developed through research at the Center on Philanthropy, and who have served us as colleagues throughout the editing process.

The Center on Philanthropy and Jossey-Bass have taken on many projects together. This is as true now as it was when the second edition was published. We owe deep gratitude to Jossey-Bass for continuing to publish books that help strengthen the nonprofit sector and especially fundraising and philanthropy. Special thanks to our editor at Jossey-Bass, Allison Brunner, who encouraged the development of this third edition.

Each of us owes a special word of thanks to our support staff and colleagues who supported our involvement in this project and picked up the slack for us from time to time. We also wish to express our deep appreciation to our colleagues at the Indiana University Foundation and the Center on Philanthropy for the professional inspiration they provide. To our families go our heartfelt thankfulness for their unending understanding, support, and sacrifice throughout the duration of this project.

Finally, special thanks to Sarah Nathan, a Ph.D. student at the Center on Philanthropy at Indiana University and a graduate assistant at the Indiana University Foundation. She did yeoman's work on the book. Not only did she coordinate the solicitation of chapters and the application of uniform standards with all the authors, but she also contributed research to a number of chapters, edited text from beginning to end, and worked with us on an individual basis as we fulfilled our editing responsibilities. We owe Sarah a debt of gratitude for her work on this edition, and we owe the Indiana University Foundation thanks for its continued support of Sarah as a graduate assistant. We hope that this work has contributed in some small way to Sarah's foundation as a scholar in the field of philanthropic studies. We look forward to great things from Sarah as she finishes her Ph.D. and becomes a faculty member and researcher in the field.

THE EDITORS

Eugene R. Tempel is president of Indiana University Foundation and professor of philanthropic studies and of higher education at Indiana University. He is a nationally recognized expert in the study and practice of philanthropy and nonprofit management, and his career includes more than two decades in higher education administration, fundraising, and teaching. For eleven of those years, he directed the Center on Philanthropy at Indiana University, a leading national resource for nonprofit education, research, training, and public service programs. Dr. Tempel is a member of several boards, past chair of the Indiana Commission on Community Service and Volunteerism, the first elected president of the Nonprofit Academic Centers Council, and a member of Independent Sector's Expert Advisory Panel that created national guidelines for nonprofit governance and ethical behavior. He is the author and coauthor of several works in the field and has won numerous awards. He earned his bachelor's degree from St. Benedict College and his M.A. and Ed.D. from Indiana University. He also holds the Certified Fund Raising Executive (CFRE) professional certification from CFRE International.

Timothy L. Seiler is director of The Fund Raising School at the Center on Philanthropy at Indiana University and is also assistant professor of philanthropic studies at Indiana University. Dr. Seiler, an alumnus of The Fund Raising School, has been a faculty member since 1986 and its director since 1994. He was also involved with the establishment of the Center on Philanthropy through service on the Policy Advisory Committee. He is an author and editor of fundraising publications and was editor-in-chief of the *Excellence in Fund Raising Workbook Series* and author of the workbook *Developing Your Case for Support*. Dr. Seiler serves the nonprofit sector not only as a fundraiser, author, and teacher, but also as a board member and campaign committee member for several nonprofits and serves as a mentor to young professional fundraisers. He earned a B.A. degree in English from Saint Joseph's College, Rensselaer, Indiana, and M.A. and Ph.D. degrees in English from Indiana University. He also holds the Certified Fund Raising Executive (CFRE) professional certification from CFRE International.

Eva E. Aldrich is associate director of The Fund Raising School at the Center on Philanthropy at Indiana University, where her work centers on the development and revision of The Fund Raising School's curriculum. Prior to joining the Center on Philanthropy, she was a member of Johnson, Grossnickle and Associates, an institutional strategy and advancement consulting firm. Ms. Aldrich serves the fundraising profession as a member of CFRE International's Exam Committee and was a member of CFRE International's 2009 Job Analysis Task Force. In addition, she has taught fundraising professionals around the globe, conducting courses in Austria, China, India, and New Zealand. She earned her B.A. *summa cum laude* from Manchester College, North Manchester, Indiana, and her M.A. from Indiana University; she is currently pursuing a Ph.D. in philanthropic studies from Indiana University. She also holds the Certified Fund Raising Executive (CFRE) professional certification from CFRE International.

THE AUTHORS

Sandra Bate, executive director of marketing at the Indiana University Foundation, leads the initiatives in market research, creative services, and interactive media that support fundraising for Indiana University. She is a former board chairperson of the University and College Designers Association and a recipient of the Steuben Award for excellence in teaching from the Council for the Advancement and Support of Education. Bate is the former director of marketing for the Indiana University School of Public and Environmental Affairs and led creative services at Indiana University–Purdue University Indianapolis. She earned her bachelor's degree in history at Bethel College, Indiana, and did her graduate work at Michigan State University.

Melissa S. Brown, associate director of research at the Center on Philanthropy at Indiana University, manages research projects and writing of *Giving USA*, published by Giving USA Foundation. Ms. Brown came to the Center in 1991 and moved to the research department in 2001. She teaches about writing grant proposals for The Fund Raising School and at Indiana University-Purdue University Indianapolis. Ms. Brown has raised funds for higher education, health care, social services, and the arts. She holds a bachelor's degree from Reed College in Portland, Oregon, and a master of governmental administration degree from the University of Pennsylvania in Philadelphia.

Dwight F. Burlingame is associate executive director and director of academic programs and chair of the philanthropic studies faculty at the Center on Philanthropy at Indiana University. He is the co-founder of the MISP Program at the University of Bologna and has taught in the program since its inception in 2001. He currently is coeditor of *Nonprofit and Voluntary Sector Quarterly (NVSQ)*, the official journal of the Association for Research on Nonprofit Organizations and Voluntary Action (ARNOVA). He also is coeditor of the Philanthropic and Nonprofit Studies book series for the Indiana University Press. Dr. Burlingame has authored more than sixty books and articles on philanthropy, libraries, nonprofits, and fundraising. The book he coauthored and edited with Dennis Young, *Corporate Philanthropy at the Crossroads*, won the Association of Fundraising Professionals (AFP) Best Research book prize. He is the editor of *Philanthropy in America: A Comprehensive Historical Encyclopaedia* published in three volumes. He earned a B.A. from Moorhead State University, an M.S. from the University of Illinois at Champaign-Urbana, a post-master's degree from the University of Minnesota, and a Ph.D. from Florida State University.

Roberta L. Donahue has over twenty years in fundraising. Currently, Ms. Donahue is director of individual giving and state foundation relations for the National Future Farmers of America (FFA) Foundation and serves on the faculty of The Fund Raising School of the Center on Philanthropy at Indiana University. A past president of the Indiana chapter of AFP, Ms. Donahue is a Certified Fund Raising Executive (CFRE) and was selected as Outstanding Indiana Fund Raising Executive of the Year in 2005. She obtained a B.A. from Marian College, Indianapolis, and an M.B.A. from the State University of New York at Binghamton.

Elizabeth A. Elkas is associate dean for development at the Indiana University School of Medicine. Over the last two decades she has helped grow a three-person shop focused on annual gifts into a comprehensive fundraising program of over two dozen fundraising professionals now planning its third capital campaign. Ms. Elkas has served on the faculty of The Fund Raising School since 1991 and has presented on major gift fundraising to the Association for Healthcare Philanthropy (AHP), Council for Advancement and Support of Education (CASE), and Association of American Medical Colleges (AAMC). She holds a B.A. in English and fine arts from Bucknell University and an M.F.A. from Indiana University.

William G. Enright is executive director of the Lake Institute on Faith and Giving at the Center on Philanthropy at Indiana University, and former senior pastor of the Second Presbyterian Church, Indianapolis. He is a graduate of Wheaton College, Fuller Theological Seminary, and McCormick Theological Seminary. His Ph.D. is from the University of Edinburgh, Scotland. Dr. Enright has had a long career in service to the nonprofit sector and is currently a director of the Lilly Endowment Inc., a trustee of Hanover College, and member of the Board of Trustees of the Foundation of the YMCA of Greater Indianapolis. He has authored several books, the latest being *Channel Marker*.

Tyrone M. Freeman is associate director of public service and The Fund Raising School at The Center on Philanthropy at Indiana University, where he teaches continuing education courses in fundraising. He has held fundraising leadership positions in community development, youth and family social service, and higher education organizations. Mr. Freeman is a doctoral candidate in philanthropic studies at Indiana University and has taught in the graduate programs for the School of Continuing Studies, the School of Education, and the School of Public & Environmental Affairs. His expertise is in the history of philanthropy, fundraising and higher education, and African American philanthropy.

Meg Gammage-Tucker is a senior consultant at Johnson, Grossnickle and Associates, a consulting firm specializing in institutional advancement, and a faculty member at The Fund Raising School at the Center on Philanthropy at Indiana University. As a nonprofit professional for twenty-seven years, she has held lead positions in institutional advancement, marketing, and fiscal affairs with a variety of education, cultural, and international conservation organizations. Ms. Gammage-Tucker earned a doctorate in political science/public administration, an M.A. in museum science, an M.P.A. from Texas Tech University, and a B.S. in sociology from Illinois State University. She holds the CFRE professional certification from CFRE International.

Kim Gattle is director of institutional advancement and fundraising for the Center on Philanthropy at Indiana University. Introduced to fundraising in a 1983 class from The Fund Raising School taught by Hank and Dottie Rosso, she is now a faculty member of The Fund Raising School. She served as executive associate director of major and planned gifts for the Indiana University School of Medicine, director of development for Walther Cancer Institute, and executive director of New Hope Development Corporation. Gattle holds her M.A. in philanthropic studies from the Center on Philanthropy and a B.S. from the University of Florida; she has studied at the University of Guanajuato in Mexico and the Instituto de Lengua Española in Costa Rica.

James M. Greenfield has served since 1962 as a national fundraising executive at three universities and five hospitals. He retired from Hoag Memorial Presbyterian Hospital in February 2001 after fourteen years as senior vice president, resource development and as executive director, Hoag Hospital Foundation, where more than $120 million was raised during his tenure. He is the author and editor of ten books and more than forty articles and chapters on fundraising management. Most recently, he is the author of *Fundraising Responsibilities of Nonprofit Boards* (2009), part of the BoardSource Governance Series. He holds the ACFRE and FAHP designations.

Ted R. Grossnickle cofounded the philanthropic consulting firm Johnson, Grossnickle and Associates in 1994. Previously, Mr. Grossnickle spent ten years as vice president of development and public affairs at Franklin College and served as the College's acting president in 1993. He has held positions at Northern Illinois University, Wabash College, and Procter & Gamble. Mr. Grossnickle sits on the board of trustees at Wabash College and Garrett-Evangelical Theological Seminary, is the vice chair of the board of visitors for the Center on Philanthropy at Indiana University, and is chairman of Achieve, LLC. He holds degrees from Wabash College and Northern Illinois University.

Sharilyn Hale, M.A., CFRE, is a passionate fundraiser currently leading Canada's largest campaign in support of affordable and supportive housing for the YWCA. An enthusiastic mentor with a heart for women's philanthropy, community development, and the global practice of fundraising, Ms. Hale is vice chair of CFRE International, the only international credential for fundraising professionals, and chaired the 2009 Job Analysis Task Force. She is an author with undergraduate degrees in theology and psychology, and an M.A. in philanthropy and development. She is also a member of the Association of Fundraising Professionals in Toronto and an active volunteer within her local fundraising community.

Marti K. S. Heil joined the Indiana University Foundation in 2009 as senior vice president for development. She directs the $1.1 billion *Matching the Promise: The Campaign for IU Bloomington* and leads the foundation's work in principal and major gifts, planned giving, annual giving, development services, and marketing. Heil formerly served Michigan State University for thirty years as associate vice president and COO for development, where she led two comprehensive campaigns and directed fundraising programs for two colleges. She received Michigan State University's university-wide Outstanding Supervisor Award for developing a collaborative and positive work environment. A graduate of Michigan State University, Heil has also served as faculty for the Big Ten Fundraisers Institute.

James M. Hodge, vice chair, Department of Development, Mayo Clinic, has more than thirty years' experience in major and principal gift fundraising. Mr. Hodge serves on the faculty of The Fund Raising School and is a frequent national speaker and workshop presenter on donor-centric, values-based, inquiry-driven philanthropy. He holds both bachelor's and master's degrees from Bowling Green State University, where he was director of development prior to joining the Mayo Clinic. He has received numerous awards for service and team excellence at Mayo and is a past recipient of the President's Award from AFP Southeastern Minnesota.

Frances Huehls is associate librarian for the Joseph and Matthew Payton Philanthropic Studies Library at Indiana University–Purdue University Indianapolis. She holds master's degrees in philanthropic studies and library and information science, as well as a Ph.D. in higher education from Indiana University. Dr. Huehls writes a quarterly literature review for the *International Journal of Educational Advancement* and is editor of *Philanthropic Studies Index* and *PRO: Philanthropy Resources Online*.

Kim Klein is an internationally known fundraising trainer and has worked in all aspects of fundraising as staff, volunteer, board member, and consultant. Ms. Klein is the author of five books including her most recent, *Reliable Fundraising in Unreliable Times*. Her classic text, *Fundraising for Social Change*, now in its fifth edition, is widely used in the field and in university degree programs. As a speaker, she has provided training and consultation in all fifty United States, five Canadian provinces, and twenty-one other countries. She has been on the Faculty of The Fund Raising School since 1981.

Xiaonan Kou is a doctoral candidate in philanthropic studies at the Center on Philanthropy at Indiana University. She is passionate about improving rural education in China and about promoting cultural and educational exchanges across countries. She cofounded Tianjin United Education Assistance Foundation in 2005. As one of the first nongovernmental, nonprofit public fundraising foundations in China, the Foundation is dedicated to helping disadvantaged students receive a better education. She received her master's degree in public policy and certificate in nonprofit studies from the Institute for Policy Studies at Johns Hopkins University.

Jeffrey A. Lindauer is associate vice president for development at the Indiana University Foundation. In this position he oversees the development service areas that provide support for fundraising throughout the University's eight-campus system. He also serves as adjunct faculty at Indiana University and is a frequent presenter at national conferences on a variety of topics. In addition to being coauthor of *Conducting a Successful Annual Giving Program*, published by Jossey-Bass, he maintains the *Getting Giving* blog at www.gettinggiving.com.

Jay B. Love is the CEO of Social Solutions. His prior positions include senior vice president of the arts and cultural division of Blackbaud, president and CEO of Master Software Corporation, and president and CEO of eTapestry. During his twenty-five years in the sector, Mr. Love has been responsible for the implementation of over twelve thousand nonprofit database systems all over the world. He currently serves on the board of the Indiana-based Gleaners Food Bank and the Center on Philanthropy at Indiana University. A member of AFP, he serves as chairman of the Industry Partners Council and a member of the ethics committee. He is a graduate of Butler University with a B.S. in business administration.

Vicky Martin has been involved in development research for over twenty years and is currently senior analyst, major gifts at the Indiana University Foundation. At the Foundation, Ms. Martin has been in several roles including director of research management and information services. As a fundraiser, she supports the Indiana University School of Library and Information Science, the Indiana University Libraries, and the Indiana University School of Continuing Studies. Ms. Martin has been active with Association of Professional Researchers for Advancement (APRA) International and APRA-Indiana for many years and in a variety of leadership roles. She is coauthor, along with Kent Dove, Kathy Wilson, and others, of *Conducting a Successful Development Services Program*, published by Jossey-Bass.

Margaret M. Maxwell has been working with nonprofit organizations and boards throughout the country in the areas of strategic planning, governance, marketing and fund development planning since 2000. She has been a faculty member of The Fund Raising School since 1990. Prior to her work as a consultant, Ms. Maxwell was vice president for The Children's Museum of Indianapolis, one of the nation's premier cultural institutions. Her museum experience includes leadership roles in fundraising, marketing, strategic planning, and earned income programs. She received both a B.A. in journalism and an M.B.A. in marketing from Indiana University.

Debra J. Mesch is director of the Women's Philanthropy Institute at the Center on Philanthropy at Indiana University. She is also professor of public and nonprofit management in the School of Public and Environmental Affairs at Indiana University-Purdue University Indianapolis as well as professor of philanthropic studies at Indiana University. Dr. Mesch received both her M.B.A. and Ph.D. in organizational behavior/human resource management from Indiana University Kelley School of Business. Debra's primary focus at the Women's Philanthropy Institute is on expanding research on women's philanthropy.

Sarah K. Nathan is a Ph.D. candidate in philanthropic studies at the Center on Philanthropy at Indiana University. Her research focuses on fraternal groups and service clubs, particularly women's participation after 1987. She is a passionate and active member of Lions Clubs International and a graduate of Concordia College in Moorhead, Minnesota.

Una Okonkwo Osili is director of research at the Center on Philanthropy at Indiana University. Dr. Osili is an associate professor of economics and philanthropic studies at Indiana University-Purdue University Indianapolis. Dr. Osili's research on private transfers in developing and developed countries has been published in several outstanding academic journals. She has served as a consultant for the United Nations Development Program, the United Economics Commission for Africa, and the Federal Reserve Bank of Chicago. Dr. Osili received her bachelor's degree in economics with honors from Harvard University and her M.A. and Ph.D. in economics from Northwestern University.

Andrea Pactor is associate director of the Women's Philanthropy Institute, responsible for operations, curriculum development, and educational services. She has been connected to the Center on Philanthropy at Indiana University since 2001, first as a graduate student in the M.A. program. She joined the staff full-time in 2005 to manage the symposium on women and philanthropy. Andrea became assistant director in 2008 and associate director in 2009. Andrea has a B.A. in history and literature from The American University in Washington, D.C.; an M.A. in museum practice from the University of Michigan; and an M.A. in philanthropic studies from Indiana University.

Gwendolyn Perry Davis is senior director of development at the University of Chicago Booth School of Business, managing a twenty-five-person team to support the number one ranked graduate business school in the United States. She has served as a board member of a number of nonprofit organizations, including as former president of the Indiana chapter of AFP. She is currently a faculty member of The Fund Raising School at the Center on Philanthropy at Indiana University.

Robert Pierpont is a faculty member of The Fund Raising School at the Center on Philanthropy at Indiana University. A 1970 graduate of Harvard's Institute for Educational Management, Mr. Pierpont became Widener University's first development officer in 1958. Subsequently, he joined Brakeley/JPJ and was vice president for development at New York's Mount Sinai Medical Center. In 1986 he founded Pierpont & Wilkerson. Mr. Pierpont served AFP as the first chair of the certification board and a member of the ethics committee. He has been awarded the AFP Founders Medal and the Henry A. Rosso Award for lifetime achievement in ethical fundraising.

Philip M. Purcell is vice president for planned giving and endowment stewardship, Ball State University Foundation (Muncie, Indiana). He received his B.A. degree from Wabash College and his J.D. and M.P.A. degrees from Indiana University. Mr. Purcell currently serves as a volunteer on the Tax Exempt Organizations Advisory Council for the Internal Revenue Service. He teaches law and philanthropy, nonprofit organization law, and planned giving as adjunct faculty for the Indiana University School of Law, the Center on Philanthropy at Indiana University, and The Fund Raising School. He has served on the board of directors for the Partnership for Philanthropic Planning and the Indiana chapter of AFP.

Jonathan D. Purvis currently serves as the senior director for capital projects at Washington University in St. Louis, Missouri. In that role he leads the team responsible for planning and implementing university-wide capital project fundraising efforts. Previously, as the executive director for the Office of Special Gifts and Annual Giving Programs at the Indiana University Foundation, he oversaw Indiana University's centralized annual giving efforts, special gift societies, and student foundation program. He earned his B.A. from Indiana University in 1998 and his M.P.A. from Indiana University in 2007.

Dean Regenovich is the assistant dean for advancement at the Indiana University Maurer School of Law in Bloomington, Indiana. He has over twenty years of development experience in major gift and planned gift fundraising, and he previously served as the director of planned giving for the Indiana University Foundation. Mr. Regenovich is a faculty member at The Fund Raising School at the Center on Philanthropy at Indiana University, where he teaches planned giving and major gift fundraising. He has an L.L.M. in taxation from the Georgetown University School of Law, a J.D. from the John Marshall Law School, and a B.S. in accounting from Indiana University-Bloomington.

Patrick M. Rooney is executive director of the Center on Philanthropy at Indiana University. A nationally recognized expert and speaker on philanthropy, he is frequently quoted by national news media and has served on advisory committees for the Corporation for National and Community Service, AFP, and Independent Sector. As the Center's director of research, he built it into one of the nation's premier philanthropy research organizations. The Center researches and writes *Giving USA* for Giving USA Foundation and has conducted research for organizations such as Bank of America, American Express, Google, Aspen Institute, Gates Foundation, and United Way Worldwide. Patrick has three degrees from the University of Notre Dame (B.A., M.A., Ph.D.), all in economics, and is a professor of economics and philanthropic studies at Indiana University–Purdue University Indianapolis.

Jeff Stanger teaches online fundraising and social media for The Fund Raising School at the Center on Philanthropy at Indiana University. He is the development director for the Salvation Army of Indiana and serves as a fundraising and social media consultant to a variety of nonprofit organizations. In addition, he cohosts a weekly radio program in Indianapolis and is the author of two novels. He holds a B.A. in journalism and political science from Indiana University.

Lilya Wagner is director of Philanthropic Service for Institutions, an internal consulting group serving North American organizations affiliated with or operated by the Seventh-day Adventist Church. Lilya was vice president for philanthropy at Counterpart International in Washington, D.C., an international development organization; prior to that, she completed fourteen years of association with the Center on Philanthropy at Indiana University, serving as associate director for public service and director of the Women's Philanthropy Institute. She is on the faculty of The Fund Raising School and philanthropic studies at the Center on Philanthropy. Her published writings include articles, book chapters, and books on philanthropy, fundraising, and the nonprofit sector.

Mal Warwick has been raising money professionally since 1979 and has gained worldwide recognition as an author, consultant, and trainer. He has written or edited nineteen books, including *Fundraising When Money Is Tight* and *How to Write Successful Fundraising Letters*. Mr. Warwick is founder and chairman of Mal Warwick Associates and cofounder of Donordigital, both of which specialize in direct response fundraising. He has been a top-rated speaker at fundraising conferences throughout North America for more than twenty years and worldwide since 1999. He has taught fundraising on six continents to nonprofit executives from more than one hundred countries.

PART ONE

FUNDRAISING: THE ART OF RELATIONSHIP BUILDING

The Fund Raising School was established to educate and train fundraising practitioners and volunteers to secure the resources necessary for nonprofit organizations to carry out their work. At the heart of fundraising is the art of relationship building—the mutual creation of that intersection between the organization's mission and the donor's philanthropic vision. Strong relationships with donors don't just happen; they require careful attention not only to donors themselves but also to fundraising fundamentals that are grounded in ethical practice.

Chapter One is by Henry A. Rosso, founding director of The Fund Raising School, and Eugene R. Tempel. This is Rosso's original classic chapter from the first edition of *Achieving Excellence in Fund Raising*, with an added commentary on the validity of the philosophy in the twenty-first century. The concept of fundraising as a servant to philanthropy sets the tone for the entire volume.

The remaining chapters in this part deal with institutional readiness for fundraising. According to the Rosso philosophy, an organization earns the privilege to ask for funds by making the case for support. Fundraising is an ongoing process of interaction between the nonprofit organization and its publics.

Chapter Two focuses on planning as the starting point for fundraising. Planning begins with a careful analysis of organizational strengths and weaknesses that affect fundraising. It also considers the threats and opportunities in the external environment. How well an organization delivers its services and modifies its programs in response to changes in the environment has an impact on its fundraising success.

Chapter Three focuses on identifying constituents for fundraising. Constituency identification is based on the question "Who cares about us?" Chapter Four notes that case development begins with the question "Why do we exist?" The answers to these two questions are essential to planning for fundraising. Organizations cannot move forward in fundraising without understanding their constituents and having a strong mission statement supported by program globalization.

Achieving excellence in fundraising depends on institutional readiness. Fundraising success is based on preparation of a fundraising plan built on the institution's case for support, its relationship with its constituents, and its interaction with its external environment. These elements lead the institution to its fundraising plan. Unless the institution has prepared itself well in these preliminary but essential areas, fundraising cannot succeed.

CHAPTER ONE

A PHILOSOPHY OF FUNDRAISING

By Henry A. Rosso

Introduction by Eugene R. Tempel

In this chapter Henry A. (Hank) Rosso offers his philosophy of fundraising, a philosophy developed over a lifetime of work as a fundraiser, consultant, and teacher. The principles on which he founded The Fund Raising School in 1974 have stood the test of time and culture; so has his philosophy for fundraising. And both principles and philosophy have been substantiated by the research on philanthropy and fundraising that is available today. That is why his original chapter in *Achieving Excellence in Fund Raising* is included in this third edition unaltered and in its entirety.

A central theme in Hank's philosophy and in the way he approached his work was "fundraising is the servant of philanthropy." He opened and closed the first chapter of his book with that theme. Fundraising is not an end in itself. When it becomes that, both the organization and philanthropy are diminished. Fundraising, in Hank's view, was only a means to an end that rested on organizational mission. The pillars that support Hank's central theme are as relevant today as they were in 1991. For example, research shows that high-net-worth donors depend on professional fundraisers and colleagues to help them make decisions about their giving (The Center on Philanthropy, 2006).

The most significant of these pillars is "Why do you exist?" This question enables an organization to articulate its mission in terms of the societal values it is fulfilling. Mission is what gives us the privilege to ask for philanthropic support. Mission is particularly important in an era in which nonprofit organizations are encouraged to develop new income sources, undertake market-based activities, form collaborations and partnerships, and approach venture philanthropists with confidence.

Hank's philosophy also rested on the role of the governing board. He saw governing boards as responsible not only for fundraising, but also for stewardship of the organization's mission and resources. The governing board today must ensure the public trust of the organization if fundraising is to be successful. Heightened calls for accountability make the role of the governing board even more important today than it was in 1991.

Fundraising as the servant of philanthropy must be part of an organization's management system. This is a pillar of Hank's philosophy of fundraising that is also critical today. Fundraising cannot be a separate, isolated activity. Ensuring trust means conducting fundraising that is based on mission by staff and volunteers who are committed to the organization and who represent the organization with integrity.

Hank believed that philanthropy must be voluntary. Today this pillar of Hank's philosophy is even more important than it was in 1991. The interest in self-expression through philanthropy calls for a more open approach by organizations. Pluralism becomes an important tenet. Another of Hank's beliefs is applicable here: "Fundraising is the gentle art of teaching people the joy of giving." To ensure long-term donor engagement and donor satisfaction that lead to increased philanthropy, fundraisers must remember that giving is voluntary.

Perhaps the greatest contribution Hank made was to teach the substitution of pride for apology in fundraising. As the number of people engaged in fundraising has grown, and fundraisers have sought a more professional approach, recognizing that fundraising is a noble activity based on organizational mission has been central to professional development. Another of Hank's statements about soliciting a gift is applicable here: "Set yourself aside and let the case walk in."

Hank's chapter is framed by the concept of fundraising as a servant to philanthropy. He explained the role of fundraising in terms that foreshadow the models currently needed to assist wealth holders in determining their philanthropy. He wrote that fundraising "is justified when it is used as a responsible invitation guiding contributors to make the kind of gift that will meet their own special needs and add greater meaning to their lives."

Today more than ever fundraisers need a philosophy of fundraising. The call for accountability, the need to inspire trust, the leadership of volunteers, the involvement of donors in their philanthropy, and the new approaches to philanthropy discussed in the following chapters all call for fundraisers to be reflective practitioners who can center themselves with a philosophy of fundraising. Hank's philosophy provides an excellent beginning for us to develop our own philosophy.

A Philosophy of Fundraising

Fundraising is the servant of philanthropy and has been so since the seventeenth century, when Puritans brought the concept to the new continent. The early experience of fundraising was simple in form, obviously devoid of the multi-faceted practices that characterize its nature in the contemporary United States. These practices now make fundraising more diversified and more complex than ever before.

The American spirit of giving is known and respected in other nations. American fundraising methods are equally known and admired abroad, as for-eign citizens who have attended classes taught by The Fund Raising School will attest. Ironically, the practice of resource development that is so much a part of the culture, necessity, and tradition of not-for-profit organizations in the United States is not sufficiently understood, often misrepresented, and too often viewed with suspicion and apprehension by a broad section of our own population, par-ticularly by regulatory bodies. Few still argue with the observation that fundraising has never been considered the most popular practice in this country.

Dean Schooler of Boulder, Colorado, a scholar and student of fundraising, takes the teleological view of a vitalist philosophy that phenomena not only are guided by mechanical forces but also move toward certain goals of self-realization. Indeed, fundraising is never an end in itself; it is purposive. It draws both its meaning and essence from the ends that are served: caring, helping, healing, nurturing, guiding, uplifting, teaching, creating, preventing, advancing a cause, preserving values, and so forth. Fundraising is values-based; values must guide the process. Fundraising should never be undertaken simply to raise funds; it must serve the large cause.

Organizations and Their Reasons for Existing

Organizations of the independent sector come into existence for the purpose of responding to some facet of human or societal needs. The need or oppor-tunity for service provides the organization with a reason for being, as well as a right to design and execute programs or strategies that respond to the need. This becomes the cause that is central to the concern of the organization. The cause provides justification for more intervention, and this provides justification for fundraising.

The organization may *claim* a right to raise money by asking for the tax-deductible gift. It must *earn* the privilege to ask for gift support by its manage-ment's responsiveness to needs, by the worthiness of its programs, and by the stewardship of its governing board. An organization may assume the right to ask.

The prospective donor is under no obligation to give. The prospect reserves the right to a "yes" or a "no" response to any request. Either response is valid and must be respected.

Each organization that uses the privilege of soliciting for gifts should be prepared to respond to many questions, perhaps unasked and yet implicit in the prospect's mind. These may be characterized as such: "Why do you exist?" "What is distinctive about you?" "Why do you feel that you merit this support?" "What is it that you want to accomplish and how do you intend to go about doing it?" and "How will you hold yourself accountable?"

The response to "Who are you and why do you exist?" is couched in the words of the organization's mission statement. This statement expresses more than justification for existence and more than just a definition of goals and objectives. It defines the value system that will guide program strategies. The mission is the magnet that will attract and hold the interests of trustees, volunteers, staff, and contributors.

The answer to "What is distinctive about us?" is apparent in the array of goals, objectives, and programs that have been devised to address the needs of the value system as well as to serve as symbols of fidelity to it.

"What is it that you want to accomplish and how do you intend to go about doing it?" is closely linked to "Why do you feel you merit this support?" People give to people with causes. To be worthy of support, the organization must show that it has not only a vision of what it wishes to accomplish but also a clear plan for making the change it wishes to effect feasible and achievable.

"How do we hold ourselves accountable?" is the primary question. It is a continuing call for allegiance to the mission. It acknowledges the sacredness of the trust that is inherent in the relationship with both the constituency and the larger community. The organization is the steward of the resources entrusted to its care.

It is axiomatic that change is a constant. Shifting forces within the environment quicken the pace of change, thus posing a new constant. Not-for-profit organizations must always be prepared to function in the center of whirling pressure.

Organizations cannot afford to be oblivious to the environment that surrounds and indeed engulfs them. Forces within the environment—such as demographics, technology, economics, political and cultural values, and changing social patterns—affect daily business performance, whether this performance pertains to governance, program administration, fiscal responsibility, or fundraising.

To Govern or Not to Govern

Governance is an exercise in authority and control. Trustees, directors, or regents—the interchangeable nomenclature that identifies the actors in governance—are the primary stewards of the spirit of philanthropy. As stewards, they are the legendary "keepers of the hall." They hold the not-for-profit organization in trust to ensure that it will continue to function according to the dictates of its mission.

The trustees must bear the responsibility to define and interpret the mission and ensure that the organization will remain faithful to its mission. Board members should accept the charge that trusteeship concerns itself with the proper deployment of resources and with the accompanying action, the securing of resources. Deploying resources is difficult if the required resources are not secured through effective fundraising practices. It stands to reason that trustees as advocates of and stewards to the mission must attend to the task of pressing the resources development program on to success.

Institutionalizing Fundraising

Fundraising projects the values of the total organization into the community whenever it seeks gift support. All aspects of governance—administration, program, and resources development—are part of the whole. As such, these elements must be part of the representation when gifts are sought. Fundraising cannot function apart from the organization; apart from the organization's mission, goals, objective, and programs; or apart from a willingness to be held accountable for all of the organization's actions.

Fundraising is and must always be the lengthened shadow of the not-for-profit entity, reflecting the organization's dignity, its pride of accomplishment, and its commitment to service. Fundraising by itself and apart from the institution has no substance in the eyes and heart of the potential contributor.

Gift Making as Voluntary Exchange

Gift making is based on a voluntary exchange. Gifts secured through coercion, through any means other than persuasion, are not gifts freely given. They do not have the meaning of philanthropy. Rarely will gifts obtained under pressure or through any form of intimidation be repeated. These gifts lose their meaning.

In the process of giving, the contributor offers a value to the not-for-profit organization. This gift is made without any expectation of a material return, apart from the tax deductibility authorized by government. The reasons for making a gift are manifold.

In accepting the gift, it is incumbent upon the organization to return a value to the donor in a form other than material value. Such a value may be social recognition, the satisfaction of supporting a worthy cause, a feeling of importance, a feeling of making a difference in resolving a problem, a sense of belonging, or a sense of "ownership" in a program dedicated to serving the public good.

Trustees, administrators, or fundraising practitioners often misconstrue the true meaning of this exchange relationship, and they violate the acknowledgement process by offering a return of substantive value. This alters the exchange, reduces the meaning of philanthropy, and diminishes the gift in its commitment to the mission. The transaction is one of a material exchange, a self-centered *quid pro quo* with none of the spirit of philanthropy in the exchange.

Substituting Pride for Apology

Giving is a privilege, not a nuisance or a burden. Stewardship nourishes the belief that people draw a creative energy, a sense of self-worth, and a capacity to function productively from sources beyond themselves. This is a deep personal belief or a religious conviction. Thoughtful philanthropists see themselves as responsible stewards of life's gifts to them. What they have they hold in trust, in their belief, and they accept the responsibility to share their treasures effectively through their philanthropy. Giving is an expression of thankfulness for the blessings that they have received during their lifetime.

The person seeking the gift should never demean the asking by clothing it in apology. Solicitation gives the prospective donor the opportunity to respond with a "yes" or a "no." The solicitation should be so executed as to demonstrate to the prospective contributor that there can be a joy to giving, whether the gift measures up to the amount asked for or not. Fundraising professionals must teach this joy by asking properly and in a manner that puts the potential contributor at ease.

The first task of the solicitor is to help the potential contributor understand the organization's case, especially its statement of mission. When a person commits to contribute to a cause and does so because of an acceptance of and a belief in the mission, then that person becomes a stakeholder in the organization and the cause and work for which it stands. This emphasizes that philanthropy is moral action, and the contributor is an integral part of that action.

Fundraising as a Servant to Philanthropy

Philanthropy is voluntary action for the public good through voluntary action, voluntary association, and voluntary giving (Payton, 1988). Fundraising has been servant to philanthropy across the millennia. Through the procession of the centuries, the thesis has been established that people want and have a need to give. People want to give to causes that serve the entire gamut of human and societal needs. They will give when they can be assured that these causes can demonstrate their worthiness and accountability in using the gift funds that they receive.

Ethical fundraising is the prod, the enabler, the activator to gift making. It must also be the conscience to the process. Fundraising is at its best when it strives to match the needs of the not-for-profit organization with the contributor's need and desire to give. The practice of gift seeking is justified when it exalts the contributor, not the gift seeker. It is justified when it is used as a responsible invitation, guiding contributors to make the kind of gift that will meet their own special needs and add greater meaning to their lives.

CHAPTER TWO

PLAN TO SUCCEED

By Timothy L. Seiler

In the first edition of *Achieving Excellence in Fund Raising*, Hank Rosso (1991) wrote the chapter titled "Understanding the Fundraising Cycle." This revised and retitled chapter retains the concepts and principles that constitute the planning model known as the fundraising cycle. The chapter emphasizes different points than Hank emphasized, but it retains the fundamental belief that the cycle is an effective planning tool to help fundraisers, both paid and volunteer, understand the manageable process that is fundraising. Each step of the process is explained in detail in the various chapters that follow.

Effective fundraising depends on effective planning and rigorous execution— and actually more planning than execution. The better the planning, the better the fundraising results. The fundraising cycle illustrates the principle that it is possible to ask someone for a charitable gift too soon. A premature gift solicitation usually leads to one of two results: either the response "No, I won't make the gift," or a token gift, one that is neither appropriate for the donor's capacity to give nor adequate for the nonprofit's need. Neither result is what a fundraiser wants to produce, and using the fundraising cycle is a way to prepare to receive the preferred response to a gift solicitation: "Yes, I'll make the gift you ask for." To borrow and paraphrase from a winemaker's advertising slogan of some years ago, "We will solicit no gift before its time."

The first thing to note about the fundraising cycle is its name: *cycle*. The fundraising process is continuous. Its ongoing nature is illustrated by the continuing

FIGURE 2.1. THE FUNDRAISING CYCLE.

Awareness of Marketing Principles

Planning Checkpoint:
Examine the Case

Strategic Checkpoint:
Demonstrate Stewardship and Renew the Gift

Planning Checkpoint:
Analyze Market Requirements

Action Checkpoint:
Solicit the Gift

Planning Checkpoint:
Prepare Needs Statement

Action Checkpoint:
Activate Volunteer Corps

Planning Checkpoint:
Define Objectives

Planning Checkpoint:
Prepare Communications Plan

Action Checkpoint:
Involve Volunteers

Planning Checkpoint:
Prepare Fundraising Plan

Planning/Action Checkpoint:
Validate Needs Statement

Planning Checkpoint:
Identify Potential Giving Sources

Planning Checkpoint:
Select Fundraising Vehicle

Planning Checkpoint:
Evaluate Gift Markets

Source: Adapted from Henry A. Rosso and Associates, *Achieving Excellence in Fund Raising* (2nd ed.), p. 24. Copyright © 2003 Jossey-Bass Inc., Publishers. Reprinted by permission of Jossey-Bass Inc., a subsidiary of John Wiley & Sons, Inc.

arrows inside the steps of the model in Figure 2.1. These arrows represent the loop formed by the interrelated steps of the fundraising process. The complexity of the fundraising process lies, in part, in the reality that various constituencies from whom gifts are sought will be at different stages in the process. The fundraiser must coordinate the various activities necessary for moving the constituencies through the phases in the cycle.

The second thing to note about the fundraising cycle is the number of discrete steps constituting the whole. Starting with the step labeled "Planning Checkpoint: Examine the Case" and proceeding clockwise around the cycle, there are fourteen steps. Soliciting a gift in "its time" comes at step thirteen. Therefore planning to solicit a gift involves twelve steps. Skipping or shortchanging any of the steps leading to the solicitation will end in less than desirable results. Soliciting the gift (step thirteen) does not conclude the process; it begins it anew. Thus the fundraising cycle is a continuous process of planning for and asking for charitable gifts.

Prior to the first step in the fundraising cycle, the nonprofit needs to understand marketing principles and how they apply to the fundraising process. Such awareness requires the nonprofit to develop feedback systems to measure and monitor the needs, perceptions, wants, and values of prospective donors. What do prospective donors seek for their own lives that they can find through involvement with the nonprofit? The better the nonprofit understands that exchange, the better it will manage its fundraising cycle.

The first step in the fundraising cycle, a planning checkpoint, is the examination of the nonprofit's case for support. The case is the sum of all the reasons why anyone should give charitable gifts to the organization. Each nonprofit must develop its own compelling case based on how it meets clearly defined and understood community needs. The case illustrates how the nonprofit serves the community, providing benefits and adding value.

The case must provide persuasive responses to these questions:

1. Why does the organization exist? The answer lies in the human/social problem or need addressed by the nonprofit. This is the organization's mission, its *raison d'être*.
2. What services or programs does the nonprofit provide to meet the need or solve the problem?
3. Why should prospective donors (individuals, corporations, foundations) provide gifts, and what benefits accrue to donors who make gifts?

These answers form the basis of the organization's mission. The next step is to analyze the market requirements. The nonprofit must test its mission as articulated through its case against the wants and needs of the market or gift sources from which it seeks charitable gifts. Only the marketplace is a true test of the validity of the nonprofit's proposed solution to the human and social problems it addresses. Such market validation is critical to successful fundraising.

If the markets do not understand or accept the importance of the needs being addressed by the nonprofit, fundraising faces a serious obstacle. Worse, if the markets do not even know of the nonprofit or the needs the nonprofit addresses, fundraising is not possible. Donors will give to those organizations they care about that address the needs they care about.

In meeting clearly identified community needs understood to be of value to the potential donors, the nonprofit can formulate compelling arguments for why its work merits philanthropic gifts.

Next comes the preparation of a needs statement. This is the organization's plan for carrying out its work toward mission fulfillment. Program plans are projected for annual needs and for longer-term needs. Financial planning follows program planning and defines the resources required for carrying out programs and delivering services. This includes descriptions of sources of revenue needed to support the program plan. This is the justification for fundraising.

The preparation of this needs statement involves the volunteer leadership of the nonprofit, especially board members, selected major donors, and other volunteers who can affect the organization and its fundraising. The needs statement shapes future fundraising goals and objectives and must include not only annual operating needs but also longer-term fundraising plans for capital and endowment needs.

The next planning checkpoint is the definition of objectives. The programs for fulfilling the mission must be translated into specific, measurable action plans for how the organization intends to provide solutions to problems it addresses. If the mission statement explains "why," goal statements answer "what," and objectives provide an answer to "how." To be credible to the market sources, objectives must be realistic and achievable within the resources available to the organization.

The mnemonic acronym **SMART** helps us memorize the qualities of an effective objective:

Specific

Measurable

Achievable

Results-oriented

Time-determined

Specific illustrations of how the organization intends to do its work provide a visible link to program budgeting and to a rationale for fundraising.

Next comes the first action step in the fundraising cycle: involvement of volunteers. Whereas earlier steps involved board members and selected other volunteers in planning, this step calls for action in developing and carrying out effective fundraising strategies. Because an effective gift solicitor is one who believes in and is committed to the cause, the earlier involvement steps prepare the volunteers to be effective solicitors of their peers. Historically, and still today, the most effective gift solicitation is that of a peer volunteer asking for gifts in a face-to-face solicitation.

One of the most effective ways to involve volunteers is in the validation of the organization's needs statement. Philanthropic support requires constant validation by the board and other volunteers. For volunteers to give and get philanthropic gifts they must reaffirm the needs statement through continued involvement in analyzing the nonprofit's plans. Such involvement is critical before launching the fundraising program or campaign.

The next step in the cycle is an evaluation of gift markets to determine their ability and perceived willingness to fund the nonprofit's programs through charitable gifts. This step includes making informed judgments about which markets to approach and the gift amounts to be sought.

The most likely sources of gifts are individuals, corporations, foundations, associations, and government agencies. The most generous source has been individuals, equaling over 88 percent of total philanthropy in recent years when individual giving, bequests, and gifts from family foundations are combined (Center on Philanthropy, 2009b). Much individual wealth has gone into family foundations and community foundations in recent years, and thus foundations have been the fastest-growing source of gift funds.

Many nonprofits will not experience such a high percentage of gift support from individuals or even from individuals combined with foundations. The focus of market evaluation should be on building and sustaining as diverse a funding base as possible. The more diverse the funding base, the more likely it is that the nonprofit can sustain itself in a volatile fundraising environment and can be more responsive to the needs of its market constituencies.

Planning continues with careful selection of fundraising vehicles (strategies). With the gift market evaluation completed, the fundraising staff and volunteers must determine which fundraising techniques will be most effective within each market. Fundraising strategies or methods include direct mail, phone-a-thons, special events or benefits (often called fundraisers), grant-seeking, personal solicitations, recognition groups, and in recent years e-mail and websites. Just as market evaluation calls for diversity of funding, so selection of fundraising methods should explore every opportunity for raising gift funds to carry out the organization's mission.

Fundraising programs include the annual fund, special or major gifts, capital campaigns, and endowment programs. The latter two often rely heavily on planned giving as a way for donors to make larger gifts than they typically make through annual funds or special gifts programs.

The successful fundraising program will analyze all the methods, test various ones, and evaluate their effectiveness through cost-benefit ratios and other measures of success. Long-term sustained fundraising effectiveness will match the various methods to the different gift sources to identify what works best in particular markets.

Identifying potential gift sources is the next planning step in the cycle. This step distills and refines the gift market evaluation into lists of specific prospective donors. The prospective donors will be present in each market: individuals, corporations, and foundations. Each prospective donor is identified and qualified by three criteria:

Linkage to the organization

Ability to give gifts at the level being sought

Interest in the work of the organization

Although many exercises in finding prospective donors begin with identifying individuals (and corporations and foundations) with the most money (ability), such exercises are futile. Lacking interest in the work and linkage to the nonprofit— often through a committed, involved volunteer—the wealthiest funder will not give just because of the ability to do so.

Volunteer involvement through a prospective donor development committee builds a priority list of specific giving sources. Furthermore, this type of volunteer involvement builds ownership of the fundraising plan and process among the volunteers.

The tenth step in the cycle is the preparation of the fundraising plan. The previous nine steps focused on analysis, or fact gathering, and planning. Preparation of the fundraising plan is a call to action. Fundraising staff drafts the plan and involves volunteer leaders in refining and validating the plan. The plan should account for proper execution by allocating the resources necessary for implementing the plan. The plan should also include the management steps of monitoring and evaluating to provide for modification if needed.

The fundraising plan needs to spell out how much money will be raised for what programs in what time frame using which methods. The plan should include roles for volunteers and staff.

Understanding of the organization's mission and its fundraising plan by those prospective donors who will be asked to make gifts is essential to successful fundraising. People give money to causes they know and care about. Thus the next planning step is the preparation of a communications plan. For effective fundraising communications must go beyond the dissemination of information. Communications must stir the emotions and the intellects of those from whom gifts are sought. Effective fundraising communications touch the heart and the head.

The goal of fundraising communications is to lead prospective donors to an understanding and acceptance of the nonprofit and its purposes and create a desire to share in seeing that the mission is fulfilled. Effective fundraising communications are a two-way interaction providing a means for donors to express concerns. Effective communications create an opportunity for the exchange of values, which is fundamental for successful fundraising.

Fundraising is about relationships built on mutual interests and concerns. One of the truisms of fundraising is that people give to people with causes. The next action step in the cycle is to activate a volunteer corps of solicitors.

Fundraising in the United States has been largely a volunteer activity, action taken by people so committed to a cause that they make their own gifts and then eagerly invite others to join the cause. It remains true today that no solicitation is more compelling than one done by a volunteer advocate who personally solicits gifts to support a nonprofit to which she is passionately devoted.

Although volunteerism in fundraising remains strong today, there is a growing trend, especially among large organizations, to rely more and more on highly trained fundraising staff to solicit, especially major gifts. This is particularly true among universities and colleges, and to some degree among hospitals and medical centers.

The effective nonprofit must renew and expand its volunteer corps of fundraisers to expand the base of donors. It is a generally accepted norm that one volunteer is needed for every five personal solicitations.

With twelve steps now completed, it is time to solicit the gift. Some gifts—from the board, the staff, and certain volunteers—will probably already have been part of earlier stages in the process. This step represents the carrying out of the fundraising plan into the broader constituency and is the culmination of all that has been done so far.

The solicitation step calls for already committed donors to visit personally those from whom gifts will be sought. The current donor makes the case for the organization, explains his own level of commitment, and invites the prospective donor to join in the fulfillment of the mission by making her own charitable gift. The solicitation step is a dignified process of asking with pride for a philanthropic gift to help carry out the important work of the nonprofit.

Soliciting and receiving the gift is not the end of the process. In fact, it is only the beginning of a deepening relationship between the donor and the nonprofit. Proper gratitude for and acknowledgment of the gift must be expressed by the nonprofit. Additionally, the nonprofit must disclose how the gift is used and demonstrate the highest level of accountability and stewardship in the appropriate and wise use of the gift.

Properly thanking donors, reporting the use of gifts, and demonstrating wise stewardship of contributed funds makes possible the renewal of the gift. The renewal process, step fourteen, leads to the beginning of the cycle anew. The case must be renewed by testing it again among the constituency. Renewal requires ongoing analysis of how effectively the nonprofit meets the requirements and fulfills the needs of its gift markets. The needs statement must be checked and rechecked to demonstrate the continuing effectiveness and worthiness of the nonprofit.

Fundraising is a multidisciplined process requiring extensive involvement of staff and volunteers in a series of interrelated steps described in the fundraising cycle. The main responsibility of the professional fundraising executive is to manage the process, serving as catalyst and coach for all involved in fundraising.

CHAPTER THREE

DEVELOPING A CONSTITUENCY FOR FUNDRAISING

By Timothy L. Seiler

E ffective fundraising requires intimate knowledge of the nonprofit's constituency—a distinct group of people with actual or potential interest in the organization. Some organizations have natural constituencies, readily identifiable and generally accessible. Schools, colleges, and universities, for example, have students and alumni. Many educational institutions expand their constituencies to include parents and grandparents of current students. Hospitals have patients, often referred to in fundraising circles as "grateful patients." Arts organizations have patrons, members, and audiences. For Hank Rosso, constituency identification and development were at the heart of fundraising.

Identifying the Constituency

Organizations without such a natural constituency still have constituencies. The organization might need to work harder to identify and build its constituency, but every nonprofit organization has its own constituency. At the very least the constituency consists of people who need the services of the nonprofit, those who provide the services and direct the programs, those who govern the organization, and those who support the cause. In developing its constituency, an organization should expend the resources necessary to identify, inform, involve, and bond the constituency to the organization. The energy, time, and money invested in constituency development will be returned in multiples by serving the nonprofit through volunteers, donors, and advocates. The bond for this philanthropic activity is the nonprofit's mission.

A synonym for *constituency* is *interested parties*. These interested parties include stakeholders currently involved with the organization, those who have been previously involved, and those with the potential for future involvement. All constituencies also have active and inactive groups, interested and uninterested, close and distant. For fundraising purposes it is essential to know the interests, needs, and wants of the people in the constituency because their level of involvement helps or hinders the nonprofit as it seeks to accomplish its goals.

A Constituency Model

A helpful way to think about an organization's constituency is to visualize a set of concentric circles (see Figure 3.1). These widening circles represent the energy of an organization and the flow and dissipation of the energy moving outward from the center. An analogy is the action of a rock thrown into a body of water. Where the rock enters the water the action (energy) is highest. As the waves radiate outward from where the rock enters the water, they become wider but weaker; that is, as the waves move farther away from the center of the action, they are more shallow and have less energy. This is how the constituency of a nonprofit interacts with the organization. The closer to the center of the action, the greater the energy, the stronger the bond. The core constituency, then, is at the center of the concentric circles. Those members of the constituency who are in the second, third, and fourth circles—moving away from the center—have a weaker bond with the organization. The farther away from the core the constituency segment lies, the lower the energy and the weaker the bond to the organization.

For the constituency model to affect fundraising positively, certain constituent groups should populate the inner circle or core. As shown in the figure, the board of trustees, the senior management team, and major donors will ideally form the core of the organization. The trustees hold the organization in public trust and are responsible for the mission, vision, and policies of the organization. The senior management team carries out the organization's programs to meet the community needs articulated in the mission. Major donors not only demonstrate their commitment to the cause through their gifts of substance but also serve as advocates for the cause. All three core components of the inner circle provide the energy for the organization and influence the direction of the organization.

Although these three groups are the critical ones to be in the central circle, large organizations might include additional groups. Alumni boards, visiting

FIGURE 3.1. THE CONSTITUENCY MODEL.

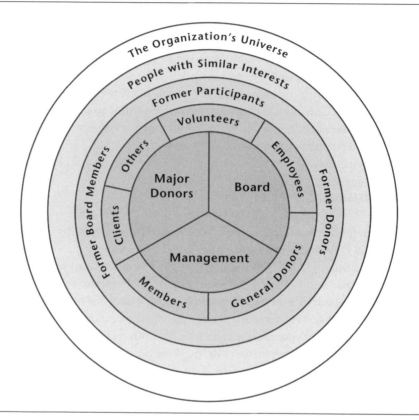

committees, foundation boards, advisory committees, and "friends of" groups, for example, might be part of the core constituency for complex organizations.

In the second circle are volunteers, for program delivery and for fundraising; clients receiving the organization's services; employees, who are not part of senior management; general donors, meaning those who make gifts more modest than those made by major donors; members, if the organization is a membership organization; and others involved with the organization, such as vendors, who have a stake in the organization but are not in the central circle.

All the components in the second circle are important because they provide a broad base of support and a potential for greater future involvement, including more strategic volunteer activity and major gift development.

The third circle—former participants, former board members, and former donors—represents a drop in energy, as these groups are farther from the core of the organization. Although "former" indicates a state of what once was and might imply something negative, this circle holds potential for reactivation and renewed involvement. Imaginative, open communications efforts might reveal that members of these groups would simply like to be invited back to participate more fully. If they once were participants, board members, or donors, they surely share the values of the organization. Exploring how to win back their affections and their loyalty might move them back into the second circle and perhaps into the core circle.

The fourth circle, people with similar interests, is an ill-defined constituency segment. Constituents here are distant from the energy center. They typically know little of the organization, and the organization rarely knows much about them. This is the segment usually approached through direct mail in an attempt by the organization to acquire new donors. It is worth probing this segment, although the organization needs to recognize that returns from this segment are likely to be low for the time and energy expended.

The very last circle is the organization's universe. Every organization has such a constituency segment and often knows little about the giving potential. Involvement will be minimal, and whatever gifts come from this circle will probably be modest in size. But the sequence of gifts might be regular and long-lasting. The donors in this segment might give year after year, and the cumulative giving becomes substantive over time. This circle, too, is worth attention and energy.

Based on the Rosso model of fundraising, several principles of the constituency circles model are important. First, because energy is at the center and flows outward, the bond is strongest at the center. Fundraising, then, begins at the center of the constituency circles and is taken to the outer circles by the board, management staff, and major donors in the inner circle. The constant challenge for the development program is to align the central players in the core circle. A dysfunctional fundraising program is one which finds the board and/or the management staff on the outer circles.

A second principle is fluidity in the circles. A major donor this year will be a general donor next year. Board members' terms expire, and they become former board members. Other changes occur in the constituency for many reasons: people change residences or occupations, donors' interests change, donors' financial capacity changes, and so forth. Patterns in constituency development show that a 20 to 25 percent change annually is to be expected. Effective constituency development requires consistent involvement with all the circles in the model.

Identifying and Attracting Likely Donors

One of the truisms of fundraising is that the best prospective donor is a current donor. Someone who has made a gift has demonstrated interest in and involvement with the organization. That donor is likely to consider another gift. Experienced fundraisers testify that every donor at one level is a prospective donor for a gift at a higher level. Working conscientiously with the constituency model will reveal the most likely candidates for renewed gifts and for increased gifts.

The most likely donors are identified by three characteristics: *linkage*, *ability*, and *interest*. Linkage is contact. Often such contact is person to person, a peer of the potential donor. The personal contact, the linkage, makes possible a personal visit to the potential donor for the organization to make its case for a gift. Linkage can also be geographic, emotional, or professional (more about this in Figure 3.2, The Wheel of Roles and Responsibilities). *Linkage* is another term for the more commonly used concept *network*. Establishing linkage means determining who knows whom and can arrange the visits necessary for successful gift solicitations.

Ability means the financial capacity of the gift source to give a gift at the level the nonprofit deems appropriate. Research by the nonprofit helps determine the capacity. Peer evaluations (linkage) of gift capacity are also effective in determining the ability factor.

Interest in the nonprofit and its work is essential. Even the most financially able prospective donor will not make a gift to an organization in which she has no interest. Interest follows information and precedes involvement.

When identifying the most qualified and most likely prospective donors, all three of these characteristics—linkage, ability, and interest—are imperative. It is most likely that these characteristics will be in greater evidence in the inner circles of the constituency model. Surely it is important to test the principles across all the circles, but the most likely prospective donors will be found in the first two or three circles.

Some aspects of the constituency arise automatically. For instance, the client base becomes an immediate adjunct of the constituency because it acts in response to services offered. Trustees, management staff, and beginning program staff become an early part of an organization because they must make available the services that are needed by their clients. Contributors, volunteers, and advocates take longer to develop. They must be sought out and invited to become the philanthropic base that will augment and celebrate the organization's work.

The fundraiser must be sensitive to the fact that there is constant interaction within and between the constituency circles and among the elements that make up each circle. Individuals gravitate toward the core circle as their interest is touched and then deepened; they drift away if their interest slackens, if they are ignored, or if their interests change or are neglected. A studied program of constituency involvement and thoughtful cultivation is necessary to maintain the vitality of the constituency base.

A responsible fundraising staff should assert itself continuously to develop an *awareness* within the constituency of the organization's mission, goals, and objectives; to foster an *understanding* of the service to that mission; and to invite constituency *commitment* to the organization through the process of making a gift. This gift-making process forges a strong bond between the constituency and the nonprofit organization and its mission.

An effective, externally oriented communication program is the first necessity. In developing any human relationship it is necessary to get the attention of the subject, the person whom the organization wants to involve. The person must be made aware that the organization exists, and that it exists for a purpose that may hold an interest to him or her. Awareness must be converted into understanding, first of the guiding mission that delineates the human or societal needs that must be addressed, and second of the programs that will respond to these needs. From awareness to understanding to acceptance is the direct path to involvement and the process that is so necessary for constituency development.

People will identify with an organization if they understand and can accept its reason for being, if they accept that the programs are valid and responsive, and if they strongly believe that the people associated with the organization are competent and trustworthy in their service to the mission.

Various techniques are applicable to this process of identifying and involving a constituency, particularly the segment of those who are likely to contribute funds and to volunteer time. One of the first and most effective instruments for constituency development is fundraising. The fundraising process is based on intelligent, purposeful communications with the amorphous and unidentified market, including prospective donors and existing donors. A sensitively managed communications program will invite interest in the organization, its mission, its goals, and its programs. The outreach or public relations effort should include periodic newsletters that contain information of interest to the reader. These publications too often are self-serving informational instruments that extol the accomplishments of staff members while neglecting the concerns, questions, and curiosity of the constituency. Periodic surveys of readers' interests and reactions to the value of the newsletter might well evoke the kind of response that will heal the myopia of an overweening self-interest.

Special events offer an opportunity to attract the attention of potential constituents. A special event may be defined as an activity that is designed to accomplish a variety of objectives, one of which is to invite possible constituents to become involved and to learn more about the organization. Events may include open houses, come-and-see tours, 10K runs, leadership dinners, fashion shows, discussions, seminars, workshops, annual meetings, and book sales.

Properly staged events can serve purposes other than just raising money. They can encourage people to become part of the organization's expanding constituency base.

It is important to know and understand the concept of constituency circles, but this understanding must be translated into an understanding of the individual constituent in order to create and maintain the exchange relationship underlying effective fundraising and giving.

Roles and Responsibilities That Influence Giving

In identifying candidates for major gifts or for volunteer leadership positions, fundraisers are well served by a model defined as the Wheel of Roles and Responsibilities (see Figure 3.2). This model shows the many roles and responsibilities assumed by individuals. The roles and responsibilities can help determine the behavior of constituents in relating to the nonprofit organization.

The individual who is a prospective major gift donor or leadership candidate is in the center of the wheel. Each spoke represents a role or responsibility demanding a portion of the individual's time, energy, ability, and inclination to be

FIGURE 3.2. THE WHEEL OF ROLES AND RESPONSIBILITIES.

involved with a fundraising program. The roles and responsibilities include family, career, religion, education, recreation, politics, and social roles.

Family is of central concern to most individuals. The family will often positively influence the gift-giving decision. But family interests can also hinder the major gift process. The fundraising executive needs to determine how the family role influences the gift-making decision.

A career or profession will often influence a constituent's ability or inclination to help a nonprofit organization. Certain professions are conventionally viewed as most likely to be major givers: attorneys, doctors, investment managers, and in the late 1990s technology investors and entrepreneurs. Other professions—educators, nurses, social workers—are generally viewed as having little capacity to give. Effective constituency development goes beyond conventional attitudes and explores each individual for capacity and inclination, ignoring convention as the sole determinant.

Religion has been and continues to be a bedrock of philanthropy. Historically, giving patterns reveal that religion influences generosity to secular causes. It is true, however, that commitments to the individual's place of worship can reduce financial capacity to give to other causes.

The role that education plays in an individual's life can be an important factor in major gift capacity. If a prospective major gift donor is paying tuition for family members enrolled at private universities, the donor's capacity to give to a nonprofit may be limited for the duration of the educational process. If the person values education because of the person's current stature, it can be a very important factor in determining interest in philanthropy in higher education.

Recreational interests can play an important role in the prospective donor's life. Some interests might be so costly as to reduce potential for gift-giving. On the other hand, recreational interests provide a forum for involvement and interaction. The astute fundraising executive will determine how the nonprofit can meet the donor's interests through recreation.

Politics, or civic engagement, plays a role in most people's lives to the degree that it influences how people interact. Those constituents most actively engaged in communities of interest and shared values have wide-ranging connections, thereby expanding constituency circles.

Social roles are important to fundraising for how they build networks and make connections. A socially active, energetic constituency will extend itself widely, creating many opportunities for delivering the nonprofit's message. Broadening social contacts will assist in establishing helpful linkages.

These roles change many times during an individual's life. The fundraiser must recognize that some of these roles might be in conflict with the organization's fundraising needs and will therefore militate against the making of a major gift. On the other hand, the roles might be compatible with the organization's needs and form a basis of linkage to the organization, thus facilitating a major gift. The role of the fundraising executive, along with volunteers, is to identify those elements that provide a basis for the exchange relationship, focusing on the compatibility of shared values.

Conclusion

Constituency development is critical for long-term, sustainable fundraising success. Most organizations will have a larger constituency than they can interact with effectively. Organizations should spend maximum time and energy identifying their constituencies and cultivating meaningful relationships with them, moving the constituents closer and closer to the center and bonding them to the core of the organization. Sensitive attention to the needs and values of the constituents will draw them more intimately into the mission of the organization.

CHAPTER FOUR

DEVELOPING AND ARTICULATING
A CASE FOR SUPPORT

By Timothy L. Seiler and Eva E. Aldrich

Nonprofit organizations know intuitively that their work merits philanthropic gift support. If they assume that their gift sources share this intuitive knowledge, they are mistaken. A case for support is a *sine qua non* for nonprofits. A case for support is the rationale underlying fundraising. For Hank Rosso (1991, pp. 39–41), it was the reason nonprofit organizations deserved philanthropic support. Without a case for support, a nonprofit does not have a right to seek support.

The case is the general argument for why a nonprofit deserves gift support. The case is bigger than the organization and relates to a cause being served. The case for support is an encyclopedic accumulation of information, parts of which are used to argue that the organization deserves gift support for doing its work.

A case statement is a particular expression of the case. A case statement is not as big as the case; rather, it is a specific illustration of some of the elements making up the case. Although the case is made up of numerous reasons why the organization deserves gift support, not every reason is included in a case statement. A case statement focuses on or highlights critical factors important in arguing for gift support. A case statement selects and articulates specific points from the overall case (Seiler, 2001; The Fund Raising School, 2009b).

This chapter moves from the development of the case to the expression of the case, distinguishing between the internal case and the external case. The role of staff and volunteers in doing the work of case preparation is also described.

The preparation of the case begins with an understanding that nonprofit organizations raise money to meet larger community needs. Unmet social needs lead to the creation of nonprofit organizations, and the case for support is built on how well the organization meets those needs. The effectiveness of the case depends on how well the cause is served.

The case is the bedrock on which philanthropic fundraising is built. It is the urgent call for a solution to a problem, the meeting of a need. The persuasiveness of the case relates directly to the nonprofit's ability to solve problems and to adjust to meet changing market or societal needs. The case for support is the expression of the cause, addressing why anyone should contribute to the advancement of the cause. The case is larger than the organization's financial needs; it is larger than the organization.

Preparation, development, and validation of the case begin with staff. If the organization has on staff a development director, she should be the catalyst in the preparation and development of the case. The development professional typically serves as an interpreter of the concerns, interests, and needs of the external constituencies while also articulating the needs statement of the organization. The development staff not only knows the organization internally but also interacts regularly with external constituencies. The staff must be able and willing to bring back inside the organization what the perceptions of the organization are among the constituencies where gift support will be sought.

It is not uncommon for fundraising staff to discover that not everything is perfect among the constituencies. Occasionally constituents are misinformed or uninformed. Sometimes there are perceptions that the organization is not effective. Perhaps constituents lack confidence that gifts are needed or that they really make a difference. Finding out how to address these concerns will strengthen the case for support. Development staff must know the organization inside and out and must represent the constituency outside and in (see Figure 4.1).

It is important to get others involved in the development of the case. When enlisting volunteer leadership for articulation of the case in fundraising, it is particularly effective to seek the ideas of key constituents—board members, volunteers, donors, and potential donors. Fundraisers can increase the enthusiasm of those who will articulate this case in their own words by giving them a role in developing and validating the case. They will question what puzzles them or challenge what disturbs them. If they are representative of others from

FIGURE 4.1. STAFF AND CONSTITUENCY PARTICIPATION IN CASE DEVELOPMENT.

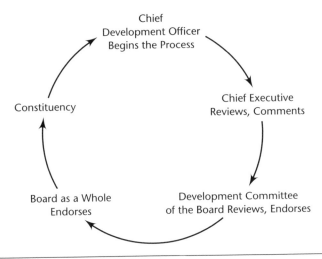

Source: The Fund Raising School, 2002.

whom gifts will be sought, their questions and challenges will strengthen the case for support.

Where to Start? With Case Resources

The development of the case begins with compiling information elements that provide the background for everything a potential donor might want to know about the nonprofit organization. These components are *case resources*, and they might already exist as documents within the organization. Case resources provide information on which the case statement is built. Case resources are a database, an information bank, from which case statements are drawn. Case resources are sometime referred to as the *internal case statement.*

Case resources consist of the following information elements:

Mission statement

Goals

Objectives

Programs, services

TABLE 4.1. ARTICULATING A CASE TO ATTRACT DONORS.

Case Components	Must Articulate
Mission statement	An awareness of the cause; insight into the problem addressed by the nonprofit.
Goals	The desired achievement that is expected to solve the problem.
Objectives	What will be accomplished by reaching the goals.
Programs and services	The nonprofit's service to people (including stories of how people benefit).
Finances	The expenses of providing programs and services, as a validation of the need for philanthropy.
Governance	The character and quality of the organization as shown in its staff and volunteer leadership and governance structure.
Staffing	The qualifications and strengths of staff.
Service delivery	The advantages, strengths, and effectiveness of the mechanics of program and service delivery.
Planning and evaluation	Program and fundraising plans and evaluation processes that demonstrate service commitments, strengths, and impact.
History	The heroic saga of founders, staff, and others, and the credibility implied by success over time.

Source: The Fund Raising School, 2002.

Finances

Governance

Staffing

Facilities, service delivery

Planning, evaluation

History

Information about all these aspects must be on hand in the organization's office and must be available, accessible, and retrievable when needed in connection with fundraising. Let's take a closer look at each of the case resources, which are summarized in Table 4.1.

Mission Statement

A mission statement is a philosophical statement of the human and societal needs being met by the nonprofit organization; it explains why the nonprofit exists. A mission statement is an expression of the value or values in which the organization believes and around which it does its work. By stating an organization's values and beliefs, a mission statement gives insight into the organization's core values.

A common misconception is that mission statements express what an organization does, as exemplified by statements such as "It is the mission of the agency to provide after-school care." This is a goal statement, not a mission statement.

Any statement containing an infinitive phrase—*to deliver, to serve, to provide*—is a goal or purpose statement, telling what the organization does. A mission statement, on the other hand, explains *why* the organization does what it does. An effective mission statement provides a base for identifying beliefs and values. A good mission statement often begins with the words "We believe" or "We value." For example, a shelter for animals might use the following as its mission statement: "Concern for Animals believes that all animals deserve humane treatment. Because we care about all animals, Concern for Animals provides shelter and food for abandoned and unwanted animals."

The following steps are suggestions for how to develop and write an effective mission statement:

1. Assert the dominant value the organization believes in.
2. Describe briefly the conditions preventing fulfillment of that value.
3. State briefly what needs to be done to alleviate the conditions in step 2.
4. Affirm that your organization challenges the conditions described in step 2, and carry out what is outlined in step 3.

The mission statement gives donors and potential donors an opportunity to identify the values they share with the nonprofit organization.

Goals

Goals answer the question "What does the organization do?" Goal statements are general expressions explaining what the organization wants to accomplish as it seeks to meet the needs or resolve the problems described in the mission statement. Goals are usually stated in ambitious terms not easily measured. Goal statements guide the organization toward fulfilling the beliefs expressed in the mission statement. Because organizations typically have multiple programs, goals will also be multiple; that is, the organization will have several program-related goals, including fundraising goals.

Objectives

Objectives differ from goals in degree of specificity. Objectives are more precise than goals; they explain how the organization expects to reach its goals. Recall the mnemonic acronym **SMART,** used to help understand how to state an objective. Effective objectives are

Specific

Measurable

Achievable

Results-oriented

Time-determined

A goal statement could be "To increase annual fund income." Objectives illustrating how to reach that goal could be "We will increase annual giving from individuals by 5 percent in the next fiscal year" and "We will increase corporate giving and corporate sponsorship by 15 percent in the next fiscal year."

Programs and Services

The programs and services component of the case resources file should include descriptions of how the organization provides service to its clients. One of the best ways to build this part of the file is to collect testimonials from clients and beneficiaries talking or writing about the organization's programs and services. Potential funders are more likely to be responsive to fundraising appeals when they recognize that real people are benefiting from the nonprofit's work. Stories of how recipients of services have benefited are an effective way to do this.

Finances

Financial information about the organization links budgeting with objectives and program descriptions. Information about finances gives a clear picture of how the organization acquires and spends financial resources. This financial overview establishes and validates the need for philanthropic gift support and justifies fundraising. The financial overview also offers the opportunity to demonstrate fiscal responsibility and accountability for prudent use of funds.

Governance

The issue of governance of nonprofits is critical in attracting charitable gifts. The governance structure of nonprofits indicates the character and quality of the institution. This part of the case resources file should contain relevant information about how the board is composed and how it functions. Complete dossiers of each board member and organizational material such as bylaws and conflict-of-interest statements should also be maintained.

This element of the case file should not be taken lightly. Governance is often a litmus test for potential contributors. The quality and integrity of the governing body indicate the strength of the nonprofit. Potential contributors have more confidence in nonprofits with boards who are serious about their commitment to governance and who hold the organization accountable to the public.

Staffing

As the governance of nonprofits is a matter of integrity and quality, staffing indicates competence and professionalism. This part of the file should illustrate the credentials and qualifications of staff, both paid and volunteer. Staffing patterns reveal how the organization delivers programs and services effectively. This part of the file should contain résumés of the staff.

Competent, skilled staff members, together with dedicated, energetic board members, offer a persuasive case for potential contributors to make charitable gifts. It is essential to keep this element of the file current. Staff should review their résumés at least annually, updating continuing education and professional development in which they participate to improve professional competence.

Facilities and Service Delivery

The next component in the case file is a description of facilities and service delivery. This should explain how people access programs and services. Occasionally facilities are distinguishing factors: visibility, accessibility, and convenience are advantages for program and services delivery.

This section might also include plans for renovation, expansion, or new construction and will help make the case for capital fundraising.

Planning and Evaluation

Information about planning and evaluation should describe the process used for planning and the measures taken for evaluation. Program plans precede fundraising plans; program plans validate the need for service, and fundraising plans demonstrate the need for philanthropic support.

Evaluation provides a means for demonstrating effectiveness and efficiency in programs and accountability and stewardship of philanthropic resources.

Planning and evaluation documents show that the organization takes its work seriously and holds itself accountable. This inspires confidence in donors and potential donors.

History

In talking about its history, a nonprofit should focus on its accomplishments in terms of service to its constituencies. The history should capture the spirit of the people, both service providers and beneficiaries. The focus should be on the organization's heroes. History is the heroic saga of the organization.

Internal Case, External Case, and the Difference Between Them

With these elements in place, the case resources file, or internal case, is ready. An operational case resources file (internal case) prepares the organization to develop expressions—that is, external case statements—for fundraising. The external case statement tells the story to the constituencies.

While the internal case is a database of information and knowledge, the external case statement orders and presents the information for purposes of communications, public relations, and fundraising. External case statements take the form of brochures, foundation (and corporation) proposals, direct mail letters, website development, campaign prospectuses, news releases, newsletters, speeches, and face-to-face solicitations. Hank Rosso defined the external case as "the case at work."

In making the transition from building the internal case to developing external case statements, the focus is on answering these questions:

1. What is the problem or social need that is central to our concern?
2. What special service or programs do we offer to respond to this need?
3. Why are the problem and service important?
4. What constitutes the market for our services?
5. Are others doing what we are doing to serve our service market, and perhaps doing it better?
6. Do we have a written plan with a statement of philosophy, objectives, and a program?
7. What are the specific financial needs against which private gift support will be sought?
8. Is the organization competent to carry out the defined program?
9. Who are the people associated with the organization: staff, key volunteers, trustees or directors?
10. Who should support the organization?

In writing case statements, it is helpful to remember that the purpose is to stimulate a potential donor to take a series of steps, ultimately ending in the decision to make a gift. The qualities that must exist in the writing and be present in the case statements to stimulate this sequence of reactions on the part of potential donors are excitement, proximity, immediacy, a sense of the future, meaning, and relevance.

Case statements need to excite the reader (or listener). Much of philanthropy begins with an emotional response to the external need as defined in the case for support. Proximity to the problem creates a sense of emotional awareness as well as a geographic proximity. How real is the problem in the potential donor's life? How important, even urgent, is it that the potential donor take action to help solve the problem? This is a sense of immediacy. What happens if the donor delays in responding to this need? In addition to immediacy—the need to act now—there should also be a sense of the future. This is not a one-time action but an ongoing process. It is unlikely that all problems can be solved now, so what does the future hold as a promise to address the ongoing problems? What is the meaning to the donor? Case statements should communicate to the donor the values and benefits of participating that are of importance to her. The mission expressed in the case should connect to the donor's values.

Qualities such as these in the expression of the case achieve the desired sequence of responses by the donor (see Table 4.2). Relevance grabs the attention of the donor and focuses on the importance of the problem or need that the nonprofit addresses. A sense of nearness will interest the donor, building a sense of concern on the donor's part. The immediacy of the problem and the sense of the future instill in the donor the confidence that the nonprofit has defined the problem accurately and offered a compelling solution. This trust leads to a conviction on the part of the donor that the nonprofit will produce the desired results in addressing the problem. Excitement about what can be done will lead to the donor's desire to be part of the program because it will bring satisfaction and enjoyment. Finally, the importance of this project or program will move the donor to take action, to become a participant by making a gift to the nonprofit.

TABLE 4.2. QUALITIES AND RESPONSES.

Case Expression Qualities	Sequence of Response
Relevance	Attention
Proximity	Interest
Sense of the Future	Confidence
Immediacy	Conviction
Excitement	Desire
Importance	Action

Source: The Fund Raising School, 2002.

Putting Pen to Paper: Strategies for Case Statement Development

Writing a compelling case statement—one that truly engages the donor's heart and mind in support of the organization—is one of the most difficult yet rewarding challenges that fundraisers will face. Too often, case expressions are written from the perspective of the organization, containing jargon and reasons that make perfect sense to those working inside the organization but have little relevance for donors or others viewing the organization from an outsider's perspective.

In writing case expressions, it is essential to keep the primary audience (usually donors) constantly in mind. How much do they already know about the cause and your organization? What do they know about your organization's values and approach? What don't they know about your cause and the challenges your organization faces in fulfilling its mission? What specific constituencies is the fundraiser trying to reach, and what stories or information will they find most appealing and compelling?

As a writer of case statements and case expressions, the fundraiser has a huge amount of information available in the case resources file. Depending on the situation, some will be vital to include in the case expression; other information will not be so important. It is up to the fundraiser to make careful and strategic choices regarding what to include and what to exclude in order to create the most effective document possible. Generally speaking, the most effective case statements and expressions:

1. Focus on making it clear to donors what differentiates the organization from others serving the same cause.
2. Engage the donor's emotions, reason, and belief in the organization's ability to get the job done.
3. Create a compelling narrative.
4. Use clear, concrete language.

Each of these elements is examined in more detail in the following section.

Differentiating Your Organization

What makes an organization stand out in a donor's mind is not how it is similar to other organizations serving the same niche but how it is different. Fundraisers thus need to think through what makes their organization unique or special. What differentiates the organization from others serving the same cause? Do the organizational values—*why* or *how* you do what you do—set your organization apart? Does the organization have exceptional leadership? Does the organization approach its work in a unique way or from a unique perspective? When writing case expressions, organizations too often waste time recounting how they are like other organizations serving similar causes. To be successful it is necessary to highlight the differences that make the organization stand out from the crowd.

Appealing to Emotion, Reason, and Organizational Credibility

Fundraisers have much to learn from classic principles of rhetoric. Namely, there are three basic types of evidence that can be used to make a convincing case to donors. You can appeal to their emotions, making them believe passionately in their hearts that supporting your organization is the right thing to do. You can appeal to their reason, convincing them intellectually that supporting your organization is the logical thing to do. Or you can appeal to the credibility of your organization, showing donors that your organization has the ability to keep its promises and successfully complete the work that it sets out to do. Examples of the different appeals are provided in Table 4.3.

Typically a successful case statement or case expression will contain all three appeals to some degree, though the proportion of each will vary. For instance, if you are writing a grant proposal for a foundation, you will likely use more appeals to reason and organizational credibility than emotional appeals because foundations want to know whether your organization is meeting a true societal need and whether your organization can execute the proposed project successfully. If, on the other hand, you are creating a case expression that is a direct mail piece aimed at acquiring first-time donors for animal rights, you might choose to focus on emotional appeals through telling stories or showing photos of animals rescued from abusive situations.

TABLE 4.3. EXAMPLES OF APPEALS TO EMOTION, REASON, AND ORGANIZATIONAL CREDIBILITY.

Emotion	Testimonials and photos of clients of your organization (with permission, of course) Ways the world will be better as a result of your organization's work
Reason	Statistics showing the success of your programs Output and outcome measurements and impacts
Organizational Credibility	Strong staff and volunteer leadership Track record of success

Creating a Narrative

It is important to remember that donors don't have as much familiarity with the organization as the fundraising team. It is therefore the fundraiser's responsibility to create a narrative that leads them step-by-step through the key points that make the case. Too often, writers of case expressions (and particularly case statements) have a tendency to forget that readers need clear transitions from one part of the document to the next. Rather than provide donors with a disjointed set of facts, it is necessary to give donors a cohesive and enjoyable narrative that tells the story of what the organization is, how it makes the world a better place, and what they can do to help.

Using Clear, Concrete Language

Unfortunately, many of us are taught in school that bigger words and longer sentences are better. The professional writing we encounter on the job usually doesn't help dispel this notion, as it is usually jargon-laden and bureaucratic in tone. To be compelling to donors, writers of case expressions have to jettison this excess verbiage and concentrate on using clear, concrete language. Clear language is easily understood. Concrete language is sense-oriented so that donors clearly see, hear, and feel the meaning.

Conclusion

The essence of fundraising success is a fully developed case for support that articulates clearly and boldly the reasons an organization deserves philanthropic gifts. Those who solicit gifts for the organization should be familiar with the case, but they should not try to memorize case statements. Their effectiveness in soliciting comes from their immersion in the cause, their passion for supporting it, and their enthusiasm for inviting others to participate. The best solicitors are those who tell the story in their own words, with the integrity of their dedication to the cause.

Written case statements are effective stage scenery, and well-produced case statements play an important role in furthering the conversation between solicitor and donor. However, donors ultimately make the gift commitment to the credible solicitor whose testimony to the value of the cause persuades the donor to join.

Developing and articulating the case for support is the first step in planning for fundraising. Reviewing and testing the case at least annually will validate that the nonprofit's mission is still compelling and its constituencies well-served.

PART TWO

STRUCTURING YOUR FUNDRAISING

Part Two outlines the total development plan and its elements. Chapter Five provides an overview of the total development plan—that is, the set of fundraising programs or activities to meet a variety of organization and donor needs through lifetime donor development. Not every organization can implement all aspects of a total development plan, but every organization can implement a plan that incorporates the concept of lifetime donor development. The total development plan reminds us of the ongoing nature of fundraising work.

The remaining chapters in this part take a look at the key elements of the total development plan. The annual fund—the topic of Chapter Six—forms the base of a successful fundraising program. Not only does it provide support for the annual operating budget, but it also uses special strategies to recruit new donors, solicit repeat or renewed gifts from earlier donors, and upgrade or increase gifts from year to year. In most cases, larger gifts solicited through the programs outlined in the other chapters in Part Two are received from donors to the annual fund.

Many organizations now operate ongoing major gifts programs as described in Chapter Seven. These might be special one-time gifts, large annual gifts, or gifts made in a capital or endowment campaign. Chapters Eight and Nine focus on the capital campaign and planned giving, respectively, and provide the structures and technical infrastructures needed to organize these two effective programs that help meet long-term major capital and endowment needs.

The total development program is based on the premise that a donor at one level is a prospect for a gift at a higher level. The fundraising vehicles outlined in Part Two must be integrated to make it possible for the organization to embrace the concept of lifetime donor development from the first annual gift to a planned gift.

Not every organization will be able to implement all levels of each program discussed here. But every organization should organize an annual fund that fits its size and scope. Other fundraising programs can be added over time as the donors to the annual fund increase and continue their gifts. Every organization can develop a program to inform donors about making bequests, and it should be the goal of every organization to develop gifts of significance and planned gifts. These not only increase total gifts and contribute to capital and endowment needs but also help reduce fundraising costs or increase returns on fundraising investment.

CHAPTER FIVE

THE TOTAL DEVELOPMENT PLAN

By Timothy L. Seiler

As development and fundraising have become more formalized and professionalized, practitioners and volunteers alike have become more cognizant
of the disciplined, systematic process that effective fundraising follows. Donors,
too, have become more aware of the heightened level of conscious activity on
the part of nonprofits to engage donors and prospective donors more fully and
intimately in the activities of the nonprofit.

The growing seriousness with which nonprofits and fundraising staff and
volunteers take fundraising is seen clearly in two venues: the increase in the
amount of continuing education and professional development and the increase
in academic programs in nonprofit management and fundraising in colleges and
universities. For example, when The Fund Raising School moved from California
to Indiana in 1987 to become part of Indiana University, there were approximately
six hundred participants a year attending about a dozen courses offered in cities
around the United States. As of this writing, more than eight thousand participants per year attend courses in cities in the United States and around the world.
The number of nonprofit academic programs in colleges and universities has
similarly blossomed during this period.

This growth reflects the maturity of nonprofits and their growing understanding of the complexity of building and sustaining a disciplined fundraising program.
More than ever before, nonprofit boards and staff realize that relying on fundraising
special events and direct mail will leave them short of the funds required to sustain

their programs—and operating at a level below their potential. Organizations are discovering that achieving fundraising success year after year calls for a fully integrated plan that develops and nurtures a diversified funding base.

Planning, Communication, and Fundraising

This chapter reflects on the components of the integrated development plan (or the total development plan) and suggests a model for building and sustaining effective fundraising and achieving excellence in fundraising.

Development as an organizational process involves fundraising but is more than fundraising. Development is growth of mission; it includes planning, communications, and fundraising.

Planning calls for vision and leadership. It means setting direction for the future by answering these questions:

Who are we?

What distinguishes us from our competition?

What do we want to accomplish?

How will we reach our goals?

How do we hold ourselves accountable?

The answers to these questions address mission, goals, objectives, programs, evaluation, and stewardship. Answering the questions provides a core script for communications. Effective communications programs include not only dissemination of information but also a means for interaction with constituencies. Good communications programs seek to engage constituencies in substantive exchange of ideas, allowing a forum for constituencies to articulate their interests and desires to the nonprofit. The best communications programs in the most effective development plans seek to nurture in-depth relationships with constituencies. They provide opportunities for constituencies to understand the organization's case for support, to endorse the case, and to become involved in the active articulation of the case.

Effective communications plans invite constituencies to join in sharing their own dreams and vision for how they can participate in fulfilling the mission of the nonprofit. Communications plans help cultivate relationships between prospective donors and the organization. They provide a means for involvement in the life of the organization.

Fundraising is an essential component of a development plan, and it often is the ultimate goal of the overall plan. Fundraising, however, is more than just asking for money. Effective fundraising includes identifying the most qualified prospective donors by focusing on their linkage to the organization and their interest in its work as well as their ability to make gifts. Fundraising involves the development of a relationship between prospective donors and the organization, a relationship fostered by mutual values and shared interests. As the organization makes its case, and as prospective donors realize how their own interests are met by the work of the organization, fundraising becomes a process of the mutual fulfillment of the donors' and the organization's needs.

Types of Gifts

Historically, organizational financial needs have fallen into these categories: ongoing program support, special purpose needs, capital needs, and endowment needs. The fundraising programs for raising the needed funds have been the annual fund, special gifts, capital campaign, and planned giving, all explained more fully in later chapters of the book. This model is still relevant today, although one modification seems to be a renaming of the special gifts program as a major gifts program. This is especially true in large fundraising programs most often found in colleges and universities, hospitals and medical centers, and large mainstream arts organizations such as metropolitan opera organizations, art museums, and urban theatre organizations. Major gifts programs are often the natural outgrowth of successful capital campaigns and are a means of continuing the higher level of giving established during the capital campaign. A total fundraising program might be illustrated with a diagram such as a four-legged stool (see Figure 5.1).

The annual fund is still the foundation of all successful fundraising. Donors contribute to the annual fund to support current, ongoing programs to fulfill the organization's mission. The ongoing programs are the organization's way of addressing the larger needs of the community. The programs provide solutions to the problems that the donor and the organization agree need to be addressed.

The annual fund also serves to bond a large number of donors to the organization through recurring gifts. As donors develop a history of giving, they grow more interested in and involved with the success of the organization. This base of regular givers becomes the most likely core group of donors for other fundraising programs such as major gifts, capital gifts, and planned gifts.

Although the special gift in response to a special need or opportunity is still a part of a total development program, the more likely formalization of this type of program and gift is the major gift. Major gifts are part of all campaigns—annual, capital, and endowment—and they are also a program; that is, it has become a common practice for organizations to maintain a major gifts program

FIGURE 5.1. THE FOUR-LEGGED STOOL OF FUNDRAISING.

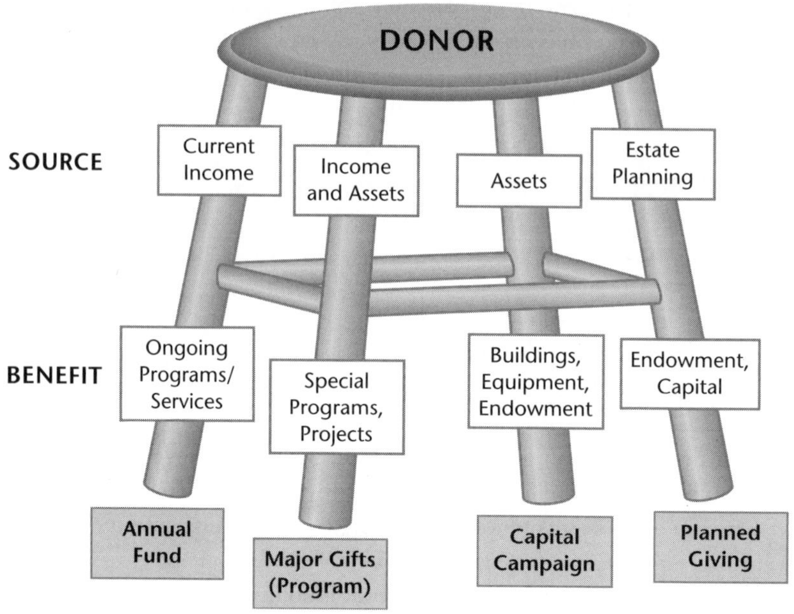

DONOR

SOURCE

| Current Income | Income and Assets | Assets | Estate Planning |

BENEFIT

| Ongoing Programs/ Services | Special Programs, Projects | Buildings, Equipment, Endowment | Endowment, Capital |

| **Annual Fund** | **Major Gifts (Program)** | **Capital Campaign** | **Planned Giving** |

Source: The Fund Raising School, 2009b, p. II-6.

alongside the annual fund. The major gift is one that is larger than the typical gift to the annual fund, raising the sights of the donor and bonding the donor even more closely to the organization.

Capital campaigns meet the organization's needs for increasing its own assets, often physical, such as renovating facilities, building new facilities, or acquiring land for expansion. Capital campaigns also support program development and expansion, and, increasingly, they support endowment. The comprehensive capital campaigns today have included all components of the integrated fundraising plan: an increase in the annual fund, capital needs (including buildings and programs), and endowment.

Because capital campaigns seek very large gifts, donors typically make their gifts from their own asset base. Their gifts will generally be pledged over a period of years, typically the number of years of the campaign itself.

In the mega-campaigns today, capital campaigns have lasted five to seven years, with some continuing for as long as ten years, although some definitions limit capital campaigns to seven years. In these larger campaigns it has not been uncommon for donors to make multiple gifts or to extend their pledges.

Planned giving has been one of the most exciting growth areas in fundraising in recent years. Planned gifts, by definition, are gifts made in the present but whose value to the organization usually occurs at a later time, generally at the death of the donor or a surviving beneficiary. The most common forms of planned gifts are wills and bequests, charitable gift annuities, charitable trusts, and pooled income funds. Other types of planned gifts are life estates, insurance, and bargain sales. In the latter part of the 1990s, as employee pension plans accelerated in value, qualified pension plans became an exciting planned gift option for many donors.

Whereas some planned gift instruments are highly sophisticated and technical and may be beyond the capacity of smaller nonprofits to manage, wills and bequests are the simplest form of planned gifts. Every nonprofit seeking to build a totally integrated development plan should be involved in planned giving at least through wills and bequests.

One of the conventional models of fundraising is the donor pyramid (see Figure 5.2), demonstrating the typical process of donor involvement from

FIGURE 5.2. DONOR PYRAMID OF FUNDRAISING STRATEGIES.

Source: The Fund Raising School, 2009b, p. IV-8.

annual gifts to special or major gifts, to the capital gift, and ultimately to the planned gift. Although there will be an occasional exception—say, a donor's first gift as a capital gift—this model still has validity today. Its primary value is in demonstrating the interrelatedness of all the components of the integrated development plan. Effective fundraising recognizes how the components are interdependent and manages the process of developing the components as mutually reinforcing.

Prerequisites for Implementing the Integrated Development Plan

When Hank Rosso originally wrote this chapter, he outlined the prerequisites: the supporting elements for successful implementation of the integrated development plan. Those elements still pertain today and are reprinted here.

Certain requisites will command the attention of the governing board and the senior management team before this broader program of fundraising can be implemented.

Governance. The statement of the overall needs, internal and external, and the plan to raise the funds that will address the internal needs must be reviewed, accepted, and approved by the governing board. It is essential that board members place their full support behind the plan by contributing financially to the best of their ability and by urging others to do so.

Management. The chief executive must serve as the principal advocate for the continuing advancement of the organization into the future. The senior management group, with the full participation of board members, must articulate the values for the organization and participate in communicating these values to the constituency. The chief executive—as the primary link to the governing board and, through the board, to the larger constituency—must constantly champion the development program and the goals that it seeks to serve.

Programs and Services Staff. Program accomplishments, not budget requirements, will attract generous gift support to the organization. The competence and the commitment of the program staff will provide the motivation for people to give and for individuals to involve themselves as volunteers. Program specialists make excellent "expert witnesses." As members of a soliciting team, they can effectively articulate the scope and worth of the programs. Key program staff members should team with board members and other volunteers to explain the organization's accomplishments to potential contributors.

Fundraising Staff. The ability of this staff to plan, organize, and administer programs will determine the outcome of the fundraising effort. However, administration is not the single factor that is most conducive to effective fundraising. Other compelling factors are adequate budget, proper office space, competent support staff, and sincere acknowledgment by program and management staff that fundraising is an integral part of the total organization.

All four of the factors that contribute to the success of a total development program are interrelated and must not remain in bureaucratic isolation. None should be seen as weaker than or subservient to any of the others. All four are integral parts of the organization's structure and therefore interdependent.

Essential Support

A number of elements must support the organization and its mission:

- Responsible board membership, competent management, quality services, concern for the individual, valid needs, and stewardship through open accountability will justify the case for philanthropic generosity.
- The mission statement, the very foundation of the organization's case position, must be a statement of shared values or a philosophical expression of the human or societal needs that the organization is endeavoring to serve. The mission is a statement of the organization's reason for being.
- Proper communication methods require an acknowledgment of the constituents' needs and wants, an awareness of their perceptions and their requirements, and a readiness to design the public relations plan that will respond to these needs.
- Acceptance of fundraising as a management function and as a management process requires the acceptance of the chief fundraising officer as an important member of the senior management team.
- The involvement of board members, administrators, and program staff members with the development function is essential to ensure that key people become fully conversant with and supportive of fundraising objectives, policies, strategies, plans, and programs.
- The need to institutionalize the development function by weaving it into the fabric and endowing it with the power and the dignity of the organization is a reality in a complex, somewhat turbulent, and always challenging environment. Fundraising must bear the mantle of the institutional mission as its symbol of honor.

To make this plan effective, the following components need to be addressed:

I. The Institutional Plan
   A. Plans must be created that reach at least three to five years forward as a design of the organization's strategy for addressing its mission, goals, and objectives.
   B. The plan should set forth details of program support, special purpose, and capital and endowment needs for the period of the plan. The dollar requirements can serve as a guide to fundraising programs for each year of the plan, as well as for the total period.
II. Full Board Involvement
   A. A sense of personal ownership is an important motivating force to inspire board members, volunteers, and staff members to give and to work for the success of the program. Ownership can be generated by encouraging people to assist in determining needs, identifying prospects, and helping with solicitation.
   B. The board is the constituency's energy center. It can mirror the constituency's interest. It should serve as a sounding board to receive and reflect the constituency's feelings about the program and about the organization's readiness for major fundraising. It can and should present and represent the organization to its constituency.
III. Case and Cases: The Primary Document
   A. Each request for gifts must have a case of its own, drawn from the organization's larger case.
   B. Each case must be exciting, compelling, and responsive to the prospective donor's interests and requirements for information.
   C. The case must describe valid needs, and it must offer various gift options that will be suitable to the contributor's situation to facilitate the donor's gift-making capabilities.
   D. The case must be renewed regularly if it is to have merit and if it is to have pertinence for prospective contributors.
IV. Volunteers for Fundraising
   A. Volunteers will play many roles willingly in the fundraising program once their commitment to the organization has been confirmed.
   B. To encourage this commitment, volunteers must be meaningfully involved, properly recognized, and given a sense of importance. They must be made to feel that they are an important part of a worthwhile team serving a worthwhile program—that their involvement is making a difference.
   C. Training for volunteers must have a major place in this transaction.

V. Planning
  A. The total development program is a full-circle approach to the organization. It examines every aspect of an organization's being. The plan's final draft must be converted into a living document with meaning for each board member, each member of any advisory body, and each staff member, as well as for strategically important leaders in the organization's service area.
  B. To be effective, the plan for total development should be prepared, evaluated, refined, and accepted by those people who possess the power to put it into action.

The integrated or total development plan will be necessary for sustainable fundraising success as the twenty-first century unfolds. Organizations that limit themselves to the lower-end activities of special events and direct mail deprive themselves of the opportunity for the high-impact major gift or the institution-changing capital or planned gift. Fundraising that proceeds with pride in mission, boldly inviting large gifts from committed donors, will raise considerably more money through a total development plan than through hit-and-miss appeals designed only to keep the doors open.

Piecemeal fundraising activities and programs that do not integrate all four components of a fundraising program—annual fund, major gifts, capital campaign, and planned giving—limit their own opportunities for long-term fundraising success.

Organizations running only an annual fund will find themselves always stressed to keep the doors open by raising only what they need, year after year. This strategy overlooks the opportunities present for occasional major gifts for special programs or projects as well as the opportunity to expand the organization's capital (assets) or the opportunity to build long-term sustainability through an endowment. At the other extreme, organizations that concentrate only on endowment fundraising miss the opportunity to build enduring relationships and to expand their constituencies—hallmarks of an annual fund.

Conclusion

The totally integrated development plan recognizes the giving patterns of the majority of donors. The annual fund builds a large base of loyal donors who give repeatedly over many years. Their deepening commitment to the organization makes them likely donors for special gifts in addition to their annual gifts. The total development program recognizes that the annual fund and special or major gifts programs form the solid base for the occasional capital campaign that expands the asset base of the organization. A carefully coordinated orchestration of all the components of the integrated program realize that the ultimate gifts made through planned giving will typically be the result of donors who have participated in the earlier stages of the total development program. This wisdom about fundraising has been substantiated through Schervish (2000b), who found that major donors had developed a philanthropic identification with the organization through what he called "communities of participation." These are the very structures that the total development program promotes.

Subsequent chapters in this book on the annual fund, major gifts, capital campaign, and planned giving address the strengths of each discrete fundraising program. Each leg of the fundraising stool plays a strategic role in the life of the organization's fundraising. The overall fundraising program (the four-legged stool), when it is fully integrated and carefully managed, positions the organization to conduct and manage fundraising most effectively.

The power and the efficacy of the total development plan lie in bringing to bear the essential elements for long-term fundraising success. These include market-oriented programs and services; well-informed constituencies capable of and willing to serve the mission; a well-defined workable plan that can be monitored, evaluated, and adapted; dedicated leadership, staff, board, and other volunteers willing to work, to give, and to ask others to give; and a high level of professional accountability and prudent stewardship.

These elements, when properly managed with disciplined attention to the demands of organized fundraising, will carry organizations to higher and higher levels of effectiveness. The total development plan will raise the funds necessary for program support, special needs, capital needs, and long-term endowment needs. The total development plan demands commitment to hard work. It requires investment of time, energy, and financial resources. However, its returns are high and position an organization for long-term sustainability and growth.

CHAPTER SIX

THE ANNUAL FUND

By Henry A. Rosso

Updates by Meg Gammage-Tucker

The annual fund is fundamental to the operational viability of nonprofit organizations. It has earned this distinction by the simple fact that it provides the foundation for all other fundraising activities. Its primary function is to establish a base of donors whose financial and volunteer support ensure fulfillment of the organization's mission. The annual fund encourages the building of relationships through a regular exchange of information and the proper solicitation and stewardship of contributions. This regular and effective interaction serves to enhance the donors' knowledge, involvement, and, ultimately, investments in the organization.

A successful annual campaign ensures a steady flow of human and financial support and is based on a carefully planned and implemented program. A successful annual fund program will also have support from a broad base of constituents including individuals, corporations, foundations, and civic and other community organizations. And all effective fundraising programs—no matter the constituency—are based on thoughtful planning and the building of solid relationships.

Constituents and the Annual Fund

People make philanthropic gifts for many different reasons, including but certainly not limited to the following:

- They are moved to give by the urgency of a current community need.
- They respect an organization's commitment to carry out programs that are responsive to a community issue.
- They know and respect someone who works for an organization.
- They believe there will be a substantial return on their investment for themselves and/or their community.
- They are drawn to the social aspects of being involved with a cause.
- Their religious or spiritual beliefs harmonize with a cause.
- They want to give something back to an organization, community, or friend.

However, people do not give to an organization simply because the organization needs money. Rather, it is generally accepted that "people give to people with causes" and "they give to people who ask on behalf of causes that matter to them."

The focus of this work is on individuals, as the bulk of the money that is given away annually in the United States—historically approximately 75 percent of the total—comes from individuals. However, as with all fundraising programs, a diverse constituent base is important. And the principles and techniques noted herein can and should be applied to corporations, foundations, and other organizations, and relationships with each of these constituent groups should be developed to the greatest extent possible.

Individuals tend to give from three sources: discretionary or disposable income, their assets, and estates. Historically, annual campaigns generally sought funding from individuals' discretionary income. For the most part, the bulk of individuals make gifts that do not compel them to give up something important in their lives or cause them to change their standard of living.

In order to grow the interest and commitment of donors to give larger gifts to support special projects, for capital purposes, or to help build the organization's endowment holdings, the interests of the contributor must be nurtured. Involvement is invited through the yearly solicitation of gifts for the annual fund. The ongoing processes of cultivation and solicitation encourage the prospective donor to become more knowledgeable and understanding of the organization's mission and programs, and therefore more supportive. The annual campaign must therefore be a thoughtfully devised and effectively executed plan that creates and enhances a strong force of advocates who will dedicate themselves to the organization's advancement through their philanthropy and volunteer activities.

Benefits of the Annual Fund

The benefits and objectives of an annual fund are as follows:

- To inform, involve, and bond constituents to the organization
- To establish habits and patterns of giving through regular and effective cultivation, solicitation, and stewardship
- To provide annual (preferably unrestricted) support for operations and programs
- To expand the donor base by soliciting gifts from new prospects and constituencies
- To build a base of donors that can be cultivated to support all types of fundraising activities (including capital, endowment, and special projects)
- To assist with identification and cultivation of lead and major donors and volunteer leaders
- To offer accountability and transparency through regular communications
- To provide an annual review of organizational priorities, the case for support, and communications
- To ensure improvement of cultivation, solicitation, and stewardship practices

As Table 6.1 illustrates, the annual fund enhances donor involvement through the major gift level.

The Annual Fund Team

Good teamwork is essential to the success of the annual fund program. Volunteers become a strategic force as advocates, peers, links to the larger community, and solicitors without a salaried interest. It is necessary to involve key volunteer leaders, beginning with the governing board, in the membership of an annual fund committee. As a management force for the annual fund, the committee should invite to its membership those individuals within the community who are willing to contribute the time, energy, and talent needed to ensure a successful, productive undertaking.

The fundraiser serves in a staff support relationship to the annual fund committee and assumes responsibility for preparing the annual fund plan in draft form for review, study, modification, acceptance, or rejection by the annual fund committee. To enhance the workability of the plan early in the planning stages, the fundraising officer must involve the chair and other strategic members of the committee. The fundraising professional should control the preparation process

TABLE 6.1. THE DEVELOPMENT PROCESS.

The Objective	The Process	What Is Required
Identify potential prospects	List development	Build lists of, identify, and research constituents
Convert potential prospects into qualified prospects	Test list effectiveness identifying linkages	Refine prospect development
Convert qualified prospects into initial donors	Build on linkages, test interest, ask, acknowledge	Solicit by personal contact via telephone, direct mail, and special events
Convert initial giver into donor of record	Build on interests and linkages, ask, acknowledge	Report use of gift, invite to renew
Increase the gift	Research, build on linkages, interests, inform, ask, acknowledge	Report, involve, invite to renew and increase gift, use gift club concept
Secure special gift ($1,000 +)	Continue research through linkages, involve, build on interests, ask, acknowledge	Describe special needs and how money is used, solicit personally, invite to gift club membership
Secure major gift ($10,000 +)	Use all linkages to validate as major prospect, ask, acknowledge, reward	Involve in institution: planning, case evaluation, needs determination, cultivation events, personal letters
Secure big gift	Continue involvement through linkages, add to interests, foster desire to give, ask, acknowledge, reward	Report, involve constituent as important advocate, involve through cultivation events, personal reports, personal contacts
Secure planned gift	Continue involvement, create feelings of belonging to and identifying with institution, foster mutuality of interests	Strengthen linkage, strengthen involvement

Source: The Fund Raising School, 2002.

while ensuring that the wisdom and involvement of the committee are effectively employed throughout planning and implementation.

After accepting the annual plan, the primary function of the annual fund committee is to execute it. In accepting the plan, the committee as a whole attests to the validity of the financial needs that justify the goal. It acknowledges that the goal is reasonable and achievable. It gives evidence of the committee members' willingness to make their own gifts at the level of their capabilities at the beginning of the program, as well as to join in the soliciting process by asking other prospects to do the same. And, although prospect research is a staff responsibility, this research can be expanded and enriched significantly through a working partnership of staff and informed volunteers who have knowledge of the financial structure of the community in which the fundraising is to be accomplished.

Setting and Achieving the Annual Fund Goal

The annual fund can be enhanced by following time-tested working principles. One of the most important principles is the "arithmetic of fundraising." In planning for an annual fund, this concept directs the fundraiser to determine the quality and quantity of gifts that are required to achieve the organization's financial goals.

Determining the number and size of gifts that are required to ensure the achievement of a fundraising goal had its genesis in the planning for capital campaigns. This planning device has been employed equally successfully in determining the course and strategies of an annual fund. The chances for success will be much stronger if a determination can be made about both the numbers required and the methodologies that must be employed to achieve those numbers.

Decisions about what strategies will be pursued should then be informed by the following:

- What quality (or size) of gifts are required and how many are needed?
- How many prospects are needed to ensure you will have enough donors?
- Does the organization's current donor base have the number of prospects necessary to support the number of gifts required?
- Is it realistic to expect that the prospects can be identified and qualified and will give to the annual fund?
- If these questions cannot be answered clearly, factually, and positively, then is the goal for the annual fund realistic?

The arithmetic concept illustrates that a large amount of the money to be raised will come from a small number of contributors who are encouraged to provide what will necessarily be larger gifts. The formula is as follows:

- The top 10 percent of the gifts received during the annual fund have the potential to produce 60 percent of the money required to meet the goal.
- The next 20 percent of gifts will account for 15 to 25 percent of the money required.
- The remaining 70 percent of gifts will cover the remaining 15 to 25 percent of funds required.

As shown in Exhibit 6.1, it is truly possible to secure 484 gifts from 960 prospects to reach the 60 percent mark, *particularly if these prospects are part of the donor base that has a history of giving to the organization.* Included in the prospect listing are individuals, associations, foundations, corporations, small businesses, and others who give to annual funds. The only relevant criterion here is—do they give to operations and/or current program support?

The range of gifts dictated by the gift range chart gives eloquent testimony to the role of the annual fund in developing an involved and informed donor base. Within the base are individuals with the capability of making an extraordinary gift to the organization, yet in many cases, the gift will not be made, simply because the organization has not asked for it. If the gift is not actively sought, the larger gift—in most cases—will not be made.

Smaller gifts—which are costly to raise—should be acknowledged properly when received, but they should be less actively solicited than the larger gifts listed in the exhibit. Although it is easy to submit to the rationale that many small gifts will be easier to secure than the two largest gifts, it will require that five hundred $100 gifts substitute for two $25,000 gifts in Exhibit 6.1; this means that four hundred prospects must be solicited to secure the substituted one hundred gifts.

Certain principles become apparent quite readily. The gift range chart gives form to planning. The initial planning focus is not on a range of activity but on the more practical aspects of fundraising: the acquisition of large gifts that will make the critical difference in achieving the goal. The chart encourages that key issues be addressed: how many gifts, and at what amount, must the fundraising team produce to make the goal? Are the prospects available? If not, what can be done about it?

Gift charts are designed to be flexible instruments. The ratio of prospects from the top of the chart to the bottom of the chart may be changed to coincide with the reality of the organization's particular donor base and the availability of prospects that are required at each gift level. Flexibility pertains also to the numbers of donors and prospects that are required at each gift level. In some

EXHIBIT 6.1. ANNUAL FUND GIFT RANGE CHART: $500,000 GOAL.

Gift Range $	# of Gifts	Cumulative # of Gifts	Prospect #	Cumulative # of Prospects	$ per Range	Cumulative $
25,000+	2	2	10 (5:1)	10	50,000	50,000
10,000	4	6	20 (5:1)	30	40,000	90,000
2,500	18	24	72 (4:1)	102	45,000	135,000
1,000	30	54	120 (4:1)	222	30,000	165,000
500	110	164	330 (3:1)	552	55,000	220,000
250	320	484	960 (3:1)	1,512	80,000	300,000
	10% of donors					60% of goal
100	1,000	1,484	3,000 (3:1)	4,512	100,000	400,000
	20% of donors					20% of goal
Under 100	3,334	4,818	6,668 (2:1)	11,180	100,020	500,020
	70% of donors					20% of goal

Source: The Fund Raising School, 2009b, p. IV-23.

situations, it may be possible to secure more than the required two gifts at the top of each chart. Do not deny the reality of the figures, but be assertive when identifying prospects. Only through continual and effective research will prospects be found.

Understanding and Using the Donor Base

Although fundraising is relatively straightforward as a concept, it is also a demanding taskmaster. Attention must be given to the simple management rules that can make a difference. One of the simplest of these rules is to scrutinize and analyze the gift potential in the donor base before making any effort to determine specific techniques.

Regularly profiling the donor base provides the organization with a wealth of information about the giving patterns of its constituency and how those patterns can be accessed and maximized. The following questions should be asked:

- How many donors give annually?
- What is the frequency of the gift? Once a year, twice a year, or more often?
- How many donors give on a monthly basis? What is the date of the most recent gift?
- What is the level of giving? How many give $10,000 or more a year? $1,000 to $5,000? $500 to $999? $100 to $499? Less than $100?
- Is there a pattern of the gift being repeated but not upgraded over the years?
- Is a regular request made that the gift be upgraded?
- Do the records identify donors who give regularly to the annual fund as well as make special-purpose, capital, or endowment gifts?
- Is there a specific person identified as the solicitor of the gift?
- What is the pattern of giving by staff members, trustees, and members of advisory councils or non-board-related support committees?

This vital information is important to fundraising and is an essential part of the fundraiser's knowledge. This information will enable the person planning the fundraising program to identify the potential gifts required by the gift range chart and to meet the organization's financial goals.

As the form in Table 6.2 shows, the data retrieved from the donor base as a result of this search can be organized easily to analyze the base's potential. These data should reflect the number and dominance of gift ranges over the past four (or more) years.

TABLE 6.2. SEGMENTING DONOR DATA.

Gift Ranges	Number of Gifts and Total Contributions ($)			
	Current Year	Last Year	Two Years Ago	Three Years Ago
$10,000+				
$5,000–9,999				
$1,000–4,999				
$500–1,000				
$100–499				
$50–99				

Source: Adapted from Henry A. Rosso and Associates, *Achieving Excellence in Fund Raising* (2nd ed.), p. 80. Copyright © Jossey-Bass Inc., Publishers. Reprinted by permission of Jossey-Bass Inc., a subsidiary of John Wiley & Sons, Inc.

By replacing numbers of gifts with names of prospects, these data can be converted to a workable form. This measurement could be applied to all gifts of $100 or more. Gifts at this level show a greater tendency to repeat and to be upgraded, thus creating the opportunity for the solicitation of a special gift, major gift, or planned gift.

In fundraising parlance, *longevity* refers to the number of years that the person has been giving, *frequency* to the number of gifts made during the year, *recency* to the date of the most recent gift, and *amount* to the dollar value of the annual gift or the cumulative value of multiple gifts made in one year. Working together, these bits of information become the determining factor in evaluating whether a donor of record might respond positively to a request for one of the larger gifts designated on the gift range chart and the mechanism for seeking that gift. Uninformed guesswork has no place in fundraising. The justification for the annual fund's goal must come in the form of accurate information that the numbers of prospects required are indeed available and that the prospects do have the ability to give at the level indicated by the gift range chart.

Annual Fund Solicitation Methods

By understanding the different ways to solicit a gift, volunteers can reduce their fear of rejection and develop realistic expectations based on their choice of solicitation. The following discussion describes the relative effectiveness, in descending order, of the various methods used to solicit gifts. As methods become less personalized, the likelihood of obtaining a gift is also reduced. Face-to-face solicitation by a peer of the prospective donor is by far the most effective method; solicitation through media is the least effective.

Personal Face-to-Face Solicitation

A personal face-to-face visit by a team is far and away the most effective method of solicitation. The team is made up of two people—a peer of the prospect accompanied by the organization's chief executive, the fundraising officer, a program person, or another volunteer. The peer is a volunteer, the best link to the prospect, and an advocate for the organization; the staff person is the expert witness, there to answer any questions and to make sure that the volunteer asks for the gift.

Solicitation by Letter from a Peer

A peer writes to friends, colleagues, and family members on personal stationery. If the prospect fails to respond to the letter appeal and the solicitor declines or fails to place a follow-up call to request the gift, then usually a gift will not be made.

Solicitation by Phone Call from a Peer

A personal telephone call placed by a peer, with or without a follow-up letter, will have a similar result as the solicitation by personal letter. The chance of eliciting a gift is far greater with a follow-up letter or even a reminder via e-mail than without such follow-up. In fact, it is often the follow-up that motivates the prospect to make the gift. Response mechanisms included in the follow-up letter or e-mail will make it easier for the prospect to make a gift.

Each of the procedures discussed so far requires some form of personal contact and follow-up with each potential donor. In Exhibit 6.1, each of the 222 prospects listed at the $1,000-and-larger gift level represents a major opportunity to secure a gift. Each prospect must be approached on a personal basis by no less than a personal visit or a personal telephone call. If at all possible, the personal approach should even be extended to the prospects in categories of $250 and larger. These prospects are too valuable to be relegated to the impersonal approaches because the remaining methods of solicitation are far less effective in obtaining substantial gifts.

Personalized Letters and E-Mail

The personalized letter should include the prospect's name and address in the letter; both letter and e-mail should use the name in the salutation. Upgrade and renewal mailings are sent to appropriate segments of these lists. Organizations have become very adept at shifting a personalized letter to personalized e-mail. Whenever possible, identify people who prefer being contacted by e-mail; build a separate list of these people, and tailor solicitations (and acknowledgments) to these e-mail prospects.

Impersonal Letters (Direct Mail) and E-Mail

Nonpersonalized direct mail and e-mail have a unique and important place in the annual campaign. The overall return on investment (ROI) for direct mail and e-mail is not as substantial as for personal solicitation, but it is a useful way to acquire new donors. And for some donors, impersonal communication is a preferred method for acquiring basic knowledge about the organization's activities.

An organization must continuously seek new donors to replace those lost through attrition. The least expensive way, with the largest reach, is through direct mail or the Internet. Mail and e-mail lists can be purchased, rented, borrowed from other organizations, or obtained from current board members and friends of the organization, government lists, and other sources. Because these lists are made up of potential prospects, the response will not be nearly as successful in raising funds as the personalized letter. However, a donor acquisition mailing can cost more than it brings in yet still be considered successful if it enables the organization to obtain new donors.

Impersonal Phone Call

Impersonal telephone calls, often made as part of a phone-a-thon or telefund, are successful for some organizations (such as universities that employ student callers). This method is not usually successful for other nonprofits that lack the staff or volunteer resources to reach enough donors. Add to this the use of voicemail and caller ID, and the organization will find it necessary to make numerous calls just to get to speak to a person and not a machine. In addition, nonprofits must maintain and honor their own internal lists of donors who do not wished to be contacted by phone.

Special Events and Benefits

These activities are staged for a variety of reasons, one of which is to raise money for current programs and operating support. Special events can produce 50-percent net revenues for the organization but are costly in terms of staff and volunteer time. The primary benefits of hosting these opportunities are to educate the community about the organization's work; to recognize and honor volunteers, donors, and other supporters; to improve the organization's image in the community; and to recruit and involve volunteers.

Door-to-Door Soliciting

Very few organizations in the United States use this arduous method of fundraising, and even then, not with a great deal of success. Local schools and a small number of well-known national organizations have had some success, especially after publicly announcing their intentions to the local community.

Internet, Traditional and Social Media, and Advertising

Access to information about nonprofits and the capability for individuals to give to organizations through their websites or social media outlets (or through charitable giving "portals" for smaller organizations) have become important to the success of many annual fund programs. All communication vehicles, from letterhead to newsletters to solicitations, should direct prospective supporters to the nonprofit's website both to learn more about the organization and to use an online mechanism for gifting. However, it is important to note that for most organizations, the Internet and social media are still more about "friendraising" than fundraising. Very few organizations currently derive a high percentage of philanthropic contributions from these sources.

Advertising space in newspapers and airtime on radio and TV are costly and require a strong emotional appeal. Most recent success through advertising campaigns has occurred following a major natural disaster (such as a tsunami, hurricane, flood, or earthquake) or repercussions of violence (such as a terrorist attack or refugees fleeing a war zone) to motivate what are essentially impulse givers to respond. Newspaper articles and feature stories are good for publicity but rarely generate much in the way of contributions.

The Annual Fund Plan and Calendar

With rare exceptions, nonprofit organizations are always in need of funding for their operations and delivery of programs and services. However, to take proper advantage of funding opportunities, the organization must allow sufficient time for planning, research, volunteer recruitment, cultivation, and solicitation of the critically important major donors.

Planning includes analysis—that is, a prodding curiosity about the diversity of financial needs that will affect fundraising plans in the fiscal year ahead. In addition to current program support, will there be a need to raise special-purpose, capital, and endowment money? How will this affect the annual fund plan?

The solicitation of gifts in person, by mail, by phone, through special events, and through grant applications is a year-round activity. A wisely developed plan will provide for multiple mail and e-mail solicitations at carefully decided times during the course of the entire year. It will also allow for a leveraging of different solicitation methods, as it is increasingly important for organizations to consider how to time their various methods of contacting donors so that donors have the opportunity to respond through the medium that suits them best. Perhaps one of the greatest advantages of a year-long annual fund calendar is flexibility. This enables work to be done with annual major gift prospects in accordance with their requirements and without the artificial constraints of an unrealistic timeline imposed by the organization. Volunteers' time must be put to judicious use throughout all of this, something that a flexible timetable also permits. Sensitivity to the importance of building and maintaining relationships with major contributors demands it.

Conclusion

The annual fund campaign requires a carefully devised plan and timetable, people with the right abilities in the right roles, and, most of all, the willingness and ability to ask for gifts. "Secure the gift, renew the gift, upgrade the gift" are the keys to its success—year in and year out.

The annual fund is the most effective strategy to invite, involve, and bond the constituency to the organization, making it a cornerstone of organizational sustainability. This strength will enhance the organization's ability to raise funds for current program support, for special purposes, and for capital projects and endowment because the organization will be asking a constituency that has been properly initiated and invested.

If done effectively, the annual fund can and should do all of the following:

- Inform, involve, and bond constituents to the organization.
- Establish habits and patterns of giving.
- Provide annual funding for operations and programs.
- Expand the donor base by soliciting gifts from new prospects and constituencies.
- Assist with identification and cultivation of lead and major donors and volunteer leaders.
- Provide accountability and transparency through regular communications.
- Offer an annual review of organizational priorities, the case for support, and communication.
- Ensure improvement of cultivation, solicitation, and stewardship practices.

CHAPTER SEVEN

MAJOR GIFTS

By James M. Hodge

Nonprofit organizations large and small rely heavily on major gifts to reach annual fund objectives as well as to ensure the success of capital campaigns. The Fund Raising School model of a total development program depends on personal solicitation of major gifts to complete the donor pyramid. The definitions of a major gift vary as greatly as the institutions themselves. One thing is certain: major gifts are inspired gifts that have a significant impact on the development program and the institution. Such gifts make it possible to launch new program initiatives, transform the physical plant, and endow vital components of nonprofit organizations. Defining major gifts by their size alone is insufficient to characterize the role they play in an organization's vitality. One group's definition may be $1,000 while another's may be $100,000.

Major gifts (also known as "gifts of significance") come in many forms. They may be substantial cash contributions, gifts of appreciated securities, or in-kind gifts such as contributions of valuable art or tangible personal property. Often major gifts are in the form of multiyear pledges given outright or through planned giving vehicles such as bequests, charitable trusts, or gift annuities. Regardless of the form they take, gifts of significance usually come from donors who have contributed several "step gifts" over a period of time. Charitable step gifts are smaller gifts given to the nonprofit that allow the organization to demonstrate how it uses contributions and how it reports on the impact of such gifts. The Fund Raising School's philosophy is that every benefactor, regardless of gift size, is a prospective benefactor for a gift at a higher level. Leaders in the field of fundraising have posited models of giving leading to major or ultimate gifts. Perhaps one of the best examples is that espoused by David Dunlop (2000). Dunlop classifies gifts as "annual," "special/capital," and "ultimate." His work details the size, frequency, types, and characteristics of gifts on a continuum. In this model, major gifts are ten to twenty-five times larger than the annual gift. They are infrequently requested and require considerable thought on the part of the benefactor prior to confirming a commitment. These and other similar models of major gifts presented by Dunlop give form and context to the work of major gift officers.

Although most models focus on the sizes, types, and purposes of major gifts, a new or perhaps renewed perspective on major gifts is emerging in the philanthropic literature as well as in the practice of development. These models involve ever-deepening relationships between the fundraiser and the benefactor, as well as between the benefactor's values and the institution's mission. Such models consider how the value systems of donors overlap with the core values and mission of the organization. These are the models of transforming philanthropy (see Figure 7.1). The theory behind such models is based on the *why* of giving far more than the *how* of giving. Gifts of significance are given to organizations that earn the trust and confidence of benefactors. Eric Uslaner (2002) observed, "Trust matters most for those activities that signify the greatest commitment to your community: donating money and especially giving time" (p. 133). Covey (2006) noted, "Trust is a function of two things: character and competence. Character includes your integrity, your motive, your intent with people. Competence includes your capabilities, your skills, your results, your track record. And both are vital" (p. 30). Big ideas compel these philanthropically minded individuals to invest in, partner with, and commit to meaningful contributions to worthy organizations.

FIGURE 7.1. STAGES OF PHILANTHROPY.

Transactions			Transformations	
Quid Pro Quo	Obligation	Gratitude	Relationship	Ownership/ Partnership

Transitions

Source: Adapted from Henry A. Rosso and Associates, *Achieving Excellence in Fund Raising* (2nd ed.), p. 90. Copyright © Jossey-Bass Inc., Publishers. Reprinted by permission of Jossey-Bass Inc., a subsidiary of John Wiley & Sons, Inc.

Relationship-based models of philanthropy require the fundraiser to be an "agent of change," as articulated by Sheldon Garber (1993) in a thoughtful essay. As agents of change, development officers are charged with articulating the institutional mission, probing the core values of prospective major benefactors through values-based inquiry, and developing a deeper sense of the role and meaning of philanthropy in one's life.

Regardless of the model of philanthropy, there are two essential aspects to the work of major gift fundraisers. Fundraisers must work with volunteers to determine both the *financial* capacity of prospective benefactors and the *inclination* those benefactors may have to make a gift to a specific organization. Determining donor capacity requires the fundraiser to explore indices of wealth from public records, garner information from volunteers who know the prospective benefactor, and draw conclusions based on interactions with the benefactors themselves. Some development offices have full-time staff whose job it is to search databases and sources of wealth to determine the financial capacity of prospective benefactors. With or without such research staff, it is imperative that the fundraiser garner all possible knowledge about prospective benefactors before formulating a request. Fortunately, in this age of information, and with powerful search engines such as Google, this research has been more readily available to all in the profession.

Arthur Frantzreb (1991), in describing benefactor research (also known as "prospect research"), states the need to know the "interests, concerns, hobbies and eccentricities; education; family history, spouse and children; experience in the nonprofit world; residences; civic, social and fraternal positions; and religion" of potential major benefactors (p. 120). This information serves as a basis for evaluating donor capacity and inclination to make a major gift. Paul Schervish, in his studies of the wealthy, has postulated that the truly wealthy have the advantage of satisfying all their comfort needs in life and that such individuals no longer have to expend energies on accumulating wealth. Rather than focusing on asset accumulation needs, the truly wealthy, those with abundance, can explore ways their resources can have a meaningful impact on the world (Schervish, O'Herlihy, and Havens, 2001, pp. 3–4). These individuals have the capacity to make a difference in the world and truly leave a legacy of compassionate, consequential change through philanthropic gifts. In a sense, this is a way to transform money into meaning in the lives of philanthropists. To attract gifts of significance, one must cultivate relationships with those of significant resources. But mere indices of wealth capacity alone do not suffice to inspire major gifts. Both an inclination to do good in the world and a specific passion for the organization are required for the realization of a major gift. Instead of merely chasing money, fundraisers and volunteers must be cognizant of signs of wealth, but they must place more emphasis on those individuals with a charitable nature.

Seeking "natural partners" is the prime responsibility of the major gift officer. Who are natural partners for one's organization? First and foremost are present donors to the nonprofit. Major gifts generally come from individuals who already embrace the institution's mission and case for support. Other potential major benefactors are volunteers who are governing board or committee members, the nonprofit's constituencies (alumni, former clients, members, and so on), and philanthropically minded individuals in the community. Studies have found that individuals who are traditionally religious or spiritual are more likely to use philanthropy to vote their values and to find meaning in their lives (Independent Sector, 2002). Indeed, historically more than half of all individual gifts to nonprofit organizations have been directed to religious institutions, and religious beliefs are cited among top motivators for giving. Searching for wealthy individuals who are spiritual and committed to making the world a better place is an important activity for major gift officers. Major gift programs must focus more time and attention on individuals who believe in the organization and wish to propel it to new levels of service, efficiency, or effectiveness.

Using benefactor wealth research and referrals from board members, volunteers, and major donors, development officers create lists of individuals with the capacity to make a difference in the organization. It is then the fundraiser's responsibility to initiate a strategy to engage those donors in the life of the organization. For it is through involvement, genuine engagement in the experiences of the nonprofit, and the impact your organization has on those whom they serve that vital social equity increases between individuals and organizations, resulting in philanthropic gifts of significance. As Pine and Gilmore note, "Experiences are events that engage individuals in a personal way. Staging experiences is not about entertaining *customers*; it's about engaging them," according to the authors of *The Experience Economy* (1999).

Numerous models describing stages in the solicitation of major gifts have been postulated over the years. The Fund Raising School (2009a) uses an eight-step model (see Exhibit 7.1). As donors are involved deeply in the life of the nonprofit organization, they develop an "ownership position" in the good that is done through the organization. As donors increase their "social equity share" in the institution and see their personal values overlap with the institution's mission, more and more significant gifts are made to further the cause. Benefactors no longer will accept being merely "deep pockets" but rather yearn for and require authentic experiences with the organizations they support. "People tend to perceive as authentic that which is done exceptionally well, executed individually and extraordinarily by someone demonstrating human care; not unfeelingly or disingenuously performed" (Pine and Gilmore, 1999, p. 49).

How does the development officer engage potential benefactors in the mission of the organization? Once natural partners are identified, it is through sincere

EXHIBIT 7.1. MAJOR GIFTS: THE EIGHT-STEP SOLICITATION PROCESS.

1. Identification
2. Qualification
3. Development of Strategy
4. Cultivation
5. Solicitation and Negotiation
6. Acknowledgment
7. Stewardship
8. Renewal

Source: The Fund Raising School, 2009a, p. V-3.

relationship building that the development officers promote major investments. Inviting donors to volunteer on important committees, raise funds, share their expertise, and serve on the governing boards are some of the most common ways of building ownership. The key is not so much a technique but rather the spirit behind the technique. Potential major benefactors are in constant demand, and volunteer burnout is rampant, but a surefire way to propel an organization in the arena of major gifts is to involve donors authentically in the mission of the nonprofit. Perhaps the highest form of reverence we can demonstrate to donors is genuinely to ask their opinions and, equally important, to consider those opinions seriously, as they may affect the institution's mission and core values. It is not through disingenuous encounters that major gifts arise. The wealthy, like all of us, are tired of being manipulated to make gifts. The proper stance to take in relationship-based philanthropy is not to manipulate but to inspire, not to push someone to make a "transaction-based" gift but rather to make the mission and its work so real and important as to impel or "pull" a donor to make a gift. Tom Morris said in his book *If Aristotle Ran General Motors* (1997), "Pull is the lure of an attractive goal or a strongly desired good, recognized by Plato and Aristotle as well as by many other great thinkers of the past . . . embodying a valued ideal. It attracts us and calls us to put forward our greatest efforts. The greater the ideal, the greater the power it can have in our lives" (p. 63).

What Works in Major Gift Fundraising

Fortunately, in the past several years, practitioners in the field of philanthropy and professors in our nation's universities have begun to explore more deeply why benefactors make major gifts and why donors say they do not make gifts. This donor-centered research is both refreshing and instructive. Recent research funded by the Bank of America and conducted by the Center on Philanthropy (2007c) finds that high-net-worth donors generally are described by several donor portraits:

- *The very wealthy*, with net worth of $50 million or more
- *Bequeathers*, whose bequests leave 25 percent or more to charity
- *Devouts*, who attend religious services at least weekly and donate to religious causes
- *Seculars*, who do not attend religious services or give to religious causes
- *Entrepreneurs*, with 50 percent or more of net worth in entrepreneurial assets
- *Dynasts*, who give money to their children for giving to charity
- *Metropolitans*, whose primary residence is in a city with a population of five hundred thousand or more
- *High frequency volunteers*, who volunteer more than twenty hours per year
- *Strategic donors*, who have foundations and/or donor-advised funds and give to few subsectors
- *Transactional donors*, who do not have foundations or donor-advised funds and give to many or all subsectors
- *Altruistic donors*, who give from a sense of meeting critical needs in society or the belief that those with more should help those with less
- *Financially pragmatic donors*, who are concerned with return on investment and feeling financially secure

This important work emphasizes understanding the interests, concerns, needs, and motivations of wealthy individuals in terms of the role of philanthropy in their lives. By developing an understanding of such motivations, the development professional can better plan how to involve a particular prospective benefactor in the work of the nonprofit.

Some benefactors make major gifts because of a sense of obligation to the nonprofit, the greater community, or the world. Gifts of significance, however, arise out of the true interests, values, and passions of the prospective benefactor (see Figure 7.1). Regardless of the particular motivation for giving, the role of the major gift officer is to engage the donor in the important work of the nonprofit and deepen the benefactor's involvement in the organization's mission and value systems.

It is also instructive to note why fundraisers fail or why donors refuse to make major gifts to nonprofits. Sturtevant (1997) identifies the most common reasons that major gifts fail to materialize: institutional leaders and development officers neglect to establish basic trust between the organization and the nonprofit's mission, vision, and services; nonprofit leaders don't help donors to connect with the institution and serve the benefactor's interests and needs; and fundraisers fail to instill a sense of urgency for the request. Donors choose not to make major gifts because of a mismatch of interests between donor and institution, a premature request before the donor was ready to give, a failure to ask for a specific amount, being asked too many times by the organization or by competing nonprofits, and a lack of connection between the solicitor of the gift and the donor. The Bank of America research conducted by the Center on Philanthropy (2009a) confirms the main reason that donors cease giving to organizations: they no longer feel connected to the organization's mission.

Inquiring and Inspiring

Given the anecdotal findings of fundraising professionals and the recent research of social scientists, we are better prepared to understand the motivations of major donors. The next question confronting nonprofits is how we can best position our institutions and our prospective benefactors for success in the area of major gifts. Hank Rosso put it best when he said, "Fundraising is the gentle art of teaching people the joy of giving." He long understood and practiced the idea of "transformational philanthropy." He knew that major gift work was the result of relationship building. And like Sheldon Garber, he understood the need for fundraisers to be agents of change in the lives of their organizations and benefactors. What skills, then, do fundraising professionals working in the area of major gifts need to succeed? Simply put, they require inquiry skills that will help them understand the values and motivations of potential major benefactors and train and manage volunteers, the ability to articulate the institution's mission, and the creativity and passion to inspire the benefactor to action. Being a successful major gift officer and volunteer fundraiser does not require having all the answers about the prospective benefactor, but it does require that fundraising professionals and volunteers know all the right questions to ask of both the institution and the donor. As agents of change, fundraisers and volunteers must be involved at the highest levels of decision making in the nonprofit. They must be not only skilled at articulating the mission but also involved in creating the mission and moving the organization to greater levels of efficiency and effectiveness.

The following are some key questions the major gift officer must ask of the institution:

- Is our mission relevant, important, and easily articulated?
- Can we use outcome measurements to determine if we are advancing the mission—that is, can we measure impact?

- How can we better involve volunteers and donors in the good that is done through our organization?
- Who best articulates our mission and vision for the future?
- Who would be a natural partner with a particular benefactor?
- Who is responsible for developing the relationship with a specific benefactor?

Every nonprofit must identify the "vision master," a leader who brings the mission to life for benefactors. Just as important, each institution must identify the staff members with the skills to transform vision to action, to make things happen so as to advance the mission through definable steps and acts. Finally, the major gift officers must be primarily responsible to advance the relationship between the prospective donor and the institution. This is where donor and institutional values overlap and the "dance of philanthropy" is performed (see Exhibit 7.1). Some institutions discover that the vision master is primarily the organization's president or chair of the board of directors. For other nonprofits, there will be many hands in the work of inspiring major gifts. It is wise to have multiple links between the nonprofit and the benefactor. This prevents reliance on a few people to raise major gifts. That can be devastating when and if the major players leave the nonprofit. Malcolm Gladwell, in his book *The Tipping Point* (2000), speaks of the need for both "sticky" messages and "contagious" messengers in order for ideas and innovations to take hold. The "sticky" message is the institution's most compelling articulation of its primary mission or cause. To attract the new, more engaged philanthropist, it is the development officer's duty to discover from inside or outside their organization those contagious people who can bring mission and impact alive for benefactors.

There are questions major gift officers must ask themselves as well. To paraphrase Payton (1988, p. 74), who posed the most piercing question of all: Do we as professionals work *for* philanthropy or *off of* philanthropy? Why are we doing this important work? For major gift work is less a job than it is a calling. Fundraising professionals are not selling products; rather, they are promoting visions and possibilities for the betterment of humankind. This is serious work taken seriously by the professionals engaged in it. It is not a vendor/vendee relationship but rather a genuine partnership we inspire with our benefactors. O'Neill (1993) saw development professionals as moral trainers. Major gift officers are indeed moral trainers whose work is about ethical inspiration (Rosso's "teaching the joy of giving"). Hence we must ask ourselves: Are we serving as role models of philanthropy? Are we making important philanthropic gifts ourselves? Do we serve as "soul models" of well-examined lives? And perhaps most important of all: Are we devoted to helping donors find meaning in their lives through acts of philanthropy? Many prospective major benefactors know how to accumulate "means" but not "meaning" in their lives. One way of looking at major gift work is that fundraisers, volunteers, and donors are on a long walk together to find meaning in life. Meaning can be found through philanthropy.

As important as it is to be an agent of change through professional intro-spection and probing the mission and values of the institution, the great work of development is done through exploring a benefactor's values in an atmosphere of trust. Using a process Dunlop (2000) refers to as "nurturing inquiry," major gift officers ask values-defining questions of donors. The classic work by Kübler-Ross (1997) on death and dying teaches that on their deathbeds, individuals do not measure the value of their lives by their net worth or accumulations; rather, they measure their life's meaning based on whether or not they made a differ-ence in the world and whether they're leaving a lasting legacy. It seems apparent that through philanthropy, development officers and volunteers can help donors provide meaningful answers to those deathbed questions. For this is the essential partnership in philanthropy: our institution's mission and the donor's value sys-tem equal more than either can accomplish separately. This makes the essence of major gift work "helping people arrive before they depart!" This requires encouraging benefactors to transform from role models in business to soul mod-els in philanthropy. These transformations are accomplished by inquiring about the donor's core values and passions through values-based questions. By asking important questions, we help donors transform from motivations that are intrinsic to extrinsic, from self-centered to other-centered, and from independent to inter-dependent. Transforming major gift work is about changing "me-centeredness" to "we-centeredness."

Questions of Values

Prior to elucidating some of the key values questions, it is important to set the rules of values-based inquiry. Before one asks important questions regarding val-ues, it is necessary to establish an atmosphere of trust. Two essential components for an atmosphere of trust are permission and protection. These are assurances to the donors that before we probe core values, we will seek their permission to enter a deeper relationship. Beyel (1997, p. 52) calls it "philanthropic informed consent." This is a discovery process whereby the development officer and the donor engage in a moral and ethical dialogue. This may be as simple as asking permission to inquire about closely held values, but more often it is an intuitive process, much like knowing when it is safe to ask an acquaintance a question we would normally ask a close friend. The second important way of establishing trust is to ensure that any information divulged will remain private and confidential.

This means that the fundraiser must guard all insights gained and not mention them to the donor's family, friends, or colleagues or in visit reports.

Some key donor questions include these:

- What values do you hold most dear?
- Who has inspired you in your life and your work?
- How does one make a difference in the world?
- What is your legacy in the world today or in the world of tomorrow? Can you finish your legacy alone?
- How much is enough money to leave heirs? Is there ever too much money to leave to heirs?
- What is the most satisfying philanthropic gift you have made and why?
- Which one of the nonprofits you support does the best job of keeping you involved in its mission? What kinds of reports do you want and expect as stewardship for your major gift?
- How do you prefer to be invited to make a charitable gift?

These are only a few samples of key questions the major gift officer must ask while developing a relationship with each benefactor. The questions are asked at appropriate stages in the relationship. They are meant to be stretching questions but can seem impertinent or assertive if they come too early in a relationship.

In addition to the individual contacts between the fundraiser and the donor, strategic questions may be considered when the donor interacts with other members of the nonprofit board or staff. One highly successful way to ask many of these questions is through a donor profile interview. In this setting, a donor is asked to participate in a profile of his or her life and philanthropy. These questions help turn dreamers into dream makers for your institution. It is a truism that once they have fulfilled their own personal goals and dreams, highly successful individuals will often transform into major benefactors who will fulfill the dreams of others through the nonprofit.

Building an Ownership Position

The most important role for the major gift officer is to forge a close relationship between a donor and the nonprofit, including its volunteers. One important device in this relationship building is philanthropic storytelling to elucidate to the benefactor great things that others have done to advance the organization's mission through philanthropy. Storytelling allows the development officer comfortably to make maps for donors to follow with their own personal gifts. A part of the cultivation and relationship-building process may be to ask the donor to make investment or step gifts to the organization. It is important to ask for these smaller gifts, as they allow the donor to open a window into the nonprofit and provide the nonprofit with the opportunity to further involve the donor through meaningful stewardship and appropriate recognition. Solicitations of step gifts allow the development officer to determine if the proposal harmonizes with the donor's core values. But rather than asking merely for any "starting gift," it is paramount to consider what sort of gift will further involve the donor in the nonprofit and might naturally lead to additional gifts. The major gift officer should ask, "Does this proposal have the potential to grow into more significant and consequential gifts by the donor?" An annual gift request for a partial academic scholarship can be a step that leads to further requests to provide full scholarships and eventually to investments to endow that scholarship in perpetuity or perhaps, through an estate gift, to name the academic unit wherein the scholarship lies.

Although step gifts are common ways to encourage major gifts, it is not unheard of for a first gift to a nonprofit to be a major gift. Development officers and volunteers must be alert to those unique individuals who can quickly catch a vision and make major initial gifts to the nonprofit. This is especially true with gifts from entrepreneurs that come at much earlier ages than were the norm from older, more traditional major benefactors. The information age and the technology it has sparked have made billionaires out of thirty-year-olds, and they are asking themselves earlier and earlier about the social responsibility that comes with their wealth.

Another way to involve donors in step gifts is to "borrow their collections." Often potential major benefactors have accumulations that can be appropriately used by the nonprofit. These may range from art collections to private planes. By borrowing these accumulations, the nonprofit recognizes their value and demonstrates to the donor that their collections, as well as their donations, will be respected and used wisely.

The Request or Invitation

Most of the work of a proposal is done prior to writing the request and making the appointments with a benefactor. Donor values have been explored, an appropriate gift amount has been considered, and the proposal team has been carefully selected and has rehearsed the solicitation in detail. The major gift officer must ask several questions: Have we come to know this donor sufficiently? Has this donor been involved meaningfully in the work of our organization? Is this an appropriate time for this request? Are we requesting a respectful amount? Will the project or the gift purpose resonate with the benefactor? Is this the inspiring team to set a vision and make the request?

In setting up the specific meeting to discuss a proposal, it is important that the potential benefactor know that the purpose of the visit is the request for financial support for an important project. This avoids fundraising by stealth or surprise and is the respectful thing to do. In some cases, saying, "We are coming with a compelling request that we believe will inspire you" is sufficient to let the prospective benefactor know that a request will be made of him or her.

Where will the major gift proposal be made? The site should be chosen with the donor's needs and comfort in mind. Usually it is at the donor's home or place of business. Sometimes it takes place at the nonprofit, particularly if the request requires a tour or on-site demonstration of how the donor's gift will be employed by the nonprofit. Public settings such as restaurants for major gift solicitations can be disastrous. Privacy and protection can never be guaranteed in such a setting. A waiter may interrupt or stumble just as the proposal reaches its apex, spoiling both mood and decorum.

Regardless of the setting, the major gift officer must be sure to ask: Who will be in attendance from the benefactor's side of the equation? Are all the decision makers at the table, or is this a meeting with the potential benefactor alone? Eventually all the appropriate leaders of the organization, the donor and spouse and family, and legal and financial advisers, as appropriate, may have to be on board. The proposal itself must be clear and include the gift amount, project goals and means of measuring the achievement of those goals, recognition options for the gift, and a plan for reporting or stewardship after the gift is made. A preproposal rehearsal will make certain that at the right time, the right person makes the right request. Part of a good rehearsal session before a major request is to brainstorm potential benefactor questions, to have ready the answers to those questions, and to determine precisely who is responsible for answering those questions about the proposal at hand. The worst possible scenario is for a potential benefactor to ask an important or unanticipated question and to be met with hesitation as to who should address that question. Sometimes volunteers prefer to tell the stories of their passion for the cause and describe the project but feel more comfortable if a member of the organization actually asks for a specific amount of money. "We are requesting your consideration of a leadership gift of [*specific amount*], which will be the catalyst for making this project a reality," is only one tried and true way of asking for a gift.

Stewardship and Recognition

Once a gift commitment is entered into, the process of stewardship begins. To ensure that there is no "donor regret"—to adapt a term from the for-profit world—the organization must provide stewardship of the gift and send regular and meaningful reports. Reports on construction progress, thank-you letters from scholarship recipients, financial reports, lab tours, photos, and personal visits with progress reports are simply the best ways to strengthen donor ties to the nonprofit. Stewardship is both ethical and essential following receipt of major gifts, and it is the smart thing to do to encourage future gifts from the benefactor.

Donor recognition is another way to involve benefactors in the nonprofit. "How would you and your family like us to acknowledge your generous gift?" is an appropriate inquiry. Recognition should be as personal as possible, reflective of the uniqueness of the nonprofit and the gift, and appropriate to the size and importance of the contribution. Other major donors in waiting will examine how your institution respectfully recognizes and exhibits stewardship for gifts of significance.

Managing the Major Gift Process

Whether a major gift officer heads a one-person shop or is a part of a large and complex major gift team, the key to major gift success is an organized system for the identification, involvement, and solicitation of potential major benefactors. The literature is rife with examples of how to manage the major gift process. Successful programs can be managed using simple index cards or sophisticated software programs. Regardless of the format, every institution must identify the top twenty-five to one hundred, or 5 to 10 percent of the institutional donor base, for potential major donors whose philanthropy can have a significant impact on the organization.

Once identified, each donor should be assigned an individual file. Files should be developed with respect for the donor and include only information that is pertinent to the relationship and the potential major gift. This information will be useful in determining what types of nonprofit projects will resonate with the donor's value system. Private and potentially embarrassing information about a donor has no place in these files. A good guide is to include only information, notes, or comments on donor contacts that could be read over your shoulder by the benefactor herself without embarrassment. Files should also include the names of natural partners who are centers of influence in the donor's life. It is vital to include information about regular meetings with institutional leaders to discuss the donor, his or her deepening involvement in the nonprofit, a realistic potential gift amount, and details of any projects of great potential interest. All encounters, engagements, and experiences with the benefactor should be appropriately documented, for these relationships are a result of the alignment of the institution and the donor, and they do not belong to development officers who manage the relationships.

Specific ways to further the donor's involvement and interests can then be documented. Essential to the management process is the appointment of the relationship manager—the person responsible for advancing the relationship using volunteers and other individuals as appropriate. Many management plans set goals for specific numbers of personal visits between the major gift officer and the potential major benefactor during a given period of time. However, it is not the frequency of the encounters that is important but rather how deep an impact the fundraiser or other institution leaders and volunteers have on a donor's sense of belonging to the nonprofit. Visit numbers are less important than meaningful encounters with predetermined objectives that increase the donor's "equity share" in the nonprofit. Fundraisers must fashion metrics based on the deepening of relationships as well as on dollar goals or number of donor contacts.

The Philanthropic Road Ahead

Much has transpired in the world of philanthropy since the publication of *Achieving Excellence in Fund Raising*, second edition. Research led by the Center on Philanthropy has revealed important evidence about who are the most generous people in the world. The Center's study showed that the most philanthropic people in America are entrepreneurs who have earned and/or hold 50 percent or more of their assets from entrepreneurial activities (2006). Entrepreneurs have shaped and reshaped our country, and they are rapidly transforming the philanthropic landscape as well. Greg Dees of Duke University was quoted thusly in the book *Philanthrocapitalism* (Bishop and Green, 2008): "Philanthropy today is best defined more broadly than giving money away, as mobilizing and deploying private resources, including money, time, social capital and expertise, to improve the world in which we live" (p. 49).

The first lesson to be learned in major gift work is to scan your institution's database for the entrepreneurs in your midst. This movement has been led by the words and the works of powerful exemplars of philanthropy and the positive impacts they have had in the world. Bill Gates, Warren Buffett, Bono, Muhammad Yunus, Steve Case, and many, many others are questioning the traditional "give, name, and go away style of philanthropy" more common in decades past. According to Bishop and Green, "One of the key elements of philanthrocapitalism is an obsession with ensuring that money is put to good use" (p. 69). They go on to say that Mario Morino, founder of Venture Philanthropy Partners (VPP), "agrees that being businesslike as a philanthropist, which he favors, is not the same thing as treating nonprofits as if they were businesses. The social sector, he says he has learned, is 'far more dependent on relationships than systems'"

(p. 91). There are indeed economic norms associated with business, while our field is grounded on social norms. The new "engaged philanthropist," however, expects nonprofits to look at and learn from the business world to gain efficiencies, learn to model new programs, replicate those models, and then scale them. These hypermanic, passionate, and results-driven philanthropreneurs will not tolerate nonprofit "business" as usual. They expect nonprofit organizations to work as hard at doing good with their gifts as the entrepreneurs worked to earn the money in the first place. They bring to the table their creative minds, their intense curiosity, their experience, and their contacts. They are attracted to new ways of doing social good and are willing to participate in venture philanthropy to change our way of serving the world, try new models, tinker with delivery systems, and quickly reinvest in success. They also know the value of leverage in their gifts and simply expect more from us. In response to this new trend toward social entrepreneurship, new low-profit, limited-liability corporations are taking hold. As Pink notes, "Dubbed an L3C, this entity is a corporation—but not what we typically think of it. As one report explained, an L3C operates like a for-profit business generating at least modest profits, but its primary aim is to offer significant social benefits" (2009, p. 24). Philanthropreneurs are both left- and right-brain sensitive and, as such, require that nonprofit organizations answer all their business questions as well as respond to their needs for purpose in their lives. Bill Gates said it well when he gave a speech on creative capitalism at the 2008 World Economic Forum: "There are two great forces: self-interest and caring for others." Steve Case invented the term "not only for profit organizations" for a blended model with both business goals and social change as dual objectives. So fundraisers must be aware of this brave new world of major gifts, for it requires that fundraisers bravely embrace it.

FIGURE 7.2. PHILANTHROPY TO BUSINESS SPECTRUM.

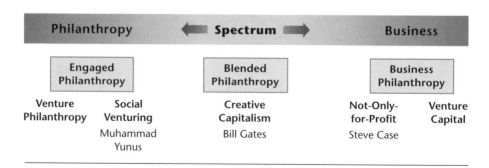

There is a new landscape of philanthropy evolving the past decade or more and spreading rapidly around the globe. It is characterized by the "philanthropy to business spectrum" depicted in Figure 7.2.

Is this a fleeting trend to ignore? Should we lie low until the new "new thing" passes over us? Reason says not. As moral trainers, relationship managers, agents of change, and provocateurs, fundraisers are ethically equipped to inspire these game-changing philanthropists. We are accustomed to working with business-minded individuals; we know what motivates them. We are well positioned to lead dialogues within our organizations as to how to navigate these relationships and potential conflicts of interest. We must ensure that we remain true to our missions and core values while embracing new ways to affect our nonprofit worlds. It will not be boring. We invite these engaged benefactors along on the philanthropic rides of their lives where one can really exchange money for meaning through partnerships with our institutions.

Conclusion

Some specific techniques of major gift work have been explored in this chapter, along with ways to approach and manage the major gift process, but when all is said and done, it is still the spirit behind the major gift process that determines its success. If, as major gift officers, we operated on the "push" or "scolding" model of development (Schervish, 2000b, pp. 2–3), we will have neither long-term success in the field nor satisfaction in our work (see Exhibit 7.2). It is through Schervish's "discernment model" that we respect donor wishes in the fundraising process.

EXHIBIT 7.2. THE SCOLDING AND DISCERNMENT MODELS.

Scolding Model	Discernment Model
You are not giving	Is there something
• Enough	• You want to do with your wealth
• To the right causes	• That fulfills the needs of others
• At the right time	• That you can do more efficiently and more effectively than government or commerce, and
• In the right way	• That expresses your gratitude, brings you satisfaction, and actualizes your identification with the fate of others?

Source: Paul G. Schervish, "The Spiritual Horizons of Philanthropy," in E. R. Tempel and D. F. Burlingame (eds.), *Understanding the Needs of Donors.* New Directions for Philanthropic Fundraising, no. 29. Copyright © 2000 John Wiley & Sons, Inc. This material is used by permission of John Wiley & Sons, Inc.

If we compete with other nonprofits for perceived limited charitable dollars, we will look like avaricious children squabbling over a parent's estate. We should adopt a supply side approach to philanthropy and not a scarcity model, as good philanthropic work is like the rising tide that lifts all ships and spirits. Schervish (2000b) helps us do just that with his idea of "supply side philanthropy." This elegant theory postulates that it is not through competition for an illusory and limited piece of the "pie of philanthropy" but rather through inspiring individuals toward gifts of significance that the true growth of philanthropy will occur. This theory implies that the only limits to philanthropy are those that we impose on ourselves and our institutions through misinformed notions of this important work and the transforming effect that philanthropy can have on the lives of our benefactors. If we follow Schervish's advice and focus on improving the quality of giving over the quantity of giving, we will achieve both greater respect for the work of fundraising and greater philanthropic success as well.

CHAPTER EIGHT

CAPITAL CAMPAIGNS

By Robert Pierpont

Acapital campaign is an intensive fundraising effort designed to raise a specified sum of money within a defined time period to meet the varied asset-building needs of an organization. These needs can include the construction of new buildings, the renovation or enlargement of existing buildings, purchase or improvement of land, acquisition of furnishings or equipment, and endowment. All of these are asset-building objectives. All can have a place in developing a goal for capital fundraising. Whatever the goal, the following are the elements of capital campaigns that have proven to be essential to success in almost all circumstances:

1. *A case rooted in well-developed, advanced institutional planning, with a sound, defensible business plan for the application of the funds needed to meet the goal.* Through their sophisticated investments or business acumen, most prospective donors have accumulated the large resources that allow them to be uncommonly generous. Because of this, organizations must be prepared to show them how philanthropic support is a worthwhile investment, while at the same time endeavoring to touch their hearts and minds with an emotional appeal. Given this, the case must address (a) how the organization will address the larger problem, and (b) what about it will appeal to the generous human spirit that characterizes those whose support is sought.

2. *A set of objectives that, when funded, will respond to a community or societal need.* The case must be larger than the organization. Organizations don't raise money simply

because they need money; they raise money when they can show how the funds will address a recognized need that transcends the organization's own self-interest. Here is a simple example: a church that wishes to establish a homeless shelter cites the fact that there are dozens of people in the community who don't have any place to get a hot meal or warm bed each night. The church could declare that they will, with the help of gifts and pledges, open a shelter to respond. On a much larger scale, an academic medical center might document the demand for additional beds and more intensive research and the need to train more health professionals, based on valid studies of shortages in these areas.

If endowment is to be part of the goal, it is important to have policies in place about how endowments are managed and how the endowment objectives have been established. Briefly, to endow an activity might require a goal of twenty times the amount to be spent for it annually. The basis for this is the policy that 5 percent of the principal will be expended each year. If an institution has a different spending policy, then a different calculation will be necessary. Five percent is fairly common and is based on the idea that over long periods of time a "balanced portfolio" of equities and debt will yield 5 percent plus a percentage about equal to the rate of inflation, which gives some assurance that the principal will maintain an inflation-adjusted value.

Including endowment raises the question: what counts? If all the funds raised are to pay for new facilities, then they are needed on a schedule that provides for timely payment of the costs. But endowment commitments are often accepted in the form of deferred or planned gifts that may not mature until the donor's estate is settled. If this is the case, the organization will need some policy about the age of donors whose gifts will count and the gift amount. Will a discounted present value be used for accounting purposes? How about for recognition purposes?

3. *An involved and committed governing board, prepared to make personally significant commitments of time and funds.* If the board has developed and adopted the plans on which the campaign is based, the board must be willing to support it collectively and individually before asking others to join them. If board members aren't willing to commit to support their own campaign with individual participation according to each member's capacity, how can they expect others to?

4. *An informed constituency with a history of support and the apparent potential to provide the funds needed to meet the goal.* Launching a capital campaign is an unlikely way to initiate an institution's advancement or development program. There are certainly exceptions, but they are rare. Successful campaigns rely most often on donors who, over the years, have been generous with annual gifts and special gifts while involved as alumni, patients, members, participants, or friends. Involvement can take many forms, but time has shown that involvement leads to investment.

To this point, involving those whose generous commitments will be needed to ensure success should be considered when initially developing the case and the campaign plan, which may mean supplementing the board's aforementioned planning with others—perhaps as members of committees or task forces or other volunteer groups—to involve them in the process to the degree that the campaign becomes theirs, as well as the board's.

5. *A chief executive officer prepared to support the campaign intellectually and emotionally and to recognize that campaigning is not the time for business as usual.* It is a great advantage if the CEO has a genuine sense of vision about what a successful capital campaign will mean to its constituents and beneficiaries and can persuasively communicate that vision. This is less a requirement for charisma than it is for sincerity. It has often been said, "People don't give to causes—they give to people with causes." A CEO who can articulate the case with conviction and who inspires confidence will add enormously to the potential for success.

6. *Adequate budget for the incremental costs of campaigning, in hand or in sight.* The budget should provide for sufficient funds to meet the expenditure requirements of an active, forward-moving campaign. Too tight a budget can be inhibiting; too generous a budget can invite questions and criticism. Campaign costs vary significantly. Small campaigns, for a few million dollars, will cost more proportionately than large campaigns for hundreds of millions. Local community campaigns should be less expensive than national campaigns with heavy travel costs and/or regional campaign offices.

As a percentage of the campaign goal, costs as low as 5 percent and as high as 15 percent may be expected—and acceptable. Emphasis on costs can be counterproductive. The better measurement is return on investment (ROI). Campaign costs of 12.5 percent, for example, should be shown as an ROI of 8:1. In other words, every dollar invested in the campaign budget will produce eight dollars of gross income or a net of seven.

Basic budget elements and their percentage of the overall budget are typically:

Personnel: 50 to 60 percent

Materials and events: 20 to 30 percent

Overhead: 10 to 20 percent

Contingency: 5 percent

These percentages are a starting point only. The multiple variables and experience in similar situations all must be weighed in developing the campaign budget.

7. *Qualified staff with the requisite campaign experience or openness to retaining outside expertise, as needed.* Campaign budgeting must also consider whether the costs are over and above ongoing fundraising operations or part of the costs will be covered by assigning present staff to campaign responsibilities. The most obvious case is when the chief development officer decides to direct the campaign by hiring a "number two" to take on the annual fundraising effort. How that change is reflected in the budget will affect the calculation of costs.

Another issue is whether in a large organization, for example, major gift officers will reorient their efforts to the capital pledges during a campaign and then return to the ongoing major or planned gifts program post-campaign. Still used, but less common, are part-time, on-site campaign directors—typically provided by a large fundraising consulting firm with a number of very experienced staff. This approach is still valid for organizations that don't have staff with the requisite experience or those that see the campaign as a once-in-a-generation event and therefore plan to return to normal operations following the intensive capital campaign. More typical is retaining periodic campaign counsel to make regular site visits to meet with senior staff, the CEO, and campaign volunteer leaders to advise and assist, by applying their years of experience in comparable situations.

8. *A Table of Gifts Needed, laying out the pattern that has been demonstrated to be necessary to meet a capital campaign goal of virtually any size.* The most demanding campaign disciplines are the unremitting focus on large gifts and the requirement that enough of these gifts must be secured at the very beginning of the campaign to establish a pattern for others who follow.

Current experience shows that 5 to 10 percent of the donors are providing 85 to 95 percent of the goal. A similar pattern holds true in the for-profit world, where sales managers note that 20 percent of their sales staff sell 80 percent of the products and that 20 percent of their customers buy 80 percent of their product.

A Table of Gifts Needed (TGN) applies this reality to capital campaigns and illustrates how many gifts of what size a campaign probably will need to reach its goal. As illustrated in Table 8.1, the TGN is an instrument that provides a method to determine the quality of gifts, the quantity of gifts, and the number of prospects that will be required to ensure achievement of the goal.

Several guidelines should be used in the formulation of a TGN:

- Above all, the lead gift should constitute at least 10 percent of the goal.
- Forty to 60 percent of the goal comes from the ten to fifteen largest gifts.
- Thirty-three to 50 percent comes from the next 100 to 150 gifts.
- Ten to 20 percent comes from all other gifts.

TABLE 8.1. TABLE OF GIFTS NEEDED (TGN) FOR A $10 MILLION CAMPAIGN GOAL.

Type of Gift	Number of Pledges	Number of Prospects	Pledge Size	Total for Size	Cumulative Total	Percentage of Goal
Lead Gift	1	5	$1,000,000 +	$1,000,000	$1,000,000	47.5%
	1	5	750,000–999,999	750,000	1,750,000	
	3	15	500,000–749,999	1,500,000	3,250,000	
	6	30	250,000–499,999	1,500,000	4,750,000	
Major Gifts	12	48	100,000–249,999	1,400,000	6,150,000	39.5%
	24	96	50,000–99,999	1,300,000	7,450,000	
	50	100	25,000–49,999	1,250,000	8,700,000	
Special Gifts	70	210	10,000–24,999	700,000	9,400,000	12%
	100	300	5,000–9,999	500,000	9,900,000	
General Gifts	All others	Many	Under 5,000	100,000	10,000,000	

Source: Adapted from Henry A. Rosso and Associates, *Achieving Excellence in Fund Raising* (2nd ed.), p. 124. Copyright © Jossey-Bass Inc., Publishers. Reprinted by permission of Jossey-Bass Inc., a subsidiary of John Wiley & Sons, Inc.

The purpose of these guidelines has not so much to do with the labels or even the arithmetic as it does with their uses:

a. To be tested in a campaign feasibility study.
b. To set levels of donor recognition. At the top, that may take the form of "naming opportunities." At lower levels, categories may be used to recognize Benefactors, Patrons, Sponsors, Donors, and so on.
c. To use levels to plan and schedule campaign phases—the ten to fifteen largest gifts initially sought can be the Leadership Gifts Phase. In the mid-range they may be organized as the Major Gifts Phase, and at lower levels, the Community or General Gifts Phase.
d. To set donors' sights on what gifts are needed to succeed.
e. To help keep score and highlight shortfalls. It is not uncommon to adjust the table during the campaign—not frequently, but to reflect actual results versus planned. When it is tempting to adjust or modify the table, it is necessary to reflect on the number of prospects needed. If all prospects have been exhausted at a level that still has not reached its total for size, then either new prospects must be identified or an adjustment must be made to make up the shortfall in that level.

9. *Prospect research and rating programs to identify and evaluate the potential sources of support in sufficient numbers to have three to five prospects for each gift needed at various levels.* The Table of Gifts Needed provides a good guide for evaluating the number of prospects needed for a specific campaign goal. The traditional ratio of prospects to gifts needed in a TGN is 5:1 for the top gift levels, 4:1 for the middle, and 3:1 for the bottom. This ratio is based in part on the reality that some donors will give at lower than expected levels. Therefore their gifts will be credited to lower levels, reducing the need for prospects at those levels.

Some believe that more accurate ratios are reversed, with 3:1 at the top, 4:1 in the middle, and 5:1 or more at the bottom. Those who use this approach are convinced that better prospect research improves the probability of strong results at the top, whereas the limited volunteer effort at the bottom requires a higher ratio because the large pool of low-rated prospects will be solicited by phone, mail, and/or e-mail.

10. *Recognition of the absolute importance of soliciting in sequence, from the top down, and establishing an early pattern of pacesetting and exemplary gifts to motivate others.* The Table of Gifts Needed and the listing of prospects by giving potential provide a guide for sequential fundraising. This is the technique of classifying prospective donors according to their assessed giving potential and then approaching top prospects first in sequence, assiduously avoiding any solicitations at lower levels until the solicitations at the top have been successful.

Sequential fundraising is based on four axioms of campaign fundraising:

- The ten largest gifts set the standard for the entire campaign.
- A failure to adhere to the top-down pattern lowers giving sights across the spectrum of donors.
- Extended solicitation and participation at lower levels will not offset major gaps in the upper ranges.
- Once the big-gift-first sequence has been seriously violated, the entire program is in jeopardy.

11. *Involved board members and other volunteers willing to serve first on a campaign planning committee and subsequently on other committees, as needed.* In recent years, boards have increasingly authorized or accepted the idea that major gifts officers are those who should do the heavy lifting of asking for gifts and pledges—even the very largest. This trend away from volunteers taking "assignments" for solicitation is inconsistent with the basic concept that "like should ask like" and that someone who has already given a generous "stretch" gift is in a good position to ask others to do likewise.

An effective current technique involves staff managing a process whereby volunteers are brought in when needed. What does this mean? Staff members are assigned a portfolio of prospects to manage through the four-step process: *identify, engage, ask,* and *recognize.* Staff then ask volunteers—preferably board and campaign committee members—to take part in research by reviewing prospective donor lists and suggesting what levels of pledge amounts might be sought on the basis of "capacity"—that is, what they could give if they would—and to comment on "inclination"—the estimated probability of getting a favorable response. They are also encouraged to share any thoughts about the best strategies needed to elicit a favorable response. The resulting information is compiled by staff and used to determine what to do next in the cultivation phase.

Here again volunteers can be critical—inviting prospective donors to attend briefings, tour facilities, or join them in their homes or clubs to meet the CEO. Examples abound. The key is that there will be a higher level of acceptance to attend such events if the invitation comes from a peer, not from staff. After each such occasion, the staff will debrief the volunteer to help to determine the next step(s) to engage the prospect. It is then up to the staff to endeavor, once again, to involve volunteers when the prospective donor is asked for a gift. This may mean yet another personal meeting or the preparation of a proposal or such other ideas as the volunteer/staff team consider appropriate.

At each step, the staff has managed the process and facilitated volunteers by doing whatever is reasonably needed to keep the focus on them, not the staff.

Remember: people give to people, and like should ask like. The four-step process is essential in the early phases when a reasonably small number of people are involved as volunteer committee members seeking the largest gifts needed. As the campaign expands to reach out to more people, and even to wider geographic regions, it will be necessary to organize committees to take assignments, solicit gifts, and report results. These efforts require skilled staff able to organize, support, and motivate volunteers and to teach them how to solicit.

12. *A procedure for testing the campaign plan in advance through a planning or feasibility study involving volunteers and staff.* A well-conducted pre-campaign planning study is the start of the campaign, because it should involve those who can give or influence the top gifts needed for a successful campaign. This may be the only time that those interviewed will focus their attention on the future of the organization in a focused, probing conversation. What happens before capital fundraising starts is the most important part of the work! Questioning, measuring, qualifying, verifying, listening to hard answers to hard questions, weighing judgments expressed by potential key volunteer leaders and potential key contributors—all these are part of strategic market testing. In straightforward terms, the study is a thorough examination of the institution's readiness to ask and the constituent's preparedness and willingness to give—and, if appropriate, to serve as a volunteer committee leader or member.

Can an organization conduct its own feasibility study? Is it necessary to retain professional counsel to conduct a study? It is quite difficult for an inexperienced fundraising staff member or the executive staff member with no fundraising experience to undertake this sensitive assignment. A staff person often does not know what questions to ask, how to evaluate the answers, or how to judge the campaign's feasibility. Objectivity is important to the process, and the staff may find it difficult to be objective. However, in exceptional circumstances, in which staff members have developed long, cordial, and confidential relationships with key leaders and donors, they may be able to test feasibility through conversations with donors known to be ready to consider the top-level gifts needed for success.

Some institutions with very sophisticated, experienced chief development officers have been through several campaigns in recent years. They frequently skip the formal study process because they and their board members have the confidence that the gifts needed are in sight—especially the very large ones needed for success.

How are the names of intended interview respondents selected? To gain the insights required to determine the campaign's feasibility, a list of key interview candidates is developed. This list can range from as few as thirty names to as many as one hundred or more. It may include senior managers, program staff members, governing board members, current major gift donors, potential big gift donors, and campaign leadership candidates. It certainly should include the prospective donors who can give or influence the top ten to twenty gifts needed.

Most interviews are in-depth, lasting about an hour. All information gathered during the interview is held in confidence; if it is divulged, it is with the promise that its source will not be attributed. Only in this manner can sensitive information critical to the success of the campaign be elicited from interview respondents.

The following questions are indicative of those that usually are asked during the feasibility study. They seek information about the nine most important components of the capital campaign.

The appeal (case). Is the case or argument for a capital campaign well defined? Does it reflect the institution's mission, goals, and objectives? Does it have strong appeal? Will the organization's constituencies understand it? Will it motivate potential donors to be unusually generous? Are the needs valid? Do they reflect a sense of urgency? Are they understood and accepted as valid by the constituency that will be asked to give?

The goal. Is the proposed goal realistic for the constituency? If not realistic, why not? What are the problems?

The prospects. How many gifts will be required and at what level? Do potential sources for these gifts exist? Are they expected to come from individuals, corporations, foundations, or associations? How many from each category and in what range? Is it possible to secure one gift that is at least 10 percent of the goal? What solicitation strategies will be required to meet the goal?

The leadership potential. If the campaign is to succeed, leaders must be able to give and to help solicit upper-level gifts, especially at the start. Can this quality leadership be enlisted first from the membership of the governing board and second from the larger constituency? Who is the best possible candidate to be the general chairperson for the campaign?

The timing. Is this the proper time for a campaign? Are conflicting campaigns in progress or contemplated in the near future? What impact will they have? What amount of time is required to ensure the success of this campaign: a year, or two, or three or more? Current practice is three to five years and not more than seven. Fundraising programs of longer duration usually cannot sustain the level of intensity that campaigning implies.

The public relations requirements. Are there public relations problems that must be resolved before any campaign can start? What public relations or promotional activity may be needed to motivate the community to support this program?

Staffing. What staffing will be required? Should an outside professional firm provide it? Should people be added to the existing staff? What are the short- and long-term benefits of these options?

The budget. What is the budget that will be required to finance the campaign? How much will it cost to raise the goal? Is that cost reasonable? Will management and the governing board make these funds available? What budget-control and reporting methods will be required for proper accountability?

The study report. It is imperative at the start to know the agreed-upon deliverables. A complete study should include a recommended campaign plan with a TGN, schedule, structure, budget, and staffing requirements, as well as any recommendations on continuing counsel, if appropriate. If outside counsel conducts the study, they should also summarize and report separately on the levels of support that they have found potentially available from the names tested, as well as who has been identified for specific leadership roles.

13. *Adherence to a schedule with deadlines for action and accountability.* It is axiomatic that campaigning, with the implicit urgency of achieving a dollar goal within a set schedule, requires a discipline sometimes cited as "no-time for business as usual." But it is this very pressure that makes a campaign a campaign. Careful advance preparation is needed, coupled with a strong sense of responsibility for getting results.

14. *Publicity and printed materials prepared in phases and released or produced as needed.* A key element of a good campaign plan is a good communications plan with provisions for timely publication of newsletters, progress reports, and for social media, PowerPoint presentations and websites. This chapter does not endeavor to cover the topic completely since it is elsewhere in this volume, but once again, in capital campaigning there are wonderful opportunities to involve volunteers, and this is one such opportunity. Media owners, editors, and others whose influence will be helpful in getting the story of the campaign out to those whose support is essential for success can be enlisted to help. Campaigning is a time to invest in the best professional help an organization can afford because the return on investment is so much higher than in any other form of fundraising.

15. *Events to announce the campaign, report progress, publicize significant gifts, and recognize donors and volunteers.* In addition to the media and publications already mentioned, remember that personal relationships are the very heart of successful fundraising and that campaigning is a great opportunity to enhance them through genuine expressions of appreciation for gifts and work. This is a great

time to unveil plaques or stage events honoring donors. Creative involvement of some of those who will benefit from what the campaign will make possible—students, clients, artists, and others—is a compelling way to tell the campaign story. Beneficiaries can also say "thank you" directly and personally and can write notes and give token gifts. In sum, celebrating campaign success at the end offers everyone the chance to join in being part of a new beginning.

16. *Contagious enthusiasm about the campaign's goals and objectives throughout the organization.* Everyone—from the organization's leadership to support staff—must be completely aware of the extraordinary activities that are going to take place during the campaign period and the wonderful future that success will mean to them and the whole organization. It is never clear who will influence the donor—positively or negatively—so the organization must make certain that everyone is on board for this venture and that each is putting on his best face.

Conclusion

A successful campaign depends on the strengths of the organization. Whether an organization is pursuing the traditional "bricks and mortar" campaign that has a specific goal related to building construction, renovation, or expansion; a special project campaign for one particular pressing need; an endowment campaign for perpetual support; or a comprehensive campaign that takes into account current program support, special purposes, capital, and endowment, careful attention not only to the discrete processes of a campaign but also to their sequential execution is essential for campaign success.

CHAPTER NINE

ESTABLISHING A PLANNED GIVING PROGRAM

By Dean Regenovich

Since the early 1900s, individuals have relied on various charitable instruments—bequests, charitable gift annuities, and charitable trusts—to fulfill their philanthropic desires. These giving arrangements became known as *planned gifts*, for they typically involve thoughtful, deliberate planning on the part of the donor and the donor's advisor. However, it was not until the mid-1970s that nonprofits experienced a significant increase in planned gifts. Most of the activity was centered on the establishment and marketing of charitable bequest programs, which continues to be the cornerstone of most successful planned giving programs because they are easy to understand and communicate to gift prospects. *Giving USA 2009* (The Center on Philanthropy, 2009b) reports that of the nearly $308 billion contributed in 2008, bequests accounted for $22.66 billion, representing 7 percent of all contributions made in 2008.

Tax legislation enacted in 1986 increased the capital gains tax, which is typically triggered on the sale of an appreciated asset. The philanthropic community—donors, professional financial advisors, and charitable organizations—responded by taking advantage of various charitable estate planning instruments to fulfill a donor's philanthropic and financial objectives. An aging donor population and an unprecedented growth in asset values further strengthened the attractiveness of various planned giving instruments such as the charitable remainder trust and charitable gift annuity. These gift instruments not only offered possible income, capital gains, and estate tax benefits, but also generated a new stream of income for the donor or an income beneficiary designated by the donor. A survey conducted in 2000 by the National Committee on Planned Giving (now known as Partners in Philanthropic Planning), reports that life income vehicles—charitable remainder trusts and charitable gift annuities—have increased in popularity, with 2 percent of Americans indicating that they have created one or both of these types of instruments. This is more than triple the 0.6 percent of 1992 respondents who reported making a "life income" planned gift.

Nonprofits responded to this "new" giving opportunity by hiring development professionals who are familiar with the technical aspects of planned giving. Many of these individuals came from the legal, accounting, and financial planning professions. Other nonprofits, primarily because of budgetary constraints, have chosen not to hire individuals who have been formally trained; instead, they have allowed fundraising staff to learn these techniques on the job. Although a formal background in the legal, tax, and financial planning areas is not a prerequisite to becoming a successful planned giving officer, a professional designation such as a J.D., C.P.A., or C.F.P. sometimes affords the planned giving officer instant credibility with donors because of the formal training it denotes.

The important point to recognize is that planned giving is a necessary component of all successful major gift programs, regardless of an organization's size, mission, age, budget, in-house expertise, or prior giving history. The Fund Raising School challenges all nonprofit organizations to work toward a total development program that includes planned giving. The material in this chapter is designed to assist in determining the level of planned giving activity appropriate for *your* organization. Your organization's planned giving program may end up looking much different from the planned giving program at the nonprofit across the street. That should not be a cause for concern, for most planned giving programs are built over time, with layers added as the organization matures and grows. This chapter also contains a brief overview of the "core" planned giving instruments as well as a discussion of the marketing of planned gifts and how to identify prospective donors of planned gifts.

Institutional Readiness

Institutional readiness depends on giving consideration to the organization and its staff, its board, its planned giving professional, and its policies and guidelines.

The Organization and Staff

Not all nonprofit organizations are prepared to implement a comprehensive planned giving program. In fact, most small to mid-size organizations, particularly relatively new organizations, do not have the financial resources and personnel to allow for a comprehensive planned giving program that includes not only expectancies such as bequests, life insurance, and retirement plan/IRA designations but also life income arrangements such as charitable gift annuities and charitable remainder trusts. What is important to recognize is that despite the age of an organization and the limitation on resources, there are ways to begin a planned giving program now that can be enhanced over time.

The first order of business is to ensure an organizational plan exists before deciding on the level and sophistication of the planned giving program. Does the organization have a strategic plan that outlines goals and objectives for the next three to ten years? Is the mission statement clear and does it accurately depict the organization as it exists today? Is there a case statement that clearly and concisely describes what the organization does, why the services provided are important to the community, and how those services will be delivered? If the organization's mission and case statement are unclear, the planned giving program will most likely experience limited success.

Because many planned gifts benefit the nonprofit organization at some future date (thus the term *deferred gift*), donors must be comfortable with the stability and permanence of the organization. How long has the organization existed? Will the organization be in existence thirty years from now to receive the planned gift? Is the organization growing or shrinking? These are some of the questions donors will ask before contemplating a planned gift, particularly because planned gifts are typically larger in dollar amount than annual fund gifts and other outright, current-use gifts.

Planned gift donors may also be interested in the financial stability of the organization. Does the organization have the capacity to satisfy current operating expenses? Does the organization have a history of balancing its budget? Will the organization be a responsible steward of the gift? Does the organization have the financial staff to account for and invest the gift properly? Will the organization ultimately use the gift in accordance with the donor's wishes? Today's donor expects greater accountability as to how the gift will be invested and used; thus organizations must be prepared to provide financial reports and information concerning the organization's overall financial performance and, in some cases, the performance of specific funds established by the donor.

People give to people with causes. Planned gifts typically come from donors who know and trust the organization. Attaining this level of comfort typically requires the development of close personal relationships with individuals over time. Thus many planned gifts come from donors who have been supporting the organization for years. To be successful in planned giving, organizations must have a knowledgeable fundraising staff capable of clearly articulating the organization's mission and programs, and a point person who has both the technical knowledge to assess a particular donor's giving options based on their philanthropic and financial objectives, and the ability to explain those options in an understandable manner.

Board Commitment

The planned giving program must have full support from the board. They must understand the role that planned giving plays in ensuring the growth and long-term stability of the organization. Additionally, they must be willing to assist the development department with the planned giving program and play an active role in the program, including the identification, cultivation, and in some instances, solicitation, of planned giving prospective donors.

Before introducing a proposed planned giving program to the board, there must first be an understanding of what "planned giving" is all about and how planned gifts benefit both the organization and the donor. Consider conducting a brief seminar for the board to address the various planned giving options and the specific benefits afforded by each option. Help them understand how planned giving complements the organization's existing fundraising efforts. It is not uncommon for boards to develop a mind-set that planned gifts will detract from current gifts, when in fact it has been proven repeatedly that a healthy planned giving program enhances current annual gifts. Don't hesitate to bring in an outside consultant or a third-party financial professional who can clearly and concisely articulate the merits of a planned giving program. Sometimes a board needs to hear this message from outsiders rather than the fundraising staff before they are convinced that a planned giving program is vital to the future financial stability of the organization.

There is no better way to begin a planned giving program than by securing planned gift commitments from current and former board members. This should be done by personally meeting with each board member individually, rather than making a broad appeal to the entire board. Due to the sensitive nature of the information surrounding planned gifts, individuals are often not inclined to discuss their planned gift intentions in front of others. By participating in the planned giving program by way of their own personal commitments, the board sends a strong message to other donors and prospects that these types of gifts are important and should be considered as a complement to their current annual gifts.

The board must be willing to provide the financial resources necessary to begin implementing a planned giving program. An effective program will be built around the development of long-term personal relationships with donors. This is a labor-intensive process that may require adding fundraising staff whose primary responsibility is to spend time outside of the office cultivating close personal relationships with prospects. Marketing the planned giving program may also require financial resources. It is not imperative that an organization purchase new print materials to promote the various planned giving instruments. At the outset, it is often sufficient to incorporate planned giving messages into existing publications such as the annual report, newsletters, and brochures.

Although most planned gifts come from donors who have an existing long-term relationship with the organization, the board must recognize that introducing a planned giving program is not likely to generate immediate results. Securing these gifts will take time. Some planned gifts may occur within a six-month period; others may take a lifetime to complete. As is true with most gifts, the donor ultimately decides when he or she is ready to make the planned gift. For that reason, when evaluating the progress of a planned giving program, particularly one that is relatively new, consideration should be given to the number of substantive contacts and personal relationships established by the fundraiser, rather than the number of commitments secured and actual dollars generated. Mature planned giving programs will ultimately generate a steady flow of gift income, but that will take time. The board can provide leadership to the planned giving program by

- Publicly endorsing the merits of planned gifts
- Identifying and cultivating prospective donors
- Introducing fundraising staff to prospective donors
- Assisting in the solicitation of planned gift prospective donors

By properly educating the board at the outset and using their time judiciously throughout the process, you are likely to find that most board members will vigorously endorse and support the planned giving program. Along the way, be sure to keep the board informed and share with them your progress and success in the planned giving area.

The Planned Giving Professional

Because of budget constraints and limited staff, many organizations cannot hire a full-time fundraising professional whose sole responsibility is planned giving. Therefore it is common for many organizations to ease their way into planned giving by providing training opportunities to existing fundraisers and marketing the more basic planned giving opportunities, such as bequests and retirement plan/IRA designations, rather than the full menu of available options.

How an organization responds to planned giving inquiries from individuals can be handled in any number of different ways. First, the organization can assign that responsibility to a fundraiser whose sole responsibility is to raise money.

Ideally, this will be a major gifts officer who is interested in learning planned giving. This approach may somewhat limit that person's ability to travel and develop personal relationships with donors, for the major gifts officer will need to devote a portion of work time to technical training, developing planned giving policies and procedures, identifying planned giving prospects, and marketing the planned giving program.

A second option is to build a network of "friends" who have experience working in the charitable estate planning and related areas. These "friends" could come from a variety of professions, including attorneys, certified public accountants, certified financial planners, bank trust officers, certified life underwriters, and stockbrokers. Although these individuals can provide the organization with the technical support necessary to respond to planned giving inquiries from interested donors, it is probably not feasible to rely on these professionals to develop the personal relationships with donors that are so critical to the success of a planned giving program—that is the job of the organization's fundraisers. Professional advisors are best suited to handle the technical functions, such as drafting planned giving instruments, accompanying the fundraising professional on a personal visit to explain a gift illustration or answer questions posed by the donor or the donor's advisor, and assisting in the development of planned giving policies and procedures.

A third option—one that is not feasible for some organizations with budget constraints—is to hire a fundraising professional whose primary responsibility is planned giving. This person may or may not have previous development experience as a major gift or annual fund officer. A growing number of planned giving officers are coming from the for-profit world. A growing number of attorneys, accountants, bank trust officers, and financial planners have made career changes and moved from the for-profit sector to the nonprofit sector, seeking either to do something different or to serve an organization about which they are passionate.

Although it is not imperative that the planned giving officer have formal training, legal or otherwise, it is advantageous if that individual has some familiarity with the technical issues involved in planned giving. Some of the best planned-giving professionals have come from nontechnical backgrounds and have learned the technical aspects of planned giving through self-study, attending seminars, and practical hands-on training.

What attributes should a nonprofit organization look for when hiring a planned giving officer? The following characteristics merit attention:

Good interpersonal relationship skills. The ideal planned giving officer has the ability to develop meaningful personal relationships with donors.

Proactive. An effective planned giving officer must spend significant time outside of the office developing personal relationships with donors, rather than be consumed with in-office administrative details. Approximately 30 to 60 percent of a planned giving officer's time should be spent outside the office visiting donors and professional financial advisors. Most planned gift donors will not come to you—it is up to you to find them and initiate the discussion. The good news is that they are likely to be individuals already known to your organization.

Simplicity and understanding. Individuals skilled in articulating the technical aspects of planned giving with simplicity and understanding will experience the most success in planned giving. This same skill is also important when training other development staff, the board, and volunteers. And don't forget to listen to what your donor is telling you.

Thirst for knowledge. The tax laws surrounding planned giving sometimes change; thus an effective planned giving officer must be willing to stay abreast of tax law changes and case law developments that affect charitable gift planning.

Ability to articulate mission and programs with clarity. Although the planned giving officer is responsible for explaining the technical aspects of planned giving and identifying the donor's financial objectives, that individual must also be able to clearly articulate the organization's mission and programs and identify the donor's philanthropic objectives.

Planned Giving Policies and Guidelines

Before embarking on a planned giving program, the organization should develop written policies and guidelines governing the program. It is highly recommended that board approval be a prerequisite to the implementation of such policies and guidelines. Once these are board approved, fundraising personnel, volunteers, and donors are subject to the parameters contained in the document, thereby positioning the planned giving program to move forward with clarity. Clear and concise written policies and guidelines also help protect fundraisers from potentially awkward situations with donors who might perceive that the fundraiser is making up rules in midstream.

The following is a list of issues a nonprofit organization should consider addressing in a policies and guidelines document:

1. Will the organization offer charitable gift annuities? How will payout rates be determined?
2. Will the organization serve as trustee of charitable remainder trusts and charitable lead trusts? If not, is it the donor's responsibility to secure a trustee?

Does the organization require a minimum charitable remainder interest before it will agree to serve as trustee?

3. Will the organization administer charitable remainder trusts or charitable gift annuities? If not, who will serve as the third-party administrator? Will a fee be charged for these services?

4. What minimum dollar amounts and minimum age requirements should be established for each of the planned giving instruments? What is the minimum gift amount the organization is willing to accept for a charitable gift annuity? What is the minimum gift amount the organization is willing to accept for it to serve as the trustee of a charitable remainder trust or charitable lead trust? Are there minimum age requirements the donor must satisfy before the organization will enter into a charitable gift annuity contract with that donor? Are there minimum age requirements the donor must satisfy before the organization will serve as trustee of a charitable remainder trust?

5. Who in the organization has the authority to accept gifts of appreciated property, particularly hard-to-value assets such as real estate and closely held stock? Is board approval required before such assets are accepted?

6. Who in the organization is authorized to negotiate the terms of a planned giving instrument—such as a charitable gift annuity or charitable remainder trust—with a donor? Is board approval required before the document may be executed?

7. Who in the organization has the authority to sign the planned giving document on behalf of the organization?

The following are guidelines to consider incorporating into a policies and guidelines document, but note that these numbers and percentages may vary from one organization to the next and are designed to provide general guidance:

1. *Percentage payout rate on charitable remainder trusts.* The percentage payout rate on charitable remainder trusts must be at least 5 percent but should not exceed 50 percent.

2. *Minimum age requirements and funding levels for charitable remainder trusts.* If the organization is willing to serve as trustee, the minimum age of an income beneficiary should be fifty-five. The minimum funding level should be $50,000.

3. *Percentage payout on charitable gift annuities.* It should be the organization's general practice to use the gift annuity rates established by the American Council on Gift Annuities.

4. *Minimum age requirements and funding levels for charitable gift annuities.* The minimum age of an income beneficiary should be fifty-five. The minimum funding level should be $10,000.

5. *Trustee.* Most organizations should not serve as trustee of charitable remainder trusts and charitable gift annuities. In such instances, the donor is responsible for selecting a trustee.

6. *Real estate and closely held stock.* All proposed gifts of real estate and closely held stock must be approved by a committee of the board before acceptance.

7. *Donor-centered philanthropy.* All arrangements entered into with donors should always have the donor's best interests in mind, provided the terms of the arrangement do not violate the organization's policies and guidelines.

8. *Legal counsel.* Donors should be advised to consult with legal counsel or a financial advisor before executing a planned giving instrument with the organization.

9. *Confidentiality.* All information about a donor or named income beneficiaries—including names, ages, gift amounts, net worth, and the like—should be kept strictly confidential by the organization unless permission is obtained from the donor to release such information.

The Planned Gift Options

Planned giving generally involves one of three gift methods—current outright gifts, expectancies, and deferred gifts. A common misnomer in the planned giving industry is that all planned gifts are "deferred gifts." Some planned gifts may be structured to provide immediate benefits to the nonprofit organization. However, in most instances planned gifts either provide deferred benefits to the organization or involve a combination of methods, whereby a current outright gift is combined with a deferred gift or an expectancy to achieve the donor's philanthropic and financial objectives. The planned gift should always be structured with the donor's philanthropic and financial interests at the forefront.

Current Outright Gifts

Gifts of appreciated assets such as stock, real estate, and tangible personal property, although given for the current use and enjoyment of a nonprofit organization, typically qualify as planned gifts. These gifts are generally made jointly by spouses because of the dollar amount and the fact that they require significant contemplation and planning—unlike annual fund gifts, which are often made spontaneously in response to a mail appeal and without spousal consent.

Stock

Appreciated stock—publicly traded or closely held—represents the most common type of noncash gift received by charities. Nonprofit organizations prefer gifts of publicly traded stock because it is easily transferable—typically by way of a wire transfer—and highly liquid—it can be sold instantaneously as soon as it is deposited into the charity's account. Publicly traded stock always has a readily ascertainable fair market value, which can be found on the Internet and in most major newspapers. Closely held stock, on the other hand, may be difficult to value and requires the services of a qualified independent appraiser, which could take several weeks to complete. Such stock may also prove to be illiquid in that it may contain restrictions prohibiting it from being given to an organization; in some cases it is not sellable because a ready, willing, and able buyer cannot be located. Most family businesses are closely held, and the owners may have a significant portion of their net worth in the business, thereby making them prime prospective donors of a planned gift.

Real Estate

Real estate is the second most common type of noncash gift. There are a number of issues a nonprofit organization should address before accepting a gift of real estate. Is the real estate subject to a mortgage or some other type of debt? Are there liens or encumbrances on the real estate? Is the donor the sole owner, or is it jointly owned with others? Once accepted, is it likely the organization can sell the property within a reasonable period of time? If this is not likely, does the organization have funds available to pay for the insurance, taxes, and maintenance of the property in the meantime? If the organization retains the property, can it be used for a tax-exempt purpose? Have environmental tests been conducted on the property to ensure that it is not contaminated?

Many organizations require board approval before accepting gifts of real estate. Some even create a real estate checklist that must be satisfied before the proposed gift is presented to the board. Because most organizations are not interested in entering into the real estate management business, acceptance of a gift of real estate may be predicated on the ability to sell the property within a short period of time.

When deciding on the most advantageous assets to give currently to an organization, donors often choose to give the most highly appreciated assets, thereby entitling the donor to a charitable income tax deduction equal to the current fair market value of the property, maximizing the deduction. In addition, if the donor gives appreciated assets to the organization and the organization, rather than the donor, sells such assets, capital gains tax is avoided because the organization is a tax-exempt entity and will not incur such tax upon the sale of the assets.

Charitable Lead Trust

A charitable lead trust is a trust that pays current annual income to the nonprofit organization for a specified period of years, with the trust principal reverting to the donor or the donor's family when the trust ends. The annual income payment made by the trust is similar to an outright gift of cash, for the charity is free to use the cash immediately—subject, of course, to any restrictions placed on the gift by the donor. The charitable lead trust is probably the most sophisticated of all the planned giving instruments, thus it is advisable to seek the assistance of an experienced charitable estate planner before entering into this type of arrangement. Charitable lead trusts are generally utilized by high-net-worth individuals with estate and gift tax concerns, thus it is likely to be of interest to only a small percentage of an organization's constituency.

Expectancies

An expectancy is a promise by a donor to make a gift to a nonprofit organization at some future date; however, that promise may be revoked any time prior to the donor's death. In other words, the charity is expecting to receive the gift at some future date, but ultimately it may not receive it if the donor changes his or her mind. As the gift is not a completed gift during the donor's lifetime, because of the allowed revocation, the donor does not enjoy the benefit of a charitable income tax deduction when the expectancy provision is created. But because the donor retains the ability to make a change and does not have to part with the asset while alive, expectancies tend to be very popular. The most common types of expectancies are bequests, retirement plan/IRA designations, and life insurance designations.

Bequests. Bequests are the backbone of all planned giving programs and, historically, are the most popular planned giving method used by donors because they are easy to understand and can be revoked any time before death. They give donors the peace of mind of knowing that they retain control of these assets during their lifetime; the funds remain available to them to satisfy unforeseen expenses such as medical or nursing home costs. Bequests are also popular with charities because they are easy to explain to donors, they require very little cost to market, and once in place, they are rarely revoked.

A bequest is a written statement in a donor's will directing that specific assets, or a percentage of the estate, be transferred to charity at the donor's death. Because many individuals choose to transfer their assets at death by will, and because bequests can be established for any dollar amount, nonprofit organizations should consider marketing bequests to their entire constituency, regardless of age and net worth. If there is one giving opportunity worthy of marketing to an entire constituency, it is the bequest. Organizations that do nothing else but regularly include sample will language in their communications have successfully implemented the cornerstone of most planned giving programs and are likely to reap dividends from this giving opportunity for years to come.

Retirement Plans and IRAs. A second type of expectancy popular among donors is the designation of a charity as a partial or full beneficiary of a retirement plan or IRA. For many individuals, retirement plan assets constitute a significant portion of their net worth. Like the bequest, this vehicle is easy to understand and easy to implement, and it keeps the door open for the donor to make a change. Naming a charity as the beneficiary of a retirement plan merely requires the donor to obtain a beneficiary designation form from the retirement plan administrator and to name the charity as the beneficiary of a percentage of the plan. The transfer will not occur until the death of the retirement plan owner. In the meantime, the donor can change the designation and increase, decrease, or totally eliminate the charity's beneficial interest in the plan. It is important to note that a donor may achieve significant income and estate tax savings by naming a charity as the beneficiary of the retirement plan assets rather than a noncharity, such as a spouse or child. In some instances, the tax savings can be as much as seventy-five cents on the dollar.

Life Insurance. A third type of expectancy, life insurance, is attractive because it affords donors the opportunity to make a potentially sizeable gift for a minimal outlay of cash. Donors may make a gift of an existing policy, either fully or partially paid, or purchase a new policy. Similar to retirement plan designations, the proposed gift to charity is accomplished by naming the charity as a beneficiary of the policy on the beneficiary designation form provided by the life insurance company. Upon the donor's death, the charity will receive all or a portion of the proceeds from the policy. The donor is entitled to a charitable income tax deduction equal to the cash surrender value of the property and any future premiums paid only if the charity is named as both the owner and beneficiary of the policy.

Deferred Gifts

Deferred gifts are irrevocable transfers of cash or property not available for the charity's use and enjoyment until sometime in the future. Although the gift is complete, thereby entitling the donor to a current charitable income tax deduction, a future event—such as the donor's death or the expiration of a specific term of years—will cause the charity's interest to come into fruition. The most prevalent types of deferred gift arrangements, both of which offer income to the donor or a beneficiary designated by the donor, are charitable gift annuities and charitable remainder trusts.

Charitable Gift Annuity. A charitable gift annuity is a simple contract between the donor and the charity whereby the donor makes an irrevocable transfer of cash or property to the charity. In return for the contributed property, the charity agrees to pay a fixed sum of money each year for the lifetime of one or two individuals. The donor need not be a life income beneficiary—payments can be made to elderly parents, children, or other loved ones. The payout rate offered by the charity will depend on the number of income beneficiaries (again, two is the maximum) and their ages. The income beneficiaries have the option to defer receiving their annuity payments until some future date provided this decision is made at the time the gift annuity contract is signed.

Many charities offer charitable gift annuities because they are easy to explain and require minimal administrative time and expense to implement. Charitable gift annuities are attractive to donors who are interested in making a gift to charity but are unable to do so because of limited financial resources. The gift annuity allows such donors to make a current gift and in return receive a stream of income for their lifetime.

Most states regulate charitable gift annuities; thus a charity should familiarize itself with state restrictions, regulations, and reporting requirements before initiating a charitable gift annuity program. The charity must be concerned not only with the requirements of the state in which it has offices but also those in states where the charitable gift annuity donors are domiciled. All states require some form of registration before the charity can enter into legally binding contracts with donors.

Charitable Remainder Trust. A charitable remainder trust is an irrevocable trust in which the donor transfers cash or property to a trustee, and in return the donor, other individuals named by the donor as income beneficiaries, or both receive income from the trust for life or a term of years, not to exceed twenty years. When the trust terminates, the remaining trust principal is distributed to the charities named as the charitable remainder beneficiaries.

There are two primary types of charitable remainder trusts—the charitable remainder annuity trust and the charitable remainder unitrust. Although both trusts are similar in many ways, the most significant difference is the method by which the annual income paid by the trust to the income beneficiaries is calculated. The other major difference is that annuity trusts do not allow for additional contributions once funded, whereas unitrusts allow for additional contributions at any time.

A charitable remainder annuity trust pays a fixed dollar amount, annually, based on the initial fair market value of the property transferred to the trust. For example, if a donor transfers $100,000 to an annuity trust and selects a payout percentage of 5 percent, the named income beneficiaries will receive $5,000 per year until the trust terminates, regardless of whether the trust principal increases or decreases in value over time. Thus annuity trusts are generally favored by donors who are more interested in receiving a fixed income instead of being subjected to market volatility and fluctuating income payments. For this reason, conservative donors tend to favor the annuity trust.

A charitable remainder unitrust, on the other hand, provides fluctuating income payments to the income beneficiaries, based on a fixed percentage of the trust principal, revalued annually. For example, as in the previous example, if a donor transfers $100,000 to a unitrust and selects a payout percentage of 5 percent, the named income beneficiaries will receive $5,000 in the first year. But if in the second year the trust grows in value to $110,000, the income beneficiaries will receive $5,500 (5 percent of the new revalued trust principal of $110,000) thereby enjoying the benefit from the appreciation experienced by the trust. Alternatively, if in the second year the trust drops in value to $90,000, the income beneficiaries will receive only $4,500 in the second year (5 percent of the new revalued trust principal of $90,000). Thus market volatility will have a direct impact on the income payments received each year by the income beneficiaries. For this reason, aggressive, entrepreneurial-minded donors tend to favor the unitrust.

With both trusts, the payout percentage provided for in the trust document must be at least 5 percent but may not exceed 50 percent. Most charitable remainder trusts contain payout percentages ranging from 5 percent to 10 percent depending on the number of income beneficiaries and their ages. Charities who serve as trustees will have a voice in determining the payout percentage, but charities who do not serve as trustees are not in a position to dictate the trust's payout percentage—that percentage is determined solely by the donor. Many charities choose not to serve as trustee because of the legal fiduciary responsibility they must assume as trustee.

Marketing Planned Gifts

Developing a planned giving program internally among staff, volunteers, and the board is not enough to market a planned giving program effectively. Thought must be given as to how the organization will inform the entire donor base about planned giving opportunities. Determining which planned giving instruments are marketed to various segments of an organization's constituency will be critical to the overall effectiveness of the planned giving program.

For organizations starting a planned giving program, it is unrealistic to expect that a comprehensive program offering every available planned giving opportunity must be rolled out all at once. Many organizations develop planned giving programs on a piecemeal basis, first introducing the revocable arrangements such as bequests, retirement plan/IRA designations, and life insurance designations, and later, once they have experienced success with the revocable arrangements, introducing the irrevocable arrangements such as charitable gift annuities and charitable remainder trusts. If an organization is not prepared to respond to inquiries concerning the more technical instruments such as charitable remainder trusts, then it is probably a good idea not to market that particular giving option. Make sure your backyard is in order before proceeding. Donors must be left with the impression that the organization is capable of answering questions accurately and fully explaining the benefits of a particular opportunity to both the donor and the organization.

Not every available planned giving opportunity will be marketed to an organization's entire constituency. In some instances it may be prudent to market a particular giving method to the entire constituency (such as bequests), but other giving methods may appeal to only a narrow segment of the constituency (such as charitable remainder trusts), and therefore are marketed in a targeted fashion to that group alone. Age, family situations (living spouse, children, grandchildren, and so on), prior giving history, level of affluence, and involvement with the organization are some of the factors to consider when determining which gift opportunities should be marketed to a particular donor.

The essence of a successful planned giving marketing program is to educate and inform constituents about the various giving opportunities available to help a donor accomplish his or her philanthropic and financial objectives. Communicating that the organization is in the planned giving business sends a message to donors that the organization is looking to the future to address long-term goals and objectives. As such, many donors choose to direct their planned gifts for endowments that perpetuate themselves because only a portion of the principal is spent each year, rather than support current operating expenses that could quickly diminish the funds. For this reason, charitable organizations should be prepared to share with their donors the various endowment opportunities offered by the organization.

Print Materials

The development of print materials may be the first step in disseminating planned giving opportunities to an organization's constituency. Print materials may include planned giving brochures, planned giving newsletters, planned giving inserts, planned giving ads, stand-alone mailings made up of a cover letter and accompanying illustrations, and the integration of planned giving messages in all communication pieces, including annual fund appeals.

Planned giving brochures and newsletters are commonly used by organizations to market planned giving opportunities. There are two basic approaches to consider with brochures. The first is the creation of a comprehensive brochure containing a brief explanation of each available planned giving opportunity—bequests, retirement plan designations, charitable gift annuities, and so on. These brochures tend to be widely distributed because they cover all available planned giving opportunities, from the most basic, bequests, to the most sophisticated, charitable lead trusts. An all-inclusive brochure may be particularly attractive to organizations with a limited budget, as design and printing expenses will be kept to a minimum.

The second approach is the creation of a series of planned giving brochures, each describing in detail a particular planned giving method. For example, individual brochures may be created for "Bequests," "Charitable Gift Annuities," "Retirement Plan and IRA Designations," "Charitable Remainder Trusts," and so on. These brochures are typically not intended for widespread distribution, but rather are available to share with donors on a limited basis during personal visits or when a donor expresses an interest in a particular giving method.

Regardless of which approach is used, there are a number of companies who offer copy-ready generic brochures that can be purchased and imprinted with the organization's name and logo. Many of these companies also give the nonprofit organization the ability to custom-tailor the generic brochure and incorporate photos, stories, and mission-related information specific to the organization. Weaving organizational information into the generic text is the preferable approach because it produces a brochure with a look and message consistent with other communication pieces.

Some organizations assume the task of preparing the entire planned brochure in-house. There is merit to this approach, in that the brochure is completely written and produced by individuals who work for the organization and therefore best know its mission. But before embarking on a project of this magnitude, those contemplating it should ask, "Do we have the staff resources and technical expertise in-house to produce an effective brochure that is technically sound, conveys a clear and understandable message to our constituency, and can be produced in a timely fashion?" Because planned giving relies heavily on relationship building, an organization may conclude that their planned giving officer's time is better spent out of the office developing relationships with key donors, rather than behind a desk preparing brochures.

Each brochure should contain a reply device giving the donor an opportunity to request additional information, indicate they have already included the organization in their will or estate plan, request an illustration, or request a personal visit from the planned giving officer. Donors who take the time to respond to mailings are prime prospective planned gift donors and should be contacted immediately to gather additional information and schedule a personal visit.

Planned giving newsletters sent on a periodic basis (quarterly, semi-annually, annually) are another way to market planned giving opportunities. Each newsletter can focus on a specific planned gift instrument and contain a testimonial from a donor who has used that particular method to benefit the organization. Some organizations have been successful in securing newsletter sponsors, such as law firms or banks, who are willing to underwrite the cost of producing the newsletter in exchange for placing the firm's name on the newsletter. Newsletters typically lend themselves to widespread distribution—all donors of record, volunteers, professional financial advisors, and so on—and the cost per newsletter drops significantly once a certain quantity is produced.

One-page planned giving inserts that accompany annual fund appeals and ads in existing organizational publications are cost-effective ways to communicate with a broad constituent base. For instance, if a university regularly sends a magazine to its alumni, an ad inside the magazine highlighting the opportunity to support the organization through a bequest or charitable gift annuity may resonate with some readers and prompt them to self-identify as planned giving prospects.

Integration with Annual Appeals

Nonprofit organizations interested in marketing planned giving opportunities to their constituency should first consider reviewing existing communications to find ways to incorporate planned giving messages into these communications. This should be the most cost-effective way to begin the marketing effort, particularly for organizations with limited budgets that do not possess the financial resources to produce newsletters and brochures. This could be as basic as including language on annual appeal slips that give donors the opportunity to check boxes indicating they have already included the organization in their will or estate plan, or to request additional information about a particular planned giving method or a personal visit from the organization to discuss planned gift options.

Stand-Alone Mailings

For the cost of a postage stamp, another cost-effective marketing strategy is the stand-alone mailing, using a cover letter and accompanying illustration highlighting a specific planned giving instrument. For example, a mailing of sample bequest language accompanied by a cover letter signed by a key board member, volunteer, or leader within the organization, extolling the importance of bequests to the long-term viability of the organization, can be done with minimal effort and expense.

Revocable planned giving methods, such as bequests, retirement plan/IRA designations, and life insurance designations, are typically marketed to a broader base of donors than are irrevocable arrangements, such as charitable gift annuities and charitable remainder trusts. Donors tend to gravitate to revocable arrangements because they are easy to understand, implemented with minimal effort, and designated for any dollar amount, and they allow the donor to change her mind anytime before death. Because revocable arrangements appeal to a narrower segment of the constituency, consider segmenting marketing messages based on age, level of affluence, prior giving history, involvement with the organization, or some combination of these factors.

Seminars

Planned giving seminars are an excellent way for an organization to educate its constituency about planned giving opportunities and create an awareness that the organization is ready to discuss and assist donors in facilitating such gifts. Seminars can be designed for a variety of audiences such as donors, volunteers, board members, faculty, medical staff, and professional financial advisors.

The audience will dictate the level of technical content presented at the seminar. It is important to make donor and volunteer seminars concise and understandable. This may be the first opportunity for a donor or volunteer to learn about these gift instruments, so it is important they leave the seminar with a clear understanding of the topics presented, as opposed to feeling confused and overwhelmed. Donor and volunteer seminars should avoid presentations involving in-depth technical discussions. Discussions about bequests, retirement plan/IRA designations, life insurance designations, charitable gift annuities, and, in some cases, charitable remainder trusts, are best suited for these types of seminars. Securing a well-respected professional advisor within the community to serve as presenter will lend credibility to the program, but first make sure this individual has the ability to present the material in an understandable fashion to an audience who do not share the professional advisor's expertise.

Seminars for professional financial advisors, on the other hand, should be more technically oriented. Many, but not all, professional advisors understand the basics of planned giving, so it is generally safe to provide a thorough discussion of the various instruments, delving into the income, capital gains, and estate and gift tax issues as well as related estate planning issues. Offering continuing education credit may make the seminar particularly attractive to an advisor and help ensure a solid turnout.

Personal Visits

Although newsletters, brochures, ads, and seminars are useful ways to market planned gifts, nothing takes the place of personal visits. A marketing program that relies primarily on print materials and overlooks the importance of the personal visit will have limited success. When an individual responds to a mailing or calls requesting information, it is imperative that the charitable organization follow up in a timely fashion. The donor may lose interest if the organization is slow to respond. Most planned gifts occur as the result of a long personal relationship with the donor, so organizations should always be looking for ways to engage and involve the donor on a personal level. Letters, e-mails, and telephone calls are not substitutes for personal visits, but rather should be used to complement the visits. Depending on their job responsibilities beyond fundraising, all fundraisers should set goals for conducting a certain number of personal donor visits per month. In the early stages of a planned giving program, it may be more realistic to measure a planned giving officer's progress on the number of personal visits made, rather than the number of planned gift arrangements closed or dollars raised.

Planned Giving Recognition Society

The primary reason for creating a planned giving recognition society is to identify individuals who have already included the organization in their will or estate plan. Donors may neglect to notify the organization that they have included it as a beneficiary in their estate plans. Such omissions are sometimes intentional; in other instances the donor simply fails to think about notifying the organization. Creating a planned giving recognition society and marketing it to the organization's constituency creates a heightened awareness among individuals that the organization is interested in learning about their future plans to benefit the organization. It also provides an opportunity to begin building a personal relationship with the donor and engage them in meaningful ways.

The charitable organization establishes which planned gift arrangements qualify one for membership in the society. Many organizations make membership all-inclusive, in that all of the various planned giving arrangements qualify one for membership, regardless of dollar amount and the ability to revoke. Some organizations require the donor to provide a copy of the legal document that references the donor's gift, whereas others are comfortable taking donors at their word and merely ask for a written statement from the donor summarizing the gift arrangement.

To help market the planned giving recognition society, nonprofits sometimes create a brochure explaining that the society exists, the organization's mission, a brief description of the planned gift methods that qualify one for membership, a roster of current planned gift donors, and an explanation of what action must be taken to become a member. These brochures are typically sent to planned gift donors of record, board members and volunteers, annual fund donors, and professional financial advisors.

An annual event exclusively for society members, such as a luncheon or dinner, is used by some organizations as a way to thank members for their participation. Most planned gift donors do not expect organizations to bestow on them tangible objects such as plaques or paperweights. In fact, some donors are adamant that the organization refrain from using gift dollars for anything other than activities and programs that directly support the mission of the organization.

Identification of Prospective Donors

Prospective planned gift donors come from all age groups (young and old), levels of affluence, family situations (married, single, multiple children, childless), philanthropic objectives (capital, endowment, operating), and financial objectives (increased income, income tax savings, capital gains tax savings, estate and gift tax savings). It is a mistake to pigeonhole planned giving prospects into a narrowly defined set of characteristics. Sometimes planned gifts are made by donors you least expect, so it is important not to overlook any segment of your prospective donor population. With that said, where do you begin? Some organizations begin the identification process by analyzing individuals who are currently on the radar screen—namely, those individuals who have previously made planned gift commitments to the organization or are supporting the organization on a regular basis through annual fund commitments. Don't feel as though the process of identifying prospective donors must begin by identifying "new" prospective donors with no previous gift history. More likely than not, those individuals who become planned gift donors have a history of giving and involvement with the organization.

Current Planned Gift Donors

Begin by identifying individuals who already have planned gift commitments in place. Perhaps they have named the organization as a beneficiary in a will, retirement plan, or life insurance policy. As discussed previously, a donor has no obligation to notify an organization that it has been included as a beneficiary. For that reason, some organizations create planned giving recognition societies because they provide an opportunity for donors to notify the organization that a planned gift commitment is already in place. Once current planned gift donors are identified, it is the planned giving officer's responsibility to contact those donors, thank them for their commitments, and attempt to begin building a personal relationship. Not only will this provide an opportunity to obtain details about their planned gift, but it may also provide an opportunity to convert revocable arrangements, like bequests, into irrevocable commitments.

Annual Fund Donors

Next, look at donors who have participated in the annual fund. In particular, look at the number of years they have participated. Donors who have made annual fund gifts for each of the last ten years, or at least eight out of the last ten years, are sending a message that they are committed to the organization and willing to support it on a consistent basis. These same donors may also be interested in learning how they can support the organization in a more significant way, either during their lifetime or at death. Because some planned gift arrangements offer income to the donor in return for their gift, in addition to providing various tax benefits, some donors may reason that they are capable of making a gift they did not think was otherwise possible, or making a gift at a level that is much higher than they ever expected.

Board, Volunteers, and Staff

Next, consider individuals who have a history of direct involvement with the organization. These individuals may be former or current board members, volunteers, administrative and professional staff, donors, and community leaders. The linkage to the organization exists, or did exist at one time, so, it is the planned giving officer's responsibility to determine if the ability and interest are present. Keep in mind that most individuals have a variety of charitable interests, thus even if the interest in the organization is not at the highest possible level, an individual may still be interested in supporting the organization, particularly through an estate plan arrangement that does not require a current outlay of cash or assets. Not all planned giving prospective donors will have a high net worth. There will be individuals of moderate wealth who are willing to entertain the idea of making a current transfer to an organization in return for a stream of income, or willing to include an organization as a beneficiary in a will, retirement plan, or life insurance policy. In addition, do not overlook donors who fall below certain annual giving levels, such as $500 or more. Some individuals, no matter how committed to an organization, may not make a significant commitment during their lifetime because they have conservative financial views, or they require the peace of mind that they will have sufficient assets available if confronted with unforeseen emergencies such as major medical expenses, or both. However, these same individuals may be willing to make a significant gift to the organization, at death, through one of the various planned giving methods.

Professional Financial Advisors

Networking with professional financial advisors, particularly those practicing in the community, can sometimes lead an organization to new prospective donors. Clients sometimes look to their professional advisors—such as attorneys, accountants, financial planners, and bank trust officers—for advice in satisfying philanthropic objectives. Many financial advisors actively promote the various planned giving instruments to their clients, recognizing that some clients will lose ownership and control over a certain percentage of assets at death unless proper planning is done. If structured properly, some planned giving instruments can allow an individual to redirect to their favorite charities dollars that would have otherwise been lost to the government in the form of taxes, thereby allowing the individual to retain control of those assets, so to speak, and determine how those hard-earned dollars are spent rather than allowing the government to make that decision.

Some organizations formalize their network of financial advisors by creating a planned giving committee that meets periodically to create gift acceptance policies, review lists of prospective donors, prepare articles for planned giving newsletters, and learn more about the organization's mission. You will find that some professional advisors welcome the opportunity to learn more about an organization's mission, the programs it offers, and the people it serves. Creating opportunities for advisors to come to an organization's site and observe firsthand how the organization is serving the community may leave an indelible mark on the advisor and cause him or her to think of the organization when discussing philanthropic alternatives with clients.

Conclusion

A successful planned giving program must be carefully planned and tailored to meet the needs of the organization. Commitment from institutional leadership is critical. As gift planners, it is our job to address the donor's philanthropic and financial objectives. Never lose sight of the significance of your organization's mission to the donor. Planned gifts are rarely made based strictly on tax and estate planning considerations. A belief in the organization's mission is generally the driving force behind most planned gifts. Once a donor has decided an organization merits the donor's support, it becomes the charitable gift planner's responsibility to help the donor understand the various planned giving opportunities and how to make the gift in the most tax-efficient manner.

Like other areas of development, success in planned giving requires the ability to develop meaningful relationships with your constituency. Understanding a donor's motivations and objectives—which is accomplished primarily through personal contacts and relationship-building—is far more important than understanding the technical nuances of planned giving. Begin to develop relationships with your top prospects, learn the gift planning process, and recognize that most planned gifts require a team effort comprising multiple individuals who understand their role and those of the others involved. Success will follow.

PART THREE

DISCOVERING WHAT DONORS VALUE

The chapters in Part Three provide insights into the various sources of philanthropic support available to nonprofit organizations. Every organization should make it a goal to create a base of philanthropic funds that includes diverse sources of support. The more funding sources in the organization's donor base, the less likely the organization is to be affected by events that might have an impact on any one of those sources, such as a corporate merger or a change in fortune of an individual major donor. The dynamics that shape philanthropy are constantly changing, and Chapter Ten comments on the changing world in which nonprofits carry out their work with donors and on the challenges and opportunities fundraisers face in raising philanthropic funds.

From this broad context, Chapter Eleven zeroes in on prospect research as an ethical process for better understanding the donor. This chapter provides best practices for understanding what information is pertinent and relevant for purposes of building the relationship with the donor so that when the donor is asked for a gift, it is done with attention to the "Six Rights of Fundraising"—the right person asking the right prospective donor for the right gift for the right program in the right way at the right time.

The remainder of the chapters in this part build on this foundation to focus on commonalities of different donor constituencies. Chapters Twelve and Thirteen focus on corporations and foundations, respectively, taking account of how the unique interests and constraints of each of these entities influences its philanthropy. Because the largest percentage of philanthropic support continues to come from individuals during their lifetimes, Chapters Fourteen through Seventeen each focus on a particular individual donor constituency. Chapter Fourteen explores women as donors, taking a look at why and how the philanthropy of women differs from that of their male counterparts. Chapter Fifteen examines high-net-worth donors, using some of the most recent research available to show the distinctive ways in which the philanthropy of donors of wealth differs from that of the general public. Chapter Sixteen on ethnicity and giving draws some cautious generalizations about how cultural factors influence philanthropy, and Chapter Seventeen looks at what the most recent research can tell us about new generations of donors.

CHAPTER TEN

CONTEMPORARY DYNAMICS OF PHILANTHROPY

By Patrick M. Rooney and Sarah K. Nathan

As fundraisers, we must master the tools of the trade and commit to best practices. *Achieving Excellence in Fundraising* will help you do both. But, perhaps more important, it will also help you understand that, as Hank Rosso said, fundraising is the servant of philanthropy. Since the publication of the first edition of *Achieving Excellence in Fund Raising* in 1991, both the nonprofit sector and the fundraising profession have been fueled by practical training and academic research, and both have grown tremendously. Even recent popular culture has embraced philanthropy. *The Philanthropist*—a short-lived NBC television series—became the chic story of a ruthless capitalist with a change of heart who traveled to the poorest and most remote places to provide humanitarian aid. From *Idol Gives Back* and *Oprah's Big Give*, to the star-studded television spectacular *Hope for Haiti*, philanthropy is now an essential element of pop culture. Although this popularity may energize the work of nonprofit professionals, it is not a new phenomenon. The contemporary dynamics of philanthropy are as diverse as the missions of the sector's multitude of nonprofit organizations. This brief introduction will only skim the surface of philanthropy's cultural roots and its role today, but it provides a basic understanding of philanthropy's importance.

Roles of Philanthropy

The root of the word *philanthropy* comes from the Greek, meaning love of humankind. A lexical history of the word uncovers a "multifaceted term, with many layers of meaning in both its historical and its contemporary usages" (Sulek, 2010). Indeed, there are many possible motivations for philanthropic activities, whether it be love of other persons, the beautiful, the good, the divine, or wisdom; personal excellence, civic virtue, or morality; rational understanding, moral sentiment, or good will; the pleasures of social interaction; and so on. But even if we use the most basic definition—love of others—as a simplified understanding of philanthropy today, it does not belie the inherent moral nature of philanthropic actions. This is why the Center on Philanthropy at Indiana University uses Robert Payton's broad definition of philanthropy—voluntary action for the public good—as a foundation for its work. In this conception, philanthropy is purposeful in both action and intention. It is much bigger than the nonprofit sector that is the focus of this book, and at the same time it encompasses the work that fundraisers do. Philanthropy is a tradition that manifests itself in the nonprofit sector.

Philanthropy defines the field in a positive way, in terms of what this sort of action does and why. It affirms a value, a concern for the well-being of people beyond oneself, and a concern for the public good. It asserts that the most important aspect of action (formal and informal) in this so-called nonprofit sector is the public purpose and mission of action (Payton and Moody, 2008, p. 36). In this context, the roles of philanthropy are generally defined as:

- *Reduce human suffering*—Through health care, human services, and international relief, nonprofit organizations seek to make life more comfortable for those who are injured or ill, to aid victims, and to assist those not able to sustain themselves. This is perhaps the oldest role of philanthropy, a role that has existed throughout recorded history.
- *Enhance human potential*—Nonprofit organizations enhance human potential through religion, education, the arts, culture and humanities, and international efforts benefiting the public, society, and the environment.
- *Promote equity and justice*—Philanthropy promotes equity and justice through human services and advocacy on behalf of those who cannot speak for themselves by promoting structures and programs in the public, private, and nonprofit sectors. Through advocacy efforts, nonprofit organizations often give voice to the voiceless.
- *Build community*—Through organizations and voluntary associations, people come together, feel they belong, and make a contribution to their neighborhood, city, state, country, or world through community building.
- *Provide human fulfillment*—Philanthropy gives all people the opportunity to become that best image we have of ourselves. Through giving and sharing, humans express their ideas and values. Peter Drucker (1990, p. xvii) best captured this notion when he said, "To make contributors out of donors means that the

American people can see what they want to see—or should want to see—when each of us looks at him or herself in the mirror in the morning: someone who as a citizen takes responsibility. Someone who as a neighbor cares."

- *Support experimentation and change*—Philanthropy supports experimentation and stimulates change by taking risks, exploring areas that the larger community or the market sector may be unwilling to enter, and often funding alternative or new solutions.
- *Foster pluralism*—Nonprofit organizations and participation in them allow for multiple responses to an issue and, at its best, includes a wide variety of voices. In a civil society in which philanthropy flourishes, parallel power structures are allowed to carry out what the government and business sectors will not or cannot do.

This understanding of philanthropy, that we care for those who need assistance in our community, is as old as the land in which we live. Traditions of sharing and generosity are ever present in Native American stories, many of which influenced early settlers (Jackson, 2008). In 1630, aboard the ship *Arbella*, John Winthrop gave his sermon "Model of Christian Charity" as a guide for the colonists' actions at Massachusetts Bay. Among the rationales he provided for charity is the inherent connections between all people, rich and poor. Because of this connection, a reciprocal obligation to care for others binds people together. Almost a century and a half later, Benjamin Franklin, although a strong individualist, participated in many voluntary associations. He first joined the Freemasons as a young printer in London and eventually organized the first Freemason group in Philadelphia. He also established the Junto, a civic club for young men, and the first volunteer fire department and public library. Franklin is also credited with "inventing" the matching gift. Historian Kathleen McCarthy (2003) reveals how generations of Americans have used philanthropy to gather, speak freely and lobby for reform, establishing an "American creed."

This tradition of voluntary association, epitomized by Franklin and others, never waned. It was documented in detail by the French political writer Alexis de Tocqueville a hundred years after Franklin. The history of philanthropy in the United States is as rich and diverse as the nonprofit sector itself; the subject certainly commands treatment that cannot be fully presented here. In recent years, scholarship on the history of philanthropy has grown; several excellent resources cited here and listed in the bibliography are recommended for further reading.

Our contemporary understanding of the sector as "nonprofit," "voluntary," "independent," or "the third" is relatively new. First studied at great length and legitimized by the Commission on Private Philanthropy and Public Needs (commonly referred to as the Filer Commission) in 1973, the nonprofit sector was recognized as a powerful force in both the economy and society. The Commission's final report emphasized the close yet sometimes adversarial relationship between nonprofit organizations and government. In many ways, the Commission is credited for the subsequent "professionalization" of the sector. Perhaps its greatest legacy will be a sector grounded in research—research that today helps identify emerging trends, challenges conventional wisdom, and provides invaluable insights into philanthropic organizations and their practices.

Size and Scope

As noted, philanthropy and nonprofit organizations have always played a significant role in American society. But they play an even more significant role today. The nonprofit sector has grown to be a large part of the U.S. economy. According to the National Center for Charitable Statistics at the Urban Institute (Blackwood, Wing, and Pollak, 2008), approximately 1.4 million nonprofit organizations are registered with the Internal Revenue Service. This number, however, is an understatement of the sector's true size because it does not capture nonregistered groups—namely religious organizations and churches, which are not required to register, as well as small, mostly informal groups. Between 1995 and 2005 the number of registered nonprofit organizations grew by 27.3 percent, from 1.1 million to 1.4 million organizations. Among those reporting public charities, human services comprise the largest subsector (32.3 percent), followed by education (18.7 percent), health (13.3 percent), and the arts (11.5 percent). Among the smaller subsectors, the environment, animal rights and protection, and international affairs have seen the greatest growth, both more than doubling in size since 1995. The growing nonprofit sector means that there are more opportunities for volunteer involvement and gift making.

Just as the number of organizations has increased, so too has Americans' generosity through charitable giving. Since 1955, the Giving USA Foundation has been calculating annual charitable giving, and it is still the only annual report on philanthropy that simultaneously estimates all of the sources (households, corporations, foundations, and bequests) and uses of philanthropy (religion, education, health, human services, and so on). According to *Giving USA 2009*, total giving was estimated to be $307.65 billion in calendar year 2008 (The Center on Philanthropy, 2009b). This was the first decline in giving since 1987 (in current or "nominal" dollars) and only the second since *Giving USA* began. As the worldwide financial crisis continued, giving in calendar year 2009 fell 3.6 percent to

$303.75 billion. This is the steepest decline in giving since recording began, but it is worth noting that it was the fourth year in a row in a which giving was over $300 billion (The Center on Philanthropy, 2010).

One of the most useful things that this data reveals is the fact that giving by individuals is *always* the largest slice of the giving pie, usually about 75 percent. In 2008, individual giving was equal to $229.28 billion, and in 2009 it was $227.41 billion. Despite the slight decline, there is virtually no difference when adjusted for inflation. When individual giving as a source is combined with bequests and giving to family foundations, the total of giving done by individuals is even greater—almost 90 percent in 2009. This is why mastering fundraising techniques is so critical to the health of the nonprofit sector: an organization can no longer rely on the generosity of one foundation or corporation. It also reminds us that people do keep giving, even in tough times.

In some ways, the story of charitable giving by subsector is the reverse of the number of organizations just reported. Giving to religious causes, only 6 percent of the total number of registered organizations, annually represents about one-third of all charitable giving. In 2008, specifically, it accounted for $106.89 billion dollars, or 35 percent of all giving. Educational causes, the second largest subsector, also receives the second largest number of contributions, 13 percent in 2008, or $40.94 billion dollars (down slightly from 14 percent the previous year). And whereas human services organizations significantly outnumber other charities, they receive only 9 percent of all gifts ($25.88 billion in 2008).

This is only a snapshot of the larger subsectors. Being informed of the data available from *Giving USA* and other sources *can* empower your work. Although organizations within a subsector may experience changes based on their own unique circumstances, national data are always useful as benchmarks. Furthermore, national averages by subsector can help fundraisers engage in meaningful conversations with staff and board members about key trends as well as greatly assist in tracking and comparing the organization's rates of fundraising growth against the particular subsector as a whole.

Fundraising and the Economic Climate

A chapter about the contemporary dynamics of philanthropy would be remiss if it did not address the financial climate and its effect on charitable giving. It is no secret that many nonprofit organizations have found fundraising a challenge since the worldwide economic recession began in 2008. This is obviously reflected in the reported 2-percent decline (5.7 percent adjusted for inflation) in giving between 2007 and 2008. This is the first decline in giving since 1987 (then due to a tax law change) and the only decline attributed to the economy. Through an analysis of giving over forty years, it is clear that changes in giving are closely tied to economic changes, especially in household wealth, household income, and, for foundations, stock market performance. When adjusting for inflation, giving usually increases in nonrecessionary years (over the last forty years, giving has grown an average of 4.3 percent per year in nonrecessionary years) and slightly contracts in recession years.

The Philanthropic Giving Index (The Center on Philanthropy, 2009d), similar to a consumer confidence index for charitable giving, reflects the decline in charitable giving over the previous year. In December 2009, fundraisers reported an extremely difficult environment for fundraising as donors continue to be wary of the economy. Fundraisers from human services organizations were generally less optimistic about the current giving climate than fundraisers from other subsectors. However, there was a hint of optimism in the fact that the index increased almost 10 percent over the calendar year 2009, suggesting that negative attitudes were lessening.

As of this writing, the economic climate is both a glass-half-empty and glass-half-full scenario. On the empty side, giving has declined dramatically, often meaning a 10-percent swing from budgeted or expected revenue to actual (on average). But viewing the glass as half-full, giving fell *only* 6 percent during the worst recession since the Great Depression and at a time the nation was fighting two protracted wars and undergoing a period of significant political change and the uncertainty that accompanies that—regardless of the parties or people in power. Organizations adopting the glass-half-full attitude have generally been successful in emphasizing their proactive response to the economic climate in ways that donors indicate are most important to them. These include better stewardship and more frequent communication about the needs they are meeting, as well as making choices that result in greater organizational efficiency and impact. At the same time, successful fundraisers know to be sympathetic when talking to potential donors and acknowledging the situation the donors may be in. For example, some telephone fundraising programs that have adjusted their message to acknowledge the economic climate have generated a better response rate.

When faced with an uncertain economy, now or in the future, the importance of staying true to the best practices outlined in this book cannot be overstressed. Fundraisers must remain faithful to the organization's mission, be creative, and keep engaging board members and asking for their help. And, most of all, fundraisers must remain positive. Fundraising is an inherently optimistic profession that serves society well, especially in times of distress.

Opportunities for Philanthropy

Clearly, an economic crisis requires creative responses by fundraisers. Other opportunities exist as well. Among the most promising is the use of electronic media outlets to fundraise, attract volunteers, and build community around an organization's mission. Both e-fundraising and social media are given ample consideration in this volume. According to social media expert Chris Brogan (2010, p. 44), "Creativity, creation, communities of interest and culture itself are at the heart of what social media is equipped to enable." This is especially important for nonprofit organizations, which may be able to reach a much broader audience for a fraction of what it once cost. Just as making connections between people is an important part of a fundraiser's job, so too are quality connections at the heart of effective social media. A willingness to experiment with different tools of electronic communication can open up new pathways to build relationships with donors, volunteers, and clients.

Another opportunity in philanthropy is recognizing the importance of small organizations and small donations. Although the research on donor behavior most often focuses on high-net-worth individuals, analysis of long-term giving patterns indicates that two-thirds of Americans donate something in any given year. This is a greater portion of the population than those who vote, making giving and volunteering more democratic than even the political process. On the other hand, the top 3 percent of income earners account for approximately one-half of all contributions by household and even more when including giving through family foundations and bequests. Although the small number of high-net-worth donors are often the focus of fundraisers' work because of their ability to provide transformative gifts, annual donors, even if their gifts are "small," should never be overlooked. The two simply require different strategies. Fundraisers need to be careful not to devalue the generosity and potential of donors who make smaller gifts and the contributions made by small nonprofit organizations. In communities large and small, "small" gifts from many donors literally keep a community and its people going, providing services that are often invisible but essential. Small gifts give people a voice and foster pluralism (Tempel, 2008). There are many opportunities for fundraisers to reach out and make connections among donors of all levels.

Conclusion

In the coming years, fundraisers will have to deal with a number of economic challenges to increase philanthropic support. Creative partnerships, engaging new types of volunteers, and attracting a new generation of donors will be necessary for organizations to continue their significant role in a larger, more effective nonprofit sector. Philanthropy takes on society's most intractable problems, including homelessness, abuse, and hunger. It gives voice to the voiceless, advocates for justice, and offers care, hope, and help. Nonprofit organizations often provide what government and business cannot or will not to solve the toughest problems and champion the public good. No matter the challenges the sector faces, philanthropy will always fundamentally be about hope, fresh starts, and new beginnings. As the institutional guardians of philanthropy, it is up to fundraisers to bear this in mind as they fulfill their role in building the nonprofit sector.

CHAPTER ELEVEN

PROSPECT RESEARCH

By Vicky Martin

Prospect research gives an organization the ability to approach the fundraising process in a strategic and efficient manner. This is accomplished through a system of information gathering and analysis focused on identifying viable prospective donors, then disseminating and tracking the information in a manner that follows a prospective donor through the complete fundraising cycle. The strategic approach provided by prospect research is particularly important in difficult economic times when the competition for private dollars is more intense than ever.

For more than twenty years, the field of prospect research has experienced tremendous growth in the number of individuals entering the field and in the scope of the field itself. The one thing that has remained constant, however, is the basic fundamentals of prospect research: the LAI principle (linkage, ability, interest). These fundamentals are the basis on which quality, comprehensive research is performed.

Linkage is one of the easiest, yet highly critical, principles to identify. Linkage is the direct connection of an individual to an organization, whether as a board member, volunteer, donor, or other stakeholder role. *Ability* refers to an individual's capability to make gifts at a designated level. Interestingly, it is also the least reliable qualifier. Studies have shown that individuals with lower giving capacity tend to give more based on percentage of income. *Interest* is arguably one of the most important indicators of a prospect's likelihood to give. The level of a prospect's involvement with the organization, as well as the prospect's belief in the mission and vision, correlates directly with the likely level and frequency of giving.

Prospect research professionals can provide thoroughly vetted prospective donor lists using the LAI principle as the foundation of the fundraising effort. The value of background preparation in terms of time saved and quality information is measureless for fundraising staff working directly with donors. Prospect research professionals recognize and use the appropriate reference materials for any given project and not only identify and qualify viable prospects but also know how to determine who is *not* a likely prospect and remove those individuals from working lists.

Conducting Prospect Research

Ideally, prospect research follows the pattern of the fundraising cycle, in which prospective donors are first identified and qualified. After this, the fundraiser develops individual engagement strategies for each donor, which is then followed by cultivation and solicitation. The cycle continues past the point of solicitation with gift acknowledgment, stewardship of the donor's gift, and ultimately renewal of the donor's commitment to the organization, whereupon the fundraising cycle begins again (The Fund Raising School, 2009a). Although prospect research clearly plays a strong role in the first three steps of the cycle (identification, qualification, and the development of individual donor engagement strategies), prospect research may on occasion be called on at other points in the cycle as well.

Prospect Identification

The work of prospect research is to identify those individuals who have the closest connection to the organization, the ability to make a gift at a defined level, and the inclination to offer financial support. The best way to begin prospect identification is to analyze key segments of the organization's pool of current donors.

Major Gift Donors. Close relationships should already be established with major gift donors, allowing fundraisers to know when the donor is ready for the next step along the fundraising cycle. Research can provide additional information on any changes that may have taken place with the donor that will help fundraisers working directly with donors and know when the time is right to begin cultivating for the next gift. Indicators may include increased annual giving, an empty nest situation and/or children who have graduated from college, a job promotion, sale of a business, or retirement.

Before undertaking the process of major gift prospect identification, the organization should be clear on the definition of a major gift. The minimum level for a major gift varies widely among nonprofit organizations. Prospect research must have an understanding about the level of prospective donor the organization hopes to identify. A prospective donor capable of making a $10,000 gift looks very different from one who qualifies at the $100,000-plus level.

Annual Donors. Analyzing the top annual donors of an organization is an excellent way to determine who may be ready for cultivation beyond their current gifts. Reviewing contact reports on these individuals should provide valid information as well. Ongoing communication with fundraisers working directly with donors, in concert with the prospect research analysis, will aid in the development of a solid major gift prospective donor list.

Board of Directors. A potential major gift prospect pool lies in the organization's board of directors. It may be surprising to learn that many who serve at a high level in a nonprofit organization have yet to make their own leadership gift. The financial involvement of an organization's board members sets the tone for the community-at-large and should be a priority for their involvement. Board members also offer a level of influence among their own social and business networks that can be very helpful in achieving the fundraising goals of the organization.

Prospect Qualification

Qualification involves determining which donors have not only the linkage to and interest in the organization that is necessary for making a significant gift but also have the ability to make such a gift.

Peer Screening. Peer screening is an important tool for qualifying prospective donors, and using the board and other high-level volunteers as peer screeners is a good way to involve them in the fundraising cycle. Asking these individuals to review lists of potential prospective donors and then share, in a confidential manner, what they know about certain individuals' giving habits, interests, and ability to give is a valuable and inexpensive way to identify potential prospective donors, as well as to productively engage these volunteers. They may also be able to open the door and provide an introduction if there has not been a close relationship to the organization in the past. Asking potential donors to engage in peer screening is also a very good way to begin engagement and involvement.

Exhibit 11.1 provides a sample peer review form. The form's appearance can vary, but this gives a good idea of the type of information a volunteer could

EXHIBIT 11.1. PEER SCREENING FORM.

Prospect Identification, Evaluation, and Validation		
Campaign or program:		
Evaluator:		
Date:		
Location:		
Prospect names	**Gift capability/ probability**	**Comments**

Source: The Fund Raising School, 2009b, p. VI-23.

be asked to share. Additionally, be sure to leave room for the volunteer to add additional names that may not have been included in a screening list.

Database Screening

There may come a time when prospect research alone cannot provide the number of prospective donors needed for organizational projects, most notably when entering a campaign. During such times, many prospective donors at differing levels of giving ability need to be identified as quickly and as accurately as possible. In these situations, it may be necessary to investigate the merits of a formal database screening (also known as electronic screening).

Database screenings are provided by a myriad of companies focused on fundraising and prospect development. Their staff typically have had experience as fundraisers in working with donors and have a clear understanding of the role of prospect research in an organization's fundraising efforts, regardless of the organization's size and scope. If an organization is considering hiring a firm to conduct database screening, it is beneficial to invite several vendors to provide a free sample screening, then present the findings to those within the organization who will have a vested interest in the results, as well as the decision makers who will ultimately determine whether the investment is merited.

It is important to understand that a database screening can be costly, depending on the number of records submitted, but the value of a mass screening for capable prospects can make it a very worthwhile exercise. Among other things, it forces the organization to consider carefully what makes best strategic sense: whether to screen the entire database, focus on only certain donor segments, or look for only certain donor characteristics. A database screening will incur not only some level of financial investment but also an investment in staff resources. The research department needs to be fully prepared to focus on the results of a screening in order to get the names of the viable prospective donors identified out to fundraisers in the field as quickly as possible. The minute data are delivered, they begin to age and get stale. Quick use of the information will net a higher return on the investment.

Data Mining

In times of economic downturn, a cash investment in a database screening may not be possible. An alternative to a formal database screening is to conduct a data mining effort. If an organization is fortunate enough to have its own market research staff, they may have the skill set to pull from the database those individuals with the predetermined markers of a potential prospect at various levels of ability. Researchers can also determine which indicators in the database to use in identifying prospective donors, run the reports, and analyze the results *en masse*.

The underlying principle in data mining is to find individuals in the database who share similar patterns (for example, giving frequency, volunteer activities, memberships), then analyze the results to determine which of those individuals may be prospective donors at various giving levels. Results can easily be housed in a spreadsheet format, making data manipulation and sorting easier to manage.

Developing Prospective Donor Profiles

The actual act of developing a profile should not be a cumbersome task. There are a seemingly infinite number of resources a researcher can turn to when developing a profile. Seasoned researchers, though, seem primarily to hone in on those resources that net the most quality information on a routine basis. *Best Practices in Prospect Research*, a report published by WealthEngine in October 2009, surveys the fee-based and free resources most frequently used by researchers across the country. According to this survey, the top five most-mentioned fee-based resources were WealthEngine, LexisNexis, iWave, Alumni Finder, and Hoovers. The top five most-mentioned free resources were Google, Zillow, newspapers, GuideStar, and magazines.

It is important to remember that no single resource will net the needed information on every prospective donor. Although the Internet and fee-based resources have increased efficiency for the researcher, not all pertinent information is found there. Prospect researchers should remember to use the resources available at public and university libraries, as well as the expertise of librarians. Although librarians are not directly skilled in prospect research, they are formally trained information professionals, and their special expertise can be of great value. Additionally, the community of prospect research professionals provides its take on informative and useful information sources, and many share this information on their research websites. Links to many of these sites can be found at the website of the Association of Prospect Researchers for Advancement (www.aprahome.org).

Recording Prospective Donor Profiles

Research profiles differ widely, based on an organization's needs. A profile is not a biography but a concise document that highlights the donor's linkage, ability, and interest. There are basic pieces of information that should be found in all profiles regardless of style.

Verified contact information. It is very easy to rely unquestioningly on the information found in the database and not take the time to verify that there have been no changes in the prospective donor's contact information. If contact information turns out to be incorrect, a fundraiser will become frustrated and perhaps come to the conclusion that research is unreliable. Verifying contact information should be the first thing a researcher does when preparing materials for the profile.

Linkage. Any and all ties to the organization should be determined and documented in the profile. This includes not only the obvious ties (donor, graduate, board member, and so on) but also any close relationships to individuals tied to the organization.

Background. Current business information and career highlights; a brief, relevant family history; and civic activities (nonprofit board memberships, corporate board memberships, educational background, and the like) are examples of some of the background information on the donor that the researcher will want to collect and record.

Giving history. All gifts to your organization as well as other philanthropic giving should be included in the profile. Where an individual puts his or her money is a prime indicator of where the person's interests lie. This exercise should offer some insight and allow a researcher to offer more accurate suggestions about the direction to take with a prospective donor.

Wealth indicators. Researching an individual's wealth as it relates to his or her philanthropic potential should be approached with a sense of reality regarding what can be found publicly, what could be perceived to be intrusive, and the limitations of research. Unless a prospect actually divulges some of his or her private financial information, public information is all that is available. This may consist of real estate holdings and market values; family foundations; some public stock holdings and options; compensation, if the prospect is a top officer of a public company; and in some instances, the percentage of ownership in a private business. Divorce settlements and inheritance could be found by searching court records, but the researcher should be aware that a prospective donor may perceive that as intrusive. It is important to be clear with fundraising staff that research can provide only indicators of a prospective donor's wealth rather than precisely pinpointing an individual's net worth, as is often requested.

Gift capacity. There are various schools of thought with regard to determining an appropriate solicitation amount. A skilled researcher will take into account not only an individual's known assets but also their inclination, based on interest and giving history, to give to the organization. Some organizations develop guidelines that use known assets and prior giving to determine a prospective donor's level of philanthropic potential. It is important to consider that this identified potential relates to total philanthropy, and any one organization is only a part of prospective donor's gift intentions. However, such guidelines can be useful as a quick determinant of gift potential and can be shared with volunteers who participate in peer screenings as well as used by research staff when a quick estimate is desired. Table 11.1 shows a set of sample guidelines. These sample guidelines can easily be adapted to any organization's giving levels.

Guidelines for determining gift capacity are easy to find through a simple Google search. The key is to find a formula that works best for a particular institution. This is done through trial and error. A researcher should work with various guidelines and test the results with fundraisers in the field to determine the method that is most comfortable and accurate for the organization.

Once gift capacity is determined, a rating code should be assigned. (See Table 11.2 for a sample rating scale chart.) Ideally, this rating will be entered

TABLE 11.1. INCOME/ASSET/GIFT RANGE GUIDELINES.

Income Level	Assets Accumulated	Suggested Gift Potential (to be given over five years or through a planned giving vehicle)	Rating
$5,000,000 or more	$200,000,000 or more	$10,000,000	$10M
$2,000,000 to $5,000,000	$100,000,000 to $200,000,000	$5,000,000	$5M
$2,000,000	$50,000,000 to $100,000,000	$2,000,000	$2M
$1,000,000 to $2,000,000	$20,000,000 to $50,000,000	$1,000,000 to $2,000,000	$1M
$500,000 to $1,000,000	$10,000,000 to $20,000,000	$500,000 to $1,000,000	$500K
$100,000 to $500,000	$1,000,000 to $10,000,000	$250,000 to $500,000	$250K
Less than $100,000	$1,000,000 to $10,000,000	$100,000 to $250,000	$100K
$100,000 to $250,000	Less than $1,000,000	$50,000 to $100,000	$50K
$50,000 to $100,000	$500,000 to $1,000,000	$25,000 to $50,000	$25K

into the organization's database so prospects rated at various levels can easily be pulled. The rating should reflect the prospective donor's total capacity for giving (for example, the dollar amount the prospect is capable of giving to the organization outright over a five-year period, or through a planned gift vehicle such as a trust or bequest). Again, the rating scale can be adjusted to match the organization's prospect pool and their giving capacity.

The ratings assigned by peer screeners should also be entered in the database. The more ratings assigned from various resources, the easier it is to make a realistic determination of a prospective donor's true potential via an average of all ratings. It is important to include a disclaimer in your prospective donor profile, indicating that the rating assigned for giving capacity indicates total capacity, as your institution is likely only a part of a donor's overall philanthropic interests.

TABLE 11.2. SAMPLE RATING SCALE FOR MAJOR GIFT PROSPECTS.

Rating	Potential Gift Amount
10	$10 million +
9	$5 million to $9.99 million
8	$2 million to $4.99 million
7	$1 million to $1.99 million
6	$500,000 to $999,999
5	$250,000 to $499,999
4	$100,000 to $249,999
3	$50,000 to $99,999
2	$25,000 to $49,999
1	Less than $25,000

Prospective Donor Profiles

Prospective donor information should be recorded in a research profile. A good example of what a research profile may look like is provided by The Fund Raising School in Exhibit 11.2. Although not all research profiles look the same, they generally include such information as the prospective donor's full name, contact information (home, business, and electronic), linkage to the organization, educational background, career-related information (including employers and positions held as well as past and current business ventures), board memberships (corporate and nonprofit), community affiliations, relation to family or private foundations, and biographical information and family history (including marital status, information about family members that may be relevant, personal interests and hobbies, and so on).

Another section of the research profile that is vital to fill in is all that is known about the prospective donor's philanthropy, including gifts to the organization and the circumstances under which they were made, gifts to other organizations, and any known political donations.

Last, it is important to record any wealth indicators that are known, including real estate holdings (including the primary residence), stock holdings and options, other tangible assets of note (art collections, boats, and so on), and history of compensation (if known).

EXHIBIT 11.2. DONOR RESEARCH PROFILE.

Prospect Profile Form

Date prepared: Date revised:

Source(s):

Cards: donor _____   prospect _____

Trustee	Donor	Friend	Mailing list	# of solicitations

Last name First/middle names Residence address/phone Business address/phone Position/title	Educational background Social/business activities Spouse name (maiden, if applicable) Marriage date
Directorship/business affiliations (shares held) Foundation affiliations Community/philanthropic/social affiliations Professional memberships	Family history (children/parents/interests/ achievements/other information)
Special interests Awards/honors/and so on Close friends/relevant personal relationships	Political affiliation Religious affiliation Military service
	Attorney Bank Trust officer Tax advisor

Source: The Fund Raising School, 2009b, p. VI-21.

Prospective Donor Management

The primary objective of a prospective donor management program is to facilitate communication between all parties involved in the relationship with a prospective donor and track the activity leading ultimately to a gift. Ideally, routine prospective donor review meetings are held in which there are conversations about fundraising activities; these activities should involve fundraisers working directly with donors, pertinent research staff and/or prospect management staff, and fundraising leadership. These discussions should include information about completed solicitations, progress in building the relationship with a prospective donor, review of portfolio, and activity with newly identified prospective donors. Regardless of the size of an organization, a prospective donor management program will provide for a necessary flow of communication, goal setting based on portfolio activity, accountability, and tools for management, all leading to strategic and focused fundraising leading to increased results.

This work is necessary not only to achieve the best fundraising results for the organization but, more important, to build the best possible relationship with the prospective donor. A strong prospective donor management process is based on the premise that it is important that care and attention be paid to the relationship with the prospective donor throughout the span of that individual's involvement with the organization. This means the engagement strategy for each prospective donor must be monitored and significant interactions with the donor that move the relationship forward documented so they become part of the organization's memory. This also allows for the fundraiser and the organization to establish and maintain efficiency and accountability in relationships with prospective donors. The resources used to provide quality prospect research (which include staff time and financial investment in resources) require that a system be in place to track the effectiveness of work done by research, to determine that fundraisers working with donors are using the research provided by pursuing face-to-face visits and further qualifying the prospective donors, to ensure that the proper interactions are taking place with prospective donors in the pool so that relationships are consistently enhanced, and to determine if additional resources are necessary, either in staff or resources. An effective prospective donor management program will ensure that prospective donors proceed through the fundraising cycle in a timely and effective manner; to do this, programs typically track and report such things as dollars raised, proposals submitted, the number of prospects in each stage of cultivation, and the number of significant contacts the organization has with a prospective donor (defined as an interaction that moves the relationship with the prospective donor forward).

Ethics in Prospect Research

It is critical that prospect research, as well as fundraising as a whole, protects the integrity of organizations by closely following a code of ethics. This code of ethics may differ from organization to organization, but the underlying principles for all remain fairly consistent. Two key documents related to ethics with which the prospect researcher should be familiar are *A Donor Bill of Rights*, developed by the Association of Fundraising Professionals (AFP), and the *APRA Ethics Statement* developed by the Association of Prospect Researchers for Advancement (APRA).

Some of the key points of *A Donor Bill of Rights* assert the right of donors to be fully informed about the organization's mission and the intended use of donations, and to be confident that the board and staff of the organization are capable of carrying out the intended work. It also upholds the need for organizational accountability and transparency. In relation to the care due to the donor, *A Donor Bill of Rights* emphasizes the right of the donor to receive appropriate thanks and to be assured that donations and confidential information are handled with all due care and respect by the organization.

The *APRA Ethics Statement* outlines the standards to which professional prospect researchers hold themselves and their work accountable. In addition to protecting both the confidential information of the individual and the institution and to abiding by all laws and institutional policies, prospect researchers are also charged with abiding by fundamental ethical principles. These fundamental principles of the *APRA Ethics Statement* include a commitment to confidentiality, accuracy, and relevance of information gathered on prospective donors; a responsibility to lead by example in creating and following policies that support ethical prospect research; honesty and truthfulness regarding their role as prospect researchers and the role of prospect research at the organization; and avoidance of conflicts of interest.

One practical application of the principles included in both *A Donor Bill of Rights* and the *APRA Ethics Statement* is that there must be a method in place for protecting donor data in the organization as well as in the research department. Sensitive information should be protected not only by the use of a secured database but also through other controls on data, such as making sure that sensitive information is not sent via e-mail, restricting access to information only to those who have a need to know it, educating staff and volunteers about the importance of confidentiality, and putting in place clear policies for maintaining sensitive information as well as consequences if those policies are violated.

Conclusion

Prospect research is a key activity of successful fundraising programs. It is also one of the most sensitive, as donor information is entrusted to the care of the organization. By understanding that prospect research plays an important role in building donor engagement and relationships, those in the research role play a vital stewardship role for the donor in making sure that the donor's confidential information is treated with the utmost respect and security. It is this accountability and care that undergirds all effective, ethical, and professional prospect research.

CHAPTER TWELVE

CORPORATE GIVING AND FUNDRAISING

By Dwight F. Burlingame

Business engagement with philanthropy has been part of capitalism for a very long time. The overarching philosophical reason why companies have supported nonprofit organizations has been to increase the environment for successful business to take place. The commonly noted argument that "the healthier the community, the more business one will be able to conduct" is globally espoused. In most countries the ability to start a company or corporation is given by the state; therefore the company has an ultimate responsibility to provide for the social and economic well-being of citizens as it conducts its business. Primary responsibility is first to employees and other stakeholders and second to the general public, whether through philanthropic gifts, taxes, or other partnerships.

During the first decade of the twenty-first century, companies and nonprofits continued to address several major social and economic issues as they sought to articulate their relationships. High on the list of causes were basic human needs (including health and education), community impact causes, environmental sustainability, and more sensitivity to demands of shareholders and consumers. Especially because of the economic recession that began toward the end of the decade, companies became more focused on making their giving collaborative, strategic, and productive. Asking how the relationship benefits each party will continue to dominate the corporate-nonprofit relationship, whether the nonprofit or the business is small or large. In the current environment, the wisdom echoed by Hank Rosso years ago is especially relevant today: "In accepting the gift, it is incumbent upon the organization to return a value to the donor in a form other than material" (Rosso, 1991, p. 6).

In the past twenty-five years, cause-related marketing, sponsorships, and various other partnerships between business and nonprofits have been the fastest-growing area of corporate financing of nonprofits. This growth represents a major swing of the pendulum in how corporations seek to engage with and articulate their relationship with the philanthropic sector. As many have noted, since the 1980s there has been a significant movement in corporate giving from philanthropy to defined and more integrated relationships (Austin, 2000; Andreasen, 2009). The most famous cause-related marketing program that started this trend was the restoration of the Statue of Liberty in 1983. American Express partnered with the restoration committee and donated a tenth of one cent for each transaction on its credit card for a three-month period. The program resulted in a $1.7 million "donation" to the Statue of Liberty fund and a reported 28-percent increase in the use of American Express credit cards over the previous year. This is truly an example of doing well while doing good.

History

For all practical purposes, corporate support of charitable activities is a twentieth-century invention. In the nineteenth century most court rulings rendered corporate giving for charitable purposes not appropriate unless such giving was business-related. Laissez-faire arguments of the time—not unlike the argument put forth by Milton Friedman (1970)—held that company management could not give away stockholders' money, as it was the "social responsibility of business . . . to increase its profits." Many point to business support of the YMCA by the railroads in the early twentieth century to provide "safe" housing for workers as the beginning of corporate philanthropy—perhaps more appropriately termed strategic corporate giving or enlightened self-interest.

The majority of corporate support of nonprofit organizations over the last century could be characterized as self-interested rather than demonstrating interest for others or for the public good. This is an important realization for anyone doing fundraising for nonprofits, for it provides the context for building a successful corporate development program—one built on seeking gifts as well as other sources of revenue that benefit both parties.

The development of regular giving programs by companies began in 1936 with what Hayden Smith (1997) refers to as the modern era. It was in 1935 that the Internal Revenue Code was amended to allow for deductions by companies for charitable gifts supporting the promotion of business purposes. In 1936 the recorded figure of corporate giving on federal corporate income tax forms was around $30 million. By 2008 this figure had grown to an estimated $14.5 billion, excluding sponsorships and other forms of partnerships. According to *Giving USA* (The Center on Philanthropy, 2009b), most of the growth in corporate giving has taken place in the last thirty years and can be explained by the removal of certain historical legal obstacles and the growth of the size and number of companies. Most important of the legal cases was the 1953 case of *A. P. Smith Mfg. Co. v. Barlow*, in which the New Jersey Supreme Court refused to overturn the decision of corporate management in regard to a gift made to a charity that had no known benefit to the business. This case reflected the growing importance placed on the role of business in society—both economic and social. Nevertheless, many companies elect to distribute profits to shareholders through dividends and leave giving to owners, and about only a third of all companies claim philanthropic contributions on their federal corporate income tax returns. Smaller firms generally donate a larger share of their income to nonprofits.

Even with the growth in dollar amounts of corporate giving over the last thirty years, on average corporate profits have risen at a much faster rate than corporate giving. For example, from 1986 to 1996 corporate giving as a percentage of profits went from 2.3 to 1.3 percent. By 2008 corporate giving as a percentage of profits had declined even further to an estimated 0.9 percent (Center on Philanthropy 2009b). Corporate giving to nonprofits in 2008 accounted for around $14.50 billion. This is a drop of 4.5 percent, or 8.0 percent adjusted for inflation, from the 2007 estimated amount. Several forms of corporate support, such as sponsorships, are not included in the *Giving USA* figures. The various changes in what businesses give and to whom can be attributed to the changing philosophy, the CEO's role, the change of corporate culture, increased global competitiveness, the changes in the economic environment, and the way in which dollars move from companies to nonprofits.

Corporate Giving for Nonprofits

As noted earlier, in 2008 corporate giving was approximately 5 percent (or just over $14.5 billion) of total charitable giving in the United States (The Center on Philanthropy, 2009b) and represented around 0.9 percent of corporate pre-tax income—down from a high point of 2.3 percent in 1986. Corporate foundations gave approximately a third of the total. In 2007 and 2008, energy and technological companies were the most generous in donations, with the financial and manufacturing industries the worst as would be expected in the 2008–2009 recession. Further, several corporations are responding to the economic crisis by putting more focus on their giving that addresses (1) those who are the most in need and (2) giving that is more local. More than one-third of corporate philan-thropic giving is through in-kind donations—most often in the form of company product.

As might be expected, the most commonly sought gift from companies is cash for special and new projects or for capital campaigns and sponsorships. However, businesses today shy away from big-ticket item requests and prefer to focus on supporting activities that address community needs met in partnership with oth-ers, including government. Corporations are most interested in supporting causes that (1) form a link between the company and the nonprofit that will benefit the company economically and socially and (2) are relatively proactive and narrow in scope. Of course, many companies still do a considerable amount of reactive giving, spread around to many different organizations.

It is important for the fundraiser to recognize that one of the major ways that companies support nonprofits is by supporting workplace charitable campaigns. Being listed as an agency in such workplace campaigns can engender more oper-ating support as well as recognition for the nonprofit. Matching gifts for employee contributions are still present, but in the last few years these have been on the decline—especially in the dollar amount of the match. In-kind contributions of company product and employee time are still common in certain industry groups such as pharmaceuticals. Employee loan programs are available in many com-munities. Research and development support from corporations is limited to a few nonprofits, primarily in the health and education field.

A report by the Business Civic Leadership Center (2008) presented results of research on how companies invest in communities. The major motivations identi-fied by respondents in the study were desire to improve the "local competitive" environment for business, to improve the quality of life in the community, and finally to retain and recruit customers and employees.

As this report suggests, corporate engagement in the future with commu-nity nonprofits will be more about how they can create a more highly qualified workforce for their core operations, not corporate citizenship or giving activities. Thus it is no surprise that childhood education programs have taken on increas-ingly higher priority for company engagement with nonprofits, and using post-secondary education support to supply a competitive workforce remains a high priority.

For additional details on how companies engage in corporate giving by size, type of nonprofit supported, regional variation, industry variation, and what corporate departments have responsibility for community investments, the reader is referred to the Business Civic Leadership Center's 2008 Corporate Community Investment Study. In addition, a recent study by the Center on Philanthropy at Indiana University (2007a) reported on themes and practices of "exemplary" giving by major corporations. Some of these themes and practices are as follows:

- Increase linkages with nonprofits through employee/director giving and volunteering, grants and gifts-in-kind to local community needs, and customer-directed giving (cause-related marketing).
- Identify focus needs that match business goals with high social impact.
- Seek external long-term commitments for important societal needs.
- Build sustainable and more long-term partnerships with nonprofits that benefit both parties.
- Increase transparency in and among all stakeholders.
- Discontinue practices that aren't creating maximum benefit.
- Measure or at least try to measure the actual social impact of the company giving programs.

Fostering corporate relations is an ongoing process. Linkage, ability, and interest are important in any fundraising effort, as The Fund Raising School has advocated for decades. The approach to the company will be determined by the case for support and the number of prospective corporate donors. A personal approach is certainly the most often preferred method. The complexity of an issue tends to drive the approach, including the amount of fundraising resources an organization may have.

After a verbal exchange or meeting, completing a contact report is crucial. This document should indicate the essence of the contact and serve as a record of the information shared and commitments, if any, made for future action. Only the necessary information that would not be embarrassing if the potential donor were to read the contact report should be included.

Once a gift relationship is established, the fundraiser needs to create a plan for managing that relationship. The first component is the delivery of the quality of service or stewardship of the gift. The second component is considering what the future relationship will bring to the nonprofit. Both components of a relationship plan should be carefully integrated with an assessment of how outcomes are to be measured by both parties. In the long term, having a clear case and clarity in how it is assessed will render more beneficial and longer-term relationships.

Models of Corporate Giving

Much of the basis for this section is drawn from an earlier work by Dennis Young and this author (Burlingame and Young, 1996), in which we developed four major models of how companies approach their giving and volunteering to nonprofits. The use of these models gives fundraisers a context in which to approach businesses for support for their missions. These are the four models:

Corporate productivity or neoclassical model

Ethical or altruistic model

Political (external and internal) model

Stakeholder model

A summary of each with implications for fundraising follows.

Corporate Productivity Model

This model comes from the basic premise that corporate giving will help the company increase profits and return more value to shareholders. Corporate giving activities must therefore demonstrate in some way the increase in profits. This may be done directly by giving cash or company product or indirectly by improving company morale or worker productivity. The notion of enlightened self-interest is very consistent with the neoclassical model as long as the focus remains on the long-term profitability of the company. It further suggests that the term *corporate philanthropy* is a bit of an oxymoron and that a more accurate term is *corporate citizenship* or *strategic philanthropy* to convey the purpose of the engagement between the company and the nonprofit. The following types of giving are clearly in line with this model:

Projects that help market company products—like sponsorships, cause-related marketing, and other partnerships

Projects that improve employee morale and thus increase productivity

Projects that facilitate the improvement of the public image of the company

Projects that lower corporate costs, such as grants for research by nonprofits that lower the company's internal expenditures for product development.

The opportunity for the fundraiser is to match organizational mission and activities with the company's desire for improved productivity along these lines. Fundraisers will want to help corporate giving personnel to understand how gifts of support to the nonprofit's functions can contribute to the company's bottom line, whether directly or indirectly.

Ethical or Altruistic Model

The classical notion of corporate philanthropy is based on the premise that businesses and their leaders have a responsibility to be good corporate citizens and that corporate giving and volunteering is a way to demonstrate corporate social responsibility to society. It also assumes that corporations have discretionary resources. When a company is in difficult economic times, one would not expect giving to be based on this model. The giving program must have the capability to alert corporate leaders to community priorities and show where the company might be a partner in seeking solutions. The following three types of giving are consistent with this model:

> Projects that address community need where the company operates or has markets
>
> Projects that appeal to corporate leadership, individually or as citizens
>
> Projects that engage employees in community efforts to address local issues

Fundraisers must be keenly aware of how gifts to their organizations will benefit the community through the engagement of employees and corporate leaders.

Political Model

The political model is played out both externally and internally in many businesses. The external form is based on the idea that corporations use giving to build relationships that protect corporate power and influence the limits of governmental influence over companies. Under this model, the corporate giving program serves as a liaison to community allies. Projects that build closer bonds between the nonprofit and the company are consistent with this model. Typical efforts substitute for government initiative or more appropriately minimize government intervention, portraying the corporation as a good public citizen. Environmental or arts projects are good examples.

The internal paradigm is built on the premise that the corporate giving officer or representative is an agent within the larger corporate game, in which the corporate giving officer needs to build internal allies and prove the benefit of giving to various areas in the company. Corporate giving programs must therefore facilitate the building of alliances with human resources, marketing, research, public relations, and like units so they can see the value of nonprofit support to their area. Giving that is consistent with this model includes employee volunteerism, sponsorships, cause-related marketing, partnerships, and educational programs for employees as well as social service projects, and research and development interest most often designed for short-term return in today's corporate environment.

Fundraisers will want to be strategic in assessing how they engage with all units of the company, not just the corporate giving unit. Projects that are relevant and meet the needs of the nonprofit while meeting the needs of the company—both internal and external—become foremost. Building the case for support is crucial in maximizing this model.

Stakeholder Model

The stakeholder theory of corporate giving is based on the idea that the corporation is a complex entity that must respond to the needs and pressures of a variety of key stakeholders including shareholders, employees, suppliers, customers, community groups, and governmental officials. Under this framework, managing the company is best accomplished by managing the various stakeholder interests. Thus, to be effective, corporate giving activities must help to address stakeholder interests. The following types of giving are consistent with this model:

Employee benefit or volunteerism projects

Community education or environmental projects

Projects that help consumers of company products or services

It does not take a major leap of faith to apply the stakeholder theory to small business owners as well. Whether in a large or small business, management interacts with a variety of interested parties. Fundraisers will concentrate their efforts on identification of key stakeholder groups and develop project proposals that will articulate the nonprofit mission in a way that appeals to defined stakeholder interests of the company. A key overall strategy for the nonprofit is to demonstrate how it is a community stakeholder championed by the corporate giving program.

The models just described provide a theoretical framework for understanding corporate engagement efforts, and they can be used as a basis for doing more empirical research on the effectiveness of various approaches. Understanding how the company works can inform a more strategic corporate fundraising program for the nonprofit. Each model attempts to bring a more nuanced understanding of corporate giving. At the same time, one should recognize that all or some of the models may be operating within any one particular corporation at any particular time. Given global and economic conditions, political activities are more complex and the variety of stakeholders more diverse. This requires increased efforts to demonstrate how corporate giving affects the double bottom line (that is, both the social return and the financial return).

Other authors, such as Sargeant and Jay (2004), have articulated a more simplistic approach by drawing a distinction only between self-interested giving and philanthropic giving that does not directly benefit the company. The Committee Encouraging Corporate Philanthropy (CECP) lists three categories of why companies give:

- Charitable—where little or no business benefit is expected;
- Community Investment—gifts that . . . support the long term strategic goals of the business and meet a critical community need; and
- Commercial—where benefit to the corporation is the primary motivation. (CECP, 2008)

CECP also noted that among its members corporate giving is divided up into three broad categories as corporate community affairs (35 percent of overall giving), corporate foundation (37 percent of overall giving), and all other groups (28 percent of overall giving), which includes support from marketing, research, human resources, and regional offices.

Marketing, Sponsorships, and Partnerships

The dramatic growth in earned revenue as the major source for support of many nonprofits has meant that the way businesses engage in their philanthropic or social role has also changed. As noted at the beginning of this chapter, since 1982 there has been a major shift from corporate philanthropy to giving that is designed to build alliances and partnerships or downright commercial relationships. Partnerships with nonprofits can and should provide strategic payoffs for both parties. In addition to the financial benefits, more control of the funds, new marketing skills, and even new knowledge about products and services accrue to both parties.

It is worth noting that there is a fair amount of confusion about the terms used in what is broadly defined by Andreasen (2009) as *cross-sector alliances*, defined as "any formal relationship between a for-profit and a nonprofit organization to pursue a social objective in ways that will yield strategic or tactical benefits to both parties" (p. 157). Thus such alliances are designed to have the same goal of traditional corporate giving—a positive social as well as economic impact. Cause marketing has traditionally been defined as "a company's providing dollars to a nonprofit in direct proportion to the quantity of a product or service purchased by consumers during a particular period of time" (Burlingame, 2003, p. 185).

When that period of engagement is extended over a longer time frame it is often referred to as "cause branding."

Sponsorships, on the other hand, are not directly tied to customer purchasing behavior, but they do mean company investments of cash or in-kind products or services in return for access to an activity, event, or cause represented by the nonprofit. Such activity is not a "gift" in the true meaning of philanthropy, but a strategic investment by the company with an expected return.

Galaskiewicz and Colman (2006) provide a useful framework by dividing the objectives of company engagement into philanthropic, strategic, commercial and political—not that different from the models of corporate giving noted by Burlingame and Young earlier in this chapter. Another paradigm used to view the impact of the corporate-nonprofit alliance has been provided by Gourville and Rangan (2004). They divide benefits for both parties according to first-order and second-order benefits. First-order benefits for the nonprofit are the contribution of cash, volunteers, or in-kind services for the cause. Corporation first-order benefits are in the form of sales. Second-order benefits are expected benefits that will result for either side in the future. Sponsorship and cause marketing campaigns are illustrative examples.

Opportunities

Various studies have reported many advantages for corporations and nonprofits that engage in cross-sector activities. On the for-profit side, cause marketing or sponsorship may influence consumer behavior by increasing the perception of the firm as "good" or as a responsible corporate citizen. This may improve employee morale, and it may also build the pool of potential applicants to work with the company. Various socially conscious investors may be more likely to support the business. Cone Inc. (2000) found that good business practice acceptance rates that include cross-sector alliances have continued to increase, and that as many as eight out of ten Americans have a more positive image of companies that support nonprofits or causes that they care about.

According to IEG Sponsorship Report (2009) and others, managers of nonprofits and fundraisers report that companies seek the following second-order benefits from their sponsorship and cause marketing activities, in addition to increasing profits and direct commercial benefit:

- Category exclusivity
- Credit on related materials
- Program naming
- Tickets and hospitality for the nonprofit events
- Access to the nonprofit's database

On the nonprofit side, cross-sector activities may have several advantages, including the following:

- Increased revenue
- New volunteers
- Enhanced public awareness of the nonprofit's mission
- Connections to the company's network of employees and other contacts
- Diversified income streams
- Access to new audiences and potential donors
- Enhanced knowledge of marketing and other corporate experience

Many examples have been reported in the press. Illustrative examples of the diverse forms of cross-sector marketing collaborations can be found in Andreasen (2009). Good contemporary sources to be consulted by the fundraiser include *Corporate Philanthropy Report*, the Committee Encouraging Corporate Philanthropy (CECP), and the Boston College Center for Corporate Citizenship websites (including the annual publication *The Corporate Citizen*).

Challenges

Potential negative effects of cross-sector activities must be examined closely by nonprofit management. A foremost concern is how the collaboration with a for-profit may affect donor activity. Will the commercial nature of the activity decrease trust in the nonprofit mission? Will donors or potential donors think they have already contributed their fair share to the nonprofit through their participation in a cause-related marketing activity, with a consequent decrease in gift income? Will potential gifts from other companies in the same industry group decrease if one company enjoys an exclusive connection to the nonprofit brand? Will the nonprofit actually waste resources if the alliance activity fails?

Sponsorship and cause-marketing activities may cause only temporary effects and not build donor loyalty over time. Ties to the nonprofit may be based on a special event activity and not in the mission of the organization. Traditional fundraising may be neglected because of the focus on earned income activities. Further, concern with the ability of the nonprofit to adjust to the business culture and be an "equal" partner in a cross-sector alliance is an issue. This is especially true when a business partner is selected. Joint promotion activities may be viewed as the nonprofit's "selling out." The private-sector marketer may insist on more publicity for the relationship than the nonprofit would ordinarily grant. Licensing agreements call for expert attention, and legal fees are not insignificant.

Marketing relationships with nonprofits can also be problematic for the corporation. The mission of the nonprofit may not be of interest to the consumer, more complicated accounting procedures need to be followed, and the commitment of time and energy from company personnel may not create expected financial payoffs. Some consumers may even view company support of cross-sector activities as exploitation. This is especially true when more money is spent for an ad campaign than is actually donated to the cause.

Such concerns can inform the fundraiser of what to be aware of in building a partnership with a corporation. Developing a plan and procedures to prevent management error should be foremost in building a successful cross-sector venture that will benefit both parties. Sponsorship and cause branding guidelines should be approved by the nonprofit board of directors. Whether part of the development office or not, effective coordination and communication with the development staff is imperative. Senior management needs also to take an active role is shaping business partnerships and assessing the benefits.

Measuring the impact of marketing alliances is probably the most important action in the current state of the art. Studies in the field often fail to apply rigorous standards in measuring effects on either or both parties.

Conclusion

Business engagement with philanthropic organizations for public purposes has been multifaceted and has had various degrees of change—back and forth—over the last hundred-plus years. Once part of direct business activity, it turned toward more focused public purposes before returning to today's environment of being mainly business-driven. Fundraisers in today's environment will want to demonstrate how corporate support helps the overall revenue picture of the nonprofit, and company giving and marketing personnel will want to demonstrate how their engagement with nonprofits helps the business be a viable economic entity while also producing social good.

A 2009 State of Corporate Citizenship in the United States report showed that CEOs' support for corporate citizenship often remains strong during a recession, but there are some gaps between those beliefs and actual practices. "Reputation was cited by 70% (of respondents) as a driver for corporate citizenship, tied for the top spot with 'it fits our company traditions and values'" (Vesela, 2009, p. 2). Helping businesses and nonprofits meet societal needs—economic and social—makes for a challenging and rewarding vocation.

CHAPTER THIRTEEN

FOUNDATION FUNDRAISING

By Gwendolyn Perry Davis

A *foundation*, as defined in *The AFP Fundraising Dictionary* (2003), is "an organization created with designated funds from which the income is distributed as grants to not-for-profit organizations or, in some cases, to people" (1996–2003, p. 53). The relationship between a foundation and a nonprofit is built on mutual desire or interest directed at improving a civic or public good. Nonprofit organizations are the mechanisms through which most foundations carry out their public responsibilities.

Foundation assets (commonly referred to as endowments) and distributions from those assets continue to shape the public discussions around global issues. With a significant number of independent foundations passing the $10 billion level in endowments, according to reports compiled by the Foundation Center (2007), top-tier foundations have the capacity to disperse funds regionally, nationally, and globally in an attempt to radically change social outcomes and enhance communities. Foundations provide a significant amount of support for the nonprofit sector—second only to individual support—and 13 percent of the actual dollars of charitable giving (The Center on Philanthropy, 2009b).

As a funding source, foundations (or grantmakers) are often attractive to nonprofit organizations because of their transparency. Matching foundation interests with nonprofit missions is easily accomplished through the public space, and application and reporting processes are clearly defined. The grantmaker's expected outcomes are generally quantifiable. For nonprofits, grants have the potential to provide significant monetary support for a program or operations during start-up or expansion.

Proposal writing and grant seeking programs are functions of a comprehensive development operation. Combining a culture that encourages appropriate relationships with grantmakers and appropriate investments in a foundation relations program will help establish systematic and measurable goals for foundation resources.

Types of Foundations

Because of the complexity of their structures, it is important to understand the characteristics of four primary models of foundations: independent, corporate, community, and operating.

Independent Foundations

As defined by the Internal Revenue Service (IRS), independent foundations are private foundations established to provide support or distributions to tax-exempt organizations through grants. Assets of independent foundations are usually established through gifts from individuals or families and often carry the names of the original funders. Independent foundations are required by law to distribute a minimum of 5 percent of their endowment annually.

During the years of wealth creation in the late 1990s, the expression "family foundation" became common to describe an independent foundation with noteworthy involvement and decision making by living family members, both immediate and extended. Interest in forming family foundations has continued during the first decade of the new millennium, and one-third of family foundations tracked by the Foundation Center were established between 2000 and 2007. By 2007, family foundations provided nearly 45 percent of all foundation grants.

Large, well-established independent foundations generally have a full-time staff, often in proportion to the size of assets. Smaller foundations may have only one full-time person dedicated to daily operations. Family foundations may include family members as needed. Independent foundations often define specific areas of interest for funding or limit grants to a specific geographical area. Examples of large independent foundations include the Bill and Melinda Gates Foundation, the W. K. Kellogg Foundation, and Lilly Endowment Inc.

Corporate Foundations

The corporate foundation is another type of independent foundation. A corporate foundation generally receives its assets from an associated for-profit company or business and often serves as a grantmaking vehicle for the company. Its mission and funding interests will often mirror the business interests of the company. A corporate foundation may work in concert with any other corporate giving program and often has a separate board of directors, usually composed of employees and individuals related to the company.

Most corporate foundation giving reflects the associated company's products, services, and consumers' interests, both current and potential. Corporate foundation decisions are often directly influenced by employee involvement and interest in the nonprofit organizations seeking support. The management of corporate foundations differs from one to the next. Many corporate foundations have staff dedicated to receiving, processing, and administering proposals and grants. Others may combine foundation responsibilities with other employee duties. The Wal-Mart Foundation and the AT&T Communications Foundation are examples of corporate foundations.

Community Foundations

Community foundation growth has slowed from the rapid expansion during the 1990s, but the popularity of the vehicle has permanently altered the philanthropic landscape. The increase in community foundation assets can be attributed to several factors, including the corresponding rise in individual donors' asset values and the seeding and incubation of small donor-advised funds. The sharing of costs, reduction in administrative duties, enhanced return on well-managed investments, and ability to remain involved in grantmaking decisions all attract donors to advised funds at community foundations.

Unlike other foundation structures, community foundations generally both receive gifts and make grants through special IRS provisions. As public charities, they must receive assets from a large pool of donors and consequently fund a wide range of community needs. By definition, most community foundations limit their interests and grants to a particular geographical area and consider it a primary mission to support communitywide initiatives and develop unrestricted funds specifically for this purpose. Community foundations are exempt from the 5-percent minimum annual distribution requirement.

Community foundations generally have several fund pools: unrestricted funds, donor-advised funds, and donor-designated funds. With a donor-advised fund, a donor retains the right to make suggestions to the community foundation as to which qualified 501(c)(3) organizations or causes should receive grant money. A donor-designated fund allows the donor to select the specific nonprofit organizations or causes that will receive grants based on the fund's income. Both funds are established with a permanent gift to the community foundation and allow the donor an immediate tax deduction under IRS rules. The community foundation usually specifies that the gift be combined and managed with other foundation investments.

Examples of community foundations include the Cleveland Foundation, the first community foundation established in the United States; the New York Community Trust; the Columbus (Ohio) Community Foundation; and the Central Indiana Community Foundation. Although the largest number of community foundations are in the state of Indiana, Michigan, and Ohio, community foundations are present throughout the United States.

Operating Foundations

Operating foundations seldom make grants to other nonprofit organizations. Because they are dedicated to conducting research and promoting programs to support the work of the original charter or governing body, the IRS mandates that they spend at least 85 percent of their income in support of their own programs. Although operating foundations are not usually a source of cash grants, they are often a resource for nonprofits engaged in complementary research, work, and programs. In addition, operating foundations often serve as conveners in a particular body of knowledge and may provide opportunities for engagement with community practitioners and experts. Examples of operating foundations are the Getty Trust and the Wilder Foundation.

Growth of Foundations in the United States

In addition to the numbers of foundations and totality of the grants awarded, the growth of independent and community foundation assets between 1995 and 1999 eclipsed any previous period of recorded growth. Many factors are believed to support the increase: a period of impressive gains in the U.S. stock markets, increased gifts to all foundation types, and the rise of mega foundations in the western portion of the United States. However, recent economic conditions have created a challenging environment for those nonprofits seeking philanthropic support from foundations. As the Foundation Center (2009) reported, foundation giving was predicted to decrease in 2009 by a percentage in the high single digits to low double digits; about two-thirds of foundations anticipated making fewer grants and/or grants in lower amounts.

Traditionally, large foundations have been located in the East and Midwest, largely as a result of the individual fortunes that established them during the Industrial Age. The gains in information technology, based largely in the West, helped fuel this geographical shift. Since 1990, nationwide, more than 33 percent of all large foundations have been established, tripling the rate of growth existing in the 1950s, when foundations experienced an 11-percent increase in number, according to the Foundation Center (2001). The average age of donors also decreased during the same period as many younger foundation donors sought to take advantage of tax incentives and establish a history of giving for their young families.

Program growth in corporate foundation grants continues to be modest, in part because of more conservative transfers in cash and assets to foundation programs.

Trends in Foundation Support

Foundations are more clearly defining their interests and expectations of grantee organizations. They are also requiring more extensive evaluation of funded programs and organizations. Foundations continue to learn from past grants and use this information to make better and more effective grants for the future. Collaboration among foundations is a key trend in combating global problems and is an expected result of their grants to nonprofits. Foundations are also emphasizing effective governance and management of organizations in making grant decisions of any type.

In conjunction with the growth of foundation assets, professional staffing has increased. Joslyn (2001) indicated that full- and part-time foundation staff had grown to more than seventeen thousand by the turn of the twenty-first century. Several trends have emerged as new directions for foundation support.

Evaluation

An emphasis on evaluation of grantees and foundation activities continues. The literature on nonprofits indicates that early attempts at evaluation by foundations served two purposes: checking for accountability to grantor financial policies and expediting grantee renewal decisions. Foundations continue to evaluate grants using these criteria, but the scope of evaluation has grown to help foundations analyze the success of a programmatic field of interest and help shape future grants. In many foundations, these learning opportunities affect future grant recipients by focusing on particular segments of a program and providing helpful advice about past successes and disappointments. For foundation grant recipients, more extensive post-grant evaluation, often by external evaluators, may be required at the conclusion of a program. An objective review of the progress of a particular grant and program is intended to help organizations focus on program results and impacts.

Collaboration

Collaboration is a mutually beneficial and well-defined relationship entered into by two or more organizations to achieve common goals. This relationship includes a commitment to a definition of authority within the mutual relationship, accountability for success, and a sharing of resources and rewards. In an attempt to avoid replication of services and funding of programs, foundations and their grantees are participating in more collaborative efforts than ever before. Foundations are also interested in seeing stronger and more inclusive programs based on the expertise and client bases of cooperative organizations. For the grantee organizations, the potential for more substantial financial support and the power of a larger group working on an identified need can have a substantial impact on a community problem.

Professionalization of Grant Application and Distribution Processes

More foundations are carefully defining their policies and procedures about distribution of funds. In an effort to fund appropriate projects and reduce the time nonprofits spend preparing proposals outside foundations' interests, most foundations clearly define interest areas, application procedures, distribution plans, and timelines. In addition, foundations now seek evidence that a nonprofit operates with effective board governance and competent staff management, a long-term fiscal and program plan, and a mission related to social needs that concern the foundation.

Charitable Gift Funds at Financial Service Firms

During the late 1990s, the charitable gift funds at for-profit financial services firms experienced an incremental rise in managed assets. The *Chronicle of Philanthropy* reported that by 2000, the assets of the top three funds had surpassed the assets of the top eleven public charities (Larose, 2002, p. 11). The premise of these gift funds, such as the Fidelity Charitable Gift Fund and the Vanguard Charitable Endowment Program, is to allow donors to make irrevocable gifts to the fund and recommendations on the future distribution of those funds. For the donor, the advantages are an immediate tax reduction, the opportunity for the corpus of the fund to increase in value with the help of professional money managers, and the ability to remain anonymous with potential grantees. In the nonprofit community, concern is expressed over the fee structure of the funds and the control given to financial services professionals rather than community and nonprofit experts. Nevertheless, according to the *Boston Globe*, in October 2009, for example, the assets of the Fidelity Charitable Gift Fund had $4.1 billion in assets ("For the Record," 2009).

Emphasis on Diversity in Board Governance

According to the U.S. Census Bureau, by the year 2025 it is expected that only half of the nation's population will be non-Hispanic white. Foundations expect this diversity to be mirrored in the leadership of nonprofit institutions in the United States.

Increasingly, foundations are requesting that nonprofit boards of directors reflect the diversity of the communities and populations they serve. Some foundations require that nonprofits actively recruit in a way that encourages diversity, and some ask for evidence of diversity in board composition. Simultaneously, the boards of community and private foundations are maturing and changing with the population shift.

Capacity Building

Campobasso and Davis, in *Reflections on Capacity-Building* (2001), define *capacity building* as the development of an organization's core skills and capabilities—such as leadership, management, finance and fundraising, programs, and evaluation—in order to build the organization's effectiveness and sustainability. It is the process of assisting a group to identify and address issues and gain the insights, knowledge, and experience needed to solve problems and implement change. Capacity building is facilitated through the provision of technical support activities, including coaching, training, operational assistance, and resource networking. As with any idea, capacity building is still broadly defined and working through an evolution of approach and application. Many foundation programs have begun to develop a focus on building internal and external resources to support nonprofit programs. Programs like the Organizational Impact Program at the David and Lucile Packard Foundation have devoted important resources to define and develop capacity building as an interest area.

Types of Support

Foundations commonly provide five types of support: operations or unrestricted, program, capital, pilot, and challenge or matching. Operations or unrestricted grants are made to support the ongoing operations of a nonprofit with no conditions for their use. Program grants support a specific set of activities and plans. Capital grants generally provide support for building construction funds, large equipment purchases, and endowment growth. Pilot grants award start-up funding for new programs at an organization for a limited period of time. Challenge or matching grants support an effort to encourage philanthropic giving in a constituent segment.

As a potential funding source, foundations have several unique features, including a requirement for independent foundations to distribute a minimum percentage of their endowment through grants to qualified 501(c)(3) organizations. There are a number of excellent resources on the current scope and size of the foundation sector. The Foundation Center, publisher of the *Foundation Directory*, and its website (www.foundationcenter.org), provide resources and publications on a range of topics from starting a foundation to measuring and evaluating programs supported by foundation grants.

Before Approaching a Foundation

Foundations are interested in funding nonprofits with diverse financial sources. It is important to consider a foundation grant as one part of a fully diversified development plan. Support from clients, friends, and community members is an important tool in demonstrating a clear mission, broad community support, and a solution-focused organization.

Preparation is key in submitting foundation requests, and the first step is researching the foundation to determine any linkages and interest. The specific strategies described here are general rules. Adaptations may be necessary, depending on the culture of the organization and foundation.

Foundations are approachable because of their clear guidelines and structured timelines, but foundation fundraising is similar to all fundraising in that the most successful partnerships are built on trusted relationships established over time.

A nonprofit with clearly established priorities from its governing board and executive staff will have fewer difficulties in determining appropriate foundations to contact than will organizations without clear operational mandates and strategic plans in place.

Making a Request

As with all fundraising, the written request or proposal is the final result of intensive and thorough preparation. In foundation fundraising, it includes a review of the requesting organization's mission, identified needs, and the foundation's preferred interests. The Fund Raising School (2009b) suggests using the LAI principle (linkage, ability, interest) in qualifying foundation prospects. Using this principle, ask three sets of questions about each prospect:

1. Does the foundation have any previous relationships with my organization? Does my organization have any friends, staff, or constituents with connections

or influence at the foundation? Determine any linkages that exist or should exist before approaching the foundation.

2. Does the foundation have the assets and make grants of the size necessary for my program? Review current and past grant information to determine typical gift size.

3. Does the foundation have any interest in funding the type of program my organization is proposing? Has the foundation funded in this grant area previously? Review guidelines and funding interests.

Several tools are available to nonprofit organizations to find information on foundations. Many nonprofit and for-profit companies produce annual compilations of foundation information for a fee, but some of the best resources cost little or nothing. Because the IRS governs foundations, each year they must make a Form 990-PF available to the public. Although this form has always been available to the public, in 1998 the IRS made obtaining the form easier and less time-consuming. Most foundations place the Form 990-PF on their websites for immediate viewing. The Form 990-PF provides basic information, including board of directors, total grant amount distributed, grant recipients, and awards. Many independent, corporate, and community foundations publish a web-based annual report, listing much of the same information and providing more detailed descriptions of their support.

Foundation guidelines are an important piece of information to determine the suitability between a foundation and a potential program. Guidelines establish the current interests of the foundation, usually by program type or geographical area; give specific procedures for preparing grant proposals; provide typical funding parameters; and define deadlines for submitting a grant request. After reviewing the selected foundation information, the organization should carefully check the application for submission instructions and formatting.

Only after completing the preliminary research is the nonprofit ready to begin an initial conversation with a foundation. The next step, preferably, is an initial phone call to the prospective foundation to discuss the proposed program or project and the likelihood of funding in the current operational year. Nonprofits may also discover more specific information about a particular foundation's operations and interests. This initial conversation with a foundation representative does not ensure that a proposal will be funded, but it does provide more information for the nonprofit organization preparing a request.

Some foundations do not accept unsolicited phone calls. In these instances, it is useful for the nonprofit to prepare a brief letter of inquiry to the foundation, indicating the parameters of the program and how the program will benefit the larger community. Unless specifically requested, do not include any budget numbers in the initial inquiry; focus instead on the proposed project. Recently, there has been a shift to sending a letter of interest, briefly describing what the nonprofit intends to do with grant funds.

The Proposal

If an initial inquiry letter or phone call has been positively received and the foundation representative encourages continuing the funding discussion, the nonprofit should prepare a proposal package. The details of the package are variable and should follow the published guidelines of the foundation.

A complete proposal package may contain the following items:

1. Cover sheet, including appropriate contact information
2. Abstract or executive summary
3. Identification of needs statement
4. Case statement
5. Proposed solution
6. Expected outcomes
7. Evaluation tool
8. Governance and staffing
9. Budget and budget explanation

Much like a well-written story, the proposal should articulate the identified need and the solutions the organization will use to solve the problem.

After assembling the proposal package, provide a copy to your organization's leadership to review before submission to the foundation. The CEO should provide a cover letter (or the cover sheet mentioned earlier) to demonstrate the organization's commitment to the proposal.

At the Foundation

Once received by the foundation, your proposal will likely follow an internal review process. Information about the process is often published in the foundation's documents. Generally, the proposal is received and recorded in a central processing area. It is then reviewed to ensure that all necessary materials are included and that it generally fits within the foundation's guidelines. In small foundations, a single person often completes both tasks. Large foundations may have these steps completed separately.

A program staff person will review your proposal to determine its applicability to foundation priorities. If this review is successful, you may be contacted for further information or to arrange a site visit. Remember that the grant officer with whom you interacted now becomes your advocate. A site visit, or program visit, is an opportunity for foundation staff to obtain clear project plans and outcomes. It is also an opportunity for the nonprofit to articulate ideas, connections, and impacts that could not be included in the original proposal. Although it is important to be prepared for the site visit, the nonprofit should not attempt to orchestrate or manipulate staff, participants, or outcomes.

The Grant Decision

If the organization has successfully received a grant from a foundation, the opportunity for an extended foundation relationship begins. Provide immediate and appropriate thanks and recognition to the foundation. Depending on the length of a program, the nonprofit may be required to submit intermediate reports, or the foundation may contact the nonprofit several times for updates on progress. Continue to remain in contact with the foundation. The program's success is important to the foundation, and its staff will provide support and guidance throughout the program's duration.

At a minimum, a nonprofit will be required to provide a post-grant evaluation at the conclusion of the program period. The level of evaluation proposed at the outset of the project will also determine the level of contact and reporting to the foundation. In addition, the relationship developed may provide future funding opportunities for new programs at the organization.

A proposal denial does not preclude a relationship with the foundation. A number of factors—including timing, the current foundation portfolio, and future commitments—may influence a decision. Thank the foundation for considering your request, and accept your current denial letter. At the conclusion of the grant process, some foundations will discuss the reasons for denials and may offer advice for resubmitting a proposal.

Nonprofits should keep in mind that the number of foundation proposals submitted is not an accurate measure of foundation fundraising performance. Strong relationships and focused proposals are keys to a strong track record with foundations.

Conclusion

Working with foundations can be an exciting and successful process for many nonprofit organizations. Clearly defined programs and strategies for research and relationship building can lead to organized and appropriate grant proposals that may result in foundation support for an organization's ongoing operations and special programs. If an organization is successful in receiving foundation support, the impact of a single grant can provide greatly needed funding to implement an important program or provide vital support for an organization. Successful foundation fundraising results from clear, specific research; a focus on similar interests; and a dedication by both the foundation and the nonprofit to support the communities and causes they serve.

CHAPTER FOURTEEN

WOMEN AS DONORS

By Debra J. Mesch and Andrea Pactor

Driven by recent research, women's philanthropy offers new energy to invigorate communities and accelerate change. Women's philanthropy is a natural but untapped resource that can change fundraising practices. Just as energy experts suggest that most of the technology needed to shift the world from fossil fuel to renewable energy already exists "just by changing our infrastructure," so too, by engaging women donors in new ways, nonprofit organizations will be on the leading edge of transformative change. This chapter will explore how the changing role of women in society has created new opportunities for women to contribute time, talent, and treasure for the common good and provide tools to help fundraisers develop strategies for working effectively with women donors.

Indicators of Philanthropic Behavior

In the past thirty years women have emerged on the philanthropic landscape as a visible and bold presence. They are changing the face of philanthropy and transforming society around the world. Women today, strengthened by increasing economic power and education, are just as likely as men to be philanthropists.

Data supports the notion that the twenty-first century may well be the age of women in philanthropy. Today an increasing proportion of women in the United States have access to wealth through resources they have either earned, married into, or inherited. The Internal Revenue Service (2008) reported in its Personal Wealth Tables for 2004, the most recent year for which data is available, that 43 percent of the nation's top wealth holders were women. Top wealth holders are defined as individuals with assets of $1.5 million or more. The assets of the 1,173,000 women in this category were valued at $4.6 trillion. The percentage of women in the workforce has had an impact too, almost doubling, from 29 percent to 59 percent, in the years 1950 to 2007 (Bureau of Labor Statistics, 2008). In addition, income for women with college degrees has increased by about 33 percent since 1979 (U.S. Department of Labor, 2008). And women are increasingly holding managerial and professional jobs, resulting in significant gains in income.

The percentage of women in college has also grown steadily, from 42 percent in 1970 to 56 percent in 2000, with women receiving nearly 60 percent of all advanced degrees awarded in 2008–09 (Blackwood, Wing, and Pollak, 2008). These data, along with women's own recognition of their power and influence in philanthropy, contribute to Lisa Witter's assessment in *The She Spot* (2008) that "Women are not a niche audience. They are *the* audience."

Gender Matters

Gender matters in philanthropy. Research finds that women's philanthropic interests and habits differ from men's because women approach philanthropy with different motivations and goals. Women are different from men in their philanthropic behaviors because of the differences in the way they have been raised and the expectations that have been placed upon them as women. In other words, women have been socialized differently from men from a very young age and this impacts how they engage with the community. Research suggests that women are relational, placing more emphasis on relationships and taking care of the individual. In contrast, men tend to prefer more nonrelational acts; for example, they may favor justice as a reason for wanting to help (Skoe, 2002). Fundraisers cannot assume that what works well for men will work well for women, too.

Although much research is needed to explore this area more deeply, significant differences between genders emerge in these areas: volunteering, motivations, and influence in decision making. Additionally, researchers are exploring gender and generational issues to learn more about how fundraisers can best approach donors of different ages.

Volunteering

An engaged donor is likely to be a loyal and generous donor, and this is especially true for women. Most of the research indicates that women volunteer significantly more than men do. Single females are 18 percent more likely to be a volunteer, and on average, they also volunteer 146 hours per year more than single men (Mesch, Moore, and Brown, 2009). Consistent with earlier findings of key predictors of volunteer behavior, that probability increases with education and income. Other researchers have found that women who volunteer are more likely to provide financial support to the same organization where they or family members contribute their time (Parsons, 2004). Volunteering implies deeper knowledge of and engagement with a non-profit organization, thus increasing a woman's likelihood of supporting its mission. Organizations that give women opportunities to volunteer at all levels of engagement, including capital campaigns and board leadership, will benefit from the new perspectives, loyalty, and robust networking capabilities that women bring to the cause.

Motivations

While research provides insight into the actions of women donors, it is also important to understand their motivations for giving. What motivates women's philanthropy, and how do those motivations differ from men's? Although it must be stated that women are not a homogenous group, they do comprise half or more of all donors. Therefore a better understanding of why women give will enable organizations to communicate effectively and help female donors achieve their full philanthropic potential.

A new study conducted at the Women's Philanthropy Institute at the Center on Philanthropy (Mesch et al., 2009) found significant differences in motivations for giving between men and women. This study looked at two motives for giving: empathic concern and principle of care. The study examined two different nationally representative data sets and found that males scored significantly lower on both of these motives for giving across both sets. That is, women, more than men, have higher empathy (feeling more concern for those less fortunate, more protective toward others in need, and more empathy) as well as more willingness to care for others who are less fortunate and to assist people in need.

A recent study conducted at the Center on Philanthropy (Brown and Rooney, 2008) found additional support for differences in motives for giving by gender:

1. Men, more than women, are more motivated by a desire to "make my community a better place."
2. Men, more than women, are more motivated to provide services where government can't or won't.
3. Women, more than men, feel a strong responsibility to help those who have less.

Another study found that the top two motivations for women who give are identifying with a certain cause and helping individuals meet their basic needs

(Mesch et al., 2009). These results support a wealth of literature that indicates men and women have different motives for giving.

This research also examined if differences in these motives result in differences in the likelihood of giving to charity. The analysis revealed that men were significantly less likely to give to charities than women. Further, when these results were analyzed across generations (Silent Generation, greater than age sixty-four; boomers, ages forty-four and sixty-four; Generation X, ages twenty-eight to forty-three; and Millennials—also known as Generation Y—ages less than twenty-eight), as well as by gender, these data found that boomer women were more likely to give to charities than all other gender and generation groups, except for Silent Generation women. Millennial men were the least likely to give among all groups in both data sets—and this group scored significantly lower on both the empathic and principle-of-care scales than any other gender or generational group. The study controlled for marital status, race, number of children in the family, geographic region, religious attendance, income, education, political party, and religious affiliation—as well as controlling for the differences in empathic and principle of care scales using two different data sets. Thus we can have confidence in the validity of the study's findings.

For fundraisers, these results suggest that there are significant differences not only in the motives for giving between men and women, but between generations as well—and that these motives affect giving to charity. Fundraisers need to be aware of these differences when working with donors across both gender and generational groups. Adapting communications and marketing strategies to address the differences the research highlights will create a stronger link between donor and nonprofit and encourage more donor loyalty.

Decisions by Married Couples

Fundraisers should not underestimate women's influence in household philanthropic decision making. Brown (2006) identified three scenarios for household decision making in her research—when the husband decides, when the wife decides, and when the couple makes their decisions jointly. Gifts are more likely to go to health, education, and religious organizations when the wife makes the decision alone, rather than if the husband alone or the couple jointly decides. However, when the woman is the sole decision maker, she gives smaller amounts to more charities. This may be a function of women's egalitarian nature and sense of "fairness." Joint decisions tend to favor the husband's preferences—but this is often a function of education and income.

Subsequent research by Rooney, Brown, and Mesch (2007) finds that households in which women take the lead in making choices or give independently from their husbands are more likely to give to education. In such instances, women also give nearly twice as much.

Fundraisers can integrate simple steps in their interactions with donors to learn more about the "who decides" question in charitable giving. They can visit with the husband and wife together and ask them to share their individual philanthropic passions. They can invite either or both donors to become more deeply involved with the organization. Internally, staff can track who signs the contribution checks and maintain records for interactions with both the husband and wife. Although there is much yet to be learned about how gender matters in philanthropy, research confirms that women are indeed an important demographic for fundraisers to engage strategically.

Fundraising Implications

Fundraisers should consider personal and operational factors when working with women donors. Personal factors, such as the donor's age and attitude about money, influence charitable decision making. Operational factors, such as whether the organization's communications and marketing strategies are geared toward women, contribute to fundraising success. A simple step such as talking to the couple instead of only to the man may result in an increased gift. Women generally outlive their male partners by 5.2 years, and they often have more control of household philanthropic decision making.

Be mindful of a woman's attitude toward money. Does she perceive herself as the guardian or the owner of the wealth? Women who did not earn the wealth but received it through inheritance, marriage, or divorce may not feel it is theirs to dispose of as they would choose. If women have earned their wealth, they are likely more financially literate and more confident philanthropists.

Although conventional wisdom suggests women take longer to decide to give a gift, cultivation and continued engagement often result in significant gifts. Fundraisers do not always know who will contribute a major gift. One fundraiser shared a story about an alumna of a women's college who had faithfully contributed $25 per year for many years. The college was overwhelmed to learn they were a beneficiary of $750,000 at her death.

Internal and external barriers impede donors and fundraisers alike. Prospective women donors may not think of themselves as philanthropists or may be reluctant to talk about money. They may be afraid of outliving their resources or may have just recently acquired the money and feel it might not be there tomorrow. Some women continue to seek anonymity in their giving. Similarly, barriers may exist within the organization that prevent fundraisers from reaching this significant potential donor base. There may be little organizational commitment to working with women as donors because of perceptions that they take longer to cultivate or reluctance to change the status quo. There may be fewer women in leadership positions in the organization. The organization may not realize the need to adjust the marketing and communications strategies to better relate to women. Most important, it may be that women simply are not asked to give.

Race and Culture

Increasingly, organizations are reaching out to engage women across race and culture in their fundraising efforts and in the life of the organization. Minter (2008) reinforces the notion that "different communities of color have different giving patterns, histories, and experiences, so it is hard to generalize. Women of color have a perspective both as a female and as a person of color so fundraisers need to honor their multiple identities."

Women of color are increasingly finding new, creative, and powerful ways to express their philanthropy. Giving circles are one way in which women of all races and socio-economic backgrounds are exploring philanthropy (Shaw-Hardy, 2009). Jane Fox-Johnson, a member of the African American Women's Giving Circle at the Washington Area Women's Foundation, said, "I love it that we influenced people's opinions about what a group of powerful black women can do." Hali Lee, founder of the Asian Women's Giving Circle in New York City, asks every member to try to raise $2,500 annually because "it is important that the women have the experience of writing a personal check *and* raising money. This is great training for future board work . . . that way we're not only raising money, we're raising philanthropists."

From the donor perspective, women in communities of color want to make sure the organizations they support reflect the diversity in their communities. They may inquire about board diversity and whether the marketing and communication materials are representative of the community. They may also ask whether inclusiveness is a value embraced throughout the agency and whether diverse perspectives are actively pursued.

Focus groups are a useful tool to help fundraisers understand the dynamics and complexities at work in communities of color. Listening carefully to the group's ideas and suggestions will help lead to a respectful and strategic plan of action.

Assess Your Current Work with Women Donors

Making a commitment to growing women's giving requires knowing the organization's current position in working with women donors and setting goals regarding where you want to be. This first set of questions relates to the work of fundraising professionals.

1. How much of a fundraiser's time is devoted to cultivating and soliciting women donors?
2. Of the last ten personal visits to donors, how many were to men, to women, to couples, to families?
3. In what ways does the fundraiser customize interaction with women donors to reflect women's interests and their communication styles?
4. Are fundraisers in the habit of asking women for major gifts?
5. Are generational and family factors considered when creating your strategy for women donors?
6. Do conversations with women donors help connect their values and vision with your organization's programs and plans?
7. Does the fundraiser help women donors see philanthropy as a way to realize their philanthropic voice?

Now consider the organization's readiness for women's philanthropy:

1. Has the organization's data regarding current giving by women been assessed?
2. Is women's philanthropy prominently featured across the institution's publications?
3. Are women prominent in leadership positions (both volunteer and staff) in the organization and in special fundraising efforts such as capital campaigns?
4. Are there established avenues for women to provide regular feedback to the organization?
5. Does the organization have a women's philanthropy council to help advise and energize women's giving?
6. Does the organization have donor education programs that help women with financial literacy, estate planning, finding their philanthropic passion, and other topics that are vital to growing women as major donors?
7. Is the organization's commitment to women's philanthropy evident in its willingness to devote appropriate financial and human resources to growing women's giving?

Reflecting on twenty years of the Women's Philanthropy Council at the University of Wisconsin, Martha Taylor, vice president of the University of Wisconsin Foundation, says, "It is important to note that the women's program is part of a team of engaging women in the life of the organization, complementing all other development efforts." Making the decision to work more deliberately with prospective women donors should dovetail with the agency's strategic plan and be in concert with its fundraising plan. Addressing issues such as time frame, allocation of time and resources, identifying and engaging key stakeholders, auditing the existing database, evaluating marketing and communication strategies, outcomes, and evaluation are necessary steps to gain support for this targeted approach and to develop a solid framework for the effort.

Action Steps

When developing or refining an initiative focused on women donors, consider the following steps:

1. Develop five goals and objectives to accomplish with this initiative.
2. Identify potential stakeholders with whom to share findings to begin building a network of support.
3. Create a set of key actions to implement in the next ninety days.
4. Create a strategic plan with measurable outcomes to guide your work.

Astute fundraisers understand that the sociocultural and economic climate has changed significantly for women over the past several decades, positioning them to be powerful forces for philanthropy in the twenty-first century. The following five examples demonstrate the impact of women's giving in recent years and provide successful models that can be adapted to fit most any organization's mission.

1. Scrutiny of the database became the basis for a new planned giving program at a Minnesota nonprofit. Fundraisers found five hundred female donors in the database over the age of fifty who had made annual gifts for three or more years. Within two years, that nonprofit raised $6 million in planned gifts and pledges from those women.
2. Martha Taylor, a cofounder of the Women's Philanthropy Institute and vice president at the University of Wisconsin Foundation, started the first women's philanthropy major gift initiative in higher education in 1988 at the University of Wisconsin-Madison. She reports that

   the impact of the work after twenty years has been the increased engagement of alumnae in the life of the University. Direct impact can be seen in the gift results and increased involvement of members of the Council and the regional groups. Indirect results are the response of all alumnae when they read the women's publications and believe they are valued by the University. We also have encouraged development officers to increase their personal visits to women. It is important to note that the women's program is part of a team of engaging women in the life of the organization, complementing all other development efforts.

3. The United Way of America formalized its national Women's Leadership Council in 2004 with a goal of increasing annual funds raised by women donors in United Way affiliates across the country from $59 million to $100 million by 2008. In 2007, more than one hundred women's councils representing forty thousand women raised $105 million, exceeding their initial goal by 5 percent. Patricia J. Mitchell, Women's Leadership Council national chair, said of the councils, "We are a powerful voice of women in philanthropy, and a powerful voice to advocate for the critical needs in our communities locally, nationally, and internationally."

4. The Tiffany Circle program of the American Red Cross began as a pilot initiative in eight cities in 2007, with a member giving level of $10,000. It, too, has been one of the organization's most successful efforts. Focused on women's and leadership giving, the pilot targeted a total fundraising goal of $1 million. Results achieved three times that, or $3 million. In addition, Tiffany Circles attracted new and different donors. More than 60 of the initial 235 members were brand-new to the organization, and four out of ten (40 percent) had previously given but never at the $10,000 level. In 2008, expanded to twenty-five cities, Tiffany Circles raised over $5.3 million for their local communities. In its first three years of operation, Tiffany Circle members have contributed $15 million to the American Red Cross. American Red Cross President Gail McGovern anticipates raising $100 million from this group by 2018 (Hall, 2009).

5. The Women's Funding Network, in partnership with philanthropists Swanee and Helen LaKelly Hunt, developed the Women Moving Millions campaign in 2007 with the goal of raising the bar on women's giving by raising million-dollar gifts from women. By April 2009, the campaign exceeded its $150 million goal by 16 percent, raising $174 million from more than ninety women.

Conclusion

As we move deeper into the twenty-first century, it is likely that more women will become active in philanthropy. Former national president of the United Way

Women's Leadership Council Pat Mitchell stated that "philanthropy is the last frontier for women." From a demographic perspective, women are the majority in the United States and about half the world population. Especially in times of economic turmoil and uncertainty, it is critical to leverage all available resources to address challenging issues in our communities across the globe.

From a social, political, and cultural perspective, recognizing that women's roles in society have changed dramatically in the last fifty years is paramount to changing the way fundraisers think about women's philanthropy. As women around the globe have increasing access to education and income, they can and do become a powerful voice for change. From a financial perspective, the long-anticipated intergenerational transfer of wealth is likely to position women firmly in the driver's seat for philanthropy. Finally, it is all about transformative change. Women provide new ideas, new visions, new perspectives, and new resources to transform society.

CHAPTER FIFTEEN

HIGH-NET-WORTH DONORS

By Marti K. S. Heil and Sandra Bate

Economic observers in America often point to mega-donors like Bill and Melinda Gates as models for America's new philanthropy. New philanthropists are, indeed, looking to entrepreneurial models and following their patterns of studying, evaluating, and then investing in making the world a different place.

In an article entitled, "Write a Check? The New Philanthropist Goes Further," the *New York Times* (Bick, 2007) highlighted a workshop for emerging philanthropists that teaches wealthy individuals to approach their giving more strategically. In addition to the new activism that characterizes a certain set of donors, the size of gifts from America's wealthiest philanthropists has become astounding: perhaps it is, indeed, that these individuals are, as Churchill suggested, making a life by what they give.

It is possible, of course, to view the mega-donors, individuals like Warren Buffet and Leona Helmsley, as isolated economic wonders. But certainly the generosity has trickled through economic classes. In the same year that Helmsley left a bequest of $5.2 billion to a charitable trust, the smallest gift listed on The Philanthropy 50, a directory of America's top donors assembled by the *Chronicle of Philanthropy* (2009), was $30.5 million.

Those who study the field of philanthropy observe that today's donors have greater wealth, are more engaged with their charities of choice, are more sophisticated in philanthropic activities, and are more knowledgeable about gifting vehicles than ever before.

These high-net-worth donors are individuals who can and do make transformational gifts to nonprofit organizations. And they are becoming more and more significant as nonprofits look to redefine and take their programs to the next level of fundraising success.

Defining High-Net-Worth Donors

High-net-worth donors, as defined by the Indiana University Center on Philanthropy in the *2008 Bank of America Study of High Net-Worth Philanthropy*, are donors with household incomes greater than $200,000 and/or net worth of at least $1,000,000, excluding their primary residence.

There are two reasons why the ranks of this new class of donors are growing so rapidly and becoming more and more significant to America's nonprofit sector:

- Demographics, specifically the swell of the baby boomer generation and the wealth that this generation has accrued and will inherit
- New concentrations of wealth in an extremely small economic class

All indicators point to the boomer generation as the largest and wealthiest economic force in our nation's history. It is estimated that by the year 2015, we will have in excess of forty-five million households composed of individuals between the ages of fifty-one and seventy. At that point, boomers are predicted to control nearly 60 percent of the country's net wealth and account for 40 percent of all consumption and income (Court, Farrell, and Forsyth, 2007).

The sheer size of the boomer generation and its marked tendency to think outside the box and create rules as it goes have forced nonprofits to think more strategically and creatively about their relationships with this new dominant economic class.

Complementing the arrival of the boomers at their economic nexus is the growing concentration of wealth in this country. Since the 1980s, some commentators contend the majority of Americans have simply not been getting bigger slices from a growing pie. Long before the recession that officially began in 2008, the gap was clear, according to analyses like that done by *The American Prospect* (2001):

	Percent of Wealth in Housing	Ratio of Debt to Assets
Middle class	66 percent	59 percent
Super rich class	7 percent	5 percent

Edward N. Wolff, professor of economics at New York University and a research associate at the National Bureau of Economic Research, concludes: "[F]or most middle-class families, wealth is closely tied to the value of their homes, their ability to save money in monetary accounts, and the debt burden they face. But the wealth of the super rich has a lot more to do with their ability to convert existing wealth—in the form of stocks, investment real estate, or securities—into even more wealth, that is, to produce capital gains" (2001).

As they produce capital gains, these high-net-worth individuals also make their mark on society through exceptionally large philanthropic deeds.

There is one other distinguishing characteristic of high-net-worth donors that is especially significant for nonprofits: they are younger than ever. In an online lecture about high-net-worth donors, H. King McGlaughon, Jr., of Wachovia Wealth Management related that while approximately one-third of high-net-worth donors are sixty-five or older, 62 percent are between the ages of thirty-seven and sixty-four. Some of the younger donors, according to McGlaughon, might be best described as silent millionaires: "[T]hey don't act rich or consume conspicuously, but they do believe in giving back to society."

Understanding High-Net-Worth Donors

The consummate fundraising professional is distinguished by a comprehensive and persistent understanding of donors. And those who excel in the field will tell you that it has never been more critical than now to build and expand that knowledge and awareness.

Developing insight into high-net-worth donors and their advisors is the first step for an organization that commits to work with these generous and highly motivated individuals. That insight begins with an understanding of lifestyles, values, wealth, and aspirations. Because high-net-worth donors have attracted the attention, both nationwide and globally, of some of the best research organizations in the field of philanthropy, there is a fast-growing body of research available to help fundraisers learn about the market.

One of the most definitive studies of high-net-worth donors is the result of a highly productive research partnership between the Bank of America and the Center on Philanthropy at Indiana University. Even a cursory scan of the study offers important perspective and awareness about the giving behaviors and thinking of high-net-worth donors. The study found that

- Eighty-one percent give to give back to the community.
- Sixty-seven percent give to make an immediate difference.
- Seventy percent say their social beliefs motivate their giving.

- Fifty-nine percent say their political beliefs motivate their giving.
- Seventy-one percent say loyalty to certain causes or organizations motivates their giving.
- Forty-six percent believe their giving has a greater impact on their own personal fulfillment than on those who receive their gifts.
- Fifty-seven percent say the leading objective for their largest gifts was general operating support.
- Forty-six percent say setting an example for children or other young people is an important motivator.
- Ninety-six percent instruct their children about philanthropy and the value of giving.
- Sixty percent involve their children in philanthropy.
- Forty percent of adult-age children of wealthy families give through their own private foundation or donor-advised fund.

There are other studies, as well, that have focused on high-net-worth donors, including *The 21st Century Donor* (Saxton, Madden, and Greenwood, 2007) by nfpSynergy, a British nonprofit consulting firm. That study concluded, "The 21st century donor is richer, more engaged, more discerning, and more in control than her 20th century predecessor."

Donor Pulse (2008), a set of reports published by the market research organization Campbell Rinker and based on the firm's Great American Donor Survey, segments data and analysis by industry, such as religious charities, the arts and humanities, or animal protection charities.

All the sources mentioned here are in agreement about at least three factors that deserve special consideration as nonprofits move to focus their work with high-net-worth donors. With each of these factors, it's clear that the term *donor-centric* is taking on new meaning across the fundraising field.

Family-Based Philanthropy

First, because much of the wealth among high-net-worth donors is family-based, their philanthropy is also commonly a family deed. Private family foundations are among the fastest-growing philanthropic organizations on the national landscape and commonly have exceptionally broad agendas (Foundation Center, 2009). An organization can realize its investment tenfold by dedicating staff to understanding this type of family-based approach to giving and strategically focusing staff work dedicated to this source.

The Paul G. Allen Family Foundation, for example, has this mission: "To transform lives and strengthen communities by fostering innovation, creating knowledge, and promoting social progress." Under that broad mission, areas of interest run the gamut from economic development to scientific innovation and artistic expression and performance. It is critical for nonprofits to acknowledge this multigenerational presence and address both the interests and the giving opportunities that span generations.

A Team of Financial Advisers

Some high-net-worth donors may desire to create a family legacy and may have tangible concerns about the impact of inherited wealth on their adult children. This leads to the second defining characteristic of high-net-worth donors: to a degree not seen before, they seek counsel and professional expertise to plan their philanthropy and to make long-term investments in nonprofit organizations.

Asset protection is exceptionally important to these donors, and working with professionals in the fields of finance and wealth management is not just comfortable for them; they also view it as the most responsible behavior. For the fundraiser, then, expanding the circles of dialogue and learning to work with teams of professionals who guide and direct the donor and donor families are new requirements for success.

A High Performance Standard for Nonprofits

The Bank of America study of high-net-worth donors concluded that wealthy individuals have exceptionally high expectations of charitable organizations. They see the following factors as most significant when they are evaluating which nonprofit organizations to support:

- Sound business practices
- Appropriate spending of revenue on overhead
- Acknowledgment of contributions and recognition of donors
- Protection of personal information
- Full financial disclosure

It is also significant for today's nonprofits to understand the impact that choice and preferences have on giving. The Bank of America study, for example, discovered that more than one-third—38 percent—of donors stopped supporting a charitable organization in the past year for one of these three reasons:

- No longer feeling connected to the organization
- Deciding to support other causes
- Feeling they were solicited too often

As always in the field of fundraising, there is no substitute for knowing and understanding donors. But particularly with the new high-net-worth class, it is critical to be as flexible as possible in matching donors' passions and preferences with an organization's funding needs and priorities. And the wisest nonprofit organization will creatively explore and expand the multitude of ways that donors can be engaged and invested in meaningful activities and relationships.

Motivating High-Net-Worth Donors

There is, of course, no better counsel to fundraisers working with donors at all levels than the four-pronged, time-tested formula for success: identify, cultivate, solicit, and provide stewardship of donors' gifts. Those four tasks encapsulate the need to be vigilant about sifting and nurturing a base of new donors while remaining fully involved with and committed to current donors.

There are six steps that will help guide the nonprofit as it seeks to refine and develop its work with high-net-worth donors: explore, evaluate, enlighten, engage, encourage, and endow.

Explore

Begin the process by creatively exploring the entire market of prospective donors for your organization. Identify those individuals with high net worth who have linkage to your nonprofit and may have interest in your work. Prospective donor profiling—a service that can be purchased from a multitude of commercial vendors—can help scale down the large numbers of prospective donors to a workable database. Peer screening by your most valued volunteers and donors can also help you identify prospective donors that might be appropriate to pursue. These prospective donors are often most influential in a wide variety of circles and networks and are generally willing to share their knowledge and expertise. Ask your best donors and volunteers who they know and who should be considered a prospective donor. You may choose to engage your very best donors as ambassadors and advocates for your organization's cause as you proceed through an exploration of prospective donors.

Evaluate

Discover the gift potential and interests of the prospective donors you have identified. Learn what family traditions and values there are and what areas of endeavor are most significant from a philanthropic perspective. Track relationships through professional networks. Develop ways to identify the donor's passions and connect those passions with the compelling needs in your organization. Research is the starting point, but the best way to determine interests is a face-to-face meeting with the prospective donor during which an open and friendly exchange of information can occur. Use your most valued and influential volunteers to help broker introductory meetings with prospective donors they know. Provide opportunities for them to be spokespeople and to share their personal reasons for giving to and being involved with your organization. Testimonials from highly respected and influential volunteers can be a powerful tool for involving new and prospective donors.

Enlighten

Enlighten and educate the donor about your organization's mission, work, and philanthropic needs. Communicate clearly, consistently, and in a style that is as personalized and trustworthy as you can create. Regular contact with these prospective donors will help open the line of communication. Share important information about your organization prior to broad publication so that your most valued donors feel like insiders to your organization. Make good use of VIP distribution mailings. It's important to understand how the prospective donors wish to be contacted and their expectations of an organization like yours. When devising a tailored communication plan for the high-net-worth donor, consider everything from social networks to e-mail to snail-mail to personal phone calls and visits. And it's critical to create multiple intersections with those who have been identified as your top prospective donors, including small, intimate events hosted by your most influential volunteers.

Engage

Build relationships with the prospective donors by actively and consistently involving them in the life of your organization, based on their interests. Examine and embrace the ways you can invite and encourage active participation of those key prospective donors in your programs and advisory groups. Because involved volunteers are always the most loyal and generous, it will be helpful to determine whether a volunteer role is right for the specific prospective donor with whom you are working. Are there consulting or advisory roles that a prospective donor might fulfill for your organization? As a rule, Boomers distinguish themselves by needing to feel they add value to a team and that an organization has a need for their involvement and gifts. Like others, high-net-worth donors enjoy being asked for their opinions; one excellent way to engage them is to solicit their guidance when your nonprofit is faced with important decisions. The goal, always, is to build a relationship based on mutual respect and trust, as well as shared interests and passions.

Encourage

This is the solicitation or invitation you extend to your prospective donor. Your goal is to gain the donor's active support through a planned and documented solicitation program. A gift at this level happens when the donor has an emotional investment and the direct impact of the gift has been demonstrated. The approach must be as distinctive as each individual; there is not one cookie-cutter solution to fundraising at this level, and high-net-worth donors require a high level of individualized attention.

It is most efficient to have specific and strategic action steps in place to engage a donor at levels on the continuum of giving. You can develop a set of tracking and monitoring reports that allows you to track the gifts of prospective donors at each phase of giving, ending with an endowment gift and a long-term investment in your organization.

Many models in fundraising focus strategically on intentionally engaging donors with the organization. The program evaluates the level of engagement the donor has and the interest and involvements that the donor has demonstrated and determines other levels of engagement that are essential before a solicitation can be made. While there is a need for strategy that outlines specific steps for the solicitation of donors, it is also especially true with high-net-worth donors that there may be a gap between an authentic relationship and a calculated set of steps. The solicitation process must be deliberate and meaningful both for the donor and the nonprofit, and it must be characterized by a high degree of specificity, direct communication, sensitivity, and responsiveness. Each important step of the process should be driven by an organization's attention to being donor-centric in its approach and still be specific, exclusive, and tailored to the particular high-net-worth donor.

Endow

It is paramount that your fundraising program have appropriate financial resources to match the significance of the task you are undertaking. The adage "It costs money to raise money" was never more true than in today's fundraising market. To position your organization so that high-net-worth donors are willing to entrust you with their discretionary dollars, you must have in place a careful strategic plan and the appropriate fundraising program.

Nonprofits that are well managed and disciplined in working with high-net-worth donors will find the rewards truly transformational. Prospective donors who are fully engaged, who understand the organization's mission and needs, and who are vested and involved members of the team will invest in and endow the organization's most valued programs. High-net-worth donors are most inclined to invest their gifts in areas within an organization in which they can have a transformational impact, and often these investments are directed towards endowments. Leaving lasting legacies in the form of endowments is consistent with the type of impact most high-net-worth donors desire to make in the organizations about which they are most passionate.

Measuring Success

The metric for evaluating fundraising success with high-net-worth donors must be a two-dimensional analysis:

- It must measure the growth, over time and perhaps even over generations, of the relationship between your organization and the donor.
- It must measure the gift and its transformational nature for your organization.

There is much discussion in the fundraising field today about the proper metrics to measure the success of fundraisers. Increasingly, there is a welcome awareness that merely "getting the gift" is not, by any measure, the totality of the work. Likewise, mission and metrics are not mutually exclusive. Gifts from high-net-worth donors are never transactional: they come only as a direct result of developing and implementing a strategic set of steps focused on building the relationship between the donor and the organization. These steps must be both based on the emotional involvement of the donor and developed over a lifetime of giving.

Evaluating productivity in a fundraising environment requires that you look at all activity related to fundraising, across all donor segments. Certainly, with high-net-worth donors, the metric for measuring success must be as customized as possible, with great emphasis on the donor's wishes, timing, gift vehicles, and personal agenda for giving. And the largest gifts often come after long periods of engagement.

With high-net-worth donors, there must be a very deliberate and careful evaluation of the value of donor engagement and recognition activities, including social events that provide access and opportunity for discourse. How comfortable is the donor at these events? Are they cost-effective? Does your staffing level permit you to lead these activities without compromising other initiatives? When considering events, the fundraiser should always ask, "Will this event directly affect the bottom line fundraising result?"

With high-net-worth donors, the organization also needs to demonstrate a high level of creativity and resourcefulness with various charitable vehicles that sometimes cannot be measured through traditional metrics of evaluating fundraising success. The Bank of America study cited donor-advised funds as one of the preferred giving vehicles for 20 percent of its respondents. But significantly, another 20 percent of respondents indicated that they would consider using donor-advised funds in the near future.

Planned giving also assumes even greater significance with high-net-worth donors. Again, the Bank of America study documented that 56 percent of wealthy donors have a charitable provision in their will, but that the total could skyrocket to 93 percent in the current year, given the statement of intent of the survey respondents. It will benefit any organization to pursue using a variety of gifting vehicles, both current and deferred, when working with high-net-worth donors.

Unfortunately, the special considerations so appropriate and rewarding for high-net-worth donors may at times lead some nonprofits to the conclusion that these donors are challenging individuals with whom to work, requiring exceptionally frequent and high-level contact. That can be true, but for the rewards that the organization will realize from high-net-worth donors, the organization's investments are well worth it.

It is also true that because of their significance to the fundraising success of nonprofits, the high-net-worth donors are among the best investments of both resources and energies. If it remains verifiable that nearly 90 percent of the funds raised by charitable organizations comes from 10 percent—or less—of the donors, making the case for exceptionally personalized, highly energized, and extremely sensitive relationship-building does not seem to be a stretch (Fabrikant, 2008).

The secret to measuring the success of high-net-worth donor–related work is to appraise the growth of the relationship over time and assess how gifts at this level have, indeed, been responsible for the organization's rise to the next level of mission fulfillment. Neither of those assessments is totally a matter of metrics. But for the organization that has been transformed by a gift from a high-net-worth donor, the recognition of the significance and impact of its fundraising strategies and initiatives will not be difficult.

Conclusion

Mega-donors have become the new models for high-net-worth donors in America. These high-net-worth donors are committed, most often, to make transformational gifts to charitable organizations.

The interests of high-net-worth donors will commonly span family generations. The donors and their families are frequently advised by a team of financial
and wealth counselors that can at times include representatives of the nonprofits
they have chosen to support. High-net-worth donors have high expectations of the
nonprofits they help sustain and choose to support, in terms of accountability and
management.

To best motivate high-net-worth donors, the nonprofit must explore and
evaluate the prospective donor base, enlighten and educate donors about opportunities for support that will match individual donor passions, engage donors
and encourage their support, and endow the fundraising program for maximum
success.

Success with high-net-worth donors is best measured when there is documented and continued growth of the relationship between the donor and the
organization. The fundraising initiative with high-net-worth donors best serves
the nonprofit when the organization can take monumental strides and demonstrate extraordinary progress toward the realization of its vision and mission
because of a donor's generosity and investments.

For those purposes, high-net-worth donors do make "a life of giving," as
Winston Churchill suggested, and so enrich the lives of millions as they transform
the work and services of nonprofits around the globe.

CHAPTER SIXTEEN

ETHNICITY AND GIVING

By Lilya Wagner

Introduction by Una Okonkwo Osili

There is a great deal of interest among fundraisers and philanthropists in understanding how the growing diversity in today's communities will affect the nonprofit sector. As Lilya Wagner notes in this chapter, there is a need to adapt strategies and tactics in order to honor and appeal to the increasingly multicultural backgrounds, traditions, and motivations of donors to charitable causes. Although to date there are only a few studies that examine closely the implications of diversity for the nonprofit sector, some authors believe that greater diversity within communities can expand the scale and scope of the nonprofit sector; others have argued that increasing diversity may reduce the willingness of individuals to give to collective initiatives.

Understanding the implications of growing diversity for charitable giving is critical because the United States relies more heavily on private philanthropy and the nonprofit sector than any other industrialized country to provide social and human services, education, arts, and culture in particular. Recent research based on data from Center on Philanthropy Panel Study (COPPS), a module in the Panel Study of Income Dynamics (PSID), provides an opportunity to look anew at the implications of an increasingly diverse donor base. These data represent the largest one-time study of philanthropy in the United States and provide a unique opportunity to study the impact of ethnic diversity on charitable giving at the household level.

The COPPS data indicate that although a greater amount of ethnic diversity tends to have a negative impact on giving to collective purposes in today's diverse communities, ethnic diversity can increase the probability of contributions and total amount contributed as more diverse groups form their own organizations— and as the size and scope of the nonprofit sector increases. It is generally thought that the three main reasons for what may be a negative relationship between diversity and a low rate of giving are the difficulty of agreeing on community-wide objectives, the tendency to keep giving within a specific ethnic group, and the high "transaction costs"—such as time spent breaking down language barriers and building trust—among different groups. However, to overcome such challenges, fundraisers and nonprofit sector leaders can strive to recognize each of the distinct groups in their communities to "forge a community identity as well as celebrating differences." Certainly, the practical advice this chapter gives to fundraisers can help accomplish just that.

Embracing Diversity in Fundraising

Hank Rosso was personally committed to extending the work of The Fund Raising School to diverse populations. The Rosso emphasis on understanding the interests and needs of the donor fits well with the engagement of diverse populations. Successful ventures between The Fund Raising School and Native Americans in Philanthropy, the Hispanic Stewardship Partnership, and the Thurgood Marshall and United Negro College Funds illustrate the adaptability.

Today nonprofit organizations are increasingly embracing diversity as a mission and organizational value. They are seeking to do the right thing as well as access the economic growth and power of Hispanics, African Americans, Asian Americans, and other diverse population groups. It's not just the right thing to do. It's a useful perspective in building and managing credible, comprehensive fundraising programs.

At the same time, diversity presents a challenge to fundraisers. No longer can they function under the assumption of "one size fits all," something the Rosso model taught us to avoid. Diverse groups have identifiable, valuable, and significant philanthropic characteristics and traits. Therefore fundraisers find that in order to be successful, they must tailor their fundraising appeals to the prospective donors' customs and sensibilities.

Not to acknowledge and work with diversity in U.S. populations is to ignore much potential of income for nonprofit organizations. Reis and Clohesy stated, "As these populations grow in numbers they will continue to grow in influence and resources. In the 21st century the philanthropy of women, communities of color and youth are likely to have a substantial influence on traditional philanthropic institutions.

Already these populations have created new philanthropic institutions and networks that more closely resemble their social and ethnic cultures and attempt to solve issues they consider to be of most importance" (2001, p. 12). Some diverse or minority populations haven't attained the income levels of majority population. But there are signs of emerging wealth and purchasing power. There is a rise in entrepreneurial activities, education levels are increasing, and individuals are flourishing in professions such as the law and medicine.

According to Anft, "Besides rising wealth, minority donors also offer great potential for generosity. Federal income-tax data suggest, for example, that black and Hispanic homeowners tend to give a higher proportion of their incomes to charity than do white homeowners" (2002).

In this chapter we consider use of terminology, challenges presented by understanding philanthropic practices of diverse population groups, the giving habits and preferences of four major ethnic population groups, cautious generalizations that can serve as a foundation for further understanding, and guidelines for developing comprehensive fundraising programs and understanding diversity among donor groups.

Defining Diversity

Use of language in defining diversity presents many challenges. Even the commonly used phrase "fundraising in diverse communities," often found in titles of books and articles, can be disputed. Perhaps it would be more correct to say, "fundraising across, within, among, for, or with" diverse communities, because any discussion of fundraising among population groups other than the majority in the United States may well imply cross-cultural fundraising for mutual benefit of various population groups.

Primary to any discussion of diverse populations, a consideration of what culture means is valuable for providing a foundation or framework. According to Wilson, Hoppe, and Sayles, "Culture strongly influences how one behaves and how one understands the behavior of others, and cultures vary in the behaviors they find proper and acceptable" (1996, p. 1). There is the external culture, which is exhibited in outward behaviors and traditions that are readily discernible, such as a performance of a mariachi band, and internal culture, which is less evident, such as the way people think about situations and conceptualize information. Culture can be most easily explained as a people's way of life. The authors of *Philanthropy in Communities of Color* explained culture in this way: "All cultures construct reality differently; within each unique cultural community, beliefs and behavior have meanings that are often not shared or understood by the outside world. Some cultural meanings are manifest and easily recognized; others are latent and subtle, requiring systematic observation in order to produce accurate analysis" (Smith, Shue, Vest, and Villarreal, 1999, p. 3).

For the fundraising professional, therefore, consideration of cultural elements is vital prior to any fundraising activity. Unfortunately, many fundraisers approach a relationship and solicitation from their own perspective, leaving themselves unprepared for cultural differences that can easily be misinterpreted and misconstrued. Smith and colleagues stated that " . . . the cultural dimensions of gift-giving, financial assistance, sharing, and the distribution of income and wealth all have a variety of meanings from culture to culture. . . . The uses of wealth, prestige, and power are also important to the cross-cultural analysis of charitable behavior" (1999, p. 3).

In addition to the difficulties presented by perceptions of other cultures, terminology also offers challenges in any discussion of diverse populations and philanthropy. Should correct designation for diverse populations be people of color, minorities, or ethnic groups? And is the correct terminology African American or black? Hispanic or Latino? Asian American and Pacific Islander? Just possibly labels get in the way more than they help when we identify and qualify donors.

Naturally, people of diverse populations would prefer to be identified by their actual country of origin or their source of national orientation. Mexicans or Mexican Americans, for example, would rather be distinctive than lumped into an overall designation. Chinese may have few similarities with Pacific Islanders, yet they usually come under the same appellation. For the purposes of this chapter, the following guidelines will be used.

To identify population groups that are often called minorities or similar terms, we will use *people of diverse populations*. Although preferences differ vastly among people of diverse populations as to specific nomenclature, for purposes of clarity and ease the following will be used, sometimes interchangeably (based on terminology found in current literature):

- African American or Black
- Hispanic or Latino
- Asian American or Asian/Pacific Islander
- Native American

Problems and Challenges of Diverse Populations and Fundraising

Jill Moss Greenberg (2002) identified six forms of bias that can serve as barriers to understanding populations outside our own source of identity and can inhibit good working relationships. These readily apply to philanthropy and fundraising.

1. *Exclusion and invisibility*. This is the most fundamental form of bias and most difficult to detect. It can range from unintentional to determined exclusion. It means excluding both people and information about people, such as their contributions to history. Exclusion and invisibility diminish the value given to some groups. If diverse population groups' philanthropy is ignored or they are considered to be poor givers or even incapable of giving, we are expressing a distinct form of bias as fundraising professionals.

2. *Stereotyping*. Stereotyping portrays members of specific groups as having characteristics in common, negative and positive. It is harmful because it indicates that a certain population group is homogeneous rather than having a range of individual roles, beliefs, preferences, and behaviors. Stereotyping is, however, different from intelligent generalization, which provides a foundation for further individual understanding of cultural and ethnic characteristics leading to philanthropic behavior.

3. *Imbalance and selectivity*. This means to present only one interpretation of an issue, situation, or group. The result is a one-sided, skewed, or simplistic view of complex issues, situations, or people. For this reason, the astute and sensitive fundraiser must move beyond generalizations and understand each donor or donor group as completely as possible; in other words, the same thorough prospect research principles must be applied to all potential donors.

4. *Unreality*. This is the tendency to exclude underlying facts or issues that clarify. Substantive or controversial topics may be glossed over, restricting information that helps understanding. Again, the implication for fundraisers is that stereotypes and sheer lack of knowledge inhibit an understanding of and respect for populations that are "new" and different from our usual donor groups.

5. *Fragmentation and isolation*. This is the tendency to isolate or separate experiences of minority groups from those of the majority population. This implies that the specific experiences are somehow unrelated to the majority population. Differentiating in this way leads to exclusion or invisibility.

6. *Linguistic bias*. Language frames perceptions, perspectives, and attitudes. Slurs can categorize people. Therefore great care must be taken to use nomenclature that is comfortable for diverse populations. This is not an easy task, as we have already discussed, but it is a necessary one.

Reluctantly, we must restrict our discussion to four major ethnic groups without sufficient consideration for subcategories. We do, however, acknowledge that African Americans, Asian Americans, Hispanics, and Native Americans have been isolated from much of the broader mainstream philanthropic discussions and therefore have created their own philanthropic structures and practices. The structures and practices differ somewhat from each other as much as they differ from the white majority in the United States, but there are also some similarities across the various groups.

In general, fundraising professionals don't approach diverse donors responsibly. Unwarranted assumptions about each population's philanthropy color our viewpoints. Finding ways to appeal to ethnic generosity is a daunting challenge. There isn't one model to do fundraising from minority groups; there are different models (Anft, 2002). Compounding the challenges is the fact that ethnic groups have been stereotyped as receivers, not givers, of charity.

The following discussion of diverse population groups' philanthropy will prove that many commonly made assumptions are indeed incorrect and even harmful.

Diverse Groups and Philanthropy

The amount of giving by diverse populations groups is estimated to be consistent with that of other populations in the United States, but the ways in which they give and to whom they give vary (Smith et al., 1999). Differences also show up among ethnic groups. Asian Americans tend to give to family- and health-centered charities, while Hispanic donors, accustomed to government and church help on social issues, give more often to religious institutions and mutual-assistance groups that provide aid to impoverished community members (Anft, 2002).

Data about the U.S. population, based on 2008 estimates from the U.S. Census Bureau, are as follows:

Percentages of U.S. Population:

Non-Hispanic Whites	65.6 percent
Hispanics	15.4 percent
African Americans	12.8 percent
Asian Americans	4.5 percent
Native Americans	1 percent
Other (single or multiracial)	0.7 percent

Hispanics or Latinos. Hispanics or Latinos are people with a family heritage from more than twenty countries. They vary greatly in levels of affluence and education.

The Hispanic Federation's 1999 Latinos and Giving survey found that two-thirds of Hispanics contribute to a charitable cause, 48 percent give to churches, and 36 percent give to a nonprofit.

According to Cortes (2001), the nation's nonprofit sector has been slow to integrate Latinos into its mainstream institutions and strategies. Organized philanthropy seems slow to respond to Latino community needs and aspirations. Mainstream nonprofit institutions neglect Latinos, and Latinos in return are less likely to view the formal nonprofit sector as a vehicle for addressing their problems, aspirations, and values. Therefore more Latino nonprofits are being formed.

Generalizing about Latino philanthropy is difficult because there are variations, even as there are also distinctive philanthropic traditions that all populations have in common. Latinos give relatively little time and money to mainstream charities except churches. They send money to family, kin, and communities outside the United States. They provide caretaking services to the young and old. They help newcomers to the United States. Hispanic philanthropy tends to be characterized by personal, intimate, one-to-one relationships (Cortes, 2001).

Philanthropy in the general U.S. tradition is not well understood by Hispanics. For them, philanthropy is a "social thing" or good for business. Giving, therefore, is mostly one-to-one donations to relatives or gifts to church. In other words, the idea of organized philanthropy is relatively new, although Hispanics give generously in informal ways and through noninstitutional means.

Fundraisers, however, have shaped the current state of Hispanic philanthropy. On the average, Hispanics receive only fifteen to twenty solicitations per year. Nevertheless, even though this population is generally being ignored by nonprofits, gifts from Hispanics tend to be consistent even if small.

Hispanic culture values one-on-one contact, and Hispanics are more cause, relationship-, and motivation-oriented. Members require a very personalized approach in order to donate to a cause. Hispanic people come from a "high context" culture; they see things in terms of relationships. For this reason, Hispanics have an initial reluctance to go outside of their arena. They will work inside their communities, then go out to support larger Hispanic projects.

Hispanics tend to give to causes that have an impact on their values, beliefs and culture. As many Hispanics in the United States have made gains in the economic status, their values and giving patterns often resemble those values. For instance, it is not uncommon for wealthy conservative Hispanics to give to traditionally conservative causes. Generally speaking, because Hispanics are still in middle or lower income brackets, the appealing causes for Hispanics are often assistance to family members in need of financial or other emergency need; activities that promote their heritage and culture; education, especially in terms of scholarships for Hispanics; social justice issues; community development; and disaster relief for communities or countries in which they have a heritage.

Philanthropy in the Hispanic community is often based on their understanding of giving. Because Christianity is widely practiced throughout Latin American countries and among U.S. Hispanics, and the act of giving is taught as a Christian principle, giving is often seen in terms of time, talent, and treasure. Therefore, giving of time through hands-on involvement such as volunteering is accorded the same value as a cash gift. Also, a cause that is church based is more likely to receive approval than one that is not.

History and politics also have an impact on giving. For instance, governments that do not have accountability to their citizens create a sense of distrust among more recent Latino immigrants. In the United States, local governments are often guilty of the same lack of response and accountability to Hispanic communities. Moreover, Hispanics have not always been treated with the same respect accorded other immigrant communities by U.S. society.

As a result, trust becomes a major issue. The person asking is very important; so are how the request is formulated and the asker's accountability.

A survey of Hispanic professionals who were asked for advice on fundraising among Hispanics yielded these recommendations (Wagner and Hall-Russell, 1999, pp. 102–103):

- "Be sincere in your approach to the community, do not assume anything, and take the time to build the trust needed in order to be accepted by the Hispanic community in which you may find yourself working."
- "Know the community, know the issues, know the language, be in a teacher mode, and don't take anything for granted."
- "Consideration and patience have to be exhibited as a result of the historical neglect by dominant institutions of the Hispanic community. A sudden rediscovery of Hispanics cannot easily undo years of neglect. Be prepared to answer questions like, 'Why are we now prospects when we weren't before?'"
- "Hispanics are always willing to help. You have to be sincere with them. You have to earn their trust because too many people have tried to use them."
- "Listen to the reasons behind established practices before proposing new ones."

African Americans. Data about African American giving in the United States indicates more than 250 years of "philanthropy among friends." Similar data also show increasingly higher rates of giving as well as the use of philanthropic activity to bring about social change.

Based upon the research of Carson (1993) and other scholars, here are eight characteristics of African American philanthropy.

- The "axiom of kinship," meaning shared values and identification with other African Americans.
- The power of "collective giving," in which each member contributes to a common pool.
- The desire to leave something as a legacy to other generations.
- Thanksgiving and joy in giving.
- The importance of seeing the "face" of the need.
- Gifts of time and talent are equally valued.
- Making giving affordable.
- Ownership of the gift.

African Americans often don't view what they do to help others as philanthropy. In a general sense, they tend to help more informally and within families and neighborhoods, and helping other African Americans usually comes first. Philanthropy is perceived as a strategic activity of larger institutions. The church continues to be the primary institution through which African Americans become increasingly engaged in helping others. Giving tends to be validated when the appeal is given by a respected, charismatic leader such as the senior pastor. To this end, a culture of trust is established. Conversely, African Americans will tend to maintain a sense of doubt and suspicion should the appeal lack leadership credibility or integrity.

Moreover, African Americans tend to be reluctant to make donations to general funds and charities, preferring to focus on specific causes and individuals. African Americans consider donations of knowledge, skill, and time to be of considerably greater value than money.

African Americans most frequently support the following causes:

- Assistance to family and friends
- Religion
- Education and scholarships
- Civil rights
- Youth programs, especially for at-risk youth
- Human services
- Health care and research
- Community and economic development

African Americans make gifts through many vehicles, including churches, mutual aid societies, fraternities, sororities and other social groups, historically black colleges, community service groups, and black federated campaigns. Making gifts on a personal or situation basis is more common than on an organization level (Hall-Russell and Kasberg, 1997).

Advice for those who might work with African American causes and donors includes the following:

- African Americans value personal contact over mass-produced solicitations; direct mail is likely to be unsuccessful.
- African Americans are less likely to have wills; only 28 percent of African Americans have wills, compared to 51 percent of whites.
- African Americans see giving motivations as "obligations."
- "Uplifting the race" is a significant motivation.

Asian Americans and Pacific Islanders. There are nearly ten million Asian Americans and Pacific Islanders in the United States and they represent more than forty distinct ethnic groups. Their most significant traditions are helping each other through mutual aid societies, family, neighborhoods, and self-help groups, although Asian American philanthropy is becoming more formalized among more recent generations.

Practices and traditions vary according to how long the donor has been in the United States; there is significant variation because immigration to America spanned from the early 1700s to the present. According to Gow Pettey (2002, p. 108), Asian Americans tend to support programs that strengthen the family, support education, health care and long-term health care for the elderly, and facilitate employer-employee efforts for the poor. They consider philanthropy as a repayment for community debts.

Gow Pettey warns that no single form of Asian American philanthropy exists. Practices are as diverse as populations themselves. The following generalizations, while made cautiously, may be presented. Extended family and ethnic members of their community are more important than organized charity. Sending money to needy relatives and friends in the home country is essential. There is often reluctance to raise money for charitable causes because of a need to "save face" and be successful. Gifts are made to reciprocate instances when they feel indebted; they want to "repay" a perceived debt as soon as possible. Asian Americans tend to give to their own community groups, thereby helping maintain ethnic identity. Planned gifts are not commonly made, and Asian Americans often make gifts to mark ceremonial events, such as births and funerals. There is a tradition of stressing group needs and values over those of the individual. They would be willing to give to mainstream groups if their family association has endorsed the idea. Giving among Asian Americans differs greatly from one generation to the next. Younger generations may abandon the idea of sending money to their parents' homelands. In general, however, most Asian Americans who still have ties to their home countries send gifts of money and material goods back to relatives and friends. Among Asian Americans, giving is often thought of as sharing, not charity.

Asian Americans use five main vehicles for charitable giving:

- Family (in America and in country of birth), extended family, and friends
- Family associations, by ethnicity
- Church or temple
- Ethnic nursing homes, community centers, cultural institutions, civic associations, and sports programs
- Mainstream organizations that have a strong history of serving Asian community

When approaching Asian American population groups, the following guidelines may help the fundraiser in tailoring the funding request:

- Approach them with quiet dignity. Cheerleading is not part of the culture.
- Serve before you ask. If Asian Americans are underrepresented as service recipients, they will likely continue to be underrepresented as donors.
- Personalize. Relationships form the cornerstone of philanthropy, and for the Asian community, this tendency is even more pronounced.
- Language is an issue. Information translated into native languages will have greater impact.
- Members of Asian community feel strong ties to organizations with which they have a history or a connection.
- Memorial gifts are a popular form of donation.
- Remember that family and community are paramount to early generations of Asian Americans.
- Different generations of Asian Americans react differently—those who have been in the United States a long time (several generations) act more like traditional donors.
- Don't insult any ethnic group. Understand holidays, ways of giving gifts, and the significance of certain colors.
- Be sensitive to labels. Explore what is accepted terminology among the population segments you serve and will ask.
- Donors continue to feel a sense of loyalty to programming that is relevant to them.

Preferred methods of solicitation are, in order of preference:

- Mail correspondence from familiar organization
- Personal solicitation from someone known
- Giving at workplace
- Mail correspondence from someone known
- Phone call from someone known

Native Americans. Not unlike other major populations groups discussed in this chapter, Native Americans are also made up of diverse subgroups. What they have in common is a strong tradition of giving and caring for each other as well as others outside of their immediate communities. Native Americans tradition-ally redistribute what they have and are very generous. The distinction between sharing and charity is also important. Black (2001) wrote,

> Native communities are comprised of a network of individuals, families and kinship relationships that is also interconnected with nature and the environment. This connection is made through spiritual values, leadership and cultural roots. Western culture, on the other hand, tends to fit life into compartments–family, volunteerism, spirituality, and community are often separate, for example. Individualism tends to take priority over community. Because of the differences in culture, a wide gulf exists between methods of Native giving and that of Western philanthropy. Goodwill efforts in the Native tradition are holistic in nature, encompassing all parts of the interconnection, whereas Western philanthropy tends to divide giving into categories. Sharing and reciprocity, rather than charity, are a hallmark of Native philanthropy [p. 41].

According to Gow Pettey (2002, pp. 124–125), the most common forms of giving among Native Americans are as follows:

- Informal personal giving
- Public charities
- Tribal giving programs
- Workplace giving programs
- Private foundations

The most common interests for donors are

- Education
- Cultural preservation

- Economic development
- Youth
- Elderly services
- Arts
- Health care
- Rehabilitation services such as drug and alcohol addiction counseling
- Environmental or natural resources
- Emergencies and disasters

Native Americans prefer to make anonymous and need-based gifts. They respond to personal appeals rather than mail appeals and prefer to give to those whom they know well. In Native American tradition, both the giver and the recipient are equally honored, and gifts are passed on. Native Americans also prefer to give directly to the recipients, which are carefully selected.

The preceding summary of philanthropy among diverse populations is concise and covers only highlights. Deeper study is required when considering the philanthropic habits and preferences of diverse populations and tailoring fundraising programs accordingly. Amassing background information will help to reduce fear of the unknown, avoid mistakes in planning an approach to groups or individuals, and remind us that despite the generalizations, the individuals with whom we speak are distinct individuals and different from each other.

Arab Americans and Other Groups. Other populations besides those related to the four major ethnic populations should also be considered. For example, attention has begun to be focused on nonprofit institutions that celebrate Arab Americans, a diverse group of people, including Muslims and Christians, who have emigrated from areas of the Middle East and North Africa. Only recently, according to Blum (2002), have organizations started to systematically cultivate and solicit individual donors.

As with the other diverse populations, complications are caused by some Arab traditions. There is an informal approach to charity. Giving is often based on emotion and not on financial tax or estate planning, and gifts go first to one's family members or directly to someone in need. Arab Americans tend to donate to their churches or mosques and to send money to family members or charities in their homeland before contributing to a U.S. organization.

Arab Americans who have been in the United States for many years may give generously to nonprofit organizations, but at the same time may not contribute to or even know about Arab American groups (Blum, 2002).

Other diversity issues are evident. These include gender, age, and ethnic groups who often do not feel comfortable in being included in the sorts of broad categories that are usually used when discussing diverse population groups. For example, many persons from ethnic groups who immigrated to the United States several generations ago may still cling to cherished traditions and characteristics that set them apart, and these will clearly define their philanthropic tendencies and preferences. Some ethnic groups, such as refugees from the Balkan states, may not find it comfortable to be lumped with white Americans. Also, recent arrivals from Africa may not be compatible with African Americans when it comes to customs and traditions.

It is not within the scope of this chapter to fully explore philanthropy among diverse populations. The purpose has been to study characteristics that provide a starting point—a framework or a foundation—for consideration of donor information and to urge the fundraising professional to not ignore differences in philanthropic attitudes and practices.

Cautious Generalizations for Diverse Population Groups and Philanthropy

Generalizations about groups can be dangerous, even if one's intentions are good. This is especially true when expressing generalizations about those with whom we lack experience or knowledge. Even if the generalizations are not offensive (unlike many that have been perpetuated over time), they may be unrealistic, unfair, and stereotypical. All diverse communities contain individuals who do not closely identify with a specific group and resent being categorized according to racial and ethnic generalizations.

However, generalizations can provide us with some basic information from which we can develop further knowledge that is more specific, accurate, and individualized.

Philanthropy in diverse populations often begins with the nuclear family. Although this is usually not considered philanthropy, it does present a groundwork for developing philanthropic habits and practices. Also, in many cultures, family reaches beyond the immediate members to include more distant relatives as well as those viewed as relatives even though not blood kin. Smith and colleagues (1999, p. 147) refer to these family members as "fictive kin."

Religion often plays a significant role. Special occasions, such as birthdays and confirmations, are a platform for giving and volunteering. The traditions of most religions all promote and teach philanthropic values, although with differing emphases.

Mainstream philanthropic organizations are often shunned. The concept of not giving to strangers is prevalent in most cases. An exception is the wealthy, who may ignore their own ethnic causes and join the ranks of other major donors giving to large organizations and well-known causes.

Other similarities in giving can be seen across cultures. People of color are generous philanthropists but in ways not recognized by nonprofit world and the IRS. Most ethnic philanthropy is informal and not recorded in tax returns and Gallup polls. The following are some identifiable similarities of giving among diverse populations:

- Convergence of wealth accumulation, education, career growth, and increased earning capacity allows many to become philanthropists in their own right.
- For many cultures, philanthropy is seen in the broadest sense—gifts of time, talent, and treasure—and revolve around family, church, and education.
- There is direct and informal support to children, the elderly, and community members.
- The level of immediate need is important.
- Planned giving is seldom a priority.
- There is some distrust of traditional nonprofits.
- Most groups are highly influenced by leaders—religious, community, professional, social, and family.
- Diverse populations often give for reasons unrelated to tax and economic issues.
- Much philanthropy is focused outside of the United States without regard for tax benefits.
- Reciprocity is an accepted concept. Helping those in ways they themselves were helped often motivates giving in diverse populations.
- Caretaking activities provided by government and nonprofit groups are usually taken for granted among populations. This is usually not the case among other ethnic groups, who see caretaking responsibilities as their own.

Responsiveness to Diversity and Differences: Steps to Take in Shaping a Fundraising Program

In commenting on the new rules for engaging donors of color, Carson said, "To engage donors of color, nonprofit organizations must understand the importance and interconnectedness of morality, market and mission" (2000, p. 74).

Newman (2002) points out that the traditional donor pyramid works well for organizations that raise most of their charitable gifts from white donors but that it is not applicable for many cultures because of its hierarchical nature and the element of time involved in the donor development process. She presents a continuum of philanthropy that begins with families concerned with survival and basic needs, moving to those who help others who have less, and concluding with people who will invest in their communities and institutions to accomplish common and visionary goals. The continuum, therefore, as it moves from left to right, involves activities she labels "survive," "help," and "invest" (pp. 14–17). Such considerations may be helpful in looking at fundraising practice and changes that may be necessary to consider when fundraising among diverse population groups.

Conclusion

A review of the literature in fundraising among diverse populations indicates that traditional fundraising principles have to be adapted to changing donor populations. The fundraising professional needs to consider variations on donor approaches, including one-on-one solicitation, direct mail, use of the Internet, and telephone solicitation. Prospect research strategies must be redefined to capture information that is relevant and suitable to diverse donor identification and cultivation. Volunteers representing various ethnic groups will need to be recruited and trained.

Before modifying or enhancing fundraising strategies and practices, however, organizations must commit to diversity, both internally and among constituents and donors; to modifying the organizational mission so that it reflects this commitment; and to providing any necessary training or programs that enhance awareness of diversity issues. To accomplish this, an organization must have top-level leadership support as well as diversity in its ranks. A needs statement should be crafted that identifies the organization's status regarding diversity, its willingness to embrace diversity, and how diversity issues fit into the organization framework. Focus groups can provide excellent feedback and advice. From there, best practices can be developed through study and research, and a transformational program can be established.

Given the diverse populations of the United States and the fact that what we now call minorities will make up nearly half of the population by 2050, nonprofit organizations have a stellar opportunity to increase giving from diverse groups in the coming years. This fact provides our organizations with numerous opportunities to understand and interact with rich differences in languages, values, and cultural practices. It is a movement away from homogenizing everyone toward accepting and embracing cultural richness in our lives.

CHAPTER SEVENTEEN

GIVING DIFFERENCES AMONG THE GENERATIONS

By Melissa S. Brown with Xiaonan Kou

As fundraisers look to the future of giving and volunteering, perhaps no other factor is as important as a consideration of the ways in which generational differences will affect the philanthropic landscape. Research related to differences in giving among the generations shows fairly clear differences in preferences and identities between those born before 1964 and those born since then. These differences are important for a number of reasons, including the need for non-profit organizations to engage the younger generations in their activities now so that Generation X and Millennial constituencies will become the donors of the future as the population ages. The figures show what is at stake. In 2009, adults under age forty-five numbered about 112 million, compared with about 119 million people age forty-five and over (Demographics Now, 2010. Author's note: Demographics Now uses estimates from the U.S. Census Bureau that are based on regular surveys of American households. For the group aged fifteen to twenty-four, the author divided the total by ten and multiplied that result by seven to approximate the number of people aged eighteen and older.). In addition, just over one-third of the families with incomes of $75,000 or more are headed by someone who is under age forty-five (Demographics Now, 2010), and that share will grow over time. This is important because donors who earn the most typically give the largest total annual amounts, and a person's highest earnings often occur between age forty-five and retirement.) The giving and volunteering patterns of people born since 1964 will become increasingly important for charitable organizations in the next two decades, and those involved in fundraising will need to take into account numerous factors that are important to Generation X and Millennial constituencies. Diversity within the organization and the organization's leadership, flexible leadership styles, rethinking appropriate pairings of volunteer and/or staff solicitors with donors, and new ways of describing how gifts achieve impact are just some of the changes under way. These are the kinds of issues that resonate now with Generation X and Millennials, and in which these younger generations differ significantly from the more traditional Before Boomer and socially conscious Boomer generations.

What Are the Generations, and How Do They Give?

There are no firm rules about when generations start and end, and almost all studies show there are "blurred areas" around whatever boundary years are selected. This chapter uses the following definitions:

- Before Boomers: Born 1945 or earlier
- Boomers: Born 1946 to 1964
- Generation X: Born 1965 to 1980 (some end this generation in 1976)
- Millennials: Born 1980 to 2000 (some start this generation in 1977 and end it in the 1990s)

Household Income by Generation

Charitable giving is often managed at the household level, especially when members of the same family share a residence. Boomers account for the largest number of households (forty-four million) in the United States in 2009. Boomers also have the largest number of households (19.3 million) with incomes above $75,000. The next largest group is Generation X, which has 34.3 million households, of which 11.5 million have incomes of $75,000 or more. Third in line are the Before Boomers, with a total of 24.4 million households, with 5.9 million having incomes of $75,000 or more. Figures for Millennials suggest that this generation is still establishing households and seeking long-term employment. Millennials account for a total of 11.2 million households, with only 2.1 million of these households enjoying incomes in excess of $75,000 (Demographics Now, 2010).

Generation X and Millennials account for 13.6 million households with incomes of $75,000 or more—twice as many as the 5.9 million Before Boomer households in this income range, and almost two-thirds of the number of Boomer households at this income level. The future of charitable giving clearly lies with Generation X and Millennials, who are now or will soon be entering peak earning years and assuming greater leadership roles.

The Effect of Cohort and Lifecycle Effects on Giving

When fundraisers look at distinctions in giving among the generations, they should consider the difference between *cohort* effects and *lifecycle* effects. A cohort effect is characteristic of people in the group throughout their lives. For instance, if people who lived through the economic scarcity of the Great Depression have had their attitudes toward money and philanthropy permanently affected as a result, that is a cohort effect. A lifecycle effect changes as people age. An example would be a young person who is more generous in her forties than she was in her twenties because as she ages, she has more disposable income to devote to philanthropy, and perhaps her values or priorities change with age. Continued research asking the same questions over time will help answer these and other questions about lifecycle and cohort effects on charitable giving and volunteering.

After controlling for a number of factors known to be associated with giving (such as income, household wealth, education level, marital status, number of children in the household, and employment status), it is clear that there are distinct differences in giving between Generation X and Millennials and the older Before Boomer and Boomer generations. For Millennials, both the probability of giving and the amount given is lower than for Boomers (Mesch, Moore, and Brown, 2009), while data available for 2006 show that Generation X also give less than Boomers, though they are just as likely as Boomers to make a gift. (In their current analysis, Mesch and colleagues use the 2007 wave of the Center on Philanthropy Panel Study, as analyzed in January 2010.)

Research has not yet determined whether lower giving from Generation X and Millennials is a cohort effect or a lifecycle effect. Lower giving by Generation X and the combined lower probability and lower amounts of giving by Millennials may also reflect the lower level of engagement of people in these generations with religious organizations when compared with Boomers and older. As much as 60 percent of household giving in the United States is directed to congregations, according to the Center on Philanthropy Panel Study, yet Generation X and Millennials are much less likely than older generations to attend worship services and less likely to give to religion, at least until marriage (Wuthnow, 2002).

Another possibility for the lower giving by generations born since 1964—and an area where it is unclear whether there is a cohort effect or lifecycle effect in place—is that when asked questions related to their care of others, Generation X and Millennials give answers different from those of the Before Boomer and Boomer generations. Wilhelm and Bekkers (2010) show that high caring scores are associated with more giving. Mesch and colleagues (in progress) have found that younger generations, both men and women, score lower than Boomers on the caring scale. Millennial men, in particular, score comparatively low on this scale and are among the least likely people in these studies to be donors.

Generational Differences in Terms of Values, Preferences, and Behaviors

Research in a variety of fields has shown stark differences between Boomers and younger generations in terms of values, preferences, and behaviors. Arsenault (2004) notes that Generation X and Millennials "want leaders who challenge the system and create change [and] who are . . . perceived as change agents who challenged the status quo" (p. 137). Schewe and Meredith (2004) assert that Generation X "shows a spirit of entrepreneurship unmatched by any other cohort" (p. 54). A Pew Research Center study (2007) found that 30 percent of Millennials mentioned financial matters—bills, debts, and the cost of living—as their most important problem. These results are before the recession that began in late 2007.

For nonprofit organizations, the generations' preferences for different leadership styles has implications for selection of executive officers, identification of spokespeople, and recruitment of volunteers, especially for fundraising activities. The fact that there are many entrepreneurs in Generation X is important because successful entrepreneurs are among the most generous high-net-worth donors (Center on Philanthropy, 2008a). Engaging Generation X entrepreneurs is likely to be a key component of fundraising now and in the coming decades. The debt levels of Millennials may require some different strategies for engaging a group that wants to change the world but feels cash-poor.

Giving Profiles by Generation

This section presents detailed information about how each generation gives, including the percentage who give and the average annual gift total for religious and secular causes. Data are for 2006 and are derived from the Center on Philanthropy Panel Study, which is part of the Panel Study of Income Dynamics (PSID) conducted by the University of Michigan's Institute for Social Research. The PSID is a longitudinal study that includes more than eight thousand families in its nationally representative survey.

Also included are insights into the motivations for giving of each generation, derived from key studies such as those conducted in 2007 by Knowledge Networks, a nationally representative sample reaching more than ten thousand people (Center on Philanthropy, 2008b), and a national donor survey reaching six thousand people in 2008 (Center on Philanthropy, 2009c).

Shared Giving Characteristics of All Generations

Giving Characteristics. Table 17.1 shows the giving for all households and by generations in the PSID and Center on Philanthropy Panel Study. A majority of households give, and more households give to secular causes than to religion. However, average gifts to religion are much higher than average gifts to secular causes.

TABLE 17.1. GIVING STATISTICS FOR ALL UNITED STATES HOUSEHOLDS (2006).

ALL GENERATIONS	Total giving	Religious giving	Secular giving
Percentage of households giving	65	43	56
Average donation per household making contributions	$2,213	$2,050	$1,011
Before Boomers			
Percentage of households giving	77	58	66
Average donation per household making contributions	$2,672	$2,203	$1,067
Average number of types of secular charities			2.4
Boomers			
Percentage of households giving	70	46	61
Average donation per household making contributions	$2,596	$2,312	$1,227
Average number of types of secular charities			2.4
Generation X			
Percentage of households giving	62	37	53
Average donation per household making contributions	$1,653	$1,649	$797
Average number of types of secular charities			1.9

(Continued)

TABLE 17.1. (Continued).

ALL GENERATIONS	Total giving	Religious giving	Secular giving
Millennials			
Percentage of households giving	39.4	19.3	32.6
Average donation per household making contributions	$753	$944	$353
Average number of types of secular charities			1.4

Source: Center on Philanthropy Panel Study, a module of the Panel Income Study of Dynamics fielded by the University of Michigan.

Religion in this case is defined as a house of worship or the organizing body of a faith group (diocese, synod, or church associations, for example). It includes faith ministries that are financed through houses of worship, such as church-based food pantries. Communities of religious practitioners, such as monastic orders, are also included. Not included are secular organizations that have been formed by religious organizations to offer other types of service, such as aid for the homeless, health care, or education.

Motives for Giving. For all generations, motives or incentives to give are similar when donors select them from a list, as in the Knowledge Networks study, the results of which are summarized in Table 17.2. People in each generation gave the statements similar answers but with different priorities (Center on Philanthropy, 2008b). Across the generations, the top five choices in 2007 for why individuals give to charity were to help meet the basic needs of the very poor; to help the poor help themselves; a feeling of responsibility to help those with less; to make the community better; and to make the world better. However, the generations rank these choices differently, which is an important consideration when fundraisers are considering how best to engage members of each generation in giving. The distinctive giving characteristics and motivations of each generation are explored in the sections below.

Before Boomers

People born before 1945 are now retired or are planning to phase out of their active professional lives. Many will continue to work either part-time or as consultants. People in these generations have been important contributors to nonprofit organizations for decades, through their volunteer work, board and committee service, and financial support. They report having strong feelings of loyalty to charities they have supported in the past.

TABLE 17.2. MOTIVATIONS FOR GIVING BY GENERATION.

	Meet basic needs	Help poor help themselves	Improve community	Improve world	Responsibility to give
Millennials	2	5	3	1	4
Generation X	1	4	2	3	5
Boomer	1	2	3	4	5
Before Boomer	1	2	3	4	5

Note: 1 indicates the motivation most frequently selected; 5 indicates the motivation least frequently chosen.

Giving Characteristics. A large percentage of Before Boomers are donors to both religious and secular causes. In this group, 57.6 percent gave to religion in 2006 (the most recent data available) and 65.7 percent gave to secular causes. On average, donors who are over sixty-five (as of 2007) supported 2.4 different types of secular charities, with health and human services being two groups that frequent receive contributions from this generation. Nearly 43 percent of donors in this group gave to human services and 33 percent contributed to health causes in 2006.

Motivations. In 2007 this generation reported wanting most to help meet people's basic needs and to help people help themselves (Center on Philanthropy, 2008b). In the National Donor Survey, men of this generation, compared with men of other generations, scored the highest on the measure of care. Women of this generation, compared with other generations of women, scored second highest, following Boomer women (Mesch et al., 2009).

Boomers

Arguably the most studied generation to date, Boomers have long been the focus of marketers and are still a dominant economic force in the United States and internationally.

Giving Characteristics. Boomers are less likely to be donors than the Before Boomer generation, but the average total (at $2,596 per donor household) is not significantly different from the average for Before Boomer households ($2,572). Similarly to the Before Boomer generation, Boomer donor households support an average of 2.4 different types of secular charities.

The two types of secular causes that Boomers most frequently support are human services (39 percent give to this type of cause) and combined purpose funds such as United Way or Jewish Federation (31 percent). This generation is more likely to support education (18 percent) compared with the Before Boomer generation (of which 14 percent give to education) but less likely to support health (25 percent, compared with nearly 33 percent in the Before Boomer group).

Motivations. Boomers in the Knowledge Networks study indicate that an important factor in their giving is their desire to help people meet their basic needs. Forty-four percent of Boomers selected this motivational statement. They also indicated that they want to help the poor help themselves (39 percent) and to make their community better (36 percent) (Center on Philanthropy, 2008b).

Boomer women top the charts in the measure of caring collected in the National Donor Survey. Men in all generations score lower than Boomer women on the measure of caring scale. Younger women also score lower in care than Boomer women (Mesch et al., 2009).

Generation X

Despite having fewer members than the Boomer or Millennial generations, this generation has become one of the major creative economic forces in recent decades. Generation X has distinguished itself through its interest in nontraditional ways to give back, including social entrepreneurship.

Giving Characteristics. Generation X does not differ markedly from Boomers when it comes to the likelihood of giving. However, charitable donors of this generation give less on average ($1,653) than Boomers, whose average is $2,596. This result is most pronounced in giving to religion, but it is also found in giving to secular causes.

Generation X's giving priorities include human services (31 percent of this generation give to this type of cause), and the average gift amount from those donors is comparatively high, at over $500. Generation X gives to education at much lower rates and amounts than Boomers do. Among Gen X, 15 percent give an average of $296 to education, compared with 18 percent of Boomers who give an average of $668.

These data do not capture other ways of giving back or providing financial support for efforts to improve the lives of others, such as social entrepreneurship, donations made directly to charities in other countries, or purchases of cause-related items and services.

Motivations. Members of this generation indicate that helping people meet their basic needs was their most important motivation (40 percent), followed by making their community a better place (39 percent) (Center on Philanthropy, 2008b). Compared with Boomers, Generation X scores comparatively low on the scales for empathy and for caring. At this point, it is difficult to tell whether this is a cohort or lifecycle phenomenon (Mesch et al., 2009).

Millennials

By some estimates, there are sixty million Millennials; other estimates put the number of Millennials even higher. But note that the definition of this generation can include people born in 2000, so many in this group are years away from adulthood. The oldest Millennials turned thirty in 2010.

Giving Characteristics. Among those over age eighteen in 2006, about four in ten contribute to charity. This is a lower percentage than expected when taking into account factors such as income, education level, marital status, and other characteristics associated with giving. The unmeasured element here is maturity or even awareness and understanding of other people's needs. Although many in this generation have had an opportunity to learn through community service, that does not guarantee development of a propensity to care and to give. There are not much data about earlier generations' giving patterns when they were in their late teens and early twenties, so it is difficult to know whether the lower amounts here are cohort or lifecycle effects.

Motivations. Millennials surveyed by Knowledge Networks say they wanted to change the world (45 percent) (Center on Philanthropy, 2008b). This was the dominant motivation for Millennial giving to charity. Compared with Boomers, Millennials score lower on measures of care, with a high degree of statistical significance (Mesch et al., 2009). This finding suggests that engaging this generation at this point in their lives might be more successful if appealing to self-interest rather than by stressing responsibility or duty to care for others.

Implications for Engaging the Next Generations of Donors

As Generation X and Millennials take their place as the next generations of donors, there are myriad implications for fundraising practice in the areas of how to engage people as volunteers, whom to recruit to leadership positions, what types and with what frequency to offer "investment" opportunities or ask for gifts, and more.

Volunteering

The nature of volunteering changes as expectations change about how much time people have available and what types of tasks they find rewarding. Generation X, which has many individualistic, creative types, might find it difficult to work in large groups on a continuing basis. Generation X is more likely to take on tasks that can give them chances to develop new skills or test limits in some way (Crampton and Hodge, 2008). However, Millennials are typically comfortable working in groups. In particular, Millennials appreciate having opportunities to play an active role in planning and executing an organization's plans (Crampton and Hodge, 2008). Speaking generally, members of this generation want to do more than implement other people's ideas. They want a seat at the table, in the center of the decision making.

Perhaps most of all, it is important to consider the differences in the social lives of single people versus those who are married or in a committed relationship. Younger generations are increasingly marrying later or remaining unmarried (Wuthnow, 2002), which creates a different social dynamic that organizations need to consider in creating relevant and attractive volunteering opportunities. Millennials in particular seem to socialize in groups of friends (Thielfoldt and Scheef, 2004). One option is to determine whether there are ways to interest teams in tackling projects where they can socialize and help your organization.

Leadership

Generation X and Millennials seek leaders whom they view as agents of positive change (Arsenault, 2004). They also have high expectations about ethnic and demographic diversity (Antigua, 2009). People in these generations might point out quickly what they think might be structural injustices in the sharing of decision making. Nonprofit organizations must actively seek qualified board members from the Generation X and Millennial generations so that the board overall includes various points of view and types of life experience.

Organizational Involvement and Fundraising

Research about Generation X is more widely available than research about Millennials; the findings show that Generation X relates to causes through their personal experiences rather than through social events (Kunreuther, 2003). They also like brevity in communications, often wanting to read something short, watch a video, or access information online (Corbo, 1997, cited in Cordeniz, 2002) and show a preference for Internet-based communication technology (Rodriguez, Green, and Ree, 2003, cited in Yang and Guy, 2006). Generation X also feels comfortable making daily decisions based on information and options available via the Internet (Yang and Guy, 2006). Most important, perhaps, studies find that Generation X values flexibility, feedback, and short-term rewards (Kalata, 1996; Tulgan, 2000; Hornblower, 1997).

For fundraising, the importance of electronic communications to reach Generation X and Millennials cannot be overemphasized. For Millennials, text messaging has replaced e-mail as the preferred communications tool. In a 2005 survey by Craver and others, Generation X and Millennials were less likely to receive appeals through the mail or e-mail than were Boomers. They were more likely than Boomers to donate in response to news reports or advertising. Compared to Boomers, Generation X and Millennials were also more open to the organizations that they have not heard about, while they were less familiar with more established organizations working on issues they cared about (Craver, Mathews, Smith & Company and The Prime Group, 2005).

However, even as social networking provides information and generates excitement, donors still want the personal touch. A study of donors finds that it is important to match the right solicitor with the right donor. Many donors say that "a personal relationship with 'someone like me' is required" if they are to be inspired to give (Forum of Regional Associations of Grantmakers, 2006).

When determining the gift amount to request, fundraisers should consider the likely financial circumstances of the Generation X and Millennial generations, who are likely to be paying off student loan debt as well as possibly devoting 30 percent or more of household income for housing. "Micro" payments, with an annual pledge paid monthly or even weekly on a credit card, can be appealing for donors in these circumstances (Appert and Erickson, 2008).

Some research also indicates that Generation X and Millennials want lots of choices so that they can customize their philanthropic experiences (Brinckerhoff, 2007). This suggests that nonprofit organizations might want to offer multiple activities or programs that a donor could support. This goes beyond gift levels to offer prospective donors options about what "impact" he or she supports.

Finally, gift acknowledgment for Generation X and Millennials should be electronic and nearly instantaneous, with continuing feedback and brief communications likely to help build interest and stronger ties between organizations and donors in these generations (Brinckherhoff, 2007). Short-term rewards are also important, as these generations want recognition in addition to feedback. Rather than relying on the traditional annual report to recognize donors, fundraisers should consider how they can use social media to thank and engage Generation X and Millennial donors.

Demonstrating Impact

All generations like to know that their investments have been well spent. However, one study of donors found that Generation X is even more outcome- and results-focused compared with other generations (Crampton and Hodge, 2008). Fundraisers should use all communications tools at their disposal to demonstrate impact in data and to show impact through stories before the request, as part of the request, and as part of stewardship (Feldmann, 2010). Trends indicate that steady, small amounts of easily found online information may be preferable to comprehensive annual reports and other more formal publications (Brinckherhoff, 2007). Direct contact with beneficiaries, too, can be powerful, as can instantaneous communications via text. Above all, communication should be genuine—Generation X and Millennials tend to distrust communications that they see as being disingenuous or "fake."

Most important, organizations must create communications that are meaningful for their younger donors. Public Allies, an organization committed to developing leadership skills for communities and civic participation, studied Millennials in 2009 and found that they are seeking a sense of mission, acknowledgment, opportunities for continuous learning, bridges across cultural distances, flexibility, and clarity and transparency of process. Although this study focused largely on work and volunteer experiences, these principles apply as well for fundraising (Antigua, 2009).

Conclusion

Engaging the generations in philanthropy—particularly the new donors of the Generation X and Millennial groups—means finding ways to share a sense of excitement and even fun about an organization's work. It also means providing multiple ways for people to engage and being willing to adopt new approaches and ideas for fundraising and building a community of supporters.

PART FOUR

THE ART OF SOLICITATION AND STEWARDSHIP

The chapters in Part Four provide information on special fundraising strategies and approaches. The special methods for fundraising presented in these chapters will aid organizations in their annual fund work and in determining the application of these strategies to the total development program.

Chapter Eighteen focuses on the art of personal solicitation, emphasizing that the act of asking for a gift, when done well, is an opportunity for growing and strengthening the donor relationship. The chapter goes on to offer practical advice on asking for a gift in a face-to-face setting.

Direct mail marketing, the topic of Chapter Nineteen, is a way of contacting large numbers of potential donors, lapsed donors, and current donors of small gifts. Less expensive than more personalized mail and telephone approaches, direct mail is generally the most effective and efficient way to build a donor base or get fundraising started.

E-mail and social media have become important tools for communicating with donors, accepting contributions from donors, recruiting new donors, renewing donors, and acknowledging gifts. Chapter Twenty outlines how these uses of the Internet can be incorporated at different levels of the total development program.

Chapter Twenty-One looks at special events, which are important to organizations. For some they are a way of recruiting new donors; for others they are a way to thank donors; still others use them as a way to engage their constituents. For all they are a public relations opportunity.

The use of the telephone in solicitation and stewardship is examined in Chapter Twenty-Two. Although the telephone has been made more problematic as an instrument of fundraising for a variety of reasons, this chapter discusses how to make the most of the telephone as a tool for effective solicitation and engagement of donors.

Finally, Chapter Twenty-Three looks at effective stewardship as a vital part of ethical and effective fundraising. Although the topics of the other chapters in this part discuss means of asking for a gift, the most effective solicitation techniques will ultimately be ineffective if donors do not receive superior stewardship from the organizations to which they give. Stewardship is what builds the foundation for a deeper donor relationship—a deeper relationship that is often signified by the donor's decision to continue to give at increasing levels over a period of years.

CHAPTER EIGHTEEN

PERSONAL SOLICITATION

By Kim Gattle

Recent research reconfirms that individuals have the capacity and inclination to give and that philanthropy has the power to create meaning in the lives of donors. People are moved to action to the extent that the action has meaning to them; successful solicitation recognizes the forces that motivate people to give. When fundraisers understand that donors will make donations to the extent that they anticipate it will be meaningful to them, it becomes clear that fundraising is about more than soliciting gifts—it is a process of inviting discovery (Ritzenhein, 2000). Successful solicitation results in a gift that is the culmination of the donor's search for meaning. It pinpoints the connection between a donor's deepest passion and an organization's greatest need.

Success occurs because and only when donors are asked clearly——and with confidence, passion, and respect—for a specific contribution. Asking is not a solo act or one-time performance. It is a process—a journey, if you will—that is guided by the fundraiser. Through this process, the donor and the organization discover and then ensure the meaning that can be realized through the gift. The journey requires patience, persistence, and expertise on the part of the fundraiser.

A successful solicitation process recognizes donors as an end in themselves rather than as a means to an end (Buber, 1958). Trust is essential to the process and has a direct impact on the size of a gift. The donor's trust in the fundraiser and organization is strengthened or weakened through each interaction in the solicitation process. The length and complexity of the process increases with the magnitude of the gift.

Throughout the process we discern what the donor and organization know and need to know about each other to create a gift opportunity that offers the essential elements of meaning: purpose, value, and efficacy (Baumeister, 1991). Donors will experience the joy of giving when they are confident they are helping someone and when the gift has the impact they desire.

The Role of the Fundraising Professional in Solicitation

A successful solicitation is not achieved through power of persuasion or charm. It is achieved by the fundraiser's ability to stir the donor's moral imagination, offer the opportunity for the right kind of gift, and ensure that the purpose of the gift fits both the donor's passions and the organization's needs. The fundraiser's role is to engage the donor with the organization in a way that is meaningful to the donor. Although this is personal and specific to each donor, it is not guesswork. There are structures and tools to achieve this goal, and there is a method that we can understand and implement. Fundraisers serve as a conduit for a meaningful relationship between the donor and the organization, helping to meet the needs of both. The potential for success is increased when fundraisers recognize the essential role they play.

Philanthropy is inherently autobiographical. Walt Whitman said, "When I give, I give myself." Giving brings to the forefront life experiences that have been transformational to the donor. Donors have a vision for what they want the world to be like, based on those experiences, and they believe the chosen organization shares that vision and will turn it into a reality.

Fundraisers are not only conduits between the donor and organization; they also serve as conduits between the donor and the donor's vision. Donors are not always aware of their true values and passions; fundraisers guide them through a journey of discovery throughout the solicitation process. The job of the fundraiser is to help donors find the meaning they are seeking through a gift to an organization. Fundraisers may see in donors the potential to create a gift—and connect the gift with their life's story—before the donors see it. Fundraisers who earn their trust will have the honor of helping donors make a gift that is both meaningful and effective.

Strategic Cultivation

Securing a gift commitment is not a moment in time; it is an evolutionary process. Solicitation is the culmination of strategic cultivation, a process through which the fundraiser designs and implements specific steps to strengthen the relationship between the donor and organization, which ultimately leads to a gift.

Why include strategic cultivation in a chapter on personal solicitation? Because asking for a gift is the natural, logical next step in the relationship when—and only when—the fundraiser knows where the intersection resides between the donor's passion and the organization's needs (Fredericks, 2006).

An organization invests in strategic cultivation only for donors whose relationship with the organization indicates both interest and capacity to give a major gift (The Fund Raising School, 2009a). All major gift decisions are the result of a complex evaluation process. The organization evaluates whether the donor has interest, capacity, and willingness to give. The donor evaluates whether the organization has the capacity—in the form of leadership, infrastructure, and expertise—to fulfill the promise of the gift. Strategic cultivation provides the information required by both the donor and the organization for evaluation, allowing the organization to design engagement activities that give the donor what she needs to deepen her commitment and, together with the organization, identify a specific gift opportunity.

Managing the Strategic Cultivation Process

The process is actively managed and implemented by the fundraiser and begins with an assessment of what the organization knows and needs to know about the donor. The fundraiser uses a series of questions to develop a predetermined but continually changing plan for strategic cultivation (The Fund Raising School, 2009a):

- What are the donor's interests, values, and passion, specific to your organization?
- What is the desired purpose and impact of the gift?
- Is the gift a priority for the organization? How will it support the mission?
- What are the long-term implications for the organization in using these funds to accomplish the goal?
- Does the gift provide enough resources for the organization to deliver the impact the donor envisions?
- Who will be involved in the solicitation—from the organization and from the donor's life?
- What assets will the donor use to create the gift? In what form and when?

The cultivation plan is tweaked after each contact and adjusted based on the donor's time line, not the organization's. Through this process the fundraiser becomes a student of the donor. In the process, the fundraiser learns to understand the donor's needs and intentions, mind-set, relationship with philanthropy, world view, perception of the organization, interest, and passions. If the fundraiser is not careful to follow the donor's time line, he takes away an opportunity for realization within the donor of what is important in the context of this relationship. Rushing the process deprives the donor of the full joy of giving and deprives the organization of the maximum amount of funding.

Through strategic cultivation, the fundraiser learns everything necessary to know about how and when to ask for a gift. The solicitation process includes more than one opportunity for asking for a gift. By repeatedly inviting the donor to become more deeply engaged in the life of the organization, the fundraiser is actually asking for the donor's involvement and support multiple times along the way. The fundraiser isn't guessing and hoping for the best or "pitching" an idea and waiting to see whether the donor will take a swing. The fundraiser also is not pestering the donor. Rather, the fundraiser is asking what is important to the donor and then listening and responding accordingly.

The Strategic Cultivation Meeting

Each contact begins with open-ended questions that explore the prospective donor's key interests in the organization. The purpose of the open-ended questions is not to ask for money but to discover the donor's passions so that when the fundraiser does ask the donor to make a gift, the fundraiser knows exactly what the donor wants to support. To gain this knowledge, the fundraiser can anticipate devoting the majority of the time spent with the donor to listening. Effective listening is characterized by the ability and discipline first to interpret and then to build on the ideas expressed by the donor.

A skilled fundraiser uses the natural flow of questions and responses to move from a broad to a specific understanding of the donor's interests. Only after the fundraiser has heard what is important to the donor can he or she share with the donor the things that are important to know about the organization. This allows the fundraiser to position the information in a framework of what is important to the donor, placing the next step in the context of the donor's values (Matheny, 1999). The fundraiser should always recap what was learned from the previous visit and never assume the donor remembers what was discussed earlier. Although it is the fundraiser's hope and intention that this gift becomes central to the donor, it will take reminders along the way.

A successful engagement activity is one in which the fundraiser learns something about the donor relevant to a possible giving opportunity and then creates a mutually agreed upon reason to meet again. The fundraiser is solely responsible to keep the relationship moving forward. The fundraiser and others in the organization will need to stay active and persistent with the donor throughout the process.

Timely follow-up signals that the organization cares about the donor's interests and needs her support. A long time span between contacts requires recapturing and refocusing the donor's attention.

Once the fundraiser has confirmed the needs of both the organization and donor through strategic cultivation, it is time to invite the donor to make a gift. Although the fundraiser enjoys getting to know the donor, encouraging her interests, and creating opportunities for meaningful engagement, when it is time to ask for a gift, the fundraiser may believe that unless he uses the right words, the donor will say "no." There are no "right words," but if the right questions are asked in the right way, for the right reason, and at the right time, the fundraiser will achieve a successful solicitation.

The Invitation to Make a Gift

Through strategic cultivation, the fundraiser has confirmed that the donor has learned everything she needs to know about the organization and that the fundraiser has learned everything he needs to know about the donor. The fundraiser knows what is meaningful to her and has confirmed her readiness to make a gift that is a high priority for the organization. Now how does the fundraiser ask for the gift in a way that will ensure it is a gift that fulfills the needs of both the donor and the organization?

Team Approach

As stated earlier, asking for a gift is not a solo act or one-time performance. Involving the organization's leadership and key volunteers throughout the solicitation process is the most effective strategy for securing a major gift. This is also true when it is time to invite the donor to make the gift. The participation of the senior executive signals to the donor that the organization recognizes that this is a very important moment. It indicates that the donor's consideration of the gift is significant to the organization and that the gift opportunity has the full strength and backing of the organization. In addition, volunteers who are recognized as important to the donor and who have made similar philanthropic commitments can share a compelling testimony about how their support for the organization has been meaningful to them.

The fundraiser provides the continuity in the relationship between the organization and the donor through strategic cultivation and continues to serve in that role after the invitation to make a gift. Thus the fundraiser is uniquely equipped to prepare the team for the solicitation meeting.

Preparing the Solicitation Team

Using the knowledge gained through strategic cultivation, the development officer provides the team with talking points for the solicitation meeting and specifies who is to extend the invitation to make the gift. The decision about whether and when to include written material during the solicitation process is specific to the donor. For example, it may be most effective to ask for the gift and follow up with a written proposal reconfirming what transpired and was agreed upon during the invitation to make a gift. Either way, it is incumbent on the fundraiser to educate the team concisely but thoroughly about all details of the gift opportunity.

The fundraiser shares a list of what he believes could be the donor's objection to making a gift based on what the fundraiser and team learned about the donor during strategic cultivation. This engenders confidence among the team and ensures that the momentum of the solicitation is not derailed by the inability to respond to questions.

The fundraiser guides the team through a rehearsal of talking points, providing the opportunity to practice key words the team members want to be sure to include in the conversation. However, it is important to emphasize that the solicitation is a conversation and not a "pitch." The team should focus on what is important to the donor.

The fundraiser gives the team a suggested time line for each segment of the meeting to help keep the conversation focused on the solicitation. Remind the team to maintain a conversational tone; the team is inviting a gift, not selling it. You and your team will know when to segue to the next stage of the solicitation meeting—and how to sculpt the conversation—by listening actively, anticipating responses, and being prepared to weave the conversation back to the invitation to make a gift. Active listening requires that team members imagine themselves in the donor's position. Team members are engaged in the conversation while observing it. The ability to be both present and transcendent allows the team to listen for concerns that may be communicated through the donor's voice and body language rather than words.

The Solicitation Meeting

Preparation is critical for success, and it represents 90 percent of the time involved in the solicitation process. By this time, the fundraiser knows all that is necessary about the donor and the gift opportunity. If the fundraiser begins the solicitation with precision and care, it will close itself (Edwards and Wood, 1992).

Start the Conversation. Begin the solicitation by thanking the donor for her past gifts, current giving, and volunteering when applicable. Thank her for the privilege it has been to learn more about her, her passion, and her vision for the future. Last, thank her for the opportunity to meet, and remind her of the purpose of meeting.

Transition to the Gift Opportunity. During strategic cultivation, the donor has expressed what she values in the organization's mission. Shift the conversation to a specific gift opportunity by referencing specific things said by the donor that reflect her passion for what the gift will support or make happen. Using her own words is critical to a successful transition to a specific ask. It allows the fundraiser to restate key points about the gift opportunity in the context of the donor's passion and values. Using words you've heard her say lets the donor know you were listening and in turn deepens her trust and commitment to make the gift. If you haven't heard the donor confirm her interest in making a gift, it is too early to make the ask.

Recount what you have learned together as a story of the relationship that has grown between the donor and the organization. This is a story animated by the donor's values, passion, and vision for the future. Tell the donor why this gift and the gift amount are being suggested and that both are based on what the donor has shared about herself and her relationship with the organization. Include a moment of drama in the story in which the future is contingent on the donor's decision to make the gift. Share the importance and urgency of the gift, not in terms of deadline but in terms of an outcome that is dependent on the donor. Focus on the needs being met through the organization, not the organization's funding needs. With sincerity, respect, and authenticity, describe the gift opportunity as something the donor is uniquely poised to take. Reference how the gift will fulfill the donor's aspirations as well as create the impact she envisions.

Ask for the Gift. Then, in three sentences or less, invite the donor to make a gift of a specific amount for a specific purpose, stating the benefits of the gift to the organization and to the donor. Ask with confidence, passion, and expectancy. Donors will be persuaded more by the depth of your conviction than by the height of your logic (Basile, 2009).

Await the Answer in Silence. The next step is the most difficult: stop talking and wait for the donor's response. Although the silence may last no more than a minute, this is a critical juncture in the solicitation meeting. Neither listening nor silence is passive. Silence is *not* waiting to talk while simultaneously crafting a response. Through silence the fundraiser creates a space in which the donor can reflect on what is important to her. By turning over control of the conversation to the donor, the fundraiser demonstrates respect for her and further earns her trust.

Negotiate if Necessary. The larger the gift, the greater the opportunity for success or failure for both the donor and the organization. Therefore, when the solicitation is made, the solicitation team should expect a "no" answer. A no is not a roadblock; it is an opportunity to find out to what the donor is saying no. Respond with confidence and patience. Acknowledge the objection and identify the concerns by listening, then begin to address the concerns through discussion and negotiation.

You may think that *negotiation*—a word more commonly associated with a competitive or adversarial exchange—would be anathema to the almost spiritual process of inviting someone to express her greatest values. However, negotiation is inherent in the determination of a gift that is significant for both the donor and the organization. It is necessary in an exchange through which the donor and organization ensure that their shared aspirations for the gift are realized.

Although it is important to ask for a specific amount within a specific time frame, be prepared to provide options on how the gift can be funded. As you move through negotiation, do not lower the amount of the gift. A set gift level and timing are required to accomplish the impact envisioned by the donor and the organization. Devaluing the gift may negatively affect the organization's capacity to deliver the outcome. To prevent this, in advance of the meeting take time to identify alternative giving opportunities that match the donor's passion, and be prepared to discuss them.

Again, there are no right words, but there are right questions and responses. The focus of your initial response must always be on the donor rather than on the organization. Your first concern is to deal with the specific concerns raised by the donor rather than closing the gift.

Close the Gift. Closure occurs when all parties reach consensus on next steps to be taken by both the donor and the organization, whether for the execution of a gift or continued exploration. Establish a specific time line for following up before concluding the meeting. In all cases, each member of the team should contact the donor again within twenty-four hours.

Close the conversation with the same confidence and specificity you had when asking for the gift. Always include an expression of gratitude for the opportunity to invite the donor to make the gift commitment, and do so in a tone that conveys your confidence that the donor will in fact make the gift.

Beyond Solicitation: The Fundraiser's Role Rightly Defined

The fundraiser's role is to help the donor discover what she would like to accomplish through the organization that is meaningful to her. Although the donor is not giving because of the fundraiser, the fundraiser's mind-set has an enormous impact on the success or failure in getting the gift. Anxiety and fear impact the fundraiser's effectiveness negatively. Asking for money is personal; it takes the fundraiser to places in a donor's life that are reserved for very few people. The fundraiser sometimes fears that he will fail to secure the gift and thus will jeopardize the organization's sustainability. Anxiety emerges when the fundraiser focuses on fear of failure rather than on what is known to be true about individuals of wealth: they have the inclination to give, and their giving provides the meaning they seek in life. The fundraiser must not lapse into the mind-set that he must convince reluctant donors to part with their money. It is important for fundraisers to recognize at all times that donors are not giving something away; they are sharing their resources so that what is important to them is available to themselves and others.

The key to overcoming anxiety is to focus on the donor and the mission of the organization. A fundraiser doesn't need to be anxious when he is secure in the knowledge that he has followed a process that assures both the donor and the organization that all of their needs have been considered and will be met. The fundraiser and donor share a vision for the future and confidence in the organization that it will fulfill that vision. As the fundraiser experiences the joy of working together with the donor toward this common purpose, fear naturally subsides (Matheny, 1999).

The job of fundraising is not really about asking for gifts (though fundraisers must ask), but about bringing a new joy to the lives of donors by helping them fulfill their need for meaning (Ritzenhein, 2000). Through this process fundraisers discover that just as donors are not simply a means to an end, neither are fundraisers. Fundraisers help facilitate and are often present at the defining and exquisite moments when donors gain awareness of their deepest passions. As fundraisers guide donors though their philanthropic journeys, fundraisers may discover the potential meaning that gifts hold for donors before the donors themselves realize what that is. At times fundraisers may assist donors in their journeys; at other times donors' visions inspire the confidence fundraisers need to move forward and ask for a gift. As fundraisers invite donors to discover the joy of giving, fundraisers experience joy themselves.

Conclusion

Personal solicitation is an opportunity and invitation to do something important, for both the fundraiser and the donor. In the words of Dag Hammarskjöld (1983), fundraisers invite donors "to read with open eyes the book (their) days are writing." Fundraisers help donors translate the life experiences and values they hold dear into a legacy of generosity. Generosity, in turn, creates the fabric of our lives and evokes the best in all of us.

CHAPTER NINETEEN

DIRECT MAIL MARKETING

By Mal Warwick

To Hank Rosso, fundraising was "the gentle art." Most fundraisers view direct marketing as anything but gentle—a set of mechanistic, marketing-driven techniques that seem to bear little relation to the major gift fundraising, planned giving, and capital campaigns that are widely considered the backbone of traditional fundraising.

The communications channels that together compose direct marketing—principally direct mail, telemarketing, e-mail, face-to-face solicitation, direct response television, and online advertising—all are tainted with a reputation of being impersonal and unwanted. As part of a comprehensive fundraising program, a strategic, donor-centric approach to direct mail marketing puts to work the methods and mechanisms of an increasingly sophisticated craft.

By providing superlative donor care to individuals recruited through one direct marketing channel or another, and by carefully tracking and respecting their behavior and their preferences, many nonprofit organizations have learned that direct mail marketing can become the engine of a dynamic and lucrative fundraising program, yielding hundreds or thousands of high-potential major and planned giving prospects.

Direct Mail at All Levels

In the years following World War II, mail was first widely put to work to raise money for the fast-growing nonprofit sector as a way to generate gifts from people who wouldn't otherwise be reached by charity fundraising drives. For two decades direct mail was seen as a cost-effective way to secure small donations, mostly first-time gifts. Its function was to recruit new donors. Many charities persisted for years without soliciting repeat gifts by mail from previous donors.

Direct mail fundraising is much different today. Fundraisers can now use direct mail marketing to work with donors at every stage, as follows:

• *New donors.* Surveys show that "I got a letter" is the reason most often cited by donors for giving a first-time gift to charity. And on a much smaller scale, Internet-based direct marketing techniques are increasingly successful at acquiring new donors. For most nonprofits, direct marketing is the most cost-effective means to make the case to broad lists of prospective donors.

• *Active donors.* An active donor is a former first-time donor who has now made a second gift. About one-quarter to one-half of first-time donors never give again to the same charity. In contrast, typically two-thirds of two-time donors give a third gift. Direct marketing, especially direct mail and telemarketing, is widely and successfully used to convert first-time donors into active donors.

• *Committed donors.* Donors who give an average of two or three small gifts every couple of years are the base of most direct marketing programs. But to generate a level of revenue that will help sustain a nonprofit organization requires either much more frequent or much larger gifts. Donors who are unable to give large gifts can express their commitment with *monthly* gifts that, over time, will mount into the hundreds or thousands of dollars in a steady stream throughout the year. Telemarketing, direct mail, and sometimes e-mail are effective tools to recruit and retain monthly or committed donors. (In much of the world outside the United States, monthly gifts are the norm, with donors enrolling as committed givers at the outset through face-to-face, direct mail, or online contact.)

• *High-dollar donors.* Most nonprofit direct mail marketing programs solicit and receive gifts of less than $200 each. Until the 1980s, larger gifts were unusual, and direct mail was only rarely used to ask for them; those that came in almost always represented the spontaneous generosity of the giver, not the fundraiser's intention. In the late twentieth century and early twenty-first century, direct marketing has been used effectively to solicit gifts of $500, $1,000, and more. The appearance, production quality, and message of high-dollar direct mail solicitations are different from the direct mail packages used to solicit small gifts, although the underlying principles are the same. Similarly, telephone solicitations for high-dollar gifts typically involve an organization's most accomplished operators and last longer than other calls.

• *Major donors.* Major donors are defined differently by different organizations. Many nonprofits classify anyone whose annual giving reaches the $1,000 level as a major donor. Others may use $25,000—or even $1,000,000. But, whatever the definition, direct marketing is coming into wider use to cultivate, inform, and occasionally solicit major donors. However, we must not confuse highly personalized direct mail packages, phone calls, or e-mail messages directed to major donors with junk mail or spam.

• *Legacy donors.* With a charitable bequest through a will or a trust, many donors can become major donors. Bequests of tens of thousands of dollars may come from donors with modest lifetime giving levels—typically a series of gifts of $100 or less over a number of years. Many legacy donors have *never* previously contributed to the organizations named in their wills. Donors in higher tax brackets or with more complex financial needs might leave a legacy through some other form of "planned giving" involving a charitable gift annuity, a pooled income fund, or a charitable trust. Direct marketing, especially direct mail, is playing an increasingly prominent role in cultivating legacy prospects and marketing bequests and other legacy giving options.

Direct marketing can be viewed as a flexible set of tools. But direct marketing is not limited to tactical applications in the fundraising process. It can play a strategic role in the life of a nonprofit organization.

Fundraising strategies assist the organization in five distinct ways, not just to raise funds but also to support the organization in the pursuit of its mission. Taken together, the five strategies—*growth, involvement, visibility, efficiency,* and *stability*—encompass the full range of strategic directions a nonprofit is likely to pursue at any given time in its organizational development. Direct marketing can be used effectively in specialized ways for each of these five strategies:

• *Growth.* If growing the donor base is the top priority, direct marketing can be uniquely useful. Donor recruitment is the classical first use of direct marketing. Most nonprofits use it to reach out widely to attract new donors.

• *Involvement.* If the priority is involving its donors—to participate in grassroots lobbying, to volunteer, or patronize its productions—direct mail, e-mail, and online advertising can be effective. Direct marketing can advertise opportunities as well as involve donors. A nonprofit group involved in lobbying might operate an online e-mail alert system or include petitions or postcards to elected officials in its fund appeals. A museum might mail or e-mail free tickets to an upcoming exhibition or discount coupons for use in its retail shop. These are all involvement devices.

- *Visibility.* Many nonprofits are hampered by low public profile and name identification. Direct marketing can often help address this problem while recruiting new donors and generating revenue. The communications can create familiarity with the organization's name, logo, and mission. Front-end premiums included in the mail—such as decals, name labels, or bumper stickers—can multiply the mail's impact by reinforcing the organization's visibility and building its brand. So can e-mail messages that are forwarded by donors to friends, family, or coworkers.

- *Efficiency.* Increased use of direct mail to recruit donors will not help lower the cost of fundraising. Direct mail donor acquisition and face-to-face recruitment through canvassing can both be cost-effective, but they're rarely revenue generators. Telemarketing is even more expensive. Online donor acquisition can also be costly because it normally requires multiple contacts. However, telemarketing, e-mail, and sometimes direct mail can help build a monthly giving program, which is more efficient. Direct marketing techniques can also be used to recruit, cultivate, and upgrade gifts of $1,000 or more.

- *Stability.* An organization that is overly dependent on one or just a few sources of revenue must diversify its fundraising program. When stability becomes a priority, direct marketing can be used several ways: launching a new, low-donor recruitment program; upgrading responsive low-level donors to monthly giving; upgrading responsive mid-level donors with high-dollar solicitations; or promoting bequests and other forms of legacy gifts.

This flexible set of approaches can work in all these circumstances. We will now examine some of the basic elements of direct marketing employed in fundraising.

Donor Acquisition and Donor Development

Donor recruitment and donor development are the yin and yang of direct marketing for fundraising. Without new donors, a donor development program will shrink. Donor attrition through death, changed economic circumstances, attraction to new causes, or other reasons will cause any donor base to decline. Conversely, donor recruitment is rarely cost efficient enough without an intensive donor development program to help a nonprofit realize true value from its new donors. Donor recruitment is usually evaluated in terms of the investment required, or "acquisition cost"—that is, the average net cost of recruiting a new donor (calculated by taking the difference between a campaign's total cost and its total revenue and dividing that by the number of donors recruited).

Donor recruitment usually uses these tactics: mailings involving tens of thousands, hundreds of thousands, or even millions of letters; extensive, high-profile online advertising campaigns; costly television advertising; or face-to-face campaigns on street corners employing platoons of canvassers. The purpose of these efforts is to bring in a large number of new donors at an affordable cost. In contrast, donor development efforts directed at previous donors are designed to maximize the value of existing donors. Donor development is intended to increase revenue and to educate and cultivate donors, increasing their loyalty and responsiveness. The most effective donor development activities are based on the relationships that donors have with the organization. Most donor development efforts are much smaller than donor recruitment efforts, using letters, phone calls, or e-mail messages (although in very large, mature programs the relative sizes may be reversed).

The economics of donor acquisition vary by method:

• Enrolling new donors on the street through face-to-face fundraising is typically expensive, ranging up to $200 per donor. Although these donors normally agree to monthly donations averaging $15 to $20 per month, a year and a half or more may elapse before a charity breaks even on the process, since the acquisition cost and attrition rates are high.

• Direct response television is also expensive. Large charities that can afford the up-front production costs can sometimes successfully recruit new monthly donors via television. But the acquisition costs per donor can be $200, $300, or more.

• Enlisting new donors online typically involves a multistage process. Prospective donors are usually first enrolled as e-newsletter subscribers or grassroots activists. Through repeated e-mail contact, a small percentage will become members or donors. Response rates to e-mail solicitations are small—just 0.15 percent (or one out of seven hundred prospects) is acceptable in most programs. Average first-time gifts frequently approach $100. E-mail may also be used to solicit repeat gifts. However, more fundraisers are experiencing equal or greater success renewing online donors by telephone or mail.

• Limitations of recruitment techniques cause most U.S. and Canadian charities to rely on direct mail for acquisition. Response rates are typically modest, ranging from a fraction of 1 percent of the number of letters mailed to as much as 7 or 8 percent, but typical acquisition rates are between 0.5 percent and 2.5 percent. The rate of response to donor development solicitations is ordinarily higher, ranging from 2 or 3 percent to as high as 50 percent. The average new gift is typically lower than gifts in a donor development mailing because low-level, first-time donors are often not included in resolicitation mailings, and some donors increase or "upgrade" their gifts when resolicited.

Strategies for Direct Mail

Because direct mail remains the dominant direct marketing method in North America, it merits a closer look.

Choosing Acquisition Lists

Donor recruitment requires great skill in the selection of lists. Most lists of prospective donors are an unknown quantity. Because they are not donors, there is no certainty that they will respond to your mailing. Several characteristics help increase the likelihood of individuals responding to direct mail; they are listed here in approximate declining order of predictive value:

- They have written your organization expressing interest in contributing.
- They have phoned or e-mailed your organization asking for information.
- They have previously given to similar causes.
- They have previously given to causes or institutions whose donors are demographically similar to yours.
- They subscribe to periodicals focused on the issues your organization addresses.
- They have previously given to other causes or institutions.
- They subscribe to periodicals whose readers are demographically similar to your donors.
- They have demonstrated their responsiveness to direct mail by purchasing goods—and they share key demographic characteristics with your donors.
- They live in neighborhoods with demographic characteristics similar to those of your existing donors.
- They appear on lists of people who claim affinity for your mission or who have contributed to similar organizations.

Two characteristics stand out above all others: demonstrated donor behavior and proven responsiveness to direct mail. Sometimes what seem to be high-potential lists do not work because they lack these characteristics. Among the best examples are lists of physicians who fail to contribute to health-related causes (unless they're already donors and direct-mail-responsive) and lists of people who have attended a charity's fundraising event. Again, choosing lists for donor recruitment mailings is an art.

Segmenting Your Donor File

Successful donor development depends on four properties of a gift that help determine its worth in the cold arithmetic of direct marketing:

- *Recency*. How recently the last gift was received is an excellent indicator of the likelihood that a donor will respond to another appeal. People who have recently given will give again. Only those who have given *very* recently—say, within the past thirty to forty-five days—are less likely to respond.
- *Frequency*. The greater the number of times a donor has given to your organization, the higher is the likelihood that she'll give again when you ask. Frequency is usually measured in terms of the number of gifts received during a recent period, typically twelve, twenty-four, or thirty-six months. Response rates will be twice as high for a group of donors who have given twice during that time as for one-time donors, and three times as high for three-gift donors.
- *Giving level*. Donors of $10, $15, or $20 gifts can be a reliable and lucrative source of funds as they give frequently. However, gifts of $50, $100, or more produce higher net income. Higher-level donors are also much more likely to upgrade (or increase) the size of their gifts over time.
- *Source of first gift*. Those who respond to direct mail have the habit of responding to direct mail. People who are accustomed to responding to telephone appeals or attending special events *typically will not respond* to direct mail. When selecting donors for a direct marketing appeal through one channel, it's not always wise to include those who've previously contributed through other channels. An important exception: donors recruited online can often be resolicited *more* successfully by telephone or mail than e-mail.

By using all four of these donor properties a fundraiser can fine-tune a direct mail or telephone solicitation so that it is as cost-effective as possible. An effort limited to donors who have given most generously, most recently, and most frequently, and who have proven responsive to appeals sent through the channel in question, will yield the greatest revenue at the lowest possible cost. Selective projects also allow concentrating on donors who have demonstrated the greatest interest in the organization's work, a high priority in donor development. A more inclusive effort may maximize the number of current donors or give everyone an opportunity to contribute at year-end.

Factors That Make the Most Difference

Half the response is determined by your organization's track record and the power of your message, the quality and visibility of your organization's leadership, ties to issues of broad public concern, and the publicity the organization gets. The other half is affected by factors under the fundraiser's control:

- *List selection.* This accounts for 25 percent of the success. The most brilliant appeal for the most dynamic organization in the world won't work if it's directed to the wrong lists of people.
- *The offer.* What you ask for, and what you tell donors they'll receive in exchange, is 10 percent of the appeal. Every appeal must be built around a connection between the offer and the market or intended audience.
- *Copywriting.* The wording of your appeal may account for 5 percent. Direct mail experts consider the letter with a conversational or personal style to be the most important element in a direct mail package. But the outer envelope, response device, and all other package elements must reinforce the marketing. The fluidity and clarity of telephone or e-mail appeals can be decisive.
- *Format.* The size, shape, and color of a mailing envelope, the character of the inserts, and the extent of personalization may all have a significant bearing on the results. So it is in online fundraising as well: the creative choices a fundraiser makes in crafting an e-mail appeal can make a big difference. The right format choices can be as important as the copy—about 5 percent of the total. For maximum impact, all the elements in a direct mail package, an e-mail appeal, or a telemarketing script must fit together to form an effective whole.
- *Design.* Once the format is set, the designer's skill with type, color, and placement can have a 5 percent influence on the outcome whether in direct mail or online.
- *Timing.* Timing usually doesn't matter all that much—except when it matters a whole lot. Seasonality—most notably, the power of the year-end holidays and the December 31 tax deduction deadline—and natural or historic disasters that preoccupy the public will have a significant impact on giving.

Elements of a Direct Mail Package

Direct mail fundraising packages in North America have four basic components: the letter, the outer envelope (or "carrier"), a reply envelope, and a response device (sometimes called a "coupon").

Many direct mail fundraising packages include other elements as well. Brochures are commonly used (although more often than not they depress response rather than enhance it). Other inserts are also popular:

- *Lift letters* (or *lift notes*) in the form of short, signed letters that highlight an important endorsement or a new argument that supports the case for giving
- *Involvement devices* such as surveys, petitions, and pre-addressed postcards to decision-makers in government or the private sector
- *Buckslips* that characteristically illustrate a premium or special benefit available to those who respond by sending gifts
- *Other items* such as copies of press clippings, memoranda from field staff, photographs, or membership cards
- *Front-end premiums* or *freemiums*, the fancy language to describe the freebies often included in direct mail packages to entice the reader to open the envelope (and to induce guilt—such items as name labels, bookmarks, decals, or calendars)

Direct mail fundraising packages vary in size, shape, color, and format. In the United States, standard, business-size letter packages are the most common and normally the least expensive, using 8-1/2 by 11-inch letterhead and #10 carrier envelopes with windows. In the simplest package, the addressee's name and address appear only once, usually on the response device, and are positioned to show through the window on the outer envelope. Larger-quantity mailings may involve unconventional shapes and sizes and include a half-dozen or more instances of personalization, in which the addressee's name appears in many different places. (In small quantities, multiply-personalized, "in-line" packages such as these are often prohibitively costly.)

More costly formats sometimes achieve higher impact. Involvement devices and front-end premiums can also be effective in boosting response, increasing the cost-effectiveness of a direct mail appeal. Direct mail package costs (including postage, printing, and the cost of "lettershopping"—addressing and assembling the contents into packages, affixing postage, and mailing) vary from a low in the range of 40 to 50 cents per package to a high of $5 or more. Ordinarily, less expensive packages are used most widely in donor recruitment efforts, and the more expensive (and more personalized) ones are used almost exclusively in donor development.

Benchmarks for Evaluation

There are three levels of assessment in a direct marketing program: individual campaigns, the direct marketing program, and the development program as a whole. To gain a full appreciation of the value of direct marketing, it is necessary to view the realities at each of these levels.

- *Individual campaigns.* Every direct marketing project looks at the rate of response expressed as a percentage, the average gift, and cost compared to revenue. A donor recruitment effort is usually evaluated in terms of the acquisition cost—the net cost to enlist one average new donor. A handful of exceptionally well-known and well-established nonprofits are fortunate enough to recruit donors at a profit; many others typically pay an average of between $2 and $25 per donor; some are willing to invest $100, $200, or even more because their donors are worth so much more to them. In the case of donor development activities, the key to assessing the results is to compare the cost of the effort with the amount of revenue it generates. Some fundraisers measure the fundraising ratio—the number of cents it costs to raise a dollar. Others calculate the ratio of revenue to cost; still others look at net per donor mailed. Typically, a donor development mailing will generate between two and ten times its cost. Donor development telephone campaigns may successfully operate at levels not much above break-even.
- *The direct marketing program.* Viewing the direct marketing program as a whole requires us to take into account the net *investment* typically required for donor recruitment campaigns. A program focused on efficiency might limit prospecting to replace donors lost to attrition; such a program could easily generate between four and eight times its costs in revenue. A growth strategy that requires heavy emphasis on donor recruitment might yield, on average, only two or three times its costs. Television and face-to-face campaigns tend to be the most expensive, the telephone somewhat less so, and direct mail and online efforts frequently the most cost-effective.
- *The development program.* The principal functions of direct marketing recruitment and donor development are to identify and cultivate prospective major donors and prospective planned giving donors. Thus viewed, the principal benchmarks to evaluate might be (1) the number of direct marketing donors who reach a predetermined threshold (say, $1,000), at which point they become candidates for cultivation as possible major donors; and (2) the number of direct marketing donors who express interest in charitable gift annuities, bequests, or other forms of legacy giving.

In other words, establishing benchmarks to evaluate the success of a direct marketing program requires a clear understanding at the outset of what the program is intended to accomplish.

Ten Keys to Success

The ten most important things about direct marketing are presented throughout this chapter. Explicitly stated, they are as follows:

1. *Direct marketing is a process, not an event.* Direct marketing is a way to communicate with large numbers of people and build rewarding relationships with them.

2. *The true rewards from direct marketing come over time.* The principal virtue of direct marketing is that it can generate steady, predictable, undesignated income. Still, the richest rewards from a direct marketing program may come in the form of bequests or other types of planned gifts—and such a gift may not come until fifteen or twenty years after a donor is recruited by direct marketing.

3. *Cost is less important than cost-effectiveness.* It costs money to raise money. Sometimes net revenue rises when an investment in a mailing or telephone campaign is increased. In any case, the sheer cost of a direct marketing project is less important than its outcome. It usually pays to invest more in top donors, less in the least-responsive and least generous donors.

4. *The list is paramount.* It's worth emphasizing over and over again: the list is by far the most important factor in any direct marketing project.

5. *Next comes the offer.* The importance of the offer you make to the recipients of your direct marketing appeal is second only to the importance of the list. If you're seeking an annual gift or membership renewal, it's important that the offer appear front and center in the appeal.

6. *Segmentation is the key to cost-effectiveness.* Whom you include in a direct marketing project and whom you exclude determines its outcome. It rarely makes sense to appeal to everyone on your donor file. Assessing the recency, frequency, giving levels, and sources of your donors, you can reserve special treatment for your top donors. Special treatment like this frequently pays off in bigger returns in the short run—and more numerous legacies over the long haul.

7. *Annual giving provides the structure for direct marketing.* One of the most basic assumptions in direct mail fundraising is that donors must be encouraged to give at least one gift per year; less frequent giving is unlikely to produce enough net revenue to justify the effort. In many organizations, either a membership program or an annual campaign or annual fund serves as the vehicle to inculcate this idea in donors' minds. Even those nonprofits that maintain neither an annual fund nor a membership campaign are likely to conduct a year-end holiday appeal every year.

8. *Testing leads to incremental improvements over time.* The distinguishing characteristic of any form of direct marketing is that its results are precisely measurable.

If you want to know which of two offers will produce the better results, you can construct a test. Testing allows direct marketers to improve results over time, by identifying (and then putting to work) the most successful lists, offers, formats, and messages.

9. *Repetition is essential.* Success in direct marketing, as in any area of marketing or advertising, requires that materials have a consistent "look and feel" over time. Repetition reinforces donors' views of an organization.

10. *Without timely and accurate record-keeping, direct marketing is impossible.* The donor database is the sine qua non of direct marketing. Without an up-to-date database, fundraisers can't measure results, segment, test, or assess the success of their development program.

Conclusion

To maximize returns and enhance the long-term value of direct marketing donors, fundraisers are using a variety of direct marketing techniques in tandem. For example, telemarketing is often effectively used to increase renewal rates, to recruit monthly donors, to upgrade donors to high-dollar annual giving clubs, or for other important tasks. E-mail and websites are used to supplement donor or member services—with free electronic newsletters, for example—as well as to attract and cultivate prospective donors or members and to reinforce appeals delivered by mail or telephone.

Fundraisers are also coming to understand that direct marketing must be seen as an essential ingredient in an organization's development program as a whole. This requires integrating direct marketing efforts (and the resulting donor or member base) with activities to secure major gifts and planned gifts. This kind of integration is easier to describe than to accomplish, but the added revenue potential it brings is too substantial to ignore. Integration—both with other forms of direct response and with other fundraising activities—is the new reality with which fundraisers must learn to live.

Direct marketing, long the stepchild of the fundraising profession, has come into its own in the twenty-first century. However, all too many fundraisers continue to think of direct marketing in yesterday's terms—recruiting and renewing donors in a stand-alone direct mail program with no meaningful connection to the broader development picture. By approaching direct marketing as the flexible set of tools that it is, and viewing it in terms of its potential to serve major gift, planned giving, and capital campaign fundraising, today's fundraisers can gain an enormous advantage for the organizations they serve.

CHAPTER TWENTY

E-MAIL AND INTERNET SOLICITATION

By Jeff Stanger

The online universe continues to change at a rapid pace. As you are reading this sentence, someone is unveiling a new widget or Facebook application that will change things yet again. Before you finish this chapter, hundreds if not thousands of people will already know about it.

That is the appeal and the concern about online fundraising and social media. It has the power to reach far more people for less investment than any traditional form of fundraising. Yet it is also a constant challenge to those who would pursue it. Attention spans are short, and distractions are limitless. One minute your donor is watching your two-minute video appeal on YouTube and the next she is watching a cat on a unicycle.

It is a challenge to stay relevant, fresh, and remarkable online. However, just by reading this book, you have a distinct advantage and are on your way to having a successful online presence. Why is this so? Because you don't need to have many technical skills or a mastery of HTML to raise money online. The secret to being successful online is to master the tried and true principles of fundraising and then apply them to the online environment. You still need to build a case for support. You still need to cultivate relationships and make a compelling ask. All of those skills are covered in this book, and in this chapter we show you how to convert those principles into widgets and tweets and many other words you are going to have to explain to various stakeholders in your organization.

Continued Growth

Despite the poor economic climate of 2009, online fundraising continued to grow at a higher rate than other traditional forms of fundraising. Network for Good reported that in 2009, they processed a record $112.7 million in gifts, representing a 58-percent increase over the $71.2 million they raised in 2008. They also reported that, although the average gift amount dropped in 2009 ($92 down from $112 in 2008), it was offset by the massive increase in total gifts (Wallace, 2010).

The effectiveness of Internet fundraising becomes magnified in times of disaster. The *Chronicle of Philanthropy* reported that online giving represented one-third of the money given to relief efforts following the tsunami of December 2004 (Barton and Wasley, 2008). Less than a year later, 50 percent of the money raised for Hurricane Katrina was collected online.

Separating the hype from reality is more critical now than ever before, as nonprofit budgets shrink and dollars become more challenging to raise. When put in proper perspective, social media and online fundraising can be valuable tools in an overall fundraising strategy. However, do keep in mind that neither tool will replace traditional fundraising or be the cure-all for bad fundraising strategy. Both are simply tools that can be used to maximize your fundraising success.

Keeping things in proper perspective becomes even more important when considering social media platforms. The explosion of Facebook pages for non-profits has led to a phenomenon called *click-through philanthropy*. The concept: people feel better about themselves when they can show they support a cause on Facebook. With one click, I can join a cause and my profile will reflect that I am socially aware, compassionate, in tune with the issues of the day. It's safe, it's free, and it does not require me to do anything. To be successful at social media, the fundraiser has to turn those click-through "do-gooders" into active participants in the organization's cause.

By the Numbers

The growth in Internet fundraising over the past decade has been remarkable. Consider the following statistics (Estes and Nielsen, 2009):

- The growth rate of online donors was 33 percent per year from 2004 to 2008.
- Offline donors declined 1 percent during the same period.

- From 2007 to 2008, online donors increased 39 percent and offline decreased 3 percent.
- In 2008, online donors accounted for 9 percent of donors and 11 percent of donations.
- The five-year cumulative donor value for those who gave in 2004 was $237 for those acquired online and $86 for those acquired offline.
- Donor retention is still lower for online donors than for direct mail donors.

The impact of social media on fundraising is growing as well. Facebook Causes have raised more than $10,000,000 in just over two years of existence. Half of that total came in the first six months of 2009. A significant portion of the increase can be attributed to the fast growth of what most nonprofits view as their prime giving demographic. According to the Facebook Press Room, women over thirty-five are its fastest-growing demographic; the second fastest is men and women over fifty-five (Facebook Press Room, 2010). It is important to note that with this type of technology change is constant, and these statistics are updated frequently.

Which online tools are most organizations using? The *Chronicle of Philanthropy*'s online giving survey (Barton and Wasley, 2008) reported that 41 percent are using blogging, text, instant messaging, or other technologies to raise money. Fifty-five percent are using Facebook, while MySpace lags behind at only 21 percent. Twitter saw incredible growth in 2009, and as of 2010, 18 percent of nonprofits report using it as a fundraising tool.

Having presented this overview of the growth and impact of online fundraising and social media, in the next few pages we will discuss websites, social media, e-mail campaigns, and peer-to-peer fundraising as available tools.

Internet-Based Fundraising Tools

An organization's online fundraising success starts at home. Or, more accurately, it starts at the homepage. Think of a website as an online reception lobby: it must be welcoming and easy to use, and it must quickly provide visitors with the information they seek. Make a visitor wait only a few seconds, and that visitor will click on something else. A common mistake made by nonprofits is putting all their efforts into their social media pages (like Facebook) and not updating their websites. This is a bad strategy because organic search continues to be the most common activity on the Web, and an organization's webpage is more likely to be the top result of a Google search than its Facebook page.

The percentage of online donations as a part of overall donations is steadily climbing. As online donations increase and put pressure on traditional forms of giving, it is more important than ever to understand this medium and the best practices for online fundraising.

It is important to remember what websites can and cannot do. When designed well, a nonprofit website is uniquely efficient for attracting new donors and creating impulse giving opportunities. They are not, however, as effective at facilitating donor relationships for the long term. These shortcomings can be mitigated by using social networking tools, e-mail newsletters, and RSS subscriptions to grow donor loyalty.

A comprehensive study was done by the Nielsen Norman Group on nonprofit website usability and donor behavior (Estes and Nielsen, 2009). Their findings point to the two most important categories of information users look for when visiting a nonprofit website:

- The organization's mission, goals, objectives, and work
- How it uses donations and contributions

In other words, "What are you doing?" and more specifically, "What are you doing with my money?" According to the survey, "Sadly, only 43 percent of the sites we studied answered the first question on their homepage. Further, only a ridiculously low 4 percent answered the second question on the homepage. Although organizations typically provided these answers somewhere within the site, users often had problems finding this crucial information."

Digging even deeper, Estes and Nielsen studied what caused people not to give, even when they had found the relevant information and had spent significant time on the website. The authors note the two most common factors cited for not giving:

- 47 percent were usability problems relating to page and site design, including unintuitive information architecture, cluttered pages, and confusing workflow.
- 53 percent were content issues related to writing for the Web, including unclear or missing information and confusing terms.

The report also notes that 17 percent of users could not find the donate button due to poor design. This underscores what author Seth Godin (2002) points out in his book *Big Red Fez* regarding website design: "We're all just monkeys looking for the banana." On a website, the banana is the most important bit of information or the call to action. Studies have shown that people expect the banana to be near the upper right-hand position of the website.

Keeping in mind that a website at its most basic is a tool to attract and retain donors, it is imperative that the site speak clearly and concisely to visitors. It must be easy to navigate and easy to understand. It's also important to understand the donor base. There is no cookie-cutter approach to nonprofit website design. Some organizations need to convey large amounts of information. They can be better served by a magazine format site. Others may be volunteer driven and require social networking tools or a higher degree of interactivity.

When evaluating an organization's site, it is important to remember the most common user complaints about nonprofit websites. First is the lack of clear information about mission, goals, and objectives. Second is difficulty in finding quickly where to donate. Third is a lack of clear communication on how gifts are used. Finally, a busy or cluttered homepage turns off prospective donors.

Because there are but a few seconds to grab a visitor's attention before she moves on to something else, here are some best practices for nonprofit website:

- Make sure the landing page says what the organization does and how it spends donors' money. This information should be clear, concise, and easy to find.
- Make the donate button blissfully easy to find.
- Put at least one donate button on every page.
- Offer fresh, updated information about the organization's current events.
- If yours is a national organization, make it easy to find links to local chapters.
- Offer the mission statement on the home page or just one click away.
- Avoid insider jargon. Have an organization outsider review copy to make sure it is understandable.
- Feature success stories or links to them.
- Provide easy access to the organization's annual report.
- Provide leadership information or a link to it.
- Include corporate partners and high-profile individual supporters.
- Keep the look and feel of local chapter sites consistent with the national site.
- Don't require registration for a donation.
- Allow donors to designate donations to a specific program or cause.
- Make your gift confirmation and thank-you personalized and memorable.

Social Media

The power of Facebook as a fundraising tool continues to evolve as more people join and more applications are being developed to assist nonprofits. As mentioned earlier, the first six months of 2009 saw a 50-percent jump in total donations through the Facebook Causes application. Still, the greatest value of Facebook to a nonprofit is a platform for engaging donors and volunteers. It provides an opportunity to grow and maintain relationships in different ways than does the organization's homepage.

Consider the following statistics from Facebook.com, as of this writing:

- More than two hundred million active users.
- More than a hundred million users log on to Facebook at least once each day.
- More than two-thirds of Facebook users are outside of college.
- The fastest-growing demographic is those thirty-five years old and older.
- The average user has 120 friends on the site.
- More than 3.5 billion minutes are spent on Facebook each day (worldwide).
- More than 850 million photos are uploaded to the site each month
- More than eight million videos are uploaded each month.
- More than 2.5 million events are created each month.
- There are more than twenty-five million active user groups on the site.
- There are more than thirty million active users currently accessing Facebook through their mobile devices.

Facebook Cause Pages

A Cause Page is an application that allows the creation of a fundraising drive to support a cause or organization. (Note: Only registered 501(c)(3) organizations can participate.) The first step is to create a profile on Facebook's Nonprofit Partner Center. For large organizations with multiple constituent groups, multiple causes and projects can be created. A Cause Page can recruit friends, spread information, raise money, and feature a specific project or do a general campaign. As of this writing, the process includes these basic steps:

1. Create a profile at the Nonprofit Partner Center.
2. Log into the Nonprofit Partner Center account (http://nonprofits.causes .com).
3. Select the Fundraising tab and choose "Create a Custom Campaign."
4. Select a title and describe the project.

5. Upload a photo that helps tell the organization's story.
6. Set a goal and select an end date.
7. Choose any affiliate causes that can promote the project.
8. Click the "Communications" tab and get the word out to supporters.

Donations are processed by Network for Good. It is a good idea to check to make sure the organization's GuideStar information is updated, as Network for Good will send donations to the address listed. It is also possible to sign up for electronic funds transfer and daily e-mails with a donation report.

Facebook Best Practices:

- Designate more than one administrator for the Page.
- Use the organization's logo as the Page picture.
- Limit status updates to one per day.
- Add the "Causes" Application for fundraising or use one of the other third-party applications available.
- Configure the settings to allow fans to post photos, videos, and links
- Add the Fan Box Widget to the website or blog.
- Add and use the "Links" application to get the organization to show up in "News Feeds."
- Add the "Notes" app and feature it as a tab.
- If the organization has a blog, set it to auto post on the page using an application like Networked Blogs.
- Add a Twitter tab to the page.
- Add a YouTube tab to the page.
- Add the MyFlickr application.
- Keep up on the latest ideas and tools via the Causes Exchange blog (www .exchange.causes.com).

Twitter

Twitter is a micro-blogging tool. Imagine Instant Messaging combined with blogging. It is a fast-growing phenomenon that is being used by nonprofits, political action committees, and candidates to advance their cause. Here are the basics:

- Twitter messages (called *tweets*) are limited to 140 characters.
- Tweets generally express "Here's what I'm doing, thinking, or feeling right now."
- Users can receive tweets on IM, mobile text, or the Web.

- ReTweets are repostings of interesting messages or article links.
- Users can follow friends, celebrities, organizations, and politicians.

Nonprofits can benefit from Twitter in several ways: tracking information related to the organization's cause, monitoring what people are saying about the organization, and listening to what motivates people around the cause. Tweets can be used to notify stakeholders of critical updates and to dialogue with constituents. Twitter has been particularly effective with disaster relief organizations in times of crisis.

The following are tips for nonprofits to make the most of Twitter:

1. *Research the audience.* Your constituents may not be using Twitter. Don't invest time in something that is not relevant to the people with whom you want to communicate.
2. *Be authentic.* The Twitosphere can see right through obvious marketing attempts. Speak with an authentic voice and expect to contribute to the conversation.
3. *Play nice.* Always ReTweet and say thanks. The better you treat your followers, the more of them you will have.
4. *Follow your followers.* This is not a monologue. This is about a conversation, and you cannot have one by not following others. People join Twitter to follow and be followed. If you do not follow them, they will consider it a snub, and you will rarely be ReTweeted. If you are concerned about all the clutter that following everybody will create, use the Favorites option to sort through messages. Remember, Twitter is a community, not an audience.
5. *Tweet blog posts.* This is a simple but often forgotten step. Most platforms (Wordpress, Drupal) have modules that import tweets into a blog and tweet blog updates.
6. *Keep the chitchat to a minimum.* Donors do not care about someone's cat. Save the cat stories for personal Twitter accounts; post only information relevant to nonprofit followers.
7. *Don't use auto-responders.*

Blogging for Nonprofits

The term *blog*, short for *web log*, was coined to describe a popular type of web page. Initially used as a type of online journal or diary, the format was quickly adapted for a variety of other uses. Blogs present information in a reverse chronological order, delivering anything from book reviews to political rants. They can include pictures, video, and probably more important to a nonprofit, a Donate Now button.

There are a number of advantages for creating a nonprofit blog:

- *It is cheap.* Wordpress and Blogger offer free blogs and reasonably priced custom templates.
- *It is easy.* Maintaining a blog is as easy as editing a Microsoft Word document.
- *It is free marketing.* Blogging is a great way to tell the story. Combining blogging with social bookmarking and targeted key words can often be more effective than a press release.
- *It can help raise money.* Think of your blog as a 24-hour fundraising professional. If the "Donate Now" button is nearby, any blog post is a mini case statement for the cause.
- *It builds credibility.* Blogging regularly with useful information makes someone an expert for the cause.
- *It keeps people informed.* Blogging allows communication with volunteers about events and the needs of the organization.
- *It creates a dialogue.* Blogging with the comments feature enabled allows dialogue with volunteers, donors, and constituents.

Basic Blogging Tips

Blogs are written in a conversational style. The language is easily digestible, with short paragraphs and sentences. The typical web user has a short attention span, and long complex sentences will not hold the reader. Blogs must be concise and conversational. One of the big mistakes nonprofits make is using inside jargon. Avoid this at all costs. Assume the reader knows very little about the organization. Whenever possible, include pictures to help you tell the story. Most important, establish a blogging policy with clear boundaries and objectives.

Along with the daily short posts you will be making, you should also add the occasional *pillar post* to the mix. Pillar posts are longer posts that contain timeless, original, and unique information. They are centered on one particular topic and offer deeper insight or expertise on that subject. Pillar posts attract links from other bloggers, are bookmarked more frequently, and are forwarded to more people than regular posts.

E-mail Appeals

Some of the advantages to e-mail appeals include reaching more people for less money than is possible offline. A 2007 report by the Direct Marketers Association states that e-mail returned $48 for every $1 invested (Email Marketers

Association, 2009). E-mail does require more attention to permission than offline appeals do. The concept of the prospecting mailing doesn't apply online; e-mail messages that the recipient did not opt in to—that is, request or agree to receive—are called spam, and sending them can have dire consequences for your organization.

In a down economy, e-mail is particularly effective in helping reduce costs and gather information. If the ratio of physical mail addresses to e-mail addresses is high, it might be possible to reduce costs by replacing a physical appeal with an online appeal. E-mail can also be used to keep top donors informed or reward brand loyalty with freebies or coupons.

To have a successful e-mail campaign, it is necessary to have e-mail addresses. Building an e-mail database takes time and focused effort; it can be started by making it very easy for website visitors to provide their e-mail addresses. Make the sign-up button easy to find, and use language that adds a sense of community to the experience. Invite visitors to join the cause.

Organizations should consider multiple ways for people to join their e-mail lists. Add an invitation to the e-mail signature. Include it on written forms for volunteers to fill out. Offer the opportunity at events. Set up polls or contests online that ask visitors to provide voluntarily their e-mails. Finally, always include a "Forward to a Friend" link in e-mails so donors can spread the word.

Some more tips for e-mail campaigns:

- Keep messages readable and simple.
- If you've got a long story to tell, consider sending only an excerpt and linking to the full story on the website.
- Use a catchy subject line. Like a headline in a newspaper, if it doesn't grab the reader, the story won't be read.
- E-mail only people who have given permission. Remind them how the organization got their information and why they are receiving the message.
- Encourage list members to add your organization to their e-mail address list. This will help spare your messages from landing in the spam or junk e-mail folder and increase the likelihood that images open properly.
- Always include an opt-out link and a valid physical address.
- Commit to replying to e-mails. This sounds obvious, but it is important to consider carefully which person in your organization will answer responses.
- Test and measure results. Share results with team members and strategize on how to improve.
- Send a test e-mail to your team first. This can help you avoid many headaches.
- Be consistent in your messaging and design.

- Handle spam complaints and unsubscribe requests immediately. This will keep the organization from becoming blacklisted.
- Avoid sending e-mails on Mondays and Friday afternoons. Most e-mails are deleted on Monday mornings.
- Create opportunities to connect with online supporters in the real world. Invite them to volunteer, take a tour, or come to a special event.
- Do not send attachments.

Peer-to-Peer Fundraising

Peer-to-peer fundraising ties into many of the tools already discussed and turns constituents into freelance fundraisers for your organization. Using viral marketing, in which current supporters spread the organization's message through their social networks, a nonprofit can launch an effective grassroots campaign for a surprisingly affordable cost. The basic premise behind a peer-to-peer campaign is simple: creating websites that allow donors to register, donate, and build their own networks with little or no technical skill required. It is donor do-it-yourself fundraising—with a little help from your organization.

Typical peer-to-peer fundraising tools include the following:

- Donation mechanism
- E-mail receipt with tax information
- A tool that allows donors to e-mail their friends
- A real-time "thermometer" that keeps tabs on progress
- Tools to allow donors to personalize their page and appeal messages.
- Tools that allow integration with social media such as Facebook and MySpace.
- Options for individuals, organizations, or businesses to participate.

The benefits of peer-to-peer fundraising include increasing individual participation, reaching new donors, minimizing costs while maximizing reach, and shortening the roll-out time for the campaign. Peer-to-peer also allows management of the brand message while enabling donors to personalize it to their experiences. It also gives top donors and supporters a simple, cost-free way to champion a cause.

As an organization adds new donors through a peer-to-peer campaign, it can strengthen the relationship with e-mail communication that is simple and inexpensive compared to print communication. Thus the cost to acquire and retain donors has been drastically reduced. Firstgiving.org, SixDegrees.org, and Chipin.com are examples of peer-to-peer fundraising platforms.

Conclusion

Online fundraising and social media are, or should be, tools in every organization's fundraising belt. They have many advantages and offer low-cost access to a wide audience. They offer the ability to communicate with donors in new ways while providing a convenient platform to donate. Yet for all of the bells and whistles—or bytes and widgets—they still require the application of the best practices of traditional fundraising. Keeping those principles in mind will help a nonprofit be successful online.

CHAPTER TWENTY-ONE

SPECIAL EVENTS

By Roberta L. Donahue

The Association of Fundraising Professionals' *Fundraising Dictionary* (2003) defines a special event as "a function designed to attract and involve people in an organization or cause." Where in this definition does it say anything about raising money? Yet there is a perception that events are a quick and easy way to do just that. Experience has shown, however, that events are neither quick nor easy. Research indicates that most events, when reviewed as stand-alone fundraising vehicles, are not cost-effective considering the staff and volunteer time invested (The Center on Philanthropy, 2008a). So why do people insist that events are a good way to raise funds? No matter what the size of an organization or the problem to be addressed, someone will suggest doing an event. As it turns out, events are neither a panacea nor a curse. They are merely one tool to help donors build a meaningful relationship with a cause.

Three key aspects of a fundraiser's work are cultivation, which seeks to engage and grow the interest and involvement of a donor; solicitation, in which a donor is asked for a gift; and stewardship, in which the relationship with the donor is further strengthened through acknowledging the donor's gift and informing the donor of its impact. Special events are best viewed through these same lenses. Too often, events are seen only as solicitation tools and, frequently, as a passive solicitation or one with little or no mission focus. Fundraisers can identify new measures of success if they use special events as a strategic means of building and strengthening donor relationships.

Cultivation Events

The goal of cultivation is "to engage and maintain the interest and involvement of a donor, prospective donor, or volunteer with an organization's people, programs and plans" (*AFP Fundraising Dictionary*, 2003, p. 35). It is interesting how well the definition of an event fits with the cultivation definition. Optimizing cultivation requires integrating strategies at all levels of the organization for different types of donors.

New prospective donors are on a fact-finding mission when they attend an event for a charity to which they do not currently contribute. Any one of a number of factors may have drawn them to the event:

- An activity, such as golf
- An invitation from a friend
- An honored guest or speaker who may hold interest for them

What portion of a cultivation event should engage the prospective donor in the work of the organization? If the purpose is to cultivate, then part of the post-event review must include how successful the cultivation element was. If a prospective donor had a wonderful time but cannot remember how the organization makes a difference, one might liken the event to an artistic commercial that sticks in the mind but leaves no memory of the actual product that was advertised.

Cultivation events for former and current donors are focused on re-energizing the bond to the mission that exists or once existed. It is the opportunity for former and current donors to share with others why they got involved with the organization and what difference they can make through their involvement, including their charitable gifts.

Once again, what portion of the event will engage the donor in reaffirming the work of the organization? If the purpose is to strengthen the relationship to the mission, what was in place to encourage that process?

Here's how one nonprofit addressed that issue. As part of a dinner/auction, the organization set a small wooden box at each place setting. Prior to beginning dinner, the host asked each guest to open the box. Inside was a wish from one of the clients (in this case, service recipients) of the nonprofit. Each guest was asked to read her client's request aloud. The prospective donors, who had come to the event only to hear the speaker, were introduced to eight lives that the nonprofit was working to change. Those current and former donors were reminded, in a very personal way, why they had become involved with the organization. During the dinner, much of the conversation centered on the dreams of the clients and personal experiences with the organization.

Solicitation Events

Solicitation events are those in which someone asks the guests for "a contribution of money, resources, a service, or opinion" (*AFP Fundraising Dictionary*, 2003, p. 111). Research has shown that the most effective way to raise money is face-to-face, so one might think that solicitation events can be very effective. Indeed, they can be, if they are approached with the same general principles that apply to personal, face-to-face solicitation.

The event must include a social time for exchange of pleasantries. This time allows attendees to get comfortable and to focus on the organization and the mission. Because donors seek positive feedback from other donors or trusted friends, this time can be crucial and must be well orchestrated. The organization's leaders, especially volunteer leaders, play an important role in meeting, greeting, and introducing guests to one another. This inclusion leads to the *involvement* phase of the event. Hosts share their own stories and invite others to do the same. Questions such as, "Did you hear about . . . ?" or "Have you heard about the difference that ABC program has made?" invite participation. Hosts must be prepared to share information or know where the answers can be found at the event. Staff and hosts must be clearly identified. Name tags for all are a must.

It is during the *presentation* that an event really differs from one-to-one solicitation. Visual aids, expert witnesses, and those who have benefited from the organization accentuate the need for financial support and embody the results of a gift. However, there must be an opportunity for prospects to engage and ask questions. This must be orchestrated to enhance success. Hosts can be strategically placed to lead discussions and answer questions prompted by the presentation.

With these steps completed, most attendees will be ready, and even expect, to be asked for a financial commitment. Many will be anxious to hear how they can be involved, having witnessed the difference they can make. The challenge is determining the right amount to solicit from each attendee. There are a variety of ways in which this can be resolved:

- Each prospective donor is given a customized pledge card with the prospective donor's name and a suggested amount.
- The host recommends a range of gifts that is appropriate for the group around the table. This works well when prospects are grouped by ability.
- A suggested minimum gift is presented by the featured speaker or another trusted representative of the organization.

In each case, the host also completes the response device and collects the responses of those with whom the host is working.

Another approach combines the best aspects of events and face-to-face solicitations. The donors join others for the presentation and the excitement of the event, but a face-to-face solicitation occurs before the end of the event or follows the event in a very timely fashion. For this approach, donors must be carefully matched with a designated solicitor already identified. This is a particularly good approach for capital or endowment campaigns.

Stewardship Events

Stewardship is "a process whereby an organization seeks to be worthy of continued philanthropic support, including the acknowledgment of gifts, donor recognition, the honoring of donor intent, prudent investment of gifts, and the effective and efficient use of funds to further the mission of the organization" (*AFP Fundraising Dictionary*, 2003, p. 113). In other words, stewardship events are an opportunity to demonstrate to donors the prudent use of their financial contributions.

Stewardship events are about the donor, not about the organization. According to Penelope Burk's *Donor Focused Fundraising* (2003), donors report that the most attractive things about donor recognition events are

- Learning more about the charity's work (28 percent)
- Seeing others who support the same cause (20 percent)
- Socializing and networking with other guests (19 percent)

That donors want to learn more about the good work the organization is doing should be no surprise. Donors may be viewed as investors or stakeholders, eager to learn how their contributions or investments make a difference. They want to understand the outcomes of the nonprofit's work. They want to build on the connection that has developed. Attendees will share stories, learn new aspects of programs, and hear testimonials that are part of casual conversation. Donors find it reassuring to be in the company of peers who are committed to a cause with no vested interest. Just being at an event with others interested in the mission builds community.

Consider the excitement and feeling of community created by alumni events and homecoming activities for universities. Or watch the excitement in the eyes of a donor who meets the student his scholarship helped. Those stewardship events are critical to building and growing the donor's belief in the mission.

What is the effect on the staff? Are events helping to build community among them? In any organization, special events can be seen as either a rallying point or an unwelcome distraction that diverts energy and resources away from the mission.

Seven key elements contribute to a successful event experience for donors/prospects (The Fund Raising School, 2009b):

- Clear purpose for the event
- Recognized organizational need
- Invitation to participate from others
- Unique opportunities
- Connection
- Tradition
- Value

What if we apply those same elements to the internal event participants—board, management, staff, and volunteers?

Clear Purpose for the Event

Integrated events clearly define what is to be accomplished for all levels of the fundraising team. Team members know the expected outcomes and recognize that this is the logical way to accomplish the goal of the event.

Recognized Organizational Need

What does the organization need from the event? Internally, there may appear to be an easy answer to this question: money. However, that may not be the real answer. As stated earlier, events do not necessarily generate substantial money. The need may have to do with something other than solicitation; it may instead be cultivation or stewardship. Based on this realization, with all the members of the leadership team in agreement, special events can be woven into the entire fabric of a donor-focused fundraising plan. Fundraisers can plan their strategies for donors around the internal need.

Invitation to Participate from Others

Rather than taking it for granted that all hands are on board, the invitation to participate can go a long way to build the fundraising team. Encouraging team members to view events as an extension of their own areas of expertise whether that is the annual fund, major gifts, or planned giving can place the opportunities presented by events in a new light.

Unique Opportunities

Events provide unique opportunities for interaction with donors and prospects. Carefully orchestrated introductions and guided conversations can enable the staff members or volunteers to learn more about donors and gain new insights into donor interests. Post-event activities should be designed in a way that continues the community feeling. Follow-up activities must be included in the original plan. Team members can weave these post-event steps into their overall plans and establish these expectations as part of early planning.

What happens post-event? The obvious tasks include thank-you notes to volunteers, sponsors, and others involved in creating a successful event. But that is just the beginning. There should be a debrief of those involved in the inner circle of the event as well as summaries from hosts, boards members, and other key volunteers engaged in conversations with current and prospective donors throughout the evening?

Donor records will reveal that many of the same donors will attend events. This raises the question: what about the other donors? They share the same commitment to the mission. They may send a gift with their RSVP but do not attend. What could be the problem? Maybe they simply don't care for special events.

If the development officer feels that a donor would be excited about the programmatic portion of the event, perhaps the speeches, the testimonials from those served, and other aspects could be brought to the donor in another fashion. This provides another opportunity to be donor-focused. Asking donors about their event preferences can stretch an event into other venues. Perhaps they would be more comfortable in smaller gatherings. A video presentation of the original program can be brought to the donors and their friends.

Connection

Events can reinforce the connection donors feel to the mission in ways that staff alone cannot. Personal stories of experiences, benefits, and histories with the organization draw others closer to the case for support. In a social setting with peers, the prospective or current donor may be more open to engaging in a way that deepens the attendee's knowledge and commitment.

To maximize the connection, hosts need guidance. They can seek pertinent and critical information that may be missing from a prospective donor's profile. Through casual conversation, a host can learn values, family history, and other involvements. But to be effective, the host must know where to steer the conversation. A report to staff, either verbal or written, helps to make sure that the information gets into the prospect file.

What traits might you look for in a host? The answer is simpler than one might think, for they are the traits of a good volunteer:

- Active supporter
- Effective advocate for the cause
- Reliable and dedicated
- Connected and respected
- Has the time to help plan and attend the event
- Willing to identify, cultivate, and ask prospects to attend event
- Represents the organization without appearing to have a vested interest
- Willing to make a gift at the event, if required

Tradition

A strong tradition of philanthropy is a valuable asset to any organization. Special events can be a part of that tradition, but tradition is not the only reason to continue an event. Staff will appreciate a traditional event if they are aware of the current benefits and how the ongoing tradition contributes to their success as fundraisers and to the success of the organization's mission.

Value

Is there a more effective/efficient way to accomplish the organization's goal besides hosting an event? If the answer is no, internal staff should see the value of proceeding. With the other key elements of a successful event clearly presented to the staff, the value to personal and organizational work will be clear.

The value will be reinforced if a review of *hard* and *soft* goals is conducted in a timely fashion and shared with the team and leadership, including volunteer leadership. The evaluation should be based on the original event plan and on the benefits to other fundraising activities. These might include the following factors:

- Did the annual fund acquire more possible contacts?
- Did the major gift officers feel that donors were brought closer to the case for support?
- Were relationships strengthened?
- Were financial goals met?
- Was the investment of time by staff and volunteers well spent?
- Do board, management staff, and volunteers still believe that this event is the most effective and efficient way to accomplish the goal?

Integrated Events

What makes integrated events different from other events? The difference between integrated events and events that happen in a vacuum can be seen from the earliest planning stage. As a part of annual and strategic planning, dates, times, locations, themes, target audiences, and objectives are reviewed and endorsed by the development team defined by The Fund Raising School (2009b):

- Chairman of the board
- Executive director
- Chief financial officer
- Development director
- Chairman of the development committee

There should be no surprises at such events. The integrated special event is clearly recognized, along with other strategies, for what it can bring to the entire fundraising plan. It is one more tool that all team members can use to evaluate and determine how the event best helps reach fundraising goals.

So what might this mean to an organization? For teams that view fundraising as a holistic and donor-centered calling, events become avenues to accomplish the mission, with the support of the team and volunteers.

For organizations struggling with competitive cultures and tight budgets, events may mean resources expended that would have been more productive as part of another solicitation process, and the result being lost opportunities. As fundraising has gotten more sophisticated, many nonprofit organizations are experiencing

- Inter-team competition
- Silos developing
- Territorialism concerning donors

One or more of these dynamics may be in play if

- Development team members refer to donors possessively as "ours."
- Donors are "protected" or "shielded" from invitations.
- Major gift officers work with their prospects in a vacuum.
- Principals of corporations are viewed as "hands off" for annual fund solicitation.
- There is a feeling of unhealthy competition between different fundraising teams or within teams themselves.

If one of these dynamics appears in a fundraising department, there's a good chance that there are others, even though they may not be blatant. The result will poor staff morale, which is very detrimental to the donors, especially those donors transitioning to a major gift.

Consider, for example, the annual fund that has been working with a donor to upgrade to a major donor level. The donor may be transitioned to a major gifts officer and the annual fund may lose the "right" to remain in contact. The major gift officer already has a full plate. A new donor, at the lower end of the major gift range, is added. The officer may not get around to contacting the original donor in a timely fashion. Now the donor is no longer receiving annual fund information and is not being contacted by the major gift officer. But the silos prevent anyone from watching to make sure the donor is not overlooked and that potential which the annual fund has established is not lost.

Coming together for an event, reviewing the target audience, and accomplishing the goals as a team can help to rebuild morale and, with further work, reinforce bonds within the team.

Conclusion

Many of the tasks of a leader, as set out in John W. Gardner's treatise *On Leadership* (1990), clearly apply to building a successful, integrated event, both internally and externally. The leader must be able to

- Explain the purpose
- Envision the goals
- Affirm the value
- Motivate staff and volunteers
- Manage all aspects of the event
- Achieve a workable level of unity internally and externally
- Serve as a symbol of ethical fundraising
- Provide for a review that allows for renewal

All of this will result in an event that helps staff at all levels reach the ultimate in successful fundraising—getting all the "right things" in place that lead to a gift that reflects the values of the donor and meets the needs of the community served by the organization: the *right* person asking the *right* prospect for the *right* gift for the *right* program at the *right* time and in the *right* way.

CHAPTER TWENTY-TWO

TELEPHONE SOLICITATION

By Jonathan D. Purvis

A nnual giving—in general, and specifically as conducted through a telephone solicitation program—is a complex and dynamic entity. To the novice and the seasoned professional alike, the number of moving parts involved in sophisticated programs can be mind-numbing. As a result, the temptation is to focus on the infinite statistical drivers of programs—completion rate, contacts per hour, attempt limits, and on and on. Although these are clearly important, the essence of worthy philanthropic endeavors is much simpler. *Fundraisers provide people with the opportunity to make the world a better place through gifts to nonprofit organizations.* If we apply that simple principle to all facets of fundraising, organizations, those served by them, and benefactors will find great success and satisfaction.

A well-designed telephone solicitation program plays an essential role in maximizing the effectiveness of any comprehensive annual giving program. Consider the following critical objectives of annual giving and the unique role that telephone solicitation plays in maximizing each one:

> *Educate the organization's constituency*—the personal interaction between a well-trained caller and a prospective donor allows an organization to test and personalize messaging across multiple constituent segments, personalize the case for support based on real-time interaction with a prospective donor, and immediately overcome both anticipated and unexpected objections.

Acquire, renew, and upgrade donors—because well-developed telephone solicitation programs allow for high-volume personal solicitation, donor acquisition and renewal rates far exceed direct mail or e-solicitation results. Furthermore, the personal and interactive negotiation inherent in phone solicitation facilitates upgrading a donor's gift amount.

Establish donor giving habits—a well-planned and executed annual phone campaign can penetrate deep into an organization's constituency and facilitate regular giving across the donor base. Conducted on an annual basis, a phone campaign is vital to creating and sustaining a culture of regular giving.

Provide donor stewardship—whether using volunteers or paid callers, the power of a live and personal thank-you is unparalleled.

Develop prospective donors for major gifts and gift planning—telephone solicitation is key to the traditional annual giving role of developing a broad donor base from which major gift and gift planning donors can be cultivated over a period of years or decades. Additionally, with proper planning, training, and care, the modern comprehensive telephone solicitation program can be leveraged to facilitate direct high-end gift solicitation and even gift planning work.

Because telephone solicitation fulfills these five objectives and provides other benefits, it can serve as the foundation on which comprehensive fundraising programs are built. The following are key concepts to take into consideration in developing an excellent telephone solicitation program.

Campaign Planning

Whether a phone campaign lasts a few weeks or is in operation twelve months a year, extensive planning is necessary to maximize results. While there is no one right way to implement a phone campaign, there are key issues to take into consideration and significant decisions to be made during the planning phase of any successful campaign.

Legislation and Regulation

Laws related to telemarketing are being introduced regularly at both the state and federal level. Although charities are generally exempt from the core elements of such legislation, it is important to remain knowledgeable of the changing regulatory landscape. Although charities are legally permitted greater latitude in use of telemarketing, it is wise to operate within a framework that will be well received by your prospects. This framework should include calling only between the hours of 8 AM and 9 PM and honoring requests to be added to an organization's internal do not call list.

Additionally, there are other regulations related to telemarketing, such as Payment Card Industry (PCI) standards, that govern the manner in which credit and debit card payment information is processed. So it is important to consult with the attorney general's office of the states in which prospective donors will be solicited or otherwise seek legal counsel before implementing any phone solicitation program.

Data

Complete and accurate data are essential to telephone solicitation. Some specific areas are critical to a successful program. At the most basic level, contact information is needed—name and phone number, but ideally home and business address as well. Related to this point, all efforts should be made to capture cell phone numbers and to distinguish this information from landline numbers in your database. Prior gift history is also essential for call planning purposes so that previous support can be properly acknowledged and the current solicitation can be appropriately structured.

Beyond these essential data, it is ideal to maintain information related to spouse and family, volunteer involvement, predictive modeling, and wealth screening. In general, the more data points in the database, the better the opportunity for strategic segmentation. Segmenting an organization's calling helps develop the most personal relationship possible between the organization and its donor base, which in turn maximizes giving.

Budget

Budget resources must always be balanced appropriately across the various functions of a development program. Likewise, developing a balanced approach to the various aspects of phone solicitation is critical to creating and maintaining success. The various elements of the program include donor renewal, lapsed donor reactivation, nondonor acquisition, pre-call emails or postcards, pledge reminder calls and mailings, and thank-you calls. It is important to plan how you will allocate your budget across the options.

In budget planning, it is important to consider the short-term and long-term implications of such decisions. Short-term returns often drive budget allocation decisions, but it is important to consider the long-term impact of annual giving and create a plan based on a multiyear view of return on investment. New donor acquisition is a critical component of any annual giving program, but is also the most costly. It is not unusual for the direct cost to raise a dollar ratio to exceed one to one in nondonor segments if only measured within a given twelve-month period. However, with careful stewardship and deliberate donor retention programming, the three-to-five-year cumulative giving of newly acquired donors will far exceed the initial budget outlay needed to acquire their support. This benefit increases when one considers the total lifetime giving of new donors. Without consistent investment in new donor acquisition, an organization's donor base will stagnate and shrink over time, limiting its fundraising potential.

Use of Volunteer or Paid Callers

The decision whether to use volunteer or paid callers can be driven by budget, organizational culture, and availability of ample committed volunteers. It can also be driven by an organization's primary objectives. There are clear advantages and disadvantages to both approaches.

On the plus side, a volunteer phone campaign not only provides a means to raise needed funds but also presents an opportunity to engage and energize a large number of volunteers in an activity that directly benefits the organization. These volunteers see the direct impact of their efforts, learn about the organization's mission, and take greater ownership in the organization. Although not every volunteer is interested in making direct solicitations, there are ample clerical duties associated with a phone campaign that engage volunteers.

On the other hand, volunteer callers are not necessarily well suited for those organizations that count on their phone campaign to maximize contacts made and dollars raised. Organizations with large donor bases, complex segmentation needs, and an extended calling schedule will likely turn to paid callers to meet these needs. With paid callers, staff can be more selective in the screening and hiring process. More extensive training and higher levels of accountability can be implemented as well. Finally, paid callers who underperform can be terminated. These factors maximize the efficiency and effectiveness of a phone program.

Call Automation

Automation presents an opportunity to increase program efficiency in large calling programs. There are a variety of automated systems with a wide array of functionality and price tags. Good systems properly implemented drive efficiency by automatically dialing the phone, adjusting solicitation levels to match prospect giving history, presenting detailed prospect information, scheduling callbacks as needed, securely processing credit card gifts and much more. Automated systems also increase efficiency when customizable reports can be generated nightly and on demand. The selection of an automated system requires research and discussion with peers who have experience with such systems. Many systems are good but not necessarily good for your organization. Take the time to find the best fit for your particular needs.

Use of a Consultant

Using a consultant to manage part of or the entire phone program is a significant decision and one that should be made in the context of an organization's overall development philosophy. For some organizations, a consultant can greatly increase the efficiency of an existing phone program or provide an easy way to begin a new one. It can also free up the time of current in-house staff to concentrate on other aspects of the development program. Some organizations have extensive in-house phone campaign experience and can effectively manage their program, tightly control their message, and take advantage of opportunities to leverage volunteer involvement. Other organizations choose a blended approach by retaining an in-house phone campaign function to address certain segments and outsourcing other segments to a consultant. In the end, the right decision is dependent on the organization's circumstances, experience, and comfort level.

In choosing a consultant, it is important to conduct extensive research. The number of companies and the breadth of services these companies offer have greatly expanded in recent years. This growth has created a buyer's market, but it has also added considerable complexity to the process of finding a company that is both reputable and a suitable fit for a given program's needs. It is critical to interview a number of companies as well as some of their current and past clients.

Selection is only the first step. The organization needs to work with the consultant before, during, and after the campaign to devise segmentation strategies, provide information for script development and caller training, ensure proper and consistent messaging, track campaign progress, handle prospect comments and questions, and other issues related to the campaign. A successful consultant-client relationship depends on a shared understanding of expectations and regular communication between both parties.

Strategy and Segmentation

Strategy and segmentation are driven by many factors, including the size of the prospect base and the desired number of contacts to be made within that prospect base. For some institutions, segmentation may be as simple as calling a segment of former donors during the annual calendar year campaign. More complex institutions may have more than a thousand individual segments called in the course of a comprehensive twelve-month continuous campaign.

A regular review of campaign strategy and segmentation can yield significant results. Year-to-year performance depends on revising prior successful segmentation plans to adapt to changing characteristics in the program. Analysis of segment performance guides changes and provides strong indicators of opportunities to expand calling, add new segments, and increase the initial solicitation amounts or, where performance results dictate the need to revise messaging, to call at a different time of year, reduce initial solicitation amounts, or cease calling altogether. Constant monitoring of segment results allows the organization to make small adjustments to maximize performance during a campaign as well as fundamental adjustments to future campaign strategy based on a greater volume of past performance data.

Anatomy of the Call

Fundamental to any successful phone campaign is the call itself. While every call is a dynamic interaction between caller and prospect, well-trained callers ensure that each call contains the following key elements.

Pre-Call Planning

This portion of the calling process should not be lengthy, but it is critical to a successful solicitation. It is critical that the caller prepare by making a pre-call review of the prospect's name, place of residence, and giving history.

Introduction

The first seconds of the call are critical to setting the stage for a successful call and building a positive relationship between caller and prospect. Confidence, professionalism, and enthusiasm are essential to a strong introduction. The introduction includes who the caller is and why he or she is calling. Also, before the solicitation is made, the caller can ask for important demographic information—mailing address, e-mail address, cell phone or landline number confirmation, and employer and business information. This early stage of the call is also critical to building a positive rapport between the caller and the prospective donor and establishing an understanding with the prospective donor that this is not a telemarketing call but rather a contact on behalf of an institution seeking support to advance a worthy cause.

The Case for Support

A caller has limited time to complete all elements of the call, so the case for support must be concise, convincing, and relevant to the prospective donor. The caller must articulate the organization's mission, why that mission matters, and the impact a gift makes in advancing that mission. Advance training helps ensure that callers are prepared to convey the case for support confidently and convincingly. Both volunteers and paid telemarketing professionals must understand and believe in the worthiness of the organization's mission to powerfully present this phase of the call.

The Solicitation

There are many benefits to a call that are not directly related to asking for support, but solicitation is the central reason for making the call. As in other phases, the caller must be confident, professional, and enthusiastic. Callers should be deliberate in their tone of voice and choice of phrasing when making the solicitation and should be clear about the action the organization would like the prospective donor to take. For example, there is a significant difference between solicitations phrased as, "Would you have any interest in giving $500?" and "It would be great if you could commit to a gift of $500 tonight! And you can put your gift to work immediately by using your credit card now." Often, the difference between a pledge and a no pledge is word choice and enthusiasm.

It is also critical that callers follow the organization's prescribed solicitation structure. The most common response to any solicitation is "no." Therefore a sound strategy uses multiple solicitations throughout the call. Callers must be prepared for initial rejection and the likely objections prospective donors will present. An important aspect of this phase of the call is to be appropriately, and tactfully, persistent in overcoming these objections by listening and demonstrating genuine concern for the prospective donor's objection, then to present reasons for giving that will resonate with the prospective donor based on the feedback provided. Each organization must determine the level of persistence with which it is comfortable, but it is not uncommon to include three or four separate solicitations in a single call. This is consistent with Hank Rosso's notion of accepting no only after four or five attempts to deal with objections.

Also, it is best to determine a specific amount for each solicitation. For prospects with a prior history of giving to the organization, it is common to determine the solicitation amount based on some multiple of the last gift amount. For example, if the donor's last gift was $50 then the first suggested pledge amount may be ten times that amount, or $500. Starting with a suggested pledge amount that is significantly higher than the previous gift amount provides the donor the opportunity to contemplate a gift amount greater than what they might have considered previously. Additionally, in the event that the initial suggested gift amount is higher than the prospect is interested in supporting, it provides significant opportunities to continue the conversation, provide other compelling reasons to give, and discuss subsequently lower gift levels that may still be an increase over the prior gift amount. For prospective donors with no giving history or other significant data point on which to base a solicitation amount, the fundraiser can create a static structure; for example, first gift amount requested = $500, second gift amount requested = $250, third gift amount requested = $100, fourth gift amount requested = $50.

The Close

The end of the call is a critical time, regardless of whether the prospect has made a pledge or not. It provides your organization's last impression on the prospect. If a pledge has been made, this is an important opportunity to secure it immediately through credit card, capture matching gift information related to the prospect's corporate employer, confirm demographic information, and, most important, thank the prospect. If a pledge has not been made, it is important to end the call on a positive note and encourage the prospect to consider support at some time in the future. Under all circumstances, the close serves as the last opportunity to ensure that the relationship between the prospect and the organization is a positive one.

Campaign Management

Performance measures and data points can be tracked throughout the course of a phone campaign. Some call center managers focus on creating new and more complicated statistics and view analysis as a rewarding challenge to the position. Others focus narrowly on one or two statistics—perhaps total dollars pledged and pledge rate. Regardless of the chosen scenario, it is important to define priority outcomes and then focus on the statistics that help achieve those outcomes.

Total dollars and donors often serve as the bottom-line outcome for a phone campaign. But more specific measures can be critical to achieving larger objectives. The following are metrics to help manage campaigns.

Record Count

The most fundamental element of phone program success is record count, so maximizing the number of records with accurate phone numbers on file should be a constant emphasis. Success in this area depends on regular record updates and data cleansing. Much of this work can be done internally through proper record keeping using regular contact with constituents. Vendors also provide services to assist with this task.

In addition to ensuring the integrity of the data in your database, it is also important that record count be scrutinized to check the accuracy of the data selection used to populate your call segments. This should be well thought out when developing the data selections, and it should also be checked in terms of record counts produced from those data selections. Comparing record counts across a number of prior years will serve as a useful way to spot check the accuracy of the record counts you have selected for each calling segment.

Completion Percentage (Total Completes/Total Records)

Completion percentage measures how deeply you are connecting with the prospective donor base. It is reasonable to expect that you can complete 75 to 80 percent of any given segment, and it is critical that you do so in order to maximize the depth of solicitations made to the donor base. The more completely an organization calls each segment, the more solicitations are made and thus more money is raised to benefit the organization.

Pledge Rate (Total Pledges/Total Contacts)

This measurement tends to dominate the focus of many phone program managers. Determined by calculating the total number of contacts (all pledges plus all refusals) and dividing by the total number of pledges, pledge rate will drive your ability to grow the number of donors to, and total dollars raised for the organization.

Average Pledge (Total Dollars Pledged/Total Pledges)

Average pledge is another core measurement for most programs. Average pledge provides a financial measure and is also a key indicator of callers' skills in negotiating a pledge that maximizes gift support. A declining average pledge can mean that callers are skipping solicitation levels or that the solicitation ladder is not structured properly. A matching gift component incorporated into each call can greatly increase the average pledge as well as the total dollars raised, so many programs will track the matching gift rate separately.

Fulfillment Percentage (Total Dollars Fulfilled/Total Dollars Pledged)

Most phone programs report pledges, but it is essential to focus on the fulfillment of those pledges. Fulfillment percentage should be tracked regularly in terms of both total dollars and number of pledges. A key related statistic is the percentage of pledges fulfilled during the call with a credit or debit card. Credit card payments should be emphasized in the close of any pledge. Successful programs should expect 30 percent or more of phone pledges to be fulfilled through credit cards. Credit card pledges are so critical that many programs monitor this statistic separately.

A low or declining pledge fulfillment percentage should prompt an analysis of the pledge reminder and stewardship process and prompt discussions related to call quality and solicitation amounts. Because fulfillment elements occur "behind the scenes," constant monitoring of this statistic is critical to success.

Completes/Contacts Per Hour (Total Completes or Contacts/Total Calling Hours)

The number of completions and contacts made in an hour is an important efficiency metric and should apply to individual caller performance, specific segments, and the program as a whole. Completions made per hour is critical to help determine the productivity of the staff and program and also to aid in performance projections.

Dollars Per Completion (Total Dollars/Total Completions)

Dollars per completion is the most important statistic for a program. It provides an instant assessment of the three most significant elements of your program: donors (pledge rate), dollars (average pledge) and data quality (contact percentage). This statistic can be measured for the overall program, but it is important at the segment level as well. For organizations with many segmentation possibilities but finite budget resources, dollars per contact is an important way to determine which segments will return the best direct results. This statistic provides an instant snapshot of the health of the program and should be monitored constantly.

Leveraging the Full Capacity of a Phone Program

With increasing demands on annual giving programs, it is important to look beyond the traditional role of a phone solicitation program. In addition to the role already described, consider the full extent to which a phone program can improve the organization's fundraising efforts. Although new ideas are always being developed and tested, consider the following:

Second solicitation program—Donors who have made a gift earlier in the year can be solicited again later in the year. With a deliberate approach and continuous stewardship, a healthy second solicitation program can yield pledge rates of 60 percent or higher, with average gifts that are comparable to or even higher than those found in the initial solicitation.

Leadership annual giving calls—Although phone programs are often used to secure smaller gifts, donors with greater capacity to give can be approached through a phone solicitation for larger gifts. This type of program requires special caller selection and training.

Wealth screening and predictive modeling—Much data analysis can be completed in-house with varying levels of sophistication. But organizations able to invest resources into professional wealth screening and predictive modeling can incorporate these into the phone program. This information will add precision to segmentation strategy, suggested solicitation amounts, and other elements of the phone campaign.

Stewardship—Proper stewardship should be a goal in choosing all elements of a phone campaign. But opportunities to elevate stewardship efforts through the phone program may not be obvious. Asking callers to personally sign thank-you cards between calls and incorporating thank-you segments into the call schedule are two common ways to add personalized stewardship. Even the most basic phone campaigns involve significant resources and infrastructure; these should be used to maximize donor stewardship activities.

Gift planning discovery calls—Organizations with an existing gift planning operation can consider adding a phone component to aid their discovery efforts. Several vendors offer this service, but some organizations are adding this element to their in-house phone campaign as well. Because gift planning is a particularly complicated element for even the most sophisticated organization, adding this element to the phone program requires deliberate planning.

Conclusion

A well-planned phone solicitation program can serve as the foundation of the annual giving program and add great value to the total development program. Phone solicitation continues to evolve in the midst of an ever-changing philanthropic and legal landscape. This constant state of evolution presents challenges but also great opportunity to continue advancing support for an organization. Successful programs are vigilant in monitoring the various elements of the program, and they are persistent in seeking outside input from peers and other professionals. By using these approaches, the program will continue to be a vital element in helping individuals make the world a better place through their support of the organization.

CHAPTER TWENTY-THREE

THE PRACTICE OF STEWARDSHIP

By William G. Enright and Timothy L. Seiler

For nonprofit organizations, stewardship typically means a management function that includes thank-you letters, gift receipts, donor acknowledgments and recognition, annual reports, prudent investment of gift funds, careful accounting, and measurement of outcomes and impact; in short, a high level of accountability to donors and to the general public.

But stewardship is much more than these practices of effective management and carries with it a deeper tradition grounded in spiritual roots. The definition of stewardship gives insight into the greater application of the concept beyond effective management. As Dan Conway wrote, stewardship is "the careful and responsible management of something entrusted to one's care by others" (2003, p. 432). Stewardship is holding gifts in trust for the public good, and serious regard for this trust is the soul of stewardship. Stewardship, then, is more than a practice; it is a practice turning on the proper understanding of an ancient metaphor. *Steward* is the metaphor; *stewardship* describes the praxis (practice).

Today, as Douglas John Hall (1990) has aptly observed, *steward* is a metaphor that has come of age. The steward metaphor ripples throughout the nonprofit and for-profit world as a synonym for both doing good things and doing things right. What does it mean to be a steward? What does a steward do?

The *steward* metaphor has its roots in the ancient Greco-Roman world. In the Greek language the word for steward is *oikonomos* or *oikonomia*, which means "household manager" or "administrator"; what today we might call a chief operating officer, or, in a specific fundraising context, a donor relations officer, or director of stewardship (Arndt and Gingrich, 1957). In practice, the household manager was often a superior or bonded slave who was given responsibility for the oversight of the household, governing the master's other servants and distributing the master's goods in accordance with the master's wishes.

As the late Hank Rosso observed, a good steward is one who practices stewardship as a spiritual exercise, serving as "the conscience of philanthropy." In the fundraising process, stewardship is the sacred trust that nonprofit organizations accept in their role as servants of the public good. They demonstrate good stewardship first by faithfulness to their philanthropic mission, their raison d'être.

Acceptance of the sacred trust in serving the public good motivates nonprofits to say thanks for the gifts they receive. Gift acknowledgment recognizes the bond between donors and funders and the nonprofit as they work together toward mission fulfillment. Nonprofits understand implicitly their responsibility to acknowledge gifts and grants, but they must take care not to handle gift acknowledgment as just an administrative management function. They must say "thank you" with a sense of genuine, heartfelt gratitude, in ways that are personal, prompt, and genuine. A recent study (Waters, 2009) on "measuring stewardship" described fundraising stewardship as consisting of four strategies: reciprocity, expressing gratitude to the donor or stakeholder; responsibility, acting in a socially responsible way for the donor or stakeholder; reporting, keeping its public informed about developments and issues; and relationship nurturing. Grateful institutions do not focus only on their mission; as good trustees they also pay attention to those who have given to them generously. People in turn give to the organizations they respect and trust, organizations with whom they have a relationship. Organizations that take stewardship seriously are careful to express gratitude to donors and funders genuinely as a strengthening of the bond between recipient and giver in service to a greater public good.

Beyond formal acknowledgment/recognition such as thank-you letters and gift receipts, those involved in expressing gratitude should consider making personal phone calls, writing short notes, or even making a visit to donors. Everyone in the nonprofit organization should take some part in expressing gratitude for philanthropic gifts. There's a special role for those involved in securing, managing, or investing financial resources—in particular board members, the executive director, the chief financial officer, the chief development officer, and other members of the fundraising team.

In addition to expressions of gratitude, stewardship calls for a high level of accountability for the wise and responsible use of gifts entrusted to the nonprofit. Organizations hold themselves accountable through their transparency and their willingness to share with donors and the public important information such as the following:

- A clear mission statement along with a description of programs, services, goals, and objectives
- Organizational charts showing the governance structure of the organization (board) and the management team (staff)
- A strategic plan, including evaluation measures
- Overviews of the organization's finances, including sources of income and a case for philanthropic support

Conventional ways of demonstrating accountability include the publication of a strategic plan, today often on an organization's website; an annual report of progress toward goals, including measurable outcomes and effectiveness in addressing community needs; individualized stewardship reports to donors invested in endowment accounts; donor recognition events, from large dinners to small, intimate visits; donor recognition societies; and other means of reporting to donors and to the general public the difference the organization makes in carrying out the responsible application of gifts entrusted to it.

Such wise and responsible use of gifts meets the definition of *prudence*, a virtue ascribed by Aristotle in his *Nicomachean Ethics* to household managers (trans. 1999). The prudent organization earns public admiration in its pursuit of excellence in working for the benefit and well-being of others. In their pursuit of excellence, prudent managers are both accountable and transparent: accountable to donors as to the uses made of the gifts given to them and fiscally transparent in making the public aware of what they have done with what has been entrusted to them. The pursuit of prudence takes the willy-nilly out of the practice of stewardship, for it is management according to plan and mission statement. In turn, prudence creates a circle of trust between the giver and the recipient, the organization and the donor. This is lived stewardship as the "guiding principle in philanthropic fundraising, defined as the philosophy and means by which an institution exercises ethical accountability in the use of charitable resources and donors exercise responsibility in the voluntary use of resources" (The Fund Raising School, 2009a, p. 5.3).

Stewardship is a recognition that what we have—as organizations and as individuals—does not fully belong to us but is "on loan" as a challenge to share our gifts for the improvement of our communities.

There's an element of the spiritual in this concept, and to practice stewardship in this way requires thoughtful consideration of how to use gifts; it calls for discernment. Discernment has different faces as it pursues excellence amidst a dizzying array of issues and choices. In a messy world, how do we assess the purity of a gift? How do we know where to give and how much to give? Given changing laws and cultural shifts, what are we to do with gifts that have become obsolete because institutions or recipients have outlived their charter or usefulness? Living as we do in a flat and global world, what does it mean to be concerned about the distant as well as the near, the world of tomorrow as well as the world of today, the nonhuman world as well as the human world? If we are to wrestle with such questions with integrity, we must take the time to think!

Discernment is taking time to think. As an exercise of the faculty of discrimination, discernment is the wide-angle lens view of a larger world, demanding that we pay attention to what is happening around us if we would court wisdom amidst the murkiness of life.

The practice of discernment has many faces. For the Roman emperor-philosopher Marcus Aurelius, discernment was pursued by keeping a diary, published as *Meditations* (Frank, 2004). Every day he took the time to ponder this question: "How will I live?" In wrestling with that question, Marcus reflected on his perceptions, his judgments of people, his desires, his wants, and his actions as he asked himself "And how well am I serving others?" Marcus's diary was his way of practicing philosophy, as for him "practice meant working daily to change his habits and way of living."

For Benjamin Franklin, discernment meant setting aside a time each day for moral reflection. Every day Franklin took a two-hour lunch break for reading and meditation. At six o'clock each evening he stopped work to devote time to the arts. He retired at the age forty-two to pursue a life of philanthropy, science, and politics. It was his practice of moral reflection that formed Franklin's sense of discernment and "added meaning" to his use of money (Wuthnow, 1996).

For Bill Gates, the pursuit of discernment means getting away for an extended period of reading and rumination. Twice a year Gates shuts down his computer and goes into retreat for what he calls his "think week." In a high-tech world in which we are always on call, Gates is a model of taking time out to think, then allowing his thinking to inform his practice of stewardship.

Today many contemporary philanthropists practice thoughtful giving by way of venture or strategic philanthropy. They go about their charitable giving as if they were making a business decision. Here money is not so much a gift to be given as it is an investment to be made in addressing a concrete human problem. Their investments are accompanied by benchmarks, which enable them to measure effectiveness. Such investors, because they have done their homework, see their investment as a longer-term relationship and the beginning of a transformative partnership (Brest and Harvey, 2008).

Through the exercise of discernment, we are put in touch with our own story and the passions and life experiences that have shaped us. The contemporary philosopher Alasdair MacIntyre notes that we humans are "essentially story-telling animals . . . tellers of stories that aspire to truth." He then writes: "I can only answer the question 'what am I to do?' if I can answer the prior question of what story or stories do I find myself to be a part?" (1984, p. 216). Discernment is the compass that gives the practice of stewardship direction and purpose.

For fundraisers who take this discernment concept seriously, their stewardship role is to guide donors to discerning how best to make philanthropic gifts. In guiding the discernment process, the fundraiser poses the following questions to donors, as suggested by Schervish in his work on the motivations of the wealthy:

Is there something

1. You want to do with your wealth;
2. That fulfills the needs of others;
3. That you can do more efficiently and more effectively than government or commerce; and
4. That expresses your gratitude, brings you satisfaction, and actualizes your identification with the fate of others? (2000b, p. 19)

As described by Schervish, such a discernment or inclination model is an honorable form of stewardship for donor and fundraiser.

Conclusion

It is through the practice of good stewardship that we as humans express love for the world. This love is often displayed by generosity to organizations voluntarily serving the greater common good, the public good, that is addressed by nonprofit organizations in their quest to create a tomorrow that is better than today. This is philanthropy, practiced most effectively through intentional stewardship—the prudent and effective use of entrusted resources for their more abundant application for the good of others. For fundraisers, stewardship is the practice of genuine gratitude thoughtfully expressed to givers. Stewardship is an understanding of fundraising as servant to philanthropy. In the words of Hank Rosso, expressed and lived today through The Fund Raising School, good stewardship views fundraising as the gentle art of teaching the joy of giving.

PART FIVE

INVOLVING VOLUNTEERS IN FUNDRAISING

Volunteers are a vital but often underused resource in fundraising, offering organizations not only their time and skills but also their social networks and community connections. This part focuses on volunteer management, leadership, and engagement for fundraising at all levels—from the first-time volunteer to the seasoned board member. It is this sort of focus on engagement of volunteers that is an important but too often overlooked aspect of building relationships with supporters throughout the organization.

Chapter Twenty-Four discusses the trustee's role in fundraising, exploring what it means to be entrusted with the welfare of the community or cause represented by the organization as well as offering practical advice for helping trustees assume their fundraising responsibilities.

Chapter Twenty-Five looks at volunteer management, focusing on how to make the volunteer experience engaging by structuring the experience so volunteers are integrated into the work of the organization in a meaningful way.

Chapter Twenty-Six takes another look at social media, this time from the perspective of how to use its capabilities to capture the imagination of volunteers and supporters and keep them connected with the organization.

CHAPTER TWENTY-FOUR

THE TRUSTEE'S ROLE IN FUNDRAISING

By Ted R. Grossnickle

Trusteeship is a covenant. As the name suggests, trustees are *entrusted* with the future of an organization and its sustained ability to carry out its mission. As David H. Smith (1995) notes, trustees as individuals should be reflective, and the board as a whole should be a "community of inquiry, more precisely, a community of interpretation" (p. ix). The best boards are those that get this right. They are reflective, internalizing the organization's mission; but they are also biased toward action, particularly in the area of securing the organization's future. As long as a trustee is engaged with an organization, there are things that the organization may rightfully expect from the trustee. One of these, of course, is fundraising.

Unfortunately, not all boards meet this standard. The expression "give, get, or get off" and the injunction to contribute "wealth, work, and wisdom" have been uttered too often by too many boards. Like magic incantations, these phrases are believed to have power by virtue of the belief that they reveal an essential collective understanding about the role of a board member. Such an unreflective approach to trusteeship ignores what Smith points out as being at the heart of the matter: the trustees' role as a collective moral authority charged with the well-being of the nonprofit organization—and, by extension, with the well-being of the entire sector. As Smith so rightly expresses,

> The fact that a board of trustees should see itself as a community of
> interpretation has very important implications for the life and ethos of the

board. It must be a community in which persons can and do talk seriously with each other about organizational purpose. The boardroom should be the place where past and future, particularity and the common good, are reconciled (1995, p. 24).

In the aftermath of the scandals inspiring the Sarbanes-Oxley Act, Smith's sentiments seem prescient. There has never been a greater need or a better time for a careful review of trusteeship and its elements. So as this chapter focuses on best practices for the trustee in fundraising, it attempts to do so within a context of the larger requirements of sound and ethical trusteeship—and indeed sees fundraising as a key means by which the role of trusteeship may be performed better and with more clarity and success. After all, fundraising concerns much more than money. In practice, fundraising constitutes one of the most effective arenas in which trustees can practice the skills that make them better trustees overall. This is because active involvement in fundraising necessarily calls for talking authentically about organizational purpose, reconciling where the organization has been with where its future lies, and harmonizing the philanthropic wishes of the individual donor with the organization's plans.

Understanding the Context for Fundraising

To be successful in the fundraising role, trustees must have a context for action. Organizations that communicate clearly to their board members why private support is required, how it is used, its role in the general budget and long-term organizational strategy, and the organization's history of support have taken an important first step to prepare their boards to be effective in fundraising. Trustees expect staff to provide them with clear and honest data, sound tactical thinking, and strategic implications leading to recommended actions. If the board is to think strategically about what best serves the organization and its fundraising, then staff must provide focused materials that raise key issues and offer relevant data for decision making.

This effort should start with a carefully planned and conducted board orientation that presents the context for the organization's fundraising, including current data as well as an overview of prior annual campaigns, capital campaigns, and other significant fundraising efforts. Providing this information as part of the trustee's introduction to this leadership role not only informs the trustee about the status of the organization's fundraising but also indicates that fundraising is indeed an organizational priority in which trustees should expect to be involved.

One of the most important things to include in the fundraising overview provided to trustees is an authentic recounting of the most important lessons learned from prior fundraising efforts—both successes and challenges. To help trustees understand fundraising at the organization, the information provided should not be limited to data alone. Experienced fundraisers know that stories— particularly the ones that over time have helped to shape the culture of philanthropy at the organization—can be a vital tool for helping trustees understand the evolution of the organization's fundraising. Stories of generosity and donor response or of gifts that have changed or transformed the organization provide trustees with a valuable sense of the role of philanthropy at the organization; over time, they create a shared history and community of understanding and interpretation around philanthropy, as Smith might suggest. Bringing questions and issues in philanthropy to life by including them in regular communications with trustees strengthens organizational fundraising by driving home the idea that philanthropy is an integral part of the organization and not just an ancillary activity for trustees.

Acting as a Sounding Board for Fundraising Strategy

A key role of a trustee is to help ensure that the organization's fundraising is based on a solid foundation. Trustees must understand the fundraising plans and strategies presented to them as well as offer constructive feedback from their perspective as volunteer leaders of the organization. To this end, the best trustees ask questions that ensure that the fundraising strategies and tactics employed by the organization are based on reliable data, good intuition, and sound practices. These questions may include the following:

- Are fundraising plans based on solid research and data? What missed opportunities could be captured? What obstacles stand in the way of success?
- Will the approach being suggested appeal to the organization's key donors?
- If a campaign is being considered, has a test of feasibility been conducted?
- Is the organization prepared to implement its fundraising plans and committed to achieving greater success?

Trustees must play an active and inquiring role in vetting organizational fundraising plans so that, in crafting its fundraising strategies, the organization has the benefit of the knowledge not only of its professional fundraising staff but also of its volunteer leadership.

Owning Fundraising Decisions

Unilateral decisions seldom work well in philanthropy and certainly do not work for boards of trustees. Every fundraising effort, whether it is for annual operations or for multiple years and hundreds of millions of dollars, should be discussed, understood, and approved by the board. Trustees must be confident that the fundraising effort has been well planned and that the goal, the volunteer leadership, the main strategic elements, and the cost all have been tailored to fit the organization's goals and needs.

This is important not only in terms of best practices but also to create ownership by the board of the organization's fundraising. If board members are asked to approve a fundraising effort, they are also implicitly being asked to support it both with a personal gift and through their ongoing efforts to help the organization raise funds. When board members vote to approve a fundraising plan in which they've been actively consulted and engaged, they own the plan. Beware the board that offers the "sure, that's fine" response to a fundraising plan. If the board has neither engaged in significant discussion of the plan nor asked probing questions, it is usually a sign either that board members are assuming little will be required of them or that they are not really planning to make significant gifts.

Once a fundraising effort is under way, trustees should receive regular updates containing not only recent gift totals but also indicators of overall success, timelines and milestones, and other information that can help them in giving informed advice and taking action to help ensure the success of the effort. Reviewing and interpreting gift results and assisting in crafting solicitation strategies for selected individuals are only two of the many ways in which board members can and should be actively engaged in organizational fundraising.

Working with Donors

Each trustee can be fully engaged in organizational fundraising without having to be an expert in every aspect of the enterprise. So many trustees worry about their ability or effectiveness in identifying, cultivating, and soliciting donors. Perhaps a sensible approach is to "lower the temperature" a bit on expectations. This is not to suggest that trustees should be let off the hook when it comes to fundraising. Rather, it may be more fruitful to recalibrate expectations by saying that some board members are adept at particular aspects of the fundraising cycle and others are not. However, each trustee has a duty to learn how to be very effective in at least one aspect of fundraising, and it is a best practice for a board to have many trustees who can participate successfully in several aspects of fundraising activity. That is how boards greatly increase support for their organizations, for it is a rare organization that achieves real greatness in philanthropy by relying year after year on only a few trustees to be actively involved in fundraising.

Donor Identification, Qualification, and Engagement Strategies

Identification of prospective donors is one area in which trustees can be of great help to the organization. Through their social and business networks, trustees are very likely to come into contact with persons who have accomplished a great deal, have the capacity to be generous, and may be intrigued about learning more about the organization on whose board the trustees serves. Fundraisers can help trustees understand that prospective donor identification is part of the fundraising process, asking trustees to share with the fundraising staff the names of individuals who might be interested in being introduced to the organization and its cause. Fundraisers should also ask trustees to participate in donor rating sessions—sometimes known as peer screening sessions—during which trustees and other key volunteers are asked to help identify which prospective donors might be interested in making a gift and what an appropriate gift range for those individuals might be.

Donor Cultivation

Cultivation of prospective donors takes trustees a step closer to authentic engagement in fundraising. Through cultivating prospective donors, trustees not only help build the relationships on which successful fundraising thrives but also have the opportunity to remember what it was that drew them closer to the organization before they became trustees. It is an incredibly rewarding feeling for trustees to see how their encouragement, personal giving, and quiet endorsement of an organization can make others want to do the same. Even more fulfilling for a trustee is to watch someone make a transformational gift to the organization that improves the lives of those the organization serves.

Throughout the cultivation process, it is important for the trustee to be reminded that interaction and coordination with fundraising staff is critical. The best results usually occur when fundraising staff have worked with the board member to create an appropriate context for introducing the prospective donor to the organization, whether that is an event, a special initiative, or a challenge. This is a case where two heads are better than one, and a close partnership between the board member and fundraising staff will almost always make the approach and engagement of a new donor easier, more fun, and more likely to be successful.

Done well, cultivation is perhaps the most important role for a trustee in the actual process of securing support. It creates a new opportunity for the organization to form a linkage with the prospective donor and a new opportunity for the prospective donor to get to know the organization from a different perspective. Put another way, boards that have most trustees actively involved in cultivation activities are generally strong when it comes to fundraising. If trustees are willing and able to bring prospective donors close to the organization's cause, these individuals will have a better understanding of and appreciation for the shared values of the organization and its leadership and will likely begin to think that they may also wish to be supportive.

Donor Solicitation

If there is one area that always seems to create the most concern, the highest drama, and the most raised blood pressure for trustees and volunteers, it seems to be donor solicitation. It is one thing for trustees to strategize donor engagement strategies. It is another not only to test those strategies but possibly put the trustees' personal influence on the line by asking them to solicit gifts.

There is a lot of unnecessary baggage associated with solicitation in the minds of many trustees, particularly those who are new to their fundraising responsibilities. Unfortunately, many trustees avoid asking for gifts for the organization because they view fundraising either as an activity that is somehow akin to begging for a handout or as a mechanistic and distasteful process whereby they are expected to pull the right lever at the right time to manipulate the "target" into making a gift. One of the best things fundraising staff can do for trustees is to educate them to understand that fundraising is fundamentally about building relationships.

Experienced trustees who embrace their fundraising responsibilities know that soliciting a gift is really a powerful moment with the donor. During this moment, the trustee risks being truly authentic, opening himself and his values to the donor by asking that person to join him in making a gift that will be an important investment in the work they both support. Because of the importance of the work and the moment, trustees who are committed to their fundraising responsibilities rarely give up at the first rejection or hard question; they do everything they can to make the donor understand that she is engaged in an honest discussion that is focused first on realizing change in the world through the organization and secondarily on the money necessary to make that happen. Although solicitation involves asking for a gift, trustees who truly understand fundraising realize that at a fundamental level, by asking for a gift they are testing their commitment to what they hold dear. This is why solicitation can be simultaneously so scary and so satisfying for trustees involved in the process. Fundraising staff can help trustees grow their understanding of the process and encourage trustees in solicitation efforts by emphasizing a solicitation approach that has integrity, avoids surprising the donor by securing permission to ask first, and more often than not creates an atmosphere in which the donor and the solicitation team can have the type of discussion that honors the mutual respect at the base of the solicitation process.

If it is helpful to have fundraising staff engaged in identification and cultivation, their involvement is absolutely imperative for solicitation. Trustees should not engage in any serious gift discussions with donors unless fundraising staff are fully aware, involved, supportive, and willing to help. Effective solicitation is a partnership between trustees and fundraising staff. Unilateral and unplanned solicitations by trustees are indicative of the enthusiastic but inexperienced amateur, not of a seasoned trustee.

Acknowledgment and Stewardship

Another way in which trustees can be actively engaged in the fundraising process is through the process of thanking donors and informing them of the positive impact of their gift on the organization. In fact, fundraising staff may be wise to encourage trustees who are otherwise reticent to be involved in fundraising to help instead in acknowledgment and stewardship efforts. After all, saying "thank you" and hearing the pleasure a donor receives from such a simple acknowledgment, or updating a donor on the success of an organization's work are elements of a low-risk enterprise that may help the reluctant trustee see the genuine joy that donors experience from their gifts. This perspective can be an eye-opener for trustees who are new to fundraising and an excellent opportunity to help them see for themselves how fundraising enriches the donor as much or more than the organization.

Acting as Organizational Advocates and Leading by Example

Another important function of trustees is to be good and ready advocates for a specific fundraising campaign or generally for the importance of philanthropy to the organization. If asked about the importance of giving, trustees must say often and with conviction that they believe in and support philanthropy and its power to make things better and stronger for the organization. Trustees can help philanthropy to grow in the organization by sharing their reasons for gifting with others, allowing themselves to be listed as donors, and having some part of their own story of philanthropic engagement with the organization told in a public forum of some sort, whether it be in the organization's newsletter or through solicitation of other donors. Although it is up to the individual trustee to decide whether or not to do this, the demonstrable impact on others of hearing why a trustee is motivated to make a generous gift has a positive ripple effect on others' giving and on the organization's overall commitment to philanthropy.

It is an undeniable fact that trustees are viewed as leaders in gifting to the organization. What they signal or otherwise indicate through their giving is picked up on by others. Donors and other organizational constituencies generally assume (often at an unconscious level or in a way they won't readily articulate) that trustees have the closest inside knowledge of what is happening at the organization. They assume trustees are doing their best to be knowledgeable regarding organizational needs and that trustees mean it when they say the organization deserves private gift support. When trustees talk about the importance of giving generously with their words but fail to demonstrate generous giving to the organization through their actions, others notice and the message falls flat.

It is true that prospective donors will not be strongly inclined to support a cause if board members do not do so, or do so only halfheartedly. Very generous donors regularly calibrate their gifts directly to what they observe as total gift support from the collective membership of the board. If trustees are not generous in their giving, these donors rightly think, "Why should I give if the leadership who are closest to the organization are not doing so?" On the other hand, if these donors observe generous giving on the part of trustees, their mental calculus runs more on this order: "This may well be a meritorious initiative because the trustees have carefully reviewed it and are demonstrating their commitment by giving generously." Many donors look to trustees to have done the "homework" about an organization's fundraising, its research, the volunteers and staff, the potential results, and the goal. They rely on the knowledge that trustees will not ask donors to support something the trustees don't believe in—and trust that board members will ask donors to help only with projects that have integrity and merit.

Donors and prospective donors are not foolish. Trustees must give donors credit for thinking deliberately and carefully about their gifting. A very wise trustee (and a national campaign chair) once said to a group of his fellow trustees, "It is one thing to think abstractly about a campaign and its case for support. It is another entirely when you realize you are expected to make a leadership gift. It has the effect of concentrating your mind on the issues at hand—and you will think differently as a result." Unless trustees are willing to act in support of fundraising for the organization, fundraising simply cannot happen—or cannot happen at the level that the organization deserves or to which it aspires.

The essential question of all trustees when it comes to fundraising is this: are they looking for others to lead, or have they decided that this is their time and their cause? For truly committed trustees, the latter is the only acceptable answer. And there are rewards to be had for a willingness to step up to the plate and accept the responsibility of fundraising for the organization. For one, there is a strong bond formed when there is a community of trustees that gives as generously as it can. Some trustees say this collective spirit of striving to grow and improve an organization through their work and their gifts is among the most meaningful relationships they have experienced in their lives. This collective spirit is nurtured and grows when it becomes not only permissible but expected for trustees to share the importance of fundraising and philanthropy as well as great examples of both with others.

This is because there are both individual and collective features to giving. Some individuals first decide to give for purely internal reasons; others may initially be influenced by what they observe others doing. Most trustees are on a journey that requires both internal reflection as well as external stimulus as they learn more and more about the organizations they serve and the fact that fundraising and philanthropy are not just organizationally necessary but personally inspirational. Often a person who serves as a trustee will give initially out of a sense of duty; that is, he has been told that giving generously is one of the expectations for trusteeship and so gives in order to not disappoint and to fulfill what he perceives as his duty. What happens subsequently is a part of the magic of fundraising and philanthropy. Trustees come to view making a gift as an integral part of organizational improvement and transformation and to see fundraising as a means of enlisting others meaningfully in support of the organization.

Organizational staff (not simply fundraising staff) have an important but subtle role here. Although trustees may not articulate this, the vast majority quietly notice and are moved to make generous personal gifts when they see a high percentage of staff making gifts to the organization. Staff should never feel that they are in a contest with trustees to make large gifts to the organization. Rather, staff can be most effective when they give generously, joyfully, and authentically in proportion to their means.

Conclusion

The work of nonprofit organizations has never been of greater importance. This is a time of many great needs as society continues to question how to balance what private individuals working together can do and what can and should be done by government. The work of a well-led and well-governed nonprofit can shine a light that brightens communities everywhere. The trustee is at the center of all of this, helping to grow the ability of organizations to do great work, alleviate suffering, make children happier and healthier, and strengthen communities and common ideals. Good trusteeship has never been more in demand nor promised greater rewards.

The best nonprofit boards have remarkable cultures that are animated by shared understanding, of which one key fact is that the organization is the single most important priority for each trustee's volunteer time, effort, and philanthropy. As Smith says, "Fidelity to a cause, commitment to the common good, willingness to become part of a community of interpretation—these should direct the action of trustees." If there is truly a best practice for trusteeship, it is this dynamic. If fundraising staff understand and can help promote a trustee culture that grows that feeling, then the organization is poised not simply to do good but to be great. Under these circumstances, almost anything is possible.

CHAPTER TWENTY-FIVE

VOLUNTEER MANAGEMENT

By Tyrone M. Freeman

Historically, the value of American volunteerism in society has been greatly underestimated and not fully recognized for its overall contribution (Ellis and Noyes, 1990). In 2008, nearly sixty-two million Americans (or 26 percent of the adult population) volunteered for nonprofit organizations, contributing over eight billion hours of service (Corporation for National and Community Service, 2010). In the midst of the difficult economic recession that year, Americans gave up many things to weather the times—including some of their charitable giving—but they held on to and even increased their volunteering. The total number of volunteers increased by more than one million that decade, and one third of them regularly gave over one hundred hours of service each year (2010).

This is important, because just as philanthropic giving is a values-based exchange between donors and recipient organizations, volunteerism, too, reflects the values and commitments of those who engage in it. People give to and volunteer for organizations that they connect with or that mean something particular to them. It is no accident that the top three types of organizations that Americans give the most money to support—religious, educational, and human services—are also the top three types of organizations for which they volunteer.

Research from the Corporation for National and Community Service has repeatedly confirmed the connection between giving and volunteering. In 2008, 78 percent of American volunteers made donations to charitable organizations, whereas only 38 percent of those who did not volunteer made charitable donations

(2010). Additionally, fundraising is the number one activity that volunteers report engaging in when they serve, followed by collection and distribution of food, general labor, and tutoring or teaching (2010). Fundraisers must keep this in mind when managing volunteers. Although having responsibility for volunteer management can sometimes feel like a distraction from the work of fundraising, it actually is of great help in meeting the organization's annual and strategic goals.

People volunteer for a variety of reasons (Musick and Wilson, 2008). Many have altruistic desires to help others by being available through service to make a difference or to support causes that will have a particular impact on community life. Some people volunteer to develop themselves as individuals or professionals by using their special knowledge or skills in service to important causes. Volunteerism is also a way in which individuals can acquire new skills or gain valuable experiences in particular areas that may lead to employment or promotion opportunities. Many professionals volunteer as a part of their transition from work to retirement, then increase their commitments in retirement. Still others volunteer out of a need for camaraderie or a sense of belonging to a community. They seek engagement in their community and in the lives of others in ways that add meaning to their lives and provide a sense of being useful and helpful to others. None of these motivations is mutually exclusive. Indeed, volunteers often have a variety of motivations animating their service, and all should be valued and respected as integral to the success of the organization's mission and fundraising efforts.

There are specific advantages to engaging volunteers in an organization's fundraising. Volunteers can enrich the organization by injecting passion and energy into the daily work. As representatives of the community, volunteers serve as ambassadors and can help build goodwill for the organization. Volunteers also bring unique blends of skills and talents that can enhance the organization's work and impact. They possess material resources and personal and professional contacts that can greatly add to fundraising efforts. No one can vouch for an organization's relevance, value, and success like a volunteer. Because of these factors, professional fundraisers should make every effort to involve volunteers in the process of securing the necessary resources to meet community needs.

The Strategic Value and Role of Volunteers

Volunteers play an important role in successful fundraising. As volunteers—that is, people who are not paid for their work on behalf of a nonprofit—they represent an internalization of an organization's values. In many ways they embody the mission and can serve as powerful advocates of its validity and impact, precisely because they are not financially compensated for their service and have no vested interest.

Volunteers have their own lives, their own jobs, and many other responsibilities and obligations related to family, work, and community. The fact that they choose to serve an organization speaks highly of its work, and this fact should be used in support of fundraising.

Volunteers provide important linkages to donors and prospective donors; they can help make connections and discern donor interests and giving capacities through their personal and professional social networks. Volunteers are essential for successful prospect research because they live out in the community among the organization's donors and can help make critical assessments of donors' likelihood for giving as well as help build meaningful and lasting relationships.

Volunteers can also serve as bellwethers for gauging the local community's needs and responsiveness to particular cases for support and fundraising campaigns. Through their local involvement as citizens and neighbors, volunteers can provide insights that can help keep fundraising activities fresh, updated, and effective.

Volunteers should also believe in philanthropic support and be donors to the organizations in which they are involved. Given the previously discussed connection between volunteerism and philanthropic giving, fundraisers are remiss in their responsibilities if they do not give volunteers an opportunity to financially support the organization that the volunteer already energetically supports through giving time and talent. This is particularly true for those volunteers who support the fundraising program. Before volunteers become involved in raising funds for an organization, they must give. No one should solicit on behalf of an organization without first making a personal gift. That is as true for volunteers as it is for staff and board members.

Volunteers also provide strategic value in planning and evaluation of fundraising activities. When examining the case for support, analyzing market requirements, and defining and validating needs statements and objectives, volunteers can provide critical feedback against which to gauge an organization's understanding, articulation, and presentation of community needs to its constituents. This can be accomplished by engaging volunteers in focus groups or by circulating drafts of documents for comments. When an organization is evaluating gift markets, selecting fundraising vehicles, identifying potential giving sources, and creating fundraising and communications plans, volunteers can provide recommendations, contacts, creative ideas, and other valuable inputs for planning and decision-making processes. Volunteers' preparedness and willingness to participate in fundraising can dramatically extend the capability of an organization's fundraising program, particularly in the case of one-person and small shop organizations.

Finally, volunteers can be highly effective solicitors and relationship builders as part of fundraising. With proper training and support, they can help solicit gifts, demonstrate stewardship, and renew gifts through strategic and meaningful engagement with donors. Volunteers can be powerful witnesses and advocates for an organization when brought before an individual donor, a foundation program officer, or corporate giving committee. They can provide the right blend of passion and energy to artfully convey the importance of the organization's mission. This is particularly true for those volunteers who have personally benefited from the organization's programs and services. Determining how to create opportunities for these volunteers to share their experiences and enthusiasm can help solidify donor relationships and illustrate an organization's impact and accountability in personal and direct ways that are nearly impossible for paid staff to accomplish. When a fundraiser contemplates his or her many roles and responsibilities, it is important to periodically stop and think about ways in which volunteers can usefully and meaningfully be engaged in the organization's work in order to be more effective and efficient in reaching fundraising goals.

Steps for Successful Volunteer Involvement

When using volunteers in a fundraising program, there are several steps for success to consider. The daily stresses of fundraising may sometimes make it difficult to do such planning and preparation. However, an initial investment of time and resources in these steps can save time, energy, and money later because fundraisers will have thoughtfully considered the intersection between the organization's needs and the volunteers' wishes and created a process that continually supports volunteer recruitment, training, engagement, and evaluation.

Analyze the Organization's Volunteer Needs

Volunteers can effectively serve in all aspects of a comprehensive fundraising program, including direct mail, events, telethons, personal solicitation, planned giving, capital campaigns, and communications (Lysakowski, 2005). To use volunteers effectively, an organization must first identify which fundraising tasks need to be completed; how volunteers can help accomplish these tasks; how many volunteers are needed; and what kind of knowledge, skills, energy, and time commitment volunteers will need to experience success. This information will help determine how volunteers can be used effectively in fundraising and help inform the creation of experiences that volunteers will find meaningful. Volunteers want to be useful, so it is important for fundraisers to provide them with concrete, organized tasks that they can complete within the constraints of their availability.

This is vital for engaging volunteers properly and keep them satisfied over the long term.

Create Volunteer Job Descriptions

Volunteer job descriptions should clearly delineate the assignments, requisite skills, knowledge, and time commitment for success. This will help identify the kind of individual who may best fit particular volunteer positions in terms of expertise, temperament, and availability. Job descriptions will also help clearly communicate volunteer opportunities and expectations for performance as well as point out the kinds of support that may be needed from the fundraising professional in charge of managing volunteer involvement. It is also useful during this step to consider any legal protections, requirements, or other best practices that should guide volunteer engagement. For instance, youth organizations regularly and commonly require background security checks for volunteers who will interact with youth program participants. Even if an organization may not need to take such steps, it is useful to think about other issues of concern that may affect volunteers—such as privacy, confidentiality of donor records, and basic ethical practices—and prepare for them.

Identify and Recruit Volunteers

It is important to approach this process with the same due diligence given to the hiring of paid positions, particularly when seeking campaign chairs and others whose service and volunteer leadership will be critical to overall success. To promote volunteer opportunities, consider word-of-mouth through the organization's network. There are also volunteer websites such as VolunteerMatch (www .volunteermatch.org) that help connect volunteers with causes. There may also be other volunteer matching networks in the community through a local United Way, community foundations, and corporations that promote employee volunteerism. Various forms of social media can also assist in efforts to promote and attract volunteers. Specific individuals can be recruited by personally soliciting their involvement. This will likely be the case for key volunteer leadership positions essential to fundraising success, so fundraisers should give careful consideration to prospective volunteers and approach them in dignified and respectful ways. As part of recruitment, a fundraiser must be prepared to make the case for why these individuals are the best candidates for such service and how their particular blend of expertise, knowledge, skills, relationships, and reputation are appropriate for the tasks as hand. Fundraisers will also want to provide volunteer candidates with sufficient time and opportunity to seriously consider their involvement and make thoughtful decisions about their commitment and participation.

Provide Orientation and Training

Even seasoned volunteer leaders need to be equipped with the basic knowledge necessary for success in their roles, whether it is general background information about the organization or the nuts and bolts of successful solicitation of donors. A firm grounding in the organization's mission and operations is essential. Never assume volunteers are fully informed. The orientation program can provide volunteers with nuanced perspectives on the organization's work and community impact. It is especially important for volunteers to be versed in the organization's finances as related to fundraising, programmatic needs, and the case for support so they can effectively and ethically interact with donors on the organization's behalf. It is also helpful to provide some sort of manual or online resource to which they can refer repeatedly to enhance their understanding of the organization.

After volunteers have received orientation, it is important to provide training that directly relates to the tasks they will perform. If volunteers will interact with donors, then solicitation training may be in order. If volunteers will be answering phones for the telethon, then their training should thoroughly review scripting, calling procedures, gift recording, and the use of related technologies. Fundraisers should refer to the volunteer job descriptions and create training opportunities that support the tasks to be completed. It is also important to think about the time commitment necessary for training to be effective. Some tasks may require only a few hours of review and practice of particular procedures before volunteers actually begin their work. Other tasks may require extended periods of training that span several weeks to prepare volunteers fully for service. It may also be necessary to use consultants, vendors, or other volunteers to provide training. Determining precise training needs and the best modes of delivery will help ensure successful entry experiences for new volunteers and continuing satisfaction for veteran volunteers.

Involve Volunteers in Designated Roles and Tasks

It is critical to be direct and concrete in assignments and to be mindful of volunteers' interests and talents. For volunteers to find meaning in their service, they must feel connected to their work and capable of successfully serving in the role that they are undertaking. Finding the proper match between their personal profiles and fundraising activities will be critical to the successful involvement and long-term engagement of volunteers. Additionally, fundraisers must ever be cognizant of volunteers' satisfaction with their service so that volunteers stay focused and committed to the work and fundraising goals are achieved.

Use Volunteer Time Carefully

Volunteers have limitations on the amount of time and energy they can devote to an organization. Their time must be used wisely and never wasted with menial tasks that do not reflect the caliber of work described to them during recruitment, orientation, and training. The goal is not simply to keep volunteers busy but rather to engage them meaningfully in advancing the organization's mission.

Evaluate Volunteer Performance

Volunteer performance should be properly and thoughtfully evaluated, for a variety of reasons. First, doing so demonstrates to volunteers their importance to the organization's mission and their intrinsic value to the organization. Second, evaluation provides useful and constructive feedback to enable volunteers to reflect upon and assess their contribution. Third, fundraisers are accountable for the work done by volunteers and as such need to ascertain that work is indeed being completed in the proper manner so that the organization's overall fundraising goals are met.

Evaluation should be performed in accordance with standard practices and acceptable procedures that align with job descriptions and the information disseminated through orientation and training. It should be provided verbally and in written form and contain a mix of positive assessments of activities successfully completed and constructive feedback on activities that need improvement and development. For areas of concern, there should be specific recommendations for ways to improve, and training and support to facilitate the desired changes.

When presented in such a fashion, evaluation provides positive reinforcement for volunteers who are doing an outstanding job for the organization. For those who are not meeting expectations, evaluation provides an effective forum for redirecting their energies and efforts and giving them opportunities and support to improve their performance. For those who continue to struggle to meet expectations in spite of adequate support and constructive feedback, evaluation provides a basis for ending a volunteer assignment and identifying a different mode of service or terminating the volunteer relationship altogether.

Provide Recognition

Recognition may be public or private, formal or informal. Regardless of the form it takes, recognition is essential to supporting volunteers, ensuring their satisfaction, and showing appreciation for their service. Given that volunteers operate from a variety of motivations for serving, rewards can help fulfill some of their needs for acknowledgment and also celebrate models of successful and effective service. It is also important that recognition be provided through an appropriate vehicle that matches the service provided. This can be in the form of letters of appreciation, plaques and awards, media coverage, and acknowledgment at dinners or other events. Depending on the organization, it may also be appropriate to provide small tokens of appreciation such as gift certificates or promotional items with organizational logos or other representations of the mission. The key is to think about meaningful expressions of gratitude, appreciation, and support for the service rendered.

Provide Ongoing Motivation and Inspiration

As fundraising staff seek to equip volunteers with the specific knowledge, procedures, and skills that will aid in their completion of assignments, they should be sure to touch their hearts as well. Tapping into volunteers' motivations will forge connections between their tasks, the organization's mission, and the difference being made in the lives of others and in the community. In demonstrating the value of volunteers' work, fundraisers help volunteers internalize the organization's vision of success. Enabling volunteers to interact with program beneficiaries and participants or to otherwise observe the organization's mission in action is another important means of inspiring volunteers. Fundraisers should never miss an opportunity to reinforce the organization's mission and connect volunteers to it.

There are many reasons for involving volunteers in the organization's mission. The key to being successful in such involvement is being clear about the organization's need for volunteers, being prepared to receive volunteers and effectively use their time and talents toward the advancement of the mission, being direct about expectations and deliberate in matching volunteer talents and interests with organizational needs and opportunities, and being constructive in evaluation and recognition of their service.

Volunteer Retention

The vast majority of volunteers continue their service annually; however, one third of volunteers lapse in their service year-to-year (Corporation for National and Community Service, 2010). This is a very high turnover rate. Although fundraising professionals may not be able to control all of the factors that contribute to it, there are steps they can take to keep volunteers happy and engaged. Providing orientation, training, continuing support, evaluation, and recognition are all critical elements of successful volunteer retention. Research shows that the more time volunteers spend in service, the more likely they are to continuing serving. Volunteer relationships are very much like donor relationships: they require the same kind of nurturing, cultivation, and stewardship in order to be rewarding for volunteers and effective sources of support for organizations. So fundraisers must diligently support and be attentive to volunteers.

Staff-Driven Versus Volunteer-Driven Fundraising Programs

As fundraising has become more professionalized and fundraising programs more institutionalized, in certain organizations there is a growing tendency to choose staff-driven fundraising over volunteer-driven fundraising. It is fairly common in colleges and universities, hospitals, and cultural institutions to observe staff-driven fundraising programs in which paid professional staff conduct all aspects of fundraising with little or no apparent volunteer involvement in the process. There are numerous arguments in favor of such approaches, having to do with the efficient use of staff time in actual fundraising rather than volunteer management as well as concerns over volunteer commitment and availability over extended periods such as those marked by annual or capital campaigns. That said, even staff-driven organizations often find ways to engage volunteers meaningfully in their fundraising, whether formally, through serving on campaign cabinets and advisory councils, or informally, through reviewing prospect lists and opening doors to donor contacts.

Ultimately, it is up to each organization to determine the extent to which it will involve volunteers in fundraising. Certainly, all fundraising should begin and end with the organization's board of directors. Nothing can supplant the leadership and involvement of board volunteers in successful fundraising. But, as has been discussed in this chapter, nonboard volunteers have much to offer fundraising programs. With adequate planning and deliberate execution, such volunteers can be successfully integrated into organizational fundraising.

Conclusion

Hank Rosso believed that volunteers were essential to successful fundraising because of their lack of vested interest in the organization, the passion and enthusiasm they bring, and the way the organization's mission resonates with the volunteers' deeply held values and personal priorities. Organizations that establish processes and procedures for regularly engaging volunteers in fundraising in meaningful ways generally experience tremendous returns on their investment. Because of this, professional fundraisers should make every effort to conceptualize meaningful volunteer involvement in their programs and execute deliberate processes for gaining volunteers' participation. Doing so will produce considerable returns that will move organizations closer to achieving overall goals in raising money to meet important community needs.

CHAPTER TWENTY-SIX

USING SOCIAL MEDIA TO ENERGIZE AND MOBILIZE YOUR VOLUNTEERS

By Jay B. Love

One cannot read any marketing- or communications-related newsletter in either the business or nonprofit world today without finding some mention of social media. In fact, entire publications are often devoted to this new phenomenon. It only makes sense to explore this rapidly growing method of communication for the much-needed mobilization of volunteers. Social media can also help motivate and energize volunteers as well.

What are *social media*? Broadly described, social media encompass the widely available electronic tools that generate interaction, participation, and collaboration. This includes blogs, videos, podcasts, photo sharing, and the use of social networks. But above all else, social media is about connecting people. According to Chris Brogan, blogger and author of *Social Media 101* (2010), "creativity, creation, communities of interest and culture itself are at the heart of what social media is equipped to enable" (p. 44).

Because social media have been with us for only the last five to seven years, most of the tips and suggestions in this chapter are from early adopters. These promising new forms of communications have not yet become mainstream. Therefore there is a unique opportunity to be slightly ahead of the large crowd coming at the high point of the bell curve of adoption.

Charities using large groups of dedicated volunteers realize that excitement and energy often flow through the organization from the bottom up rather than from the top down. If such behavior truly enhances the volunteer experience and boosts the number of volunteers, then using user-generated content or social media is logical, if not absolutely necessary.

Whenever groups of people are assembled, whether in a volunteer capacity or not, *buzz* (which most would define as a rush or a feeling of energy or excitement) is seldom generated from the top down. True buzz—such as people climbing on a bandwagon for a political candidate or clamoring to see a new movie or signing up to volunteer at a charity event—flows outward from the center of any group of people. Ideas, opinions, and views being passed from person to person to the next person create the energy.

This is what social media is all about. Each of the growing number of social media channels—such as Facebook, Twitter, My Space, LinkedIn, and YouTube—is based on the principle of everyday people from all walks of life creating and sharing content. Content is always changing and seldom boring, because it is about real people and their hopes, dreams, day-to-day experiences, and, best of all, opinions. That is why it is not uncommon for many to check Facebook or Twitter pages multiple times in a day.

Each time someone checks social media sites, he or she often adds content. The content can be words stating what a person thinks or feels or pictures, charts, slide decks, and video. In recruiting or communicating with assembled volunteers, organizations use words, pictures, charts, slide decks, and perhaps even video to generate energy and excitement.

For organizations seeking to use social media strategically, there can and should be much more to any social media posting or entry than just random thoughts. This is especially true when one is focused on recruiting, exciting, and organizing volunteers. Any method of creating a social media plan or strategy must be well thought out. Such plans, especially in their infancy, should be simple and straightforward.

One such strategy in this realm is the POST Method (Li and Bernoff, 2008):

P = People (Who are you trying to engage?)

O = Objectives (What are you trying to achieve?)

S = Strategies (What will it look like when you are done?)

T = Technologies (What are the tools you plan to use?)

Before exploring the various social media channels and specific tips for using them, one must consider disclosure and privacy issues. A commonsense approach can provide an excellent foundation as a team proceeds with portraying an organization on social media channels.

Here are some general guidelines to consider:

1. Provide only the information that the organization is at ease with sharing in public. Any post could easily appear in a newspaper or be used in a court of law.

2. Organizations should not hide behind typical press release–type messaging. Posts must look and sound like they are from a real person and be conversational in nature. The audience should start to really know the organization and its personality. Represent the organization as in any face-to-face conversation.

3. Personal life and work life become blurred in the social media world. On the personal side, if this is not the case, the passion for what you do and what you believe in does not come through. It is very difficult to maintain a separation between the "work you" and the "after-work you" in the social media world. Let them blend together as much as possible. This is true even with sharing of video, pictures, and slides. Of course, it should go without saying that everything you do should be guided by good taste.

4. Many of the social media sites will allow the use of various settings to control some aspects of privacy. Understand exactly what those settings can and cannot do to limit sharing of certain information (for example, sharing digital photos with just family and personal friends rather than a massive Twitter or Facebook fan base).

5. Any personal social media personas must be consistent with your organization's brand or they should be eliminated or a replacement persona created. People will eventually find out who you are by connecting the dots.

6. As many people as possible from the organization should be involved as contributors to social media sites. Anyone who might interact with volunteers is a candidate to engage and mobilize. When several people are involved, the privacy issues and concerns apply to all.

7. Organizations should share as much as possible within the preceding six privacy guidelines. Only by openly sharing can the charity emerge as real and engaging to all who are interested. Constituents love relevant information and insights. In fact, the more devoted the organization's following, the more they'll clamor for just about any information!

Most Common Social Media Platforms

This is an overview and foundation for moving forward with specific ideas and suggestions for using social media to attract, energize, and mobilize volunteers. What follows are various best practices, ideas, and examples to use in this realm. Most of them can be applied to online use of social media for all aspects of a charity. We focus on what have become the major social media players in 2010: Twitter, Facebook, YouTube, Flickr, LinkedIn, and any blog pages on your website.

Twitter

Twitter has had a huge influence on communicating in a rapid-fire fashion. There are many success stories in the world of Twitter. One need do no more than recall the most recent presidential election in the United States to see how effective Twitter can be in energizing and mobilizing hordes of people. Barack Obama's team was masterful in their usage of Twitter and other social media tools.

The first step in using Twitter is to customize the background to reflect the organization's mission and brand, as illustrated in Figure 26.1.

As you can see, it is best if the organization is instantly recognizable. The saying "A picture is worth a thousand words" certainly applies to all social media. Another nice touch to add to the Twitter background is to list the "handles" and pictures of all individuals who contribute to the postings.

There is no better way to make your social media presence come to life than with pictures of people engaging in and supporting your cause. Just as pictures in your background add value, so do pictures of people engaging in the organization's work. Twitter knows this and makes it simple to add them via www.TwitPic.com.

FIGURE 26.1. LAKE INSTITUTE TWITTER PAGE.

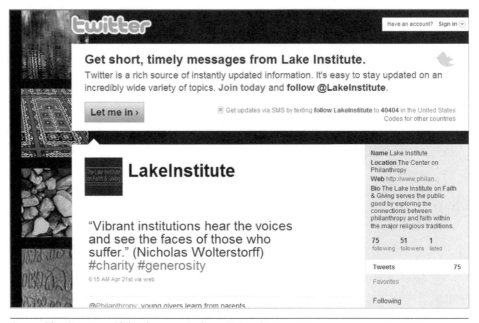

Source: The Center on Philanthropy at Indiana University.

One of the best ways to build a following in Twitter is immediately to follow nearly everyone who follows your organization. This is especially true in building a base of volunteers. Send a personal follow-up message to everyone who follows the organization. This not only allows you to thank them, but also provides an opportunity to present upcoming volunteer activities. This could spark interest in one of your volunteer events.

Another method to add as many followers as possible is to connect to the top communicators on Twitter in your area via www.Twitterholic.com. The Top 100 Twitterholics in your area can spread the word to tens of thousands of followers or more.

Once one starts using Twitter, it is best to become an active participant. This means not only posting messages but also commenting on, replying to, and retweeting the posts of others. Active participation in as many discussion threads and groups as possible is important.

If a charity's cause or anything related to it becomes a trending topic on Twitter, the organization's constituents can jump in on multiple conversations. This method helps the organization gain traction. Typing in any key words relating to a cause allows one to view what others are reflecting on. It can be simple to comment or retweet with one's knowledge of the cause. Do not be too self-serving—the crowd on Twitter and other social media sites can see through such actions.

Some posts can be opportunities for volunteers. However, do not make that subject the only one. Your personality and passion for the cause must surface as you make other posts as well as comment on the posts of others. In essence, you become a conversationalist as you progress to becoming a catalyst.

Once the posting is going smoothly, you can see how much traction the organization is getting by looking up the organization's name on www.search.twitter.com.

You can use Twitter to promote a topic or an upcoming event with the use of *hashtags*. Hashtags—identified by the # symbol—act as keyword tags that group tweets with common themes. Using hashtags allows you better to organize conversations around a cause or event. It also makes it much easier to search for, monitor, and report on the frequency of tweets directly related to the organization. This can make your Twitter effort much faster and more likely to succeed.

It is worth a reminder at this point that a social media strategy must be part of an overall outreach and communication strategy. There will be many methods for communicating, especially as it applies to energizing and mobilizing volunteers. Cross referencing and cross branding must be in place for outreach to be truly successful.

Every item of outgoing communication to volunteers—whether it is a letter, e-mail, phone call, or an actual event—must highlight the organization's social media presence and how the public can link up with the organization. You must strive to build vibrant communities on all of the top social media sites that constituents and potential volunteers visit. Volunteers will begin coming forward in a big way to follow a "buzz."

The meshing of overall communication strategy applies to the website, blogs, annual report, other printed materials, and any other method of communicating the cause. In every single instance of communication it must be obvious and simple to connect with the organization and, most of all, with other constituents on social media sites. Once others outside of your organization are touting your cause and recruiting volunteers, you have triggered the "viral effect" of the Web, which happens when the message and engagement spread like a virus—and can spread the word about your organization far and wide.

Facebook

Now let's move on to the current king of social media, Facebook. In fact, if your time allows focus on only two social media sites, they should be Twitter and Facebook, with the occasional upload to YouTube.

As is the case with Twitter, with Facebook the organization must join in at first and figure out what people are doing and saying about the organization. Many nonprofit organizations are already doing a great job with their Facebook presence. Several examples and key elements leading to their success follow.

Brand and mission must be easily visible and inviting to connect with, as illustrated by Figure 26.2.

Facebook is continually updating its site, so options for customizing are always being improved. One of the biggest innovations for nonprofits was creating and allowing the use of "causes" or user-created advocacy groups. This special feature allows organizations to create a special section in Facebook to spread the word and raise money for their cause. This can also include helping individuals become aware of volunteer activities. Tools and advice for launching a Facebook cause are available at www.exchange.causes.com.

One of the keys to driving volunteer activity and engagement is to create a strong sense of community by having discussion areas and involvement areas. The tabs in the sample pages in Figure 26.3 capture this ability. The ability to have lively discussions and "spread the word" is critical in engaging and recruiting volunteers. The mission comes through clearly thus providing a call to action.

This is a great way to tap into the daily if not hourly usage of Facebook by millions of people. Your message can be stronger if your constituents are uploading photos and videos of their experiences with your organization. Showcasing the

FIGURE 26.2. THE FUND RAISING SCHOOL FACEBOOK PAGE.

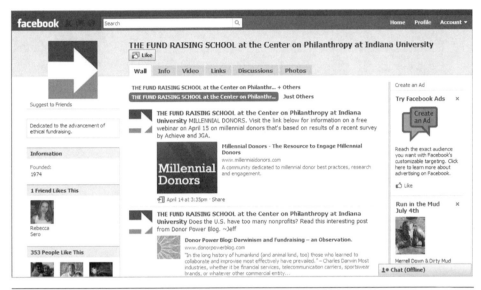

Source: The Center on Philanthropy at Indiana University.

fun and sense of reward from being involved or volunteering will be a magnet for others to become involved.

The tabs in Facebook can be modified. They are an excellent way to integrate with other social media outposts. The more cross posting, the better your overall communication and outreach will be.

This outreach can be further enhanced by allowing personal blogs to be part of your Facebook presence. This is especially true if the blogs provide insights into your team as well as the personality of key volunteers allowed to post. The blogs must be updated frequently and read like a regular conversation rather than a press release. Being open, forthcoming, and willing to share is key to social media success. Success means letting go of some of your fears and letting your following (fans) take over part of the message and outreach. They may do a better job than your own staff in this area.

Using an events tab is a way of introducing your Facebook fans and followers to the possibility of volunteering. The events tab introduces all of the past and upcoming events as shown in Figure 26.4. This not only prompts interest but should ignite many online conversations. Someday more registrations and volunteer signings may be done on social media sites than on charity websites.

FIGURE 26.3. DISCUSSION BOARD FROM THE FUND RAISING SCHOOL FACEBOOK PAGE.

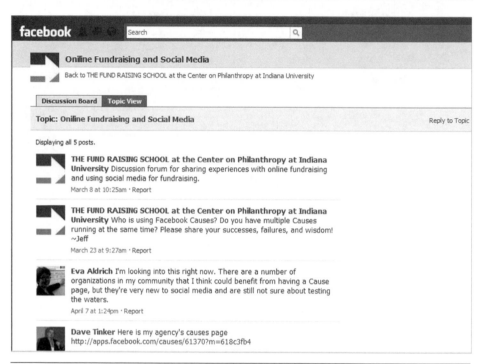

Source: The Center on Philanthropy at Indiana University.

YouTube

If a picture is worth a thousand words, a video just may be worth ten thousand words. Today, nothing else comes close to engaging and motivating as well as an inspiring video. The use of video through YouTube continues to grow and flourish. Many national organizations such as the Salvation Army and Habitat for Humanity have used YouTube videos to recruit and thank volunteers.

In addition, YouTube's Nonprofit Program allows the creation of a designated nonprofit channel (www.youtube.com/nonprofits). Its capabilities include help with premium branding, increased uploading capacity, access to the YouTube volunteers platform (www.youtube.com/videovolunteers), and use of the Google Checkout "Donate Now" button.

As with other aspects of connecting on social media, the more interaction that occurs, the better and faster your message will be spread. In the case of

FIGURE 26.4. EVENTS PAGE FROM THE INDIANA UNIVERSITY FACEBOOK PAGE.

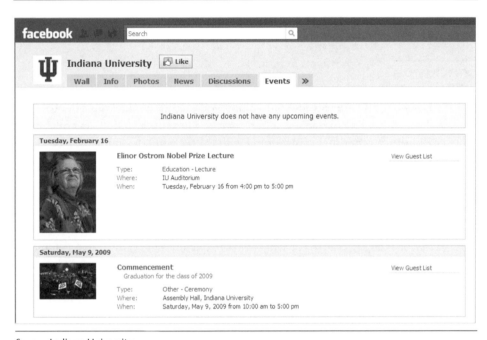

Source: Indiana University.

YouTube, if your supporters and volunteers are uploading videos to spread the organization's message, you are poised to reach viral status. Nonprofits that have achieved viral status are realizing large benefits in growth and reach.

Flickr

Although video is exciting and growing rapidly, pictures remain important. In the age of digital photos, every social media post or blog post can be enhanced by pictures. This is true even if they are taken with a cell phone. There are numerous websites for sharing photos. One of the largest and most popular is Flickr, a photo management and sharing application (www.flickr.com/about/). It has a variety of capabilities including RSS feeds, public and private settings, and compatibility with mobile devices.

One of the useful features for helping to mobilize your volunteers is the mixing of maps and photos (www.flickr.com/map/). The photo link can actually point to a site where volunteers are engaged, aiding the cause and having fun. For example, tag a photo of an event location and it will be searchable using the map feature. Or add photos from a fundraising event and tag them with the organization's address.

Conclusion

Providing an easy way for your volunteers to connect with your organization from the key social media sites should be part of your organization's overall fundraising and volunteer strategy. Beginning with the website, this initiative must permeate all communication vehicles and processes. Every outgoing newsletter or e-mail should help supporters find your organization in social media.

This chapter has explored just a few of the various social media sites active in 2010 that could play a major factor in energizing and mobilizing your volunteers. There are others, and new ones will keep developing. It is wise to start with a few, maybe even just one, so you can begin to experience the vast wave of communication that is sweeping through these channels. Staying active on a site requires the time and attention of persons with knowledge of the medium. Within weeks your organization will be able to join in and initiate conversations that will carry your message far and wide. No matter what the cause, advocates will connect and perhaps even take your message viral. With a message that illustrates the importance of your cause and the prospect of exciting experiences for volunteers, you can use the medium of social networking to energize and mobilize the organization's volunteers and constituents.

PART SIX

MANAGING THE FUNDRAISING PROCESS

Hank Rosso, founding director of The Fund Raising School, was known to say, "You can raise a lot more money with organized fundraising than you can with disorganized fundraising." Part Six covers the various aspects of managing the fundraising program. Fundraising is a management function that should be integrated with other management functions of the organization. This part of the book provides insights into management and leadership that will help fundraisers manage the total development program.

Chapters Twenty-Seven and Twenty-Eight explore the key factors for successful leadership and management of fundraising, with a focus on the concept of an expanded fundraising team working together for the good of the organization. Chapter Twenty-Nine looks at organizational responses to internal strengths and weaknesses and external opportunities and threats as key considerations affecting successful decision-making for managing and leading fundraising; Chapter Thirty examines donor database management as a key aspect of effective fundraising management.

It costs money to raise money, and the successful fundraising program has a budget to support the necessary activities. The successful fundraising manager understands the benefits and costs of various fundraising activities and can assess the risks and potential returns of new fundraising initiatives. Chapter Thirty-One provides guidance in developing fundraising budgets and analyzing fundraising costs. Investment in fundraising and concepts of return on fundraising investment are explored.

Marketing and communications are increasingly vital aspects of fundraising, and Chapter Thirty-Two examines these topics in the context of strengthening the total development program. Chapter Thirty-Three looks at working with consultants, exploring not only how they can play valuable roles in the fundraising process but also how to manage consultant involvement for best results.

This part concludes with Chapter Thirty-Four, which offers a consideration of grassroots organizations and how they can be successful in their fundraising by using special approaches adapted to their unique circumstances.

CHAPTER TWENTY-SEVEN

MANAGING THE FUNDRAISING PROGRAM

By Elizabeth A. Elkas

The work of a fundraising manager parallels that of a master gardener. Both require an investment of time to prepare the ground and design the layout; plant good-quality seeds; acclimate to the climate and growing conditions; hire a talented team of "groundskeepers"; invest in the proper tools; provide cultivation or pruning when needed; and supply ample water, nutrients, and, of course, nurturing. Both the wise gardener and the wise fundraising professional take satisfaction in bounteous results, but even then their work is not done. Like a garden, the fundraising program needs perennial attention for continued yield and growth.

Today a number of critical issues confront fundraising managers and their organizations, including these:

- Answering the demand for more services from limited resources
- Experiencing rapid change in the environment
- Finding a balance between the urgent needs of today and goals of the future
- Addressing the call for greater accountability from board members and donors
- Defining leadership roles of the board, staff, and volunteers
- Keeping pace with the latest changes in technology for efficiency and up-to-date information
- Energizing and unleashing inner motivations of staff and volunteers

The high hurdles that nonprofit managers must jump over to accomplish their mission can be daunting. Skilled fundraising managers are in the "delicate position to assert quiet leadership, of having to accomplish much through persuasion" as they inspire people to focus their efforts for the benefit of the organization (Rosso, 1991, p. 131). It's not a task for those lacking determination, but much can be done to accentuate an individual's managerial abilities.

Fundraising Managers and Their Responsibilities

"Nothing great was ever achieved without enthusiasm," wrote Ralph Waldo Emerson in 1841. While Emerson's observation remains applicable to leaders in many professions, it is especially true in the work of fundraising management. To complement their optimistic outlook, fundraising leaders must develop systems for communication to flourish, productivity to increase, and organizational goals to be realized. Several tenets hold true for fundraising leaders, perhaps none as essential as an earnest belief in the mission of the organization, a desire to champion the cause, and an appreciation of the philanthropic process. The successful leader is a mentor, a careful and thoughtful listener, trustworthy and fair in providing feedback, and one who can be entrusted with confidential information. Without micromanaging, the chief fundraising leader is available to staff, communicates regularly with people throughout the organization, and can present the case for support with influence and conviction. Such leaders set goals that are a stretch yet attainable, and they are proud to be known as fundraising professionals who abide by an ethical code through words and actions.

Recognizing that some of the best ideas evolve from the staff, talented fundraising managers are both problem solvers and solution enablers who encourage the people around them to think and act creatively for the good of the organization. Successful fundraising management is the convergence of good relationships with people and good business management practices. The key word is *relationships*. Relationships are built around people with shared goals, the same ethical values, excitement for the mission, and a clear path to effective results.

What is a successful fundraising program? What can we do to reach our goals—and to reach them faster? How do we measure our results? Will we be able to grow the program to the next level? Can we raise more money, given the resources on hand? Is the staff able to carry out our goals? These are all good questions to be asked and answered by those who want to see their non-profits serve the public interest. Each question points to effective fundraising management.

Meeting the Challenge Through Basic Management Functions

The management process used by The Fund Raising School includes six separate functions that represent planning, implementation, and assessment. The functions are analysis, planning, execution, control, evaluation, and professional ethics. When these pieces are woven together, they create a living document that addresses every element of the fundraising program.

Analysis

The management process begins with a measurement of present resources at hand. Ultimately, a thorough analysis answers the question "Where are we today?" It is also helpful to conduct a SWOT (strengths, weaknesses, opportunities, and threats) appraisal to determine the nonprofit's current vitality. The results will determine the nonprofit's "holes" and the work that needs to be done.

Planning

As important as the actual plan itself is the *process* of planning. Too little planning or no planning at all results in unclear or, worse yet, unrealistic expectations from the CEO, board, staff, and volunteers. The causes of no planning and its results are usually the same: fear, mistrust, inertia, and apathy. Conversely, excessive planning paralyzes people, and in the end they accomplish little for fear of making a mistake. Flexibility is essential, and change should and will happen along the way.

It is recommended that plans be developed and refined at least annually. This process is known as *strategic planning* (covering the next six to twelve months). A long-range plan (generally one to five years or more) may also be prepared, reviewed, and updated annually, thereby ensuring its relevance to the present as well as future growth and direction. Individuals in important decision-making roles (the CEO, board, staff, major donors, constituents, and volunteers) should be called on to participate in the planning process, and their input should be integrated into the plan, not tacked on as an addendum to the final product.

The best outcomes occur when the fundraising leader gives staff and volunteers the freedom to take prudent risks and think innovatively. Done correctly, the planning process is an energizing experience, empowering each participant as a stakeholder. An added benefit is that of building confidence, understanding, and collegiality within the team.

Execution

At last—it's time to turn the key and step on the gas. The fundraising leader does this by implementing the plan and assigning responsibilities. A plan never executed is nothing more than a concept car that never hit the street.

Planning is not a one-time deal. You wouldn't think of exercising once a year and proclaiming, "I'm glad that's over for another twelve months!" Just as a regular workout invigorates and builds muscle (and perhaps causes a bit of pain), managers need to keep up with implementation or else the process is certain to unravel and be forgotten.

It is the role of the chief fundraiser to lead the organizational charge with a commitment to invest time in the process. Keep in mind that staff members who help to devise the plan are filled with expectation and excitement and have an earnest desire to see that the plan is implemented. Copies of the plan should be distributed to all key partners to help make everyone comfortable with it. Delegating responsibilities within the plan and implementing its initiatives will help build stronger and more capable staff eager to promote cooperation instead of competition. Along the way, it's wise to check that people know what you are asking them to take on, thereby confirming their understanding and ownership of the process. Without such affirmation, communication can become splintered and the plan a burdensome workload. Time management is especially important for staging the desired outcomes of the plan.

Control

Control is the process of building procedures, policies, and reporting mechanisms into your system. It is designed specifically to manage people *and* paper. It's the end point of all the hard work, creativity, and hours that went into execution. For example, if the nonprofit sought a solution to its problem with sending acknowledgment letters within forty-eight hours of receiving the gift, the control is the system by which this was addressed, remedied, and maintained. Measures—through staff and resources—are put into place to accomplish the desired outcome. Control is the effective implementation of systems and guidelines to establish standards within the organization.

Evaluation

Managers need to regularly ask questions of themselves: Are we accomplishing what we set out to do? How well is it working? How do we compare our results to others providing similar services? The candor with which they answer these questions and benchmark against others is often telling of the success they will realize. Evaluation is the process of holding the mirror to one's self to assess programs and people. Managers who address problems with tact, concern, and dignity will be regarded as competent and efficient leaders who engender the respect of their staff. The evaluation sequence naturally leads back to analysis, thereby making it an ongoing cyclical process.

Professional Ethics

It's the responsibility of the fundraising leader to demonstrate a professional stance to all, including the CEO, board, staff, donors, volunteers, constituency, and community. Fundraisers must act ethically, using judgment that reflects not only the highest standards of the organization and the profession but also the self-worth of the individual. With today's heightened competition for donor dollars—especially those coveted leadership gifts needed to reach annual and capital campaign goals—the fundraising manager must champion what is right and acceptable in the realm of gift receiving among staff and volunteers and not exert undue pressure on reaching dollar goals at the expense of ethics. "The practice of gift seeking is justified when it exalts the contributor, not the gift seeker" (Rosso, 1991, p. 7). The fundraising leader knows the balance between meritorious staff recognition and adulation. Organizations such as The Fund Raising School, the Council for the Advancement and Support of Education (CASE), the Association of Fundraising Professionals (AFP), and the Association of Healthcare Philanthropy (AHP) have done an exceptional job in responding to the need for professionalism by developing certificate programs and certification.

The Management Matrix

The six components just described—analysis, planning, execution, control, evaluation, and professional ethics—are the elements of the management matrix (see Table 27.1). The matrix forms a superstructure or grid for integrating the management elements into a cohesive and comprehensive fundraising *management process*. Think of it as going to a team of doctors for a complete head-to-toe history and physical. The results reveal the nonprofit's current state of health and provide a prescription for a healthy future. Fundraising managers can use the management matrix as a tool, probing each area of the grid to determine the effectiveness of their fundraising operation, recognizing that a strength or weakness in one area will certainly have a spillover effect for other components on the grid. The process of working through the matrix and periodically updating it is highly valuable for measuring the progress of the ever-evolving fundraising program.

TABLE 27.1. THE MANAGEMENT MATRIX.

What must be managed	Analysis	Planning	Execution	Control	Evaluation	Professional Ethics
Institutional Readiness (Internal and External) Case Communications Constituents Stewardship						
Human Resources Staff Boards Committees Campaign Leadership Volunteers						
Markets Individuals Corporations Foundations Government Coordinating Agencies Associations						
Vehicles Annual Fund Capital Campaign Major Gifts Endowment Planned Giving						
Strategies Direct Mail Internet Phone Solicitation Personal Solicitation Proposals Events						
Other						

Source: The Fund Raising School, 2009b, p. III-14.

Fundraising Staffing

Regardless of the size of the nonprofit, hiring staff is a big investment and a critically important management function. As with any job, fundraisers function best when they know exactly what their fundraising leaders expect of them and how they can be most effective. That makes a comprehensive job description essential. Not only should the description be part of the office records, but it should also be shared with candidates during the interview process and be available for all those on staff to see. Job descriptions give staff members a sense of the magnitude and responsibility of their positions and serve as a guidepost for future performance reviews and professional growth.

Professional Staff Responsibility

Although fundraisers are hired primarily to raise money, at times the purpose of their job is reshaped and they are asked to take on additional duties to meet organizational needs. To stay focused, it's helpful for both the manager and fundraiser to have clearly written expectations. Many nonprofits have established specific, ambitious goals for the number and type (cultivation, solicitation, and so on) of donor contacts per month and year, target goals for current and planned gift dollars to be raised, and a minimum number of proposals to be presented. The number must be developed with input from the fundraiser to reflect the organization's maturity, donor base, and staff size. A large and established nonprofit may expect major gift officers to carry portfolios numbering 75 to 150 prospects who each have the gift potential of $100,000 or more. The number of meaningful donor contacts anticipated per month could be in the upper ranges of twenty-five to forty. For gift officers assigned to solicit principal gifts, the total number of prospects is considerably smaller but the dollar potential is significantly larger. Conversely, a small new organization may look for its lone fundraiser to raise a small amount—for example, the $35,000 annual fund—on a part-time basis. It is extremely helpful, yet too often neglected in small shops, to determine goals for the number of contacts and gift ranges for prospects.

What is more difficult for a fundraising manager to measure on paper, yet critically important, is the *quality* of a contact with a prospective donor. For example, is the donor feeling more involved and gratified about the relationship with the animal shelter's fundraising staff and programs (in addition to her love for the animals)? The fundraiser must be capable of progressively and carefully building relationships with people in a position to respond financially. Reflective fundraisers and their managers are well aware of this dynamic and track such relationships accordingly. Professional staff should be encouraged to establish long- and short-term goals, create job descriptions for new staff, serve as liaisons to board members and volunteers, be accountable for human and monetary resources utilized, and think creatively of ways to meet the nonprofit's mission. In shops of more than one person, it's beneficial for staff to meet biweekly or monthly to discuss current activity and progress.

Staff Retention

One of the most challenging issues for fundraising managers is staff retention. Fundraising professionals leave one job for another all too frequently, and their departures can pose serious problems for the nonprofit. The financial and emotional costs of recruiting and training new staff members are high (from hundreds to many thousands of dollars); a serious factor is the loss of unrealized income for the organization during the time the position is open. It typically takes six to twelve months before a new employee is prepared to actively solicit and receive substantial new donor dollars. When a gift officer, especially one who is more senior, chooses to leave for another job, out walks every relationship she has worked hard to nurture between the donor and the organization. Connectivity to the donor is jeopardized or may even be lost altogether; if the relationship does continue, it may never regain the same depth.

Salary is an important factor in staff retention. Competition for professional staff has skyrocketed along with the growth of U.S. charities (Schwinn and Sommerfield, 2002). Many nonprofits are in a tug-of-war offering very attractive recruitment packages (including perks) to lure talent, especially senior professionals. Staff may also be inclined to leave when they perceive—or know for a fact—that they are not fully valued or appreciated by their boards or bosses or have limited authority or influence. Those who work long hours can experience burnout, or they may be handed unrealistic expectations—including a constant pressure from the board for them, as fundraising experts, to handily fix all money woes. Successful fundraisers can thrive on gentle pressure, but they may buckle under impossible demands! Setting realistic and attainable goals with the staff member is paramount.

Although it is good that fundraisers are able to move on to better-paying and more challenging positions, ultimately it is better for the organization to retain the staff in which it has invested. Flexible work hours and higher levels of staff recognition are among the positive ways to deal with pressures staff feel both internally and externally. Who wouldn't want to work in a caring, energetic, and fun environment of professionals who share an esprit de corps? Like all professionals, fundraisers seek genuine understanding and appreciation for a job well done, making opportunities for growth and promotion within the organization very attractive to staff.

Physical space is also important; fundraisers look for a functional and appealing work environment outfitted with up-to-date technology and a budget to purchase the supplies and equipment needed to do their work. The fundraising manager's job is to hear the staff's current desires and to look ahead to meet future needs. The payoff will be a gratified and productive team of professionals who want to invest their future in the organization because they can see a meaningful place for themselves there.

Support Staff Responsibilities

Often the first face encountered by an organization's external constituency, a welcoming support staff assistant makes a positive difference in setting the tone for clients, donors, and board members. Consider this example: a support assistant at an Indiana health care nonprofit was assigned to call donors who made gifts of $100 or less. She reached a woman to thank her for her recent $100 gift—the first personal call the donor had ever received from the organization. When the donor realized that the caller simply wanted to express thanks and was *not* asking for another gift, she was dumbfounded. The support staff member tried to conclude the call by saying, "I enjoyed talking with you. You have a nice day," but the donor interrupted, saying she had never before received such a call asking "for nothing." The donor requested further information from the organization—and eventually left a $1.5 million bequest. All thanks to the sincere manner and quick thinking of a support staff member. Each contact with our donors and our constituency is a seed planted for the future, and everyone in the organization serves as a fundraising seed-planter, whether or not it is written in the person's job description. Clearly, support staff members are an indispensable part of the fundraising team. Effective support staff and volunteers are the backbone of a growing shop; as such, they should be encouraged to continue their education and, if possible, receive financial help with attending courses and seminars for professional growth. This is an appreciated vote of confidence and a morale booster.

Staff Evaluations

Staff members, both professional and support, should undergo regular one-on-one evaluations with the fundraising manager to provide feedback on performance. This may take place on a periodic basis but should certainly be conducted no less frequently than once a year. In advance of the meeting, it's helpful to encourage staff to assess their *own* performance and suggest how to improve it. The meeting itself is an ideal time to earnestly praise positive elements of staff performance and discuss how to further improve it, point out difficulties they may be having, solve problems, seek their ideas, and set future goals. Likewise, if criticism is called for to change a person's behavior, it should be done in the most constructive way possible. It's also a good time for managers to ask staff how they can help them do their jobs more effectively. People want to feel valued by the organization and their colleagues. A kind word or deserved praise goes far in sending a message of value. Given the fact that few nonprofits are in a position to compensate at a high dollar level to show appreciation, recognition of deserving staff is especially important. The evaluation, if done with honesty and care, is a lift to the individual as a contributor to the success of the mission and also serves to enhance his or her feeling of self-worth.

Policies and Procedures

It is vital for fundraising operations to be guided by clear policies and procedures for all of the following functional areas.

Gift Processing and Acknowledgment

The standard for gift acknowledgment is high, yet appropriate: within twenty-four to forty-eight hours after receiving the gift, the nonprofit should contact the donor to extend an expression of gratitude. There is no better way to demonstrate to the donor the value your organization places on the gift, and it also demonstrates accountability. Responses may be handled a variety of ways, including by personal visit, letter, e-mail, or phone call. All gifts should be acknowledged, and written documentation, including a mention of the gift amount, is generally required for tax purposes.

Internal Gift Reports and Communications

Do you know where your fundraising dollars stand as of today? What gifts and pledges are expected in the coming months? How much did it cost to raise a dollar for your annual fund? Referring to this information frequently is invaluable to fundraising managers as they plan ahead and look to help the organization reach its funding goals. Still, it is surprising that not all fundraising managers have access to this data so they can respond accordingly with cultivations and solicitations. If possible, such vital information needs to be shared with appropriate staff on a monthly or even a weekly basis.

Managing the Stewardship Program

Not surprisingly, the best future donor is one who already gives to the organization. Therefore developing a comprehensive stewardship program is one of the wisest investments in a healthy future. To yield effective results year in and year out, however, relationships with donors must be managed scientifically, which requires hard work, notes Kathleen Kelly (1998). Many nonprofits are strategically investing in staff and resources to expand their stewardship programs. Customized donor plans that address the donor's specific interests are clearly part of good planning, research, event, communication, and major gift elements. A stewardship plan has succeeded if the donor feels warmly gratified by the people within the nonprofit and seeks deeper connectivity. A fundraising leader will look to exert positive influence to grow this aspect of the fundraising program over time.

Conclusion

Managing the fundraising program takes patience, determination, good humor, and, more than anything, a plan of action. In an environment of nonprofit boards demanding (as well as wanting and needing) to raise more money to serve an escalating number of constituents, fundraising leaders are tasked with making it all happen. Rather than allow themselves to be tugged off course with the urgent rather than the important, they would be wise to study the current ground conditions, then map out the nonprofit's goals and strategy toward reaching them. Sequential planning works! The process provides a firm base on which to grow all elements of the program. Planning may be accomplished through the management matrix, using the grid to measure and monitor the status of all elements of the organization: human resources, organizational readiness, various markets, vehicles, strategies, and physical resources. While the process of planning is time-consuming, the reward is worth the labor. By engaging all stakeholders in the process, integrated planning creates a team of people that communicates more effectively in an organized and functional office setting. This enables the leader to articulate the plan for a sustainable future, knowing that the right level of resources have been identified. It also brings about ambitious yet achievable goal-setting. And, best of all, it leads to a vigorous group of committed people—the board, staff, donors, and volunteers—who stretch to help realize more and larger gifts to advance the mission.

CHAPTER TWENTY-EIGHT

LEADERSHIP AND TEAM BUILDING

By Lilya Wagner

Books, articles, e-newsletters, and other resources on leadership are plentiful, but rarely are such materials specifically geared to fundraising professionals. That may be partly because many fundraisers simply don't view themselves as leaders, much less as needing leadership skills, traits, or training. Yet when we review the best in leadership literature and other such sources of information, it's evident that fundraisers who do their job well actually perform according to best practices in leadership. A corollary to that fact is that those who don't do as well often lack the conviction that they and their work have much significance, and they view themselves as technicians in secondary roles.

This chapter will present leadership information in three parts. The first presents some of the best in leadership literature and practice, particularly in the context of current leadership requirements and organizational needs. Second is a discussion of how these leadership concepts apply and can be used effectively in fundraising. The third section presents suggestions on how fundraisers might implement leadership best practices to achieve the level of professionalism necessary for their own satisfaction and for the benefit of their organizations. So although this chapter will present some leadership *theories*, the main focus is on the *practice* of leadership and how it can best support the profession of fundraising.

As Figure 28.1 indicates, various views on leadership give us choices of what we want to be and how we want to act in our professional roles as fundraisers.

FIGURE 28.1. THE LEADERSHIP LADDER.

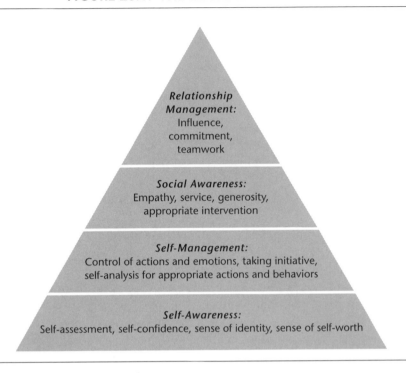

Choices can also distort reality, as these choices may represent stereotypes. Therefore awareness and self-awareness are important to beginning to understand how fundraisers can become leaders—not necessarily leaders at the top, but leaders found at any rank and level.

As already mentioned, leadership literature is plentiful. Some is pop psychology; at the other end of the spectrum are the well-researched scholarly theories. From Greek, Roman, and biblical times to the current millennium, leadership continues to fascinate and perplex. There are multiple definitions of leadership, as well as how leadership is developed—if, indeed, it can be.

Overview of Leadership Literature

Leadership can be present at all levels of an organization. Although structures and hierarchies exist, each individual can demonstrate and practice leadership competencies.

One of the newer concepts of leadership is described in "Wanted: Leader-Builders" (Yearout, Miles, and Koonce, 2000). The authors believe that leader-builders have the following traits:

- An unusually strong vision of the future
- Remarkably consistent behaviors
- Strong emphasis on development and replenishment of the leadership talent pool
- Identification of specific leadership competencies to support strategy
- Strong, strategic alignment
- A high degree of team unity
- Strong commitment to continuous organizational renewal

Leaders often challenge the process as they search for opportunities and take risks, and in doing so they share a vision with those whom they lead. As leaders envision the future, they engage others by enlisting their involvement, by promoting collaboration, by fostering their growth, and, most significant, by recognizing individual differences and therefore contributions, and celebrating accomplishments with a sense of "we did it," rather than taking sole credit.

Effective leadership combines individual traits and competencies according to the demands of the situation in a particular group or organization. Most successful leaders adhere to group norms and demonstrate their leadership by helping the group achieve its goals. Effective leadership is the successful influence of the leader that results in goal attainment by the influenced followers. Leaders are agents of change whose actions affect other people more than other people's actions affect them—they are not dictators who force others to do what they themselves want done.

Therefore we may conclude that leaders define objectives and thereby maintain the direction for meeting goals, as well as provide the means necessary for meeting the goals. Leaders work with groups in positive ways to facilitate their action and interaction, and develop satisfaction with the movement toward goals.

David D. Chrislip and Carl E. Larson cowrote *Collaborative Leadership: How Citizens and Civic Leaders Make a Difference* (1994), a resource that is particularly appropriate for fundraisers to consider because of the need for collaboration in achieving funding goals. They identified the skills for a new kind of leadership that differed from the existing predominant forms of leadership—tactical, positional, competitive. They suggest a new type: that of collaborative leaders. The primary role of collaborative leaders is to promote and safeguard the process. Four principal directives characterize collaborative leadership:

- *Inspire commitment and action.* Collaborative leaders catalyze, convene, energize, and facilitate others to create visions and solve problems. They create new alliances, partnerships, and forums.
- *Lead as peer problem solver.* Collaborative leaders do not do the work of the group for the group. Ownership of the process is shared. They are active and involved. Their role is to serve the group and the broader purpose for which it exists. They rely on credibility, integrity, ability to focus on the process.
- *Build broad-based involvement.* Collaborative leaders include a relevant community of interests, embracing more people rather than fewer.
- *Sustain hope and participation.* They convince participants that each person's input is valued, sustain confidence, and sustain commitment to the process.

In a booklet on the leadership edge, published by the American Society of Association Executives, the seven skills of the twenty-first century leader were enumerated (Bethel, 1993). All of these are appropriate for the fundraiser to consider:

- *Servant Leadership*—True leadership begins with the desire to serve others. Fundraisers work not for their own benefit but for the good of the client and all other constituents.
- *Creating and Communicating Vision*—Fundraisers create a compelling vision of the future as they raise funds to support that vision, and they must be able to communicate that vision internally and externally, to all constituents.
- *Promoting and Initiating Change*—Fundraisers advocate and initiate change that recreates the organization in response to a constantly changing environment.
- *Building Partnerships*—Individual competence, worthy as it is for the fundraiser, is not enough. Alliances and partnerships will build the strength of the organization and the professional.
- *Valuing Diversity*—Demographic and geographical barriers are breaking down, and dealing with diversity of every kind is not just necessary, but a strengthening factor in competing for financial support.
- *Managing Information and Technology*—The welter of information is boundless, and the fundraiser must learn how to manage information, avoid overload, and keep human needs and concerns in balance with technology.
- *Achieving Balance*—The fundraiser can easily become overwhelmed by demands from the "them" element and forget to keep a balance in his or her own needs.

Applying Leadership Principles for Fundraisers

Fundraising is a challenging and meaningful profession. Fundraisers have to be part of the forward momentum or they will be left floundering in the "but we've always done it that way" mentality. The world needs fundraising leaders who can maintain a competitive advantage and have innovative ideas while holding on to time-tested principles. Knowing the difference between getting things done and getting things done better than ever is an art. Fundraising leadership at every level means being innovative, building on ideas, and being adaptable, open to change, organized, entrepreneurial, and confident. Most of all, fundraising success demands that professionals know how to lead others toward a mutual vision.

Understanding the leadership principles that can appropriately apply to the fundraising professional requires an understanding of the fundraising context. A fundraising professional can or may need to practice leadership in two spheres of influence. First is the human element, consisting of the team and constituents with whom the fundraiser interacts and on whose behalf he or she practices the best in leadership principles. Second are the processes and activities by which fundraising is accomplished on behalf of the organization and personnel as well as its constituents. The fundraiser's responsibilities are equally important, complex, challenging, yet fulfilling in both relationships and responsibilities, and these are often intertwined and interdependent.

When considering the first, human element of fundraising, leadership traits are essential as fundraisers work with volunteers in seeking major gifts; in identifying, researching, and evaluating prospective donors; in implementing cultivation and communication efforts; and, in particular, when working with the president (or other designated or elected leader of the organization) and the board. The best fundraisers also "pay it forward" by identifying, training, and mentoring leaders to eventually take their place.

In terms of the second element, fundraising management, fundraisers apply leadership concepts when they examine, evaluate, and monitor a fundraising program while remaining alert to new situations and possibilities and seizing new opportunities. To do so, professionals in fundraising must keep abreast of trends and developments in the field and constantly seek to improve and refine the fundraising effort.

One specific way in which relationships and responsibilities are combined lies in the necessity of examining, evaluating, and monitoring the fundraising program so that fundraisers can meet agreed-upon or expected goals set by staff, CEOs or people in a similar position, volunteers, donors, and constituent representatives. This must be accomplished while attending to pressures from donors, demands from superiors, and desire for assistance from staff, all while trying to keep abreast of trends and developments in the field so that organizations remain competitive.

Today's climate for fundraising presents many challenges to fundraisers and makes it necessary to note carefully how leadership traits can help surmount these ever-present challenges. The pressures are many—demands for accountability, declining trust in nonprofit organizations, lack of trust that proper stewardship is practiced, lack of time, and a media corps that watches every move and is as ready to criticize as to publicize.

In accomplishing all this and more (and the tasks are well-defined in a myriad of fundraising volumes), fundraisers find themselves pressured to play many leadership roles. Fundraisers also must be able to answer questions like the following:

- Why are we what we are?
- What is important to us?
- What relationships are valuable and valued?
- Are we committed to problem solving?
- What legacy will we leave for our organization and its heirs?
- What is the need for community, internal and external?
- Can we and do we manage change?

Fundraisers must answer these to the satisfaction of those they lead at every level, from the boss to the staff and the community as well, including donors and volunteers. The answers are then realized through the actions for which fundraisers take responsibility—and thereby demonstrate leadership. The implications of leadership in providing tangible as well as philosophical responses to these questions are evident.

Let's revisit one of the theories that is most applicable in developing an understanding of how leadership traits coalesce in meeting both human and organizational goals—that of Chrislip and Larson (1994):

- Fundraisers inspire commitment and action and bring people together to create a common and workable mission with the intent of solving problems.
- Fundraisers serve as leaders in solving these problems because they inspire ownership. While they themselves are involved, they also lead in a shared process. While they serve the group, they also motivate and lead in taking action.
- Fundraisers therefore build broad-based involvement that includes a range of talents, interests, abilities to get work done, and movement toward a monetary as well as a tangible goal.
- Fundraisers inspire hope as they promote and achieve participation by giving their broad team of individuals the confidence to carry out the process and the commitment to achievement. Leaders also need to remain focused, to be sensitive to others by understanding who the people are in their sphere of

influence, what their positions on issues are, and how to best communicate with them.

• Such complex relationship-building and responsibility-sharing may lead to unavoidable or even desirable conflict, and fundraising leaders need to be able to not just tolerate such situations but handle them adroitly. Inevitably this requires flexibility and the ability to change course if necessary and adopt new approaches in both relationships as well as responsibilities.

• Ultimately, leadership is action, not ego. Leaders act not only for themselves but also for the benefit of others. Therefore fundraisers can and must exert leadership because they are not working just for themselves but, more importantly, for the good of others.

The illustration in Figure 28.2 (adapted from Nanus and Dobbs, 1999) may clarify how both relationships and responsibilities are part of the fundraiser's world, requiring leadership practices that combine these parts of a whole.

The key stakeholders may be the board and committees, other volunteers, community leaders, and other interested parties. In practicing leadership skills, fundraisers need to find out who these persons or groups are, what they value about the organization, and their needs and expectations.

FIGURE 28.2. LEADERSHIP RELATIONSHIPS AND RESPONSIBILITIES.

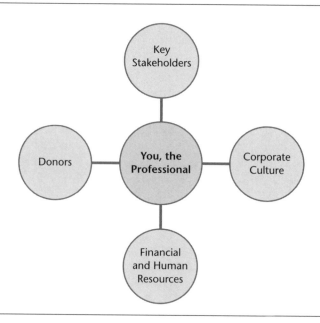

Donors are the lifeblood of organizations. Fundraisers need to determine how well donors' needs are met, their potential for giving and what difference this could make to the organization, and how to add to the donor pool.

Corporate culture includes the structures of the organization, its culture, and its values as well as its policies. Fundraisers need to know how the organization works in fulfilling the mission and relating to donors.

Financial and human resources answer the questions of who will do what, and how much it will cost. Fundraisers need to determine whether the resources are available and how effectively they are used.

By nurturing the best qualities in each of these areas, fundraisers can lead from any level of responsibility or position and motivate, influence, and change both themselves and their organizations.

Developing Fundraisers as Leaders

It is far too common for fundraisers to lack awareness of leadership and its possibilities and opportunities and to therefore feel "I'm not a leader." Consider, for example, these statements (Chrislip and Larson, 1994):

- We have expertise, but usually someone else has the authority.
- We don't make the final decision; if we're lucky, we influence the decision.
- We work with people who have more clout than we do—financial, decision making, political, and social.
- Our roles are viewed differently by different people. Our most important role of providing organizational support isn't always recognized or understood.
- Our reputation as individuals and members of a profession may not be as valued as the doctor, lawyer, or professor. But our function often helps them be successful.
- Users of our services often see us as less important, subordinate, or peripheral. We are tolerated, maybe even respected, but not fully valued.

These statements are inherent in the two predominant styles of leadership in our culture—*tactical leadership* and *positional leadership*. Both of these styles propagate the "them and you" culture under which we often work.

Tactical leadership is often defined by metaphors—*win the game, defeat the enemy, apprehend the suspect*. As the term *tactical* implies, much depends on a plan for achieving an objective, and people are led in an effort to accomplish the plan. Tactical leaders can be coaches, military leaders, film directors, presidents of colleges. In this kind of leadership, a clearly identified leader who may have assumed the position in a number of ways—ranging from force to mutual consent by the members—may set the goal, convince us that we must work to achieve that goal, organize and strategize, and deal with us as part of the effort to reach the goal.

Positional leadership identifies someone at the top of the organizational structure. This leader is in charge of an organization or unit and is similar in many ways to the tactical leader. This leader's purpose is to perform a set of tasks or activities.

These types of leadership are often ingrained in us. Our presidents or executive directors, our boards, the vice presidents or directors of development, all tell us what to do, and sometimes how to do it. We are judged by how we perform according to the set goals and standards. This reinforces the concept of "them versus you."

However, in contrast to the two theories or perceptions of leadership—tactical and positional—that we often experience as fundraisers, we can consider an alternative style, often described as collaborative, or leading from any level. Warren Bennis (1996) provided a fine perspective on this kind of leadership: "Today's leaders must have more than just absolute power to win respect and followers. . . . They must be willing to inspire a more collaborative approach that lets them tap into the endless source of ideas, innovation, know-how and knowledge of the people they lead" (p. 13).

In developing an appropriate leadership approach, fundraisers may wish to consider the following concepts or characteristics that build their strengths and capabilities to lead:

1. Develop an intellectually rich and stimulating vision, not just for themselves but also for those with whom they work and, in some way, also lead. Fundraisers' lives should stand for something, and in this way they can help transform their organizations.
2. Be conscious of the importance of building character, not ego. This calls for honesty and empathy. Donors will then know fundraisers have their interests at heart when asking for money. Also, colleagues and constituents will trust fundraisers because their behavior aligns with their words.
3. Be considerate of others' needs and desires, and share power. The credibility of fundraisers grows as others are put first. Fundraisers can mentor, support appointed leaders, and build a team for fundraising while providing professional opportunities for those who look to fundraisers for guidance. Teamwork is vital to fundraising, and fundraisers understand that power comes in many forms—information sharing, influencing, and motivating others, for starters.
4. Express appropriate concern for the whole. Fundraisers' allegiance to an organization and therefore to donors who support the cause embodies the work of fundraising. Fundraisers should be passionate about their work *and* commit the right amount of time, attention to detail, and energy to accomplishing it.

5. Be willing to experiment and take risks. This means fundraisers need to commit to communicating effectively as well as managing themselves, their tasks, and their relationships, while also respecting and following the administration's lead.
6. Celebrate the present while looking ahead to the future. Fundraisers provide recognition, celebrate achievements, and bring energy and enthusiasm to the organization because ultimately fundraising is about getting worthwhile causes to succeed and getting things done!

Making the changes that may be necessary in order to develop and provide leadership in fundraising programs takes two capacities—the intellectual (the head) and the emotional (the heart). Fundraisers can think about why there is a desire to be a leader at whatever level or rank an individual holds and can analyze and plan how to effect change.

Before considering how to develop leadership skills in the profession of fundraising, take a look at the hierarchy of capabilities explained by Jim Collins in the *Harvard Business Review* (2001). He discusses Level 5 leaders and how necessary they are to organizational change and good leadership. Let's study how one gets to that level.

According to Collins, at Level 1 is the highly capable individual who makes productive contributions through talent, knowledge, skills, and good work habits.

At Level 2 is the contributing team member who adds to the achievement of group objectives and works effectively with others in the group.

At Level 3 is the competent manager who organizes people and resources toward the effective and efficient pursuit of predetermined objectives.

At Level 4 is the effective leader who catalyzes commitment to and vigorous pursuit of a clear and compelling vision and stimulates the group to high performance standards.

Finally, at Level 5 is the executive who builds enduring greatness through a paradoxical combination of personal humility plus professional will (Collins, 2001). Level 5 leadership is essential for taking an organization from good to great.

Good-to-great leaders attend to people first, strategy second. They maintain the belief that they can surmount obstacles and prevail at the end. Level 5 leaders understand that transformations do not happen overnight but in incremental steps. And Level 5 leaders are disciplined in thought and action. As Collins noted, "There are two categories of people: Those who don't have the Level 5 seed within them and those who do!" (p. 74). Those who do have Level 5 possibilities may—under the right circumstances, such as self-reflection, acquiring a mentor, having a significant life experience—begin to develop a Level 5 capacity. Not all who are Level 5 leaders are top executives. At the heart of this theory is the fact that Level 5 characteristics, moving from good-to-great, can be found or developed in most of us.

In planning for leadership development, fundraising professionals should develop a "backward plan." This type of planning has become increasingly popular because it may be more realistic than some traditional plans. First, identify the outcome to be achieved. Think about how fundraising professionals should be perceived in their role as leaders. Then work backward, identifying the steps to take in order to get there. Organize and reorganize these steps so that there is logical flow between all of them until the desired outcome is reached.

Conclusion

In *How to Think Like Leonardo da Vinci* (Gelb, 1998), in a section titled "Fix Your Course to a Star," the author explains, "The most carefully crafted strategies rarely work out exactly according to plan. But the best improvisers do not just 'wing it,' they start with a well-made plan and then adapt gracefully to changing circumstances. You are the captain of your own ship, but you can't control the weather. Sometimes life brings us smooth sailing; other times we get squalls, hurricanes, and tsunamis. Leonardo counseled, 'He who fixes his course to a star changes not.' Fix your course to a star, and be ready to navigate through storms and uncharted icebergs" (p. 256).

CHAPTER TWENTY-NINE

ORGANIZATIONAL STRENGTHS AND VULNERABILITIES

By Eugene R. Tempel

Fundraising is an active management process that is built on organizational strengths. And fundraising fails because of organizational vulnerabilities. Public perceptions about whether an institution is well organized have a great deal to do with fundraising success. This chapter examines the various organizational factors that enable fundraising to succeed as well as those that sometimes cause it to fail.

Strengths and Vulnerabilities

Often an effort to provide for the public good begins with a single individual acting on his or her own. Others may be drawn in to help support the effort with time or talent or money. Success may lead to organized voluntary association, or, ultimately to the formation of a nonprofit organization, eligible to receive philanthropic contributions qualifying for the U.S. Federal Charitable gift deduction by the Internal Revenue Service. It is through these formal organizations—meeting the requirements of 501(c)(3) of the Internal Revenue Code or being organized as a church—that most philanthropic gifts are made. A nonprofit organization is able to engage volunteers and raise philanthropic dollars based on organizational strengths that reflect its understanding of the external environment. An inability to engage volunteers and raise funds is often a reflection of organizational isolation and weaknesses that leave the organization vulnerable to decline.

For an organization to be successful in fundraising, it must be connected to its external environment. To remain viable, the organization must understand the changing needs of that environment and integrate the environment's capacity to support the organization's need for human and financial resources into the organizational plan. The organization must have management structures in place that interpret its mission in relation to changing external needs. An organizational tendency toward an open system or a closed system relative to the external environment has an impact on fundraising ability.

For nonprofit organizations to be successful in the twenty-first century, they must operate as open systems (Kahn and Katz, 1978), understanding that they are interdependent with their external environment, even if they are highly institutionalized with values that appeal to a narrow base of supporters. Research indicates that philanthropic giving is closely related to growth of the economy (The Center on Philanthropy, 2009b). Changing needs in society call for adaptations by nonprofit organizations. So do changing donor preferences.

Nonprofit organizations have a natural tendency to become closed systems. The attempt to build endowment reflects that tendency. A fully endowed nonprofit organization can become a closed system irrelevant to the common good and vulnerable to decline.

In the twenty years since the first edition of *Achieving Excellence in Fund Raising*, nonprofit organizations have begun functioning more as open systems. Professional management, competition, calls for transparency and accountability, changing donor behavior, and scholarship on best practices have all been responsible for this change. Traditionally higher education institutions functioned as though they could shape and control their outside environments. The intense marketing programs that colleges and universities have in place today indicate they have come down from the "ivory tower," a tag that indicated they were out of touch with the real world. Many higher education institutions have developed elaborate feedback systems to determine student preferences and develop new services and arrangements to respond to them, and sophisticated advertising and communications and incentive programs to recruit the students they want.

When organizations desire or require a broad base of support or seek wider influence, they must be managed as open systems. Open-system theory assumes that organizations are not independent of their external environments, but that they have impact on, and are affected by, their environments. According to open-system theory, organizations depend on a hospitable and supportive environment to ensure supplies of human, fiscal, and material resources, as well as for consumption of goods and services.

To function successfully as open systems, organizations must continually monitor the environment and either adapt to changes or attempt to change inhospitable elements in the environment. Organizations that fail to adapt or fail to influence the environment eventually produce unwanted goods or unneeded services and lose their ability to attract vital resources.

Fundraising success depends on an organization's ability to adapt to surrounding conditions. A nonprofit organization exists to provide services for which there is a public or societal need, often on a small or local level. If that need is otherwise met, then the organization's rationale for existence disappears. If it continues to provide staff and programs to fill the outdated need, then it will be viewed as wasteful, inefficient, and unresponsive. Its sources of support will diminish, and it will be forced to close. For example, the Young Men's Christian Association (YMCA) was established in the nineteenth century in response to the need for a healthful Christian environment for young men who moved from rural areas to the cities for jobs. Had the YMCA not adapted to a new environment by abandoning its lodging business when that migration ended and shifted to filling other needs in the urban environment, it might not exist today. Similarly, the March of Dimes was founded in 1938 as the National Foundation for Infantile Paralysis, largely through the efforts of President Franklin D. Roosevelt. When a vaccine for polio was developed and the disease was eliminated in the United States, the organization lost its rationale for existence. In this case, the organization found another health problem—birth defects—that required a solution; thus it adapted to serve other social needs.

Responding to changes in the environment is not as simple as meeting current needs. Organizations that respond to changing needs by dramatically altering their own institutional value systems also risk their future. If traditional contributors fail to support an old institution in its newest efforts, then their contributions may be lost before a new support base is established. For example, consider a small Roman Catholic arts college built on the tradition of providing a well-rounded education based on Catholic values in a highly personal environment. The college might respond to declining enrollments by orienting itself toward meeting needs for continuing education in local workplaces. However, the college risks losing its entire traditional student base as well as its existing alumni support. The college may gain an expanded new student body and obtain private dollars from the community, but it will be a different institution with different potentials for fundraising.

Philip Kotler has made significant contributions by adapting marketing principles from business to nonprofit organizations (Andreasen and Kotler, 2007). He devised a scale that described an organization's orientation in one of three ways: unresponsive, casually responsive, or fully responsive.

Unresponsive organizations function as closed systems, as bureaucracies. They do not encourage customers to submit inquiries, complaints, or suggestions; they do not determine customer satisfaction or needs nor do they train staff to be customer oriented. The casually responsive organization begins to look externally in its planning. It encourages its constituents to provide feedback, and it periodically measures constituent satisfaction. The fully responsive organization shares the characteristics of the casually responsive organization but also tries to improve its services based on new needs and preferences and prepares its staff to be customer oriented.

Many nonprofit organizations cannot and should not become fully responsive to the market in order to enhance their fundraising. They must remain in harmony with the values and mission on which they were founded. Organizations with strong internal value systems that give rise to their missions should become highly responsive by actively involving their clients and potential contributors in the organization's affairs. Fundraising success depends on the sensitive inclusion of potential supporters in the life and spirit of the organization.

Kotler comes to the same conclusion (Andreasen and Kotler, 2007): "If a manager wishes the organization to be wholly customer-driven, he or she must directly confront the often unspoken fear that this type of marketing orientation will ultimately cause artists, surgeons, librarians, museum directors, and other nonprofit professionals to bend their professional standards and integrity to 'please the masses.'"

Nonprofit organizations today are vulnerable to concepts of social entrepreneurship and market orientation. Donors often push nonprofits toward operating more market-based services, using a business model, with a focus on the bottom line. Some nonprofit organizations have had to deal with external pressures to balance bottom-line interests of donors and board members with a top line, mission-driven orientation.

Although nonprofit organizations do not exist to generate profits, their long-term survival depends to some extent on good business practices. Nonprofits that develop surplus income protect themselves from fluctuations in client fees and fundraising levels. Surplus revenue also assures contributors that the organization has a future. Organizations that strive to provide the most effective services with the fewest resources are the most likely to generate surpluses. Organizations that are viewed as effective and efficient also have the best opportunity to attract philanthropic dollars. How well a nonprofit organization is managed also has an impact on its ability to raise money.

Accountability is a major force in nonprofit organizations today. Accountability encompasses not only how well a nonprofit is managed but also how well a nonprofit communicates its management and outcomes to its constituents. It is an organizational strength for a nonprofit organization to hold itself accountable to demonstrate good stewardship to its constituents.

Business techniques may be useful in managing nonprofit fundraising. However, the values and beliefs that give rise to these organizations often lead them necessarily to defy good business marketing practices. New service initiatives that abandon mission to enhance revenue production can harm philanthropic efforts. And when unpopular causes must be pursued, if the organization is to remain faithful to the requirements of its mission, then it must defy marketing information in favor of its mission.

Sometimes fidelity to mission leads to conflict with sources of support. A conservative funding source might hesitate to support an organization that is serving a controversial cause because its employees, customers, or stockholders might object. A for-profit industry that manufactures a product to reduce tooth decay might be threatened by the successful efforts of a nonprofit organization that seeks to eliminate tooth decay. Organizations that understand and manage this complexity put themselves in a position of strength when raising funds.

Fundraising is an effective test of organizational viability. As such, fundraising can become the catalyst for organization renewal and commitment. To be successful in fundraising, the organization must be viewed by potential supporters as responsive in its delivery of quality services. These services must be provided to constituents in an effective and efficient manner. Potential supporters must understand and accept the value systems that affect these services. An organization that lacks internal meaning has no basis for stimulating philanthropy.

By managing tensions between responsiveness to changing environmental factors and pursuing its mission, an organization can enhance its strengths and minimize its vulnerabilities. A simple SWOT analysis (strengths, weaknesses, opportunities, threats) will enable an organization to conduct and know better how to succeed with its fundraising (Kearns, 1996). SWOT analysis can help an organization build on its strengths, minimize its weaknesses, and deal with opportunities and threats in its external environment. Thus the organization can reduce its vulnerabilities in organizational readiness, human resource, markets, vehicles, and management—the factors that are essential to successful fundraising.

Organizational Readiness

The premise of this chapter is that effective fundraising is built on organizational strengths and that organizational weaknesses and vulnerabilities can undermine fundraising efforts. With this in mind, an organization preparing itself for fundraising must analyze its strengths and weaknesses and inventory those resources that are essential for successful fundraising.

Fundraising based on the strengths of the organization assumes a dignity that flows from those strengths, obviating any need on the part of staff or volunteers to apologize for the solicitation process. Fundraising based on values and mission is a meaningful part of philanthropy. To take its case for philanthropic support to the public, the organization must have prepared itself internally to focus on its strengths.

An essential readiness element is the organizational plan. The plan accurately attests to the organization's stability and its future, based on an assessment of current and future social and human needs within the scope of the organization's mission. One of the greatest strengths that the plan can bring to the fundraising process is the affirmation that the organization is confident of its future and empowered by its vision for a better society.

An effective plan must go beyond a description of programs. Programs must be drafted in economic terms if they are to provide a suitable foundation for fundraising. The plan must project annual income and expense requirements for each program, both those in existence and those planned for the future. Equally, the plan should identify the anticipated special purpose, capital, and endowment needs for the designated period. The organization is strongest when the prospective donor can accept the validity of the income and expense projections relative to past accomplishments and future program delivery. If financial accountability through the planning process can demonstrate efficient use of resources for effective programs, then good stewardship has begun.

The organization's financial plan should go beyond ordinary income and expense projections. It should state the amounts that must be raised for current program support through the annual fund; the amounts required for special projects, some immediate and urgent, others deferrable; the amounts required for capital projects; and endowment and cash-reserve requirements. This comprehensive financial analysis, with its realistic assessment of anticipated revenue and gift production, forces careful evaluation of program proposals and responsible decisions when priorities are set.

Before the planning process can be initiated, the process itself should undergo scrutiny from the professional staff and volunteers of the organization to determine the extent to which it has involved the organization's primary constituency. The sensitive and responsive plan involves the professional staff and volunteers from the governing board as the plan's architects. Both groups must commit themselves to implement the plan and to evaluate it on a continuing basis, or the organization will be vulnerable during the fundraising process. The organization can benefit by creating ownership of the plan among its constituents. This can be done by inviting leaders in the constituency to become part of the planning activity. The more the organization's mission is affirmed through planning, the better the chances of winning the constituency's endorsement when the plan is finished. The plan will give substance to the various programs that have been devised to respond to the designated human and societal needs. From these program descriptions can be drawn the four, five, or more of the most salient and exciting expressions that will animate the case.

Human Resources

The first human resource strength in organizational readiness is the governing board. A thoughtfully structured, involved, and dedicated board of trustees is a symbol of responsible governance and an asset to the fundraising process. Conversely, a passive, uninvolved, and disinterested board is a problem that continues to confront organizations in the twenty-first century.

It is essential that board members be actively involved in planning, from the beginning delineation of the planning format, through the periodic review, and as part of the final acceptance of the plan with its definitions of program and financial priorities. By accepting the plan, board members accept the responsibility to give and to ask others to give according to their means against the financial needs. This is trusteeship at its best. Finally, the board members must have integrity and credibility with the community, serving as the organization's first point of accountability to the public and as stewards of the public trust.

The board has a direct responsibility to press for the success of the organization's fundraising programs. To accomplish this, the board should include a fundraising or a development committee as a standing committee. This committee should include in its membership those board members who have the strongest interest in the organization's mission and whose linkage with the community helps initiate fundraising. This committee should meet regularly and actively develop, implement, and evaluate fundraising plans. Committee membership can be extended to those who, although not on the board, would nevertheless be willing to give, ask, and work as advocates of the organization.

The second point of strength is the professional staff: the CEO, individuals responsible for managing programs and finances, and the fundraising staff. The nonprofit entity's viability depends on long-term delivery of quality services that the public perceives as needed. This focuses attention on the CEO and the program staff. Filled by capable people, these positions provide an organizational strength. The CEO is a key strength in the fundraising process as a link to engage the board and to represent the organization in engaging donors and prospects.

The CEO also sets the stage for organizational support of fundraising. Lack of CEO understanding, involvement, and support is a key weakness.

For long-term fundraising to succeed, it requires the attention of someone who is competent to plan, organize, and manage the fundraising process. The amount of time and the level of professionalism required of fundraising management positions varies by organization, ranging from volunteer to minimal part-time to full-time with a multiple-member professional staff; this often depends on the organization's age and size. The fundraising position of an organization is enhanced if it has full-time professional staff members at the helm who are dedicated to involving board members, other volunteers, and administrative, program, and support staffs to assist in the fundraising process.

The governing board and CEO must be prepared to become involved in fundraising. Board members must accept ownership of the organization and support it financially as a necessary first step in establishing organizational readiness. The final assessment of readiness is determining the ability of board members, fundraising professionals, the CEO and key staff members to come together as a fundraising team. There must be an understanding of and a commitment to the concept that successful fundraising depends on the active participation of board members, the CEO and key staff members on the team, both in the development and organization of fundraising programs and in asking for gifts.

Acceptance of this concept by all is essential to the fundraising process. Under the definition of this process, the fundraising staff will provide the management services for the fundraising program. The volunteers will provide the linkage and the leverage to the gift-making potential of the community. A properly developed governing board and volunteer and professional staff members represent necessary strengths for undertaking fundraising.

Sources of Support

Philanthropic funds originate in general areas of the economy referred to as *gift sources* or *gift markets*. The five gift sources for fundraising activities are individuals, corporations, foundations, associations, and government. To some extent, every nonprofit organization has potential supporters among these markets. Opportunities for fundraising come from recognizing the potential for support among specific subsectors of each market. Proper prospect-development practices will make it possible to identify, cultivate, and solicit prospective donors in each subsector.

Government funds are *not* philanthropic funds. But it is important to recognize that government funding has become a larger rather than a smaller source of revenue for nonprofit organizations. The end of the first decade of the twenty-first century saw a new infusion of federal stimulus funds to some nonprofits. A slowed economy is likely to affect continued growth of government funding and make it challenging especially for small neighborhood organizations and church and parachurch activities that provide neighborhood services.

The second decade of the twenty-first century sees a continued change of gift markets to those from which organizations sought funds at the beginning of the last decade of the twentieth century. Foundations have continued to be an important source of funds, but not as significant as they once were; corporations take a more strategic approach and continue to be affected by a slowed economy; individuals are more likely to be interested in program-related projects that allow them to express their own values and interests, many with private foundations to make their giving more formal. Understanding the values, interests, and needs of donors has always been important to fundraising, but is even more important to success today. Being patient with loyal donors who face a more uncertain economic future, increasing health care costs, and diminished assets is key to success.

Organizations today must have specific information about the prospect's interests and linkages and ability and willingness to give. By accepting this basic principle of fundraising, the practitioner can understand that the organization will approach fundraising markets from its strongest position when its involves it board members, nonboard volunteers, and staff members in identifying, understanding, engaging, and soliciting potential contributors from any of the gift sources.

Fundraising Vehicles

A nonprofit organization maximizes its potential for philanthropic support it if utilizes the full array of fundraising vehicles in a total development program. These include annual giving, special gifts, major gifts, the capital campaign, and planned giving. The organization's fundraising plan must take into account the human and financial resources it can commit to different fundraising activities. Today that includes use of a website for solicitation and acceptance of gifts and taking advantage of the various e-philanthropy and social networking opportunities available to it.

Organizations that depend too heavily on the annual fund through direct mail, telephone, and special events fundraising are vulnerable to high fundraising costs. Organizations that are dependent on one or two large individual, corporate, or foundation sources are vulnerable to the changing interests and funding capacities of these sources. The more comprehensive the fundraising plan is in using all the fundraising vehicles available to approach the full scope of funding sources, the stronger it will be.

For small nonprofit organizations, this can be a challenge, especially with major and planned gifts. But every organization can encourage bequests or giving through wills and use volunteer or pro bono consultants or a local community foundation to help with special opportunities for other types of planned gifts.

Management

Most experts agree that nonprofit organizations are more professionally managed today than they were a decade ago. But a Kellogg Foundation initiative, Knowledge Management in Nonprofit Management Education, for the first decade of the twenty-first century is based on the evidence that professional talent is not uniformly distributed throughout the nonprofit sector. There is, however, some acceptance of the notion that even unsophisticated nonprofits are fairly efficient in the use of funds and effective in providing good services (Drucker, 1990).

Poor management, whether actual or perceived, is a deficiency that leaves a nonprofit organization vulnerable to failure in fundraising. Sound management staff and processes are an organizational strength on which successful fundraising can be built.

The most successful organizations have a management team of administrators, program managers, and fundraising managers who operate the organizations to some extent as an open system. This management team involves its various constituents—clients, donors, trustees, volunteers, vendors, the community, and its own staff—in continued analysis and planning before executing programs and exercising management control over its programs. The successful organization involves the same constituents in evaluating its programs as the management process of analysis, planning, execution, control, and evaluation begins another cycle.

Fundraising is a management process, based on the strength of an organization's programs to fulfill the organization's mission. Therefore the organization must be well managed. Transparency and accountability are the focus of management today. Organizations must illustrate to the public that they are good stewards of contributed funds and that the organization's programs are making a difference. In the strongest organizations, the fundraising manager has persuaded the board of trustees and the CEO to dedicate significant portions of their time and energies to the organization's fundraising effort.

Fundraising involves engaging constituents with the organization and helping them identify with organizational values and missions. It requires a comprehensive view of client constituencies, volunteers, advocates, and prospective contributors. Fundraising demands mastery of the professional technical skills required for fundraising and the ethical values that foster and protect philanthropy. It includes the management of planning and other efforts that precede many of society's voluntary actions for the public good.

Accountability

It is appropriate to end with a final word on accountability. The organization that makes itself as transparent as possible, holds itself accountable to its constituents and demonstrates good stewardship of mission and human and physical resources can engage in fundraising from a position of strength. The fundraising climate of the twenty-first century leaves organizations vulnerable to fundraising failure if they do not (1) communicate with their key constituents; (2) invite them inside their planning, management, financial, and evaluation processes; and (3) report accurately on expenditure of funds. Accountability is not just a buzzword of the last decade. Accountability has become an essential concept for nonprofit organization viability and success in the twenty-first century.

Conclusion

Fundraising success or failure is often related to organizational dynamics rather than fundraising strategies. Successful fundraising is built on strengths. Fundraising often fails because of organizational weaknesses or vulnerabilities.

First, to be successful in fundraising, organizations must operate as open systems while being true to their mission. Understanding the dynamics of the external environment whose gift support is sought is a key organizational strength. A sound plan for the future, developed with the involvement of key constituents, is an organizational strength in fundraising. It is also essential to have the CEO and the board involved in the process. Finally, the organization must have a communication plan through which it holds itself accountable to the public.

If organizations operate as closed systems, focused internally with no plan for the future based on external needs, they are vulnerable to decline and failure in fundraising. Simply doing good work is no longer sufficient to ensure long-term success. More sophisticated donors and funders today are holding organizations to higher standards of accountability. Doing so demands professional management approaches that lead to organizational readiness for fundraising.

CHAPTER THIRTY

DONOR DATABASE MANAGEMENT AND SEGMENTATION

By Jeffrey A. Lindauer

W hen the first edition of this book was written, few could foresee the impact of electronic data on the fundraising profession. What was once a need for simple mail-merge technology for the annual year-end letter has become a desire to maintain a cornucopia of knowledge on which competent fundraisers can base their work. As costs to acquire and save data decrease and the capability to analyze data expands, the question of *what data should be captured?* has changed to *what* shouldn't *I capture?*

In its most basic form, the fundraising database is composed of the information necessary to facilitate the fundraising process. For some organizations, the need may be as simple as recording the name, contact information, and gift history of a small number of donors. This will facilitate a prompt gift receipt and personalized thank-you letter, and the information can be used to produce the annual honor roll of donors. In subsequent years the same data can be used to renew their generous support.

For others, the need for data has expanded to a comprehensive collection of data elements including an almost limitless number of attributes such as event attendance, volunteer activity, linkage indicators, wealth and asset information, predictive modeling data, marketing segments acquired from external vendors, contacts with the organization, online behavior, and more. If the information is available, it can be stored in a database, analyzed, and used to increase the effectiveness and efficiency of the organization.

Although it has become easier to store, analyze and use vast amounts of data, it is important to remember that fundraising is, at the end of the day, about people. The process of asking for money will ultimately determine the overall success of any fundraising program. Those who are most successful are able to leverage the data they have at their fingertips to more effectively manage both resource allocation and their personal relationships with others. Simply collecting data for the sake of doing so is a certain path to "analysis paralysis" for many fundraising professionals.

Sample Data Elements

The data elements that an organization could acquire and store are limited only by the imagination of those responsible for capturing them. For the purposes of this discussion, data are considered to be more fundamental in nature, captured for individual donors and prospective donors, and used for the purpose of increasing the effectiveness of the solicitation process. To fully list any and all possible data elements would be a herculean task.

The Basics

While nonprofit organizations may differ greatly in their ability to collect, maintain, and use data, certain core data elements are essential for all. Few would disagree that simple contact information such as name, address, phone number, e-mail, employment information, and historical giving transactions are a requirement for any organization to capture and maintain.

These core data elements allow fundraisers to perform the main functions necessary to maintain a fundraising operation. Direct mail solicitations, telemarketing, e-mail, personal solicitations, gift receipts, thank-you letters, honor rolls, invitations to special events, and more can be generated with this minimal amount of data. Employment information not only helps with matching gift procurement but also provides helpful information when determining a prospective donor's ability to give.

Core data elements are often acquired at the time of the first gift to an organization. Data are captured from gift cards, information provided on a check, or online giving forms. RSVPs to organizational events and volunteer opportunities also provide opportunities to capture data on new prospective donors and update data on those already in the database. Information may also be acquired through list brokerage firms who specialize in renting or selling lists of potential donors based on criteria the nonprofit would work to determine.

Solicitation History

In addition to the basic giving history of each donor, the database should contain a solicitation history. This information is valuable on both a micro and a macro level. For the individual, it is helpful to know which solicitations (both personal and mass) have been made, when they were made, and the outcome. This information may be tracked by coding each appeal (and segment within each appeal) with a unique code. That tracking code is applied to the individual's record at the time of solicitation and again on the gift transaction, should the donor make a contribution.

On a macro level, this data enables the nonprofit to analyze the success of each individual solicitation, watch for over- and undersolicitation and generally monitor donor response to appeals at every level. As a management tool, this information is extremely valuable to determine future solicitation activity and to allocate resources most effectively.

Event and Activity Data

As the organization begins to expand its data catalog beyond the basic data elements just outlined, a logical next step is the recording of interactions with the organization and members of its staff. Keeping a comprehensive record of these interactions begins with the recording of attendance at any functions held throughout the year. This may include fundraising-specific events, such as an annual fundraising auction, or attendance at board meetings. Any such activity should be recorded, as these data are critical as the organization works to build a historical account of each donor's and each prospective donor's relationship with the nonprofit entity.

To further enhance future use of the data, event activity should record not only those who attended but also who was invited to each event and the RSVP status of each invited guest. Those who respond in the affirmative but never show up should be distinguished from those who attend every event. This data can provide important insight into individual donor behavior as well as assist in the analysis of the effectiveness of each individual event.

In addition to event attendance, many volunteer and other types of activities may be available to those interested in the organization. Each volunteer activity, its duration, and related information should be recorded. This will provide information to the organization when volunteers are needed in the future and also indicate which individuals have the greatest linkage and interest.

Personal Interaction

In addition to events and activities involving many players, a historical account of personal interactions with each individual should be recorded. The relationship between donors and organizations often outlasts the tenure of staff. As members of the organization's team come and go, it is helpful to have detailed accounts of prior interactions, from phone calls to personal notes to face-to-face visits. The reports filed on each contact should ideally include information that employees should know as they pursue the relationship in the future.

After each contact with donors or prospective donors, staff should be encouraged to document pertinent details of the discussion. This may include specific interests of the donor, funding opportunities, and particular concerns. As others currently on staff or those who join the staff into the future begin to work with that same donor, the historical record will help them understand what has happened in the past and plan appropriately to continue the relationship.

Ideally, data on the nature of each contact will include not only the substance of the discussion, but also the type of interaction (phone, e-mail, personal contact), circumstances, and next steps required to move the relationship forward.

Wealth and Ability

As the nonprofit becomes more sophisticated, it may look to enhance its database with additional data elements beyond those most readily available. Additional research to determine the ability of each individual can uncover prospective donors who would not otherwise be considered for a more substantial gift.

Internally, members of the staff can conduct research using many common tools. These may range from simple and inexpensive Internet search engines to robust data repositories available for a significant subscription fee. Publicly available information will allow the organization to gather considerable data related to an individual's wealth. Home ownership and values, publicly held stocks, and other financial information are available on many individuals in the database.

For large organizations and those with little time to invest in internal research, there are many vendors who can conduct this type of screening. Outsourcing may be limited to a select few individuals or the entire database of names, depending on the need and budget available.

In addition to specific wealth information that may be acquired, others involved with the organization often can provide information on their peers. Engaging loyal donors and volunteers to help identify others who may be able and willing to support the organization can provide valuable wealth data. In addition to the data received on others, this volunteer activity can strengthen the relationship with the individual.

Regardless of the source of this valuable information, wealth and ability information should be stored in the database. This data may be used to further segment prospective donor pools for various methods of solicitation and to determine ask amounts. As a prospective donor's wealth increases, so too can the time and energy invested in the prospective donor. Over the long term that investment may yield significant rewards.

Unique Data Elements

Beyond those fundamental elements already mentioned, a nonprofit may have valuable data that is unique to their organization. Institutions of higher education, for example, have degree data, lists of classes taken by each individual, favorite professors, Greek affiliations, and more. Organizations in the medical field may have extremely private medical information such as an individual or their family member's experience with a particular disease and information about the doctors and specific specialty areas that may have been influential in the treatment process.

Each organization must determine for itself which data it wishes to maintain and how these may be used in the future. An evaluation of the value of the data compared to the costs necessary to acquire and maintain them should determine the willingness to add each specific element to the database. When in doubt, it may be wise to do so, as a future application may warrant the data, and once it is gone it may be difficult to retrieve.

Leveraging the Power of Data

As a database and the number of elements captured grow, so do the possibilities for its use. From basic segmentation of membership lists and annual fund appeals to identifying major gift prospective donors, data play an important role in the fundraising process.

At the most basic level, the use of data should lead to increased efficiency and effectiveness. It allows the organization to best allocate its finite resources to solicit the right people for the right gift at the right time.

Linkage, ability, and *interest* are fundamental concepts on which every fundraising program is based. Data can play a key role in determining an individual's level of each. Data can be leveraged to identify the best approach for each prospective donor. In some cases, data may even determine that the best approach is no approach at all.

Linkage is usually very easy to determine if data are available in the system. Board members, donors, friends, and volunteers all have varying levels of linkage. So do those in others' networks of friends and acquaintances. If the data are in the system, the relationship can be determined. In many ways linkage, like interest, relates to a donor's propensity to give. Those who are most closely associated with the organization today (or who can be brought into the fold in the future by others) are better prospective donors than those without linkage.

Ability may be determined by giving history, wealth data, or even by comparing zip codes to historic U.S. Census Bureau data. Knowing what a prospective donor may or may not be capable of giving is an important factor when determining how an organization should approach them.

Interest is simply the interest an individual has in the nonprofit and its work. Those with great interest in an organization are more likely to give, and as this interest increases, often the size of the gifts (within the individual's ability level) does too. Interest is often determined much as linkage is. Active attendance at events and meetings, volunteering, interactions with staff, and other data points may point to greater interest. For others, the determination of interest is more difficult. Data may show that they refuse to attend events and don't volunteer, but they do write three checks annually. They may be as interested as anyone but aren't the type of person to attend events or volunteer. Determining the proper formula to identify true interest will help answer the question.

One could combine linkage and interest into one metric: "propensity to give." Ability stands on its own as "ability to give." It is true that ability may drive propensity in some cases, but often the two are considered distinct. Figure 30.1 presents a chart depicting the possible combinations of these traits.

When determining the best allocation of resources on individual prospective donors, it would be ideal to plot every prospective donor on such a chart. Knowing where each prospective donor falls on the chart allows the nonprofit

FIGURE 30.1. PROPENSITY AND ABILITY.

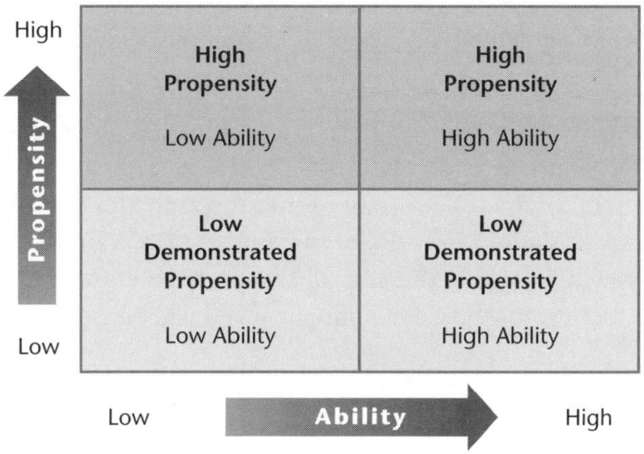

to make the best possible connection with them. Gone are the days of "one size fits all" fundraising approaches; the allocation of resources and strategy can and should vary widely by prospective donor type.

High Propensity, High Ability

Prospective donors with the greatest propensity and ability to give are the most valuable prospective donors available to the organization. They are truly the best of both worlds, having a keen interest in your success and the means to make a substantial gift. Ample resources should be allocated to this segment. These prospective donors warrant considerable investment of the organization's time and efforts. These are, or likely will be, the most significant donors to the cause.

High Propensity, Low Ability

Many prospective donors have a great desire for the organization to be successful, but lack the financial means to make major gifts. These individuals are often consistent annual fund donors, albeit with less significant gifts. They are your best friends, your greatest advocates, your key volunteers. The organization may wish to work with this segment to upgrade their giving to appropriate levels but cannot expect a major gift in the near future. These loyal individuals may be prime candidates for exploring planned giving opportunities. Prospective donors may be surprised that they can make a gift much larger than they ever thought possible through their estate, real estate, or life income arrangements. By marketing to them appropriately about these opportunities, you may generate significant income from the resulting planned gifts.

Low Propensity, High Ability

Every organization has individuals with great wealth who either have never given or give dramatically less than they are able to. They have financial ability, but their linkage and interest are lower than other donors'. The nonprofit may choose to invest in this segment as an attempt to generate further interest. The marketing team may send high-end newsletters, and the individual could be invited to take a closer look at the organizational mission without a fundraising goal in mind. Resources are allocated to these "projects" with the knowledge that not all will be converted, but those who do become involved will be well worth the effort.

Low Propensity, Low Ability

Some prospective donors simply aren't interested and don't have the ability to support the organization. In some cases, the costs to maintain contact with these individuals outweighs the current or future return on the investment. The allocation of resources to those who fit this category may be significantly reduced and, in some cases, even eliminated. Those resources may then be allocated more effectively with the remaining prospective donors in the database.

Putting It All Together

It is easy to determine where some prospective donors should fall on the ability and propensity chart. One who has obvious wealth and a consistent history may be an automatic candidate for the high propensity, high ability segment. One who has no giving history or involvement and little wealth may score just the opposite.

For most, however, data can provide a "best guess" solution. An organization may use the data to "score" each variable on a scale to best identify each prospective donor's true position on the chart. Gift frequency, gift size, activities, and volunteerism may result in a higher propensity score, whereas home value, salary, location, stock holdings, and, again, gift size may be used to compute the ability score. With the two sets of data, you can determine the best allocation of resources for each individual.

This type of activity can be taken to a more scientific level by using a predictive model to programmatically score each prospective donor in the database, using a combination of weighted measures on each piece of data in the system. A predictive model is best created by looking at past activity to identify those factors that determine donor behavior. Some characteristics are universal, others unique to the organization creating the model. Once you identify those factors that influence giving behavior, that information is used to find individuals who closely fit those criteria and score them appropriately. This takes the guesswork out of the process and helps avoid making false assumptions. No model is perfect—there will always be outliers who defy explanation—but a good predictive model will help the organization execute the proper strategy for a variety of populations within the database.

Predictive models can be created in-house using off-the-shelf software or by outsourcing with professional service bureaus who specialize in predictive modeling for nonprofits.

Conclusion

Data are the lifeblood of any organization. As such, they should be treated like any other important asset. Investments must be made to acquire, maintain, and use data on an ongoing basis. As data become stale, inaccurate, and incomplete, they become useless. Every attempt must be made to maintain and grow a robust database to ensure success.

This discussion represents only a brief overview of a few representative ways data can be used to enhance a fundraising program. To become more knowledgeable and truly begin to explore the ways data can be used to facilitate success, the reader should turn to peers and professional organizations for further information. As technologies improve and fundraisers continue to create new and imaginative ways to use them, this field will continue to reap great rewards for those who can leverage the power of data.

CHAPTER THIRTY-ONE

BUDGETING FOR FUNDRAISING AND EVALUATING PERFORMANCE

By James M. Greenfield

According to James Connell (2001), budgets are useful both for planning and evaluation in fundraising because of their measurement of fiscal performance. Consider this: Your current fundraising budget is $131,115. Your goal is to raise $600,000 using a variety of solicitation methods. At fiscal year-end, you have raised $561,235, 94 percent of your goal, at a cost of $135,850, 108 percent of your budget. How should this performance be evaluated? Failed to make goal by $38,765? Overspent budget by $4,735? Or should your evaluation focus on net income of *$425,385* received at a fundraising cost of *$0.24* per dollar raised, with a return on investment (ROI) of *313 percent* in twelve months?

The first lesson about budgeting for fundraising is that results should demonstrate efficient use of budget dollars in the effective application of solicitation methods. Clearly, spending $0.24 to raise $1.00 with a return on investment (ROI) of 313 percent would be considered an astounding performance for any for-profit business or corporation. It also seems fair to ask: Where else can a nonprofit organization realize such fiscal profitability?

The second lesson about budgeting for fundraising is to understand that fundraising does not perform the same for every nonprofit organization, and nonprofit organizations are not all the same in how they conduct fundraising. As a result, there are no uniform guidelines for evaluating fundraising performance. It is not clear what the cost ratio should be, other than low. It also is not clear that simple bottom-line analysis of gross revenue measured against fundraising expenses is sufficient data to understand how each solicitation method in use is performing.

Organizations should be cautious about comparative analysis of fundraising performance between nonprofits, including between like organizations in the same community or geographic area. Such assessments can be counterproductive and lead to misinterpretations and incorrect assumptions. Why? These other nonprofits are not using the same solicitation methods to the same audiences for the same purposes at the same time, nor do they have the same donors, volunteer solicitors, priority of needs, or history of service.

In the absence of uniform guidelines for fundraising performance, several self-appointed enterprises called *charity watchdogs* have created their own evaluation criteria to measure and report nonprofit performance, including fundraising results. For example, a nonprofit organization can earn between one and four stars from Charity Navigator (www.charitynavigator.org) depending on the percentage of expenses spent on administration and fundraising. The American Institute of Philanthropy (www.charitywatch.org) produces a *Charity Rating Guide & Watchdog Report,* which scores some five hundred nonprofits with a grade from A to F based on three categories: Percent Spent on Charitable Purpose, Cost to Raise $100, and Years of Available Assets. "In these cases, the impression of donation worthiness is based primarily on financial efficacy rather than on effectiveness in program delivery" (Hager, 2004, p. 2). An additional consequence is that these watchdog actions "can cause great damage to charities that depend on public goodwill and financial support" (Hopkins, 2002, p. 446).

Another independent evaluator is the Better Business Bureau, with its enriched analysis program. The BBB, considered the "Good Housekeeping Seal of Approval" for nonprofits, is neither a watchdog nor a rating agency but conducts voluntary charity reviews for many of the larger nonprofits engaged in national and global fundraising. Their *Standards for Charity Accountability* lists charitable organizations that have met or failed their 20-point "Standards for Charity Accountability" in four broad areas: Governance and Oversight; Measuring Effectiveness; Finances; and Fundraising and Informational Materials. Two criteria, Standard 8 and Standard 9, are linked to fundraising costs as follows:

8. Spend at least *65 percent* of its *total expenses* on program activities.
9. Spend no more than *35 percent* of *related contributions* on fundraising.

These evaluating agencies rely mainly on data taken from the Annual Information Return (IRS Form 990) required by the Internal Revenue Service for all nonprofits except religious organizations. A new and improved IRS Form 990, effective beginning with the 2008 fiscal year, provides greater disclosure of financial details and governance operations. The main depository for public access to annual IRS Form 990 data is GuideStar (www.guidestar.org). GuideStar is not a watchdog but provides Internet access to details taken from IRS 990 returns plus actual copies of 990 forms of nearly all nonprofits with operating budgets at $250,000 and above. According to Mark Hager in *Exploring Measurement and Evaluation Efforts in Fundraising* (2004):

> However, the widespread availability of the information necessary to do these kinds of calculations has driven people to make giving decisions based exclusively on the measurement and evaluation of fundraising revenues and costs. To some donors, the cause matters less than the ability of the organization to demonstrate that it is a good steward of the money that the public entrusts to it. In turn, organizations begin to control their public *financial* face so that it projects the kind of image that attracts donors and grant makers while keeping watchdogs, regulators, and bad press at bay.

Budget Preparations

Budgets for fundraising must compete with essential operating expenses needed for charitable programs and services that have first priority in meeting current mission objectives, not the other way around. As a result, fundraising budgets often are squeezed into minimal support with maximum expectations. "The reality is that most institutions aren't spending enough on fundraising because their leaders fear public criticism or donor backlash. We need to talk instead of why institutions are under-investing in themselves. That's the real challenge" (Jaschik, 2005, p. 31).

To meet this challenge and to secure a budget for fundraising that will deliver maximum performance, fundraisers and the organizations they serve need to acknowledge several principles associated with budgeting for fundraising:

1. Nonprofits must recognize that the fundraising program is a *profit center*, not just another cost center competing for scarce budget dollars.
2. Fundraising is an investment strategy with expectations for high profitability at an average 300-percent return in twelve months. To achieve this level of efficiency, continued investment will be required for at least three years for each solicitation method used.
3. Donors and volunteers make investment decisions about their time and money with the expectation of a healthy return that benefits both the organization and the community it serves. As a result, they require quantitative and qualitative

reports to confirm that the funds they provided were well used to achieve the intended outcomes as benefits delivered back to the community.

4. Fundraising budgets should be prepared for each and every solicitation program. Each is a separate financial and human enterprise with its own share of direct, indirect and overhead expenses (see Table 31.1). Each requires support for preparation and planning, materials design and production, gift and data processing, donor acknowledgments and recognition, stewardship of the donor relationship and the donor's funds, and more. Each also requires staff time for budget preparation; expense monitoring; preparing gift reports; tracking cultivation and solicitation progress; and multiple meetings with volunteers and committees, professionals and management staff, current and prospective donors throughout the fiscal year.

5. Individual fundraising methods perform at different levels of effectiveness and efficiency. Each has a separate performance guideline with the potential to achieve reasonable cost levels after three years or more of continuous effort (see Table 31.2). Direct mail acquisition and benefit events are less efficient than other methods but are essential to the primary task of creating and maintaining a base of loyal donors with reliable annual gift revenues.

6. Budgeting for fundraising is a fiscal strategy with specific revenue goals linked with the organization's most urgent funding priorities. It is not an independent revenue strategy unrelated to donor interests or donor preferences for how these funds will be used for charitable purposes.

7. Fundraising expense reports should reflect how staff is using budget funds by monitoring each solicitation's performance and analyzing results throughout the fiscal year. Regular gift reports reveal details of these combined activities and aid in their management during the year.

8. Fundraising performance evaluation requires analysis of several factors beyond a simplistic year-end bottom-line measurement of expenses to dollars raised. To demonstrate success with each fundraising method requires an assessment of their individual productivity as well as profitability.

9. Complete expense details for each solicitation activity should include all their direct, indirect, and overhead expenses before performance is measured against revenues received.

10. The intent of all these assessments is to understand accurately how each solicitation method is performing and how their budgets were used to produce these results. In addition, these measurements are especially valid when preparing new budgets and forecasting future revenue results with reliability.

TABLE 31.1. DIRECT, INDIRECT, AND OVERHEAD EXPENSE CATEGORIES.

Direct costs	Printing, postage, meetings, equipment rentals, food and beverages, entertainment fees, travel expenses, telephone, consultants and other purchased services, office equipment, donor recognition, and so on
Indirect costs	Staff salaries and benefits, overtime, meeting support, legal and accounting, computer and Internet use fees, data processing, donor communications, staff education and training, gift processing and gift reports, newsletters and brochures, office furnishings and supplies, and so on
Overhead costs	Electricity, heat, insurance, rent, water, depreciation assessments, and so on

TABLE 31.2. REASONABLE COST GUIDELINES FOR SOLICITATION ACTIVITIES.

Solicitation Activity	Reasonable Cost Guidelines
Direct mail (acquisition)	$1.25 to $1.50 per $1.00 raised
Direct mail (renewal)	$0.20 to $0.25 per $1.00 raised
Membership associations	$0.20 to $0.30 per $1.00 raised
Activities, benefits, special events	$0.50 per $1.00 raised (gross revenue and direct costs only)
Donor clubs and support group organizations	$0.20 to $0.30 per $1.00 raised
Corporations	$0.20 per $1.00 raised
Foundations	$0.20 per $1.00 raised
Capital campaigns	$0.10 to $0.20 per $1.00 raised
Planned giving/estate planning	$0.20 to $0.30 per $1.00 raised

Source: James M. Greenfield. *Fundraising Fundamentals: A Guide to Annual Giving for Professionals and Volunteers,* 2nd ed. New York: John Wiley & Sons, Inc., 2002, p. 499. Reprinted with permission.

Collecting detailed expenses and attributing them accurately to each solicitation program is a major challenge. Without such information, however, volunteers and managers are handicapped in supervising these activities for maximum results during the year. Segregating expenses by each solicitation program is possible with the assistance of the budget or accounting staff. It may be necessary to expand their chart of accounts to track expenses by individual solicitation method, grouping not by category of costs (such as postage and printing) but by segregating postage and printing expense for each and every mailing. Only by segregating each mail activity and tracking donor renewal separate from new donor acquisition can the actual performance of each mailing be calculated.

And without good internal accounting support, an accurate assessment of individual solicitation activities is not possible. As a result, the organization's leaders will lack a true understanding of its fundraising performance and must rely on inadequate data (that is, gross revenue minus expenses) to estimate new budgets and forecast future revenues.

Fundraising budgets should be prepared using traditional categories of labor and nonlabor expenses including indirect and overhead costs, as shown in Table 31.1. These expenses are combined into the annual fundraising budget and represent the estimated amount of effort required to meet assigned revenue goals with maximum effectiveness and cost efficiency. However, accounting reports and budget summaries do measure neither effectiveness nor efficiency, and results analysis are usually reported only in the form of bottom-line cost ratio summaries.

Cost benefit analysis for nonprofit organizations should focus first on results achieved in the form of quantified services delivered back to the community its mission serves—certainly a better indication of accountability than the single measurement of a ratio of fundraising costs to funds raised. Nonprofit economists Steinberg and Morris (2010) explain:

> The ratio of costs to donations is idiosyncratic for each charity, so no one-size-fits-all constraint will be helpful. Some charities will be forced to spend too little on fundraising, hindering their ability to pursue their charitable mission. Other, more popular charities can comply despite wasteful practices. More fundamentally, the efficiency with which a charity passes through and applies donations to its mission is unrelated to the cost ratio. The cost ratio reflects average behavior, rather than the behavior resulting from an increase in giving, and pass through rates depend on the latter.

Not every nonprofit organization is able to mount the full array of solicitation activities listed in Table 31.2. Newer organizations with start-up fundraising programs begin with traditional methods such as direct mail acquisition and renewal, membership associations, activities, benefits and special events, donor clubs and support group organizations, and volunteer-led solicitations. These are annual fundraising programs designed to build a base of reliable donors, a process that requires a minimum investment of three years to achieve the productivity and profitability rates shown in Table 31.2. It is these same annual donors who will become potential major gift prospective donors in time, provided the organization engages them in positive relationships beyond their annual gifts.

A nonprofit organization's funding priorities can and do change each year, and some flexibility is required in overall budget applications. In addition, external sources can reduce their gifts, grants, and contributions, resulting in income falling below expectations. During the lengthy economic recession that began in 2007–2008, donors of all types reduced or discontinued their financial support, waiting until a more positive outlook allowed them to feel comfortable again in sharing their personal resources. Planned solicitation activities can be modified to respond to such circumstances and expenses adjusted, but often not rapidly enough to achieve net revenue goals forecast months before.

From time to time, nonprofit organizations also may require new capital investments in buildings, equipment, or endowments (or all three) and more sophisticated fundraising strategies will be needed, such as support for a capital campaign lasting three to five or even up to seven years. These additional expenses of staff and operating costs must be added to the fundraising budget needed for continued production of annual contributions to sustain current operations. Major gift solicitations are efficient as well as effective in raising large sums, but they also are more intense work, require greater preparation, and need volunteer leadership and commitment to be successful. The potential for success rests in large part on the positive relationships established with current donors over time. No one is likely to make their biggest gift *first*! Major donors also will conduct their own investigations into organizations that solicit them to determine their worthiness before investing their personal assets of any size. And prospective donors will study the organization in detail, review its overall fiscal stability, compare program expenses to administrative and fundraising costs, and more; all these data, filed in IRS Form 990, are available on GuideStar. Soliciting these major gift prospective donors will require extensive personal, face-to-face discussions led by board members, volunteers, and senior staff before a major gift decision can be achieved.

Finally, as more and more organizations develop Internet-based fundraising tools, it is important to consider their budget implications. However, no studies to date have established reasonable cost guidelines for broad application to the multiple areas of online, Internet, or social media fundraising. One estimate, in the *Philanthropic Giving Index*, is that online giving represents between 1 percent and 5 percent of total donations (The Center on Philanthropy, 2007b)—too small a sample to establish a sector-wide guideline. The challenge is that attempting to establish cost guidelines similar to those for direct mail, benefit events, capital campaigns, and other traditional solicitation strategies will always be problematic. Today's technology applications are often used as additions to existing fundraising programs and back-office work such as prospect research, gift acknowledgment, donor communications, and the like; therefore electronic solicitations are difficult to segregate from all other fundraising budgets as direct and indirect expenses. It is difficult to calculate identifiable charges for APS, EFT, ISP, open and click-through rates, blog mentions, tweets, and other person-to-person forms of social media; these occur in such volume and variety that it is impossible to accurately attribute them to budget categories as day-to-day expenses (be it for advocacy, direct programs and services, administrative, or fundraising activities). Sector analysts have only just begun to examine expense questions and calculate comparative costs. Although there are no prescribed standards as of this writing, it is important for nonprofit professionals to consider and study this phenomenon as the technology evolves.

Budget Summary

After individual budget plans have been prepared for each solicitation program, they are consolidated into a budget summary for all fundraising activities. Following internal reviews and approvals, this budget becomes part of the organization's overall fiscal plan submitted to the board of directors or trustees for approval. Because fundraising is directly linked to revenue production, this budget should also illustrate expected results, with some evaluation criteria to validate the positive returns to be achieved from this investment (see Table 31.3). In this table, 2010 reports net revenue of $425,385, an increase of $41,070 over 2009, with fundraising costs at $0.24/$1.00 raised and ROI of 313 percent. These figures reflect solid improvements within one year's time and demonstrate a consistent performance to add credibility to the request for a budget increase of $10,000

TABLE 31.3. SUMMARY BUDGET REQUEST WITH ESTIMATED EXPENSE AND NET REVENUE.

	2008	2009	2010	2011
Expenses				
Labor costs	$66,009	$74,164	$79,800	$84,300
Nonlabor costs	50,541	49.376	56,050	61,550
Total budget	$116,550	$123,540	$135,850	$145,850
Gift revenue				
Gross revenue	$448,765	$507,855	$561,235	$611,235
Less expenses	116,550	123,540	135,850	145,850
Net revenue	$332,215	$384,315	$425,385	$465,385
Performance evaluation				
Cost of fundraising	$0.26	$0.24	$0.24	$0.24
Return on expense	285 percent	311 percent	313 percent	319 percent

for the coming fiscal year (2011), with the projection of another $40,000 in net revenue.

The three years' worth of performance data in Table 31.3 also offer solid evidence that this fundraising program is growing in productivity and has demonstrated reliability to generate increased net revenues. Perhaps the right question to ask is, will a budget increase *above* $10,000 produce even greater net revenue? To answer, because past performance has shown that $10,000 has produced new net revenue of $40,000, why not invest more budget in such a successful program?

Performance Evaluation

Two factors are necessary for evaluating fundraising performance. First is the direct comparison between how each solicitation method is performing and where the budget was applied to achieve these results. Second is the comparison of current performance with prior years' results to determine a reasonably reliable forecast based on demonstrated outcomes (see Table 31.4).

A comprehensive evaluation of fundraising performance requires a detailed comparison between gift revenue and expenses for *each* solicitation activity. After three years of continuous operation, these individual results can be measured against the reasonable cost guidelines in Table 31.2. In addition, performance

TABLE 31.4. REPORT ON THE OVERALL RATE OF GROWTH IN GIVING.

	Two Years Ago	Last Year	Annual Rate of Growth	This Year	Annual Rate of Growth	Cumulative Rate of Growth
Participation	1,355	1,605	18%	1,799	12%	31%
Income	$448,765	$507,855	13%	$561,235	11%	24%
Expenses	$116,550	$123,540	6%	$135,850	10%	16%
Percent participation	39%	44%	13%	52%	18%	31%
Average gift size	$331	$316	–5%	$311	–2%	–13%
Net income	$332,215	$384,315	16%	$425,385	11%	27%
Average cost per gift	$86.01	$76.97	–11%	$75.51	–2%	–13%
Cost of fundraising	$0.26	$0.24	–8%	$0.24	–0%	–8%
Return on expense	285%	311%	9%	313%	1%	10%

data in Tables 31.3 and 31.4 provide essential information when preparing a new fundraising budget.

Fundraising is intended as a growth program. To maintain growth in the numbers of donors and dollars received requires a fundraising strategic plan with the following ingredients: a sound case statement; volunteer leadership; adequate staff, budget, systems, and space; and a dedicated effort throughout the fiscal year. Close tracking of the number of donors and their gift revenue, percent participation, and average gift size for each solicitation program in use allows the organization to monitor progress, discover problems or improvements, and make adjustments during the year. Success can be defined as more donors acquired, more donors renewed, increasing net revenues, declining fundraising costs, and rising return on expense percentages. Any change in these key indicators during the operating year requires immediate study to discover the reason or reasons and to make the adjustments to reverse any negative trends before fiscal year-end.

Analysis of Table 31.4 shows a rapid growth in numbers of participants at the cumulative rate of 31 percent over three years. This effort suggests a solicitation strategy invested largely in new donor acquisition and current donor renewal, unlikely areas for average gifts of $300 or more each year. In reality, this overall program has maintained average gifts in excess of $300 due to budget commitments to solicitation methods other than donor acquisition and renewal, with focus on major gifts, corporate and foundation grants, and planned gifts and estate planning, all of which are performing at average gift levels above $300. On balance, these nine performance indicators are useful assessments and provide reliable evidence to validate continued investment in this fundraising program. All that is needed for complete understanding of this program are a few gift reports.

Gift Reports

Gift reports are needed to track how each solicitation method is performing. To achieve this level of detail requires preparation of three basic reports that track three sets of figures: number of gifts, gift income, and average gift size. Begin with Table 31.5, which lists audiences selected for solicitation and their responses. Adding average gift size illustrates how effective these solicitations have been to motivate generosity, trust in the organization, and belief in its appeal message. Table 31.6 illustrates where donor preferences in giving are matched to funding priorities cited in appeal messages. The average gift size shown here illustrates to what degree donor interests and understanding of how their funds

TABLE 31.5. GIFT REPORT ON SOURCES OF GIFTS RECEIVED.

Sources of Gifts	Number of Gifts	Gift Income	Average Gift Size
Trustees and Directors	15	$28,500	$1,900
Staff and employees	235	19,650	84
New donors (acquisition)	625	18,950	30
Prior donors (renewed)	690	59,635	86
Corporations	22	106,500	4,840
Foundations	28	185,000	6,607
Associations and societies	4	30,000	7,500
Bequests and estates	2	100,000	50,000
Unsolicited gifts	39	9,500	244
Other gifts received	9	3,500	389
Total	1,799	$561,235	$312

TABLE 31.6. GIFT REPORT ON PURPOSES OR USES OF GIFTS RECEIVED.

Purpose or Uses of Gifts Received	Number of Gifts	Gift Income	Average Gift Size
Unrestricted funds	658	$101,850	$155
Temporarily restricted funds			
Programs and services purposes	345	129,457	375
Capital and equipment purposes	165	50,500	306
Education and training purposes	240	45,000	118
Research and study purposes	118	63,800	541
Client financial needs purposes	114	18,600	163
Staff and employee purposes	22	8,500	386
Other restricted purposes	120	8,028	67
Subtotal	1,782	$434,235	$244
Permanently restricted funds			
Unrestricted endowment	6	$45,000	$7,500
Restricted endowment	11	90,500	8,227
Subtotal	17	$135,500	$7,971
Grand total	1,799	$561,235	$312

TABLE 31.7. GIFT REPORT OF SOLICITATION ACTIVITIES AND RESULTS (BY PROGRAM).

Solicitation Activities	Number of Gifts	Gift Income	Average Gift Size
Annual Giving Programs			
Direct mail (acquisition)	456	$10,050	$22
Direct mail (renewal)	408	25,855	63
Membership associations ($100)	319	31,900	100
Activities, benefits, special events	380	40,800	107
Donor clubs and support group organizations ($250)	125	31,250	250
Associations and societies	4	10,000	2,500
Volunteer-led personal solicitation	55	19,880	362
Subtotal	1,747	$169,735	$97
Major Giving Programs			
Corporations	22	$106,500	$4,840
Foundations	28	185,000	6,607
Capital campaigns	–0–	–0–	–0–
Bequests and estate gifts	2	100,000	50,000
Subtotal	52	$391,500	$7,529
Grand total	1,799	$561,235	$312

will be used coincided with appeal priorities. The third report, Table 31.7, tracks each solicitation method and its revenue results, essential information to manage each fundraising activity. Average gift size in this example reveals how each solicitation program is meeting its assigned goals of numbers of donors, dollars and gift levels.

Numbers of donors is a critical factor to track in all three reports. In every organization, some donors will leave and replacements must be found. New donor acquisition is much more expensive and time consuming than renewal. Losing ten donors who gave at the $1,000 level may require securing a hundred new donors with an average first-time gift of $100 each, which is not easily achieved. Maintaining constant contact and spending time on personal relationships with current donors is an essential strategy. Being ignored is the reason most often cited by donors for leaving a nonprofit organization (Sargeant and Jay, 2004).

The information board members and management staff require for basic performance evaluation is greater than a one-year, bottom-line summary of expenses and gifts received. In Tables 31.3 and 31.4, the current fiscal year revenue received was $561,285. Hidden in this figure were two bequests for $100,000—gifts that cannot be repeated (see also the bequest details in Tables 31.5 and 31.7). To assume that the next fiscal year will perform above $561,285 is unrealistic, as only $461,285 in new gifts actually was raised. Further, if this $100,000 in bequest revenue is removed from current fiscal year analysis, fundraising costs will increase to $0.30 and ROI drop to 240 percent—a prime example that simple "bottom-line" analysis is a poor data source for understanding actual performance, especially when setting new fundraising goals.

Take this analysis one step further. Review Table 31.3 again, noting that coming fiscal year estimates are $465,385 in new net revenue from a modest budget increase of $10,000. Factor in the $100,000 in two one-time bequests in the current fiscal year, and another net revenue gain of $40,000 in the coming fiscal year is an unrealistic expectation and unlikely to be achieved.

Conclusion

The three years of results in Tables 31.3 and 31.4 provide a comprehensive analysis of fundraising performance. In addition, Tables 31.5, 31.6, and 31.7 reveal the "devil in the details": two bequests can cause a significant misinterpretation of results. Gift reports do indeed tell all and are essential to any accurate understanding of actual performance. Adding analysis of three prior years' results can provide benchmarks for setting new goals and are essential data when attempting to estimate the capacity of this program to deliver increased levels of net revenue with reliability. In the end, reliability is what every nonprofit organization should use for its fundraising budget and revenue assumptions.

CHAPTER THIRTY-TWO

MARKETING AND COMMUNICATIONS FOR FUNDRAISING

By Sandra Bate

One of Hank Rosso's most classic and lasting definitions is the simple but elegant phrasing he used to describe fundraising itself: the "gentle art of teaching people the joy of giving."

In that simple definition, Rosso, perhaps unwittingly, went so far as to suggest a brand for fundraising: an art that is kind, gentle, and focused on teaching about human joy and gifts. Facilitating that art—making it possible—is the work of marketing in a fundraising environment.

In the first edition of *Achieving Excellence in Fund Raising*, Rosso also stressed the concept of exchange that underwrites giving. "Gift making is based on a voluntary exchange," he said. "The contributor offers a value to the nonprofit organization . . . In accepting the gift, it is incumbent upon the organization to return a value to the donor" (1991, p. 5).

The best thinkers and teachers in fundraising and marketing agree on one primary principle: our work begins and ends with exchange.

Toward an Understanding of Marketing

Marketing facilitates, eases, and assists in one primary function: to make possible an exchange of items of value. A donor brings a gift, a donation, or a contribution of some item of value. It may be cash, a treasured art collection, used clothing, or a commitment of time and talent as a volunteer. In exchange, the organization offers gratitude, appreciation, a sense of affiliation, and tax benefits to the donor.

This concept of exchange is at the core of every contemporary definition of marketing. The American Marketing Association (AMA, 2009) defines marketing as the process for "creating, communicating, delivering, and exchanging offerings" that have value for customers, clients, partners, and society at large.

To Philip Kotler, the concept of exchange is central to marketing. "Through exchanges, social units—individuals, small groups, institutions, whole nations—attain the inputs they need. By offering something attractive, they acquire what they need in return. Since both parties agree to the exchange, both see themselves as better off after the exchange" (Kotler and Fox, 1995, p. 6).

Historic Role of Marketing for Nonprofits

Perhaps because so much of fundraising practice focuses on communication and relationship building, marketing's role in a fundraising environment has not always been clear. In the corporate world, marketing was traditionally intermingled with sales. In the nonprofit sector, marketing commonly competes with such donor-focused activities as event and donor appreciation initiatives. There has also been considerable confusion between marketing and promotion, which, indeed, is only one aspect of marketing.

Kotler and Andreasen's *Strategic Marketing for Nonprofit Organizations* (1996), first published in 1975, was one of the major influences in the expansion of marketing to nonprofits. Kotler stated, "I share a lot of the responsibility for the broadened use of the term marketing. In 1969, we claimed that marketing can be used not only by profit-making organizations but also by nonprofit organizations such as museums, churches, charities . . . that want to attract clients, volunteers, and funds" (p. 7).

As marketing was adopted in the nonprofit sector, the traditional four P's of marketing—product, price, place, and promotion—began to undergo adaptation. Human services and social causes replaced traditional products, with increased subjectivity and emotion. Price was measured in noneconomic indicators such as time, commitment, and advocacy.

The concepts intrinsic to marketing are at the core of good fundraising: identifying and understanding needs and wants, targeting and segmentation, an organization's brand and positioning, and effective communication. Marketing initiatives are blended to facilitate exchanges that are at the very heart of fundraising.

The Marketing Cycle

Marketing is a process, a continuing cycle with marketing goals met and adjusted along the way. Analysis begins where the service of a nonprofit organization is

FIGURE 32.1. THE MARKETING CYCLE FOR NONPROFIT ORGANIZATIONS.

delivered. Analysis causes modifications to the service, requiring new communication and delivery. The cycle is ongoing in a marketing-responsive organization, as shown in Figure 32.1.

Practitioners argue that to be most effective, management of the marketing cycle must be a nonprofit executive priority. This is often difficult because of staff and financial limitations. A marketing committee led by a competent volunteer is better than no marketing focus. But most effective is a fully integrated, cohesive marketing unit that has a seat at the senior management table. David Packard, cofounder of Hewlett-Packard, concluded, "Marketing is far too important to leave to the marketing department." In a fundraising organization, marketing assists strategic planning and analysis, market research, and communication. The goal is to influence attitudes, awareness, and actions of both active and prospective donors.

The Marketing Plan

To become marketing oriented, a fundraising organization should start with a marketing plan, which includes six traditional steps:

- Conduct a broad and unbiased *situation analysis* of your organization and the environment in which it operates. Itemize the forces that affect your effectiveness, analyze your resources, conduct a strengths, weaknesses, opportunities, and threats (SWOT) analysis, and describe and profile your donor and client markets.

- Define your marketing *objectives*—the broad outcomes you are seeking—in ranked order. Focus on what you want to achieve, and be realistic, quantifiable, specific, and measurable. Be clear and concise in stating your organization's objectives. Here, for example, is an example of a statement of objective that is simple and straightforward: *We will increase planned gifts by 10 percent in 2012.*

- Choose the *strategies* you will pursue to achieve your objectives. Strategies are general statements that relate what you must do to meet your objective. To increase planned gifts by 10 percent in 2012, for example, you may choose to educate your forty-five- to seventy-year-old donors about the tax benefits of planned gifts.

- Develop *tactics* that will lead to the accomplishment of your strategies. Complete with a time schedule and specific assignments for staff and volunteers, your agenda of tactics will serve as your work plan. Here are two examples of the tactics you might pursue to increase understanding of the tax benefits of planned gifts: (1) host a brown bag seminar at the local library; (2) conduct an e-mail campaign featuring accountants discussing estate planning.

- Set a *budget* for the tactics you will pursue. Be realistic and obtain quotes for services, production, mail, and distribution so you have a good idea of what investment will be required to achieve your success.

- Define your *controls* and review processes and identify metrics that will help you assess whether you are progressing toward your objectives. It is always wise to delegate responsibility for the control of a marketing plan to a representative group, to assure that the organization's broadest interests are being served.

The Role of Market Research in Fundraising

Market research takes the guesswork out of fundraising. It substitutes knowledge and data for assumptions, hunches, folklore, and urban legend. It can help achieve efficiency and increase fundraising success. It will minimize risk in decision making and planning by helping determine where energies and resources should be invested.

Market research is about gathering, recording, and analyzing data. For a fundraiser, market research data are always "donor-centric." They can be as simple as a demographic profile: Where do your donors live? What are their age and education levels? How much do they earn and where are they employed? How many children do they have and what are their ages? Or data can be as complex as a psychosocial analysis of how your donors trust your organization's brand and identity. Between those two poles, there are a thousand stops along the way.

Market Research and Donor Data

The distinction between market research and researching an organization's in-house donor base is significant. Most organizations have the ability to access a database that has a tremendous amount of helpful information for the fundraiser. In addition to the basics—who the donors are, how much they have given, and their addresses, phone numbers, and e-mail addresses—it ideally permits a wide amount of segmentation, a giving history for each donor, an assessment of giving capability, and a record of donor contact. Market research, focused externally, answers questions to inform decisions and facilitate fundraising planning and analysis. It provides perspective and documentation. It also assists fundraisers by providing the means to test and evaluate creative communication strategies long before they are refined and sent to donors.

Organizations can learn much through market research: What words and phrases best resonate with your donors? Do they understand and have empathy with your mission? Who are your competitors for the donor's annual gift? Is email or print the preferred channel? Did the donor read your annual report? What kinds of photo images best communicate your work? What news sources does your donor trust? What obstacles do you face with your donor in increasing the size of an annual gift? How does a recessionary economy make your donors feel about giving to you? The list of "we'd like to know" items can quickly grow and become unwieldy. There can be a tremendous appetite for information. It is not uncommon, for example, to hear managers say, "It sure would be interesting to know if . . ." The marketing manager's task here is a quick rejoinder: "Interesting, yes, but not actionable for us now." The difference between "nice to know" and actionable research—information on which you can plan, strategize, and build—is crucial and must not be minimized.

Setting Market Research Agendas

A market research agenda is based on a segmentation and prioritization of your markets. This should be done in your marketing plan. It designates the markets you will focus your energies and resources on and the order in which you will do so. For most nonprofits, this process entails a mix of current, former, and prospective donors.

But each market has segments that are important not to neglect. For example, the current donor market may include these segments:

- First-time donors
- $1,000 and above donors
- Donors who pledge
- Donors who give online

To set a research agenda, the fundraiser must decide what she needs to know to be effective when asking for the gift, providing stewardship of the gift, and renewing the gift. If one of your priority markets is composed of donors who pledge online, it will be helpful and actionable if you know how donors want to receive pledge reminders and how frequently they want to be reminded. Do they prefer an e-mail or a letter? A postcard or a brochure? How often do they wish to be reminded? Traditionally, organizations have assumed and guessed. Today's market researcher says, "Let's ask them."

Methods of Market Research

Market research is both quantitative and qualitative. Quantitative research includes such methods as surveys and web analytic inquiries. Quantitative research focuses on numbers and statements of fact. After well-crafted quantitative market research, for example, you can, with some confidence, make statements like "Eighty percent of our donors are unsure of the value of unrestricted giving to our organization."

Qualitative market research is more concerned with subjective factors such as expressions, feelings, and emotions. Questions are often not answered with a mere yes or no. A qualitative study might, for example, produce statements like: "If they had to choose, our donors would color us green, and they think we're more like an iPhone than a Dell computer."

Primary and Secondary Research

Primary market research includes original research—studies done specifically for a certain market and a certain organization. It is preferred because it is most specific to the organization's immediate information needs. Some nonprofit marketers determine that they can neither conduct nor buy their own primary research. That may be true, but secondary market research resources should be explored, because there are many trusted sources that can provide critical information.

For example, national trade and professional associations, local chambers of commerce, community libraries, online discussion groups, business development agencies, and state and federal government offices provide a wealth of data that can sometimes satisfy the need for information. For example, anyone who visits such portals as www.usa.gov will discover what Wendy Boswell, the guide to Web search for About.com, calls an "absolutely mammoth" resource.

The only caveat about secondary research is that you must always, always, always consider and evaluate the source of your information.

Types of Market Research Tools for Fundraisers

The types of market research that might be helpful in an organization's planning are listed here, along with a representative question that each type might answer.

Brand Testing: How is our organization perceived?

Concept Testing: Will this idea work with our donors?

Copy Testing: Does this copy communicate? Is it memorable?

Donor Satisfaction Studies: Do donors like the event we sponsor?

Focus Groups: How do first-time donors evaluate our proposed ad campaign?

In-Person or Telephone Interviews: Are legacies a goal for our donors?

Mall Intercept: What does the person on the street think about holiday giving this year?

Mystery or Secret Shopping: How easy is it to make an online gift to one of our competitors?

Online Panels: Do our donors understand our mission?

Segmentation Studies: Into what subgroups can our donors be divided?

Surveys: Who are our competitors? What do they do better than we do?

Website Analytics: What sections of our website do people visit and how much time do they spend there?

Web Intelligence Review: What are people saying online about us?

The research tool selected must match both the nonprofit's personality and the informational need. There must be a high degree of resonance between your organization and the type of research you pursue.

Sophistication of Market Research

As market research has become increasingly significant in the nonprofit sector, some organizations, with the very best intentions, are pursuing amateur research agendas. A word of warning is appropriate.

Research, by its very definition, must be sophisticated enough to be objective, reliable, and valid. The science of research is ever-expanding, and as the complexity of media increases, so does the possibility of significant error in market research. Go carefully into market research experimentation, and solicit the very best professional assistance that you can either purchase or barter. Look to volunteers whose expertise can assist you in the design and testing of research instruments. Purchase professional assistance in setting your agenda and determining what tools you will use. Then consider purchasing an evaluation of your research.

Research with fatal flaws—such as an incorrect sample, a built-in bias that affects objectivity, or a measure of something other than what you intended—will not only fail to provide answers but also can substantially harm your reputation and community standing. If you cannot assume reasonable confidence of success, it is better to use discussion groups and dialogues to gain feedback and input.

Communication: Building Awareness and Motivating Action

Building awareness is the marketing function traditionally best known and understood. In many circles, in fact, promotion and advertising—two trusted methods of building awareness—are commonly assumed to be the whole of marketing. They are in fact only one step in the marketing cycle, and they do not precede research.

For the nonprofit fundraiser, awareness is not defined as it may be in commercial initiatives. In retail marketing, awareness is measured by both top-of-mind brand consciousness and personal experience in a store or an online shopping venue. In contrast, the critical marketing requirements for the nonprofit fundraiser are to build awareness of

- The organization's identity and brand
- The organization's mission and work
- The organization's need for private support
- The ways a donor can support the organization

Communicating with a Purpose

There are two types of communication messages: those intended to influence attitudes and those intended to influence actions. Often communications intended to influence attitudes are based in public or media relations activities. These might include news releases, speeches, board and community presentations, and special events.

Communications intended to influence actions are generally based in advertising and promotional initiatives. These might include collateral material, newsletters, websites, advertisements, direct mail, and print and electronic solicitations with specific calls to action.

In fundraising, crafting, testing, revising, distribution, and analysis of these influential messages must be centralized and integrated. This ensures that all marketing tools, approaches, and resources can be used to maximize impact on donors and prospective donors, as well as other significant markets and publics. In building awareness, there is little room for uncoordinated and inconsistent messaging.

Planning a Communications Campaign

A formalized market research program of collecting, organizing, and assessing data about primary markets helps fundraisers build awareness through marketing communications. Four steps in planning depend on accurate and timely knowledge about the markets you are attempting to reach.

Define your market. Be as specific, focused, and segmented as your resources will allow. Rather than taking a scattered approach, hoping all messages and all words will reach all donors, target the segment that holds the best promise of return.

Define your message. Be as concise, clear, and direct as you can. Know what each market segment knows about you, so in a solicitation, you can avoid unnecessary communication and can ask for the gift. Clearly. Quickly. Now.

Test your message. Online focus groups have increased the ability to pretest messages prior to production. Test the colors, the design, the words you use. Do donors understand the iconic photography you're using? Do they prefer black and white to full color? Do your messages look organized and economical or expensive and lavish?

Define your media. Choose the media that will offer you the best access at the best cost. A personalized, one-off proposal to a donor will have the greatest impact, and at the right level of request that kind of focused messaging is proper. Harmony between your organization and the media you select is important. Hot air balloons may reach a certain segment of your market on a fall afternoon, but what does it say about the organization? Your executive director may be very skilled at Twitter, but is tweeting right for your audience and consistent with the significance you want your donors to connect to your communications? When you are choosing media, remember what Marshall McLuhan, the famed social critic and one of the first fathers of the electronic age, said: The medium is the message.

Media Selection

From the medium of print to the latest social media, interactive websites, web banners, and instant messaging, the list of media available in marketing for fundraising is long. In evaluating media, be sure to measure return on investment (ROI). You can assess cost and define the number of people in your audience, and if your communication effort has a measurable outcome, you can know at the end of a campaign if you achieved your goal. This kind of specificity in reporting requires tracking and recording. With websites, evaluating ROI has been greatly enhanced with tools such as Google Analytics, permitting you to see who comes to your website, how they navigate once there, and how long they stay.

Marketing researchers should select media intrinsic to the process and work closely with media buyers. The team ideally includes a researcher who knows and understands the market and the market's preferences, creative strategists who craft and design effective messaging, media experts who buy time and space to distribute the message, and analysts who can measure success.

The affordability of electronic communication is a complex issue. Many nonprofit managers still contend that e-mail is free. Indeed, depending on the volume of email you distribute, the cost is low—much lower than direct mail and print advertising impressions. But media decision makers must also take into account the reality that e-mail from nonprofits may have hit a wall in terms of market penetration and effectiveness.

Currently, Email Marketing Metrics (www.mailermailer.com) says that the average nonprofit can count on approximately 17 percent of its e-mail recipients to open their email. Of those, 2 percent are likely to click through to the intended message. To properly estimate the cost of e-mail, these open and click-through rates need to be used rather than audience size figures. This more honest evaluation substantially increases the per-unit cost for e-mail.

The Creative Work: Themes and Technique

The adventure begins when your creative staff is together for that first brainstorming session. And there is much advice on working with creative people. In fact, you can find whole books and articles with titles like *Working with Creative People in 12 Steps* (Sterling, 2005) or "5 Reasons Creatives Hate Working for You" (Collin, 2009). To negative messages like the latter, a good marketing manager will say "Nonsense!" Give the creatives good direction, good resources, and good freedom and let them do what they do best: communicate.

Start with a common understanding of what the donor wants and needs to hear at various junctures in her or his relationship with your organization. With this understanding, writers and designers can craft and deliver stories and profiles with the facts and feelings about giving gifts.

Donors generally want to hear about the impact of their gifts, so there should be creative techniques to tell the stories of a nonprofit's fundraising priorities and programs. One recent article told the story of a gifted sculpture from the sculpture's perspective. Rather than hearing the words from a donor or a fundraiser, the sculpture itself noted its new surroundings and commented on the reaction of visitors when they walked past.

Marketing managers must respect the creative minds that can conceive and implement new themes and techniques for telling age-old stories. Is the frequent, disorganized, and sometimes noisy brainstorming that the creative team wants to do worth the effort? Yes, when it results in telling stories of gifts that have great impact and that also accomplish the donor's original intent.

Other Communication Issues

Branding, message repetition, production quality, viral marketing, graphic design, copywriting and editing, internal communications, social media, donor honor rolls, annual reports, website design, and vendor relationships must be considered in crafting a strategic marketing communications plan. Information about those topics not fully covered here is readily available online from relatively trustworthy sources.

Gaining exposure to successful marketing and advertising agency shops and enrolling in workshops and seminars are two other ways the manager can quickly learn techniques and best practices for nonprofit fundraising communications. There are also highly respected consulting firms who specialize in marketing for nonprofits and who can assist with the development of communication strategies and marketing assessments.

Trust and Responsibility: An Ethical Framework

The Association of Fundraising Professionals (AFP) Code of Ethical Principles and Standards of Professional Practice calls for integrity, honesty, truthfulness, and the obligation to safeguard the public trust. It addresses professional fundraisers who serve the ideal of philanthropy. For marketing managers linked to fundraising organizations, there is another call to the highest form of responsibility and trust, documented by the American Marketing Association (AMA).

The organization's website (www.marketingpower.com) identifies these ethical norms for marketers:

- Do no harm.
- Foster trust in the marketing system.
- Embrace ethical values.

These are the ethical values called for by the AMA:

- Honesty: Be forthright in dealings with customers and stakeholders.
- Responsibility: Accept the consequences of marketing decisions and strategies.
- Fairness: Balance justly the needs of the buyer with the interests of the seller.
- Respect: Acknowledge the basic human dignity of all.
- Transparency: Create a spirit of openness in marketing operations.
- Citizenship: Fulfill the economic, legal, philanthropic, and societal responsibilities that serve stakeholders.

Conclusion

Marketing for a fundraising organization focuses on facilitating and consummating exchanges: items of value for items of value. Central to marketing activity in the nonprofit sector are three tasks:

- Analyzing the environment in which a organization conducts its business and defining opportunities and threats facing the organization
- Crafting the objectives, strategies, and tactics by which the organization will choose to understand, prioritize, and communicate with its many markets about its fundraising priorities
- Establishing a budget and management controls to monitor progress toward the achievement of marketing goals

Fully functional and respected marketing as a nonprofit management tool fulfills tasks at the core of fundraising success: it calls attention to an organization and finds the right words, phrases, images, and themes that translate that organization and its mission to a host of different market segments. It measures and understands how the organization is perceived and how those perceptions are changing over time. It increases awareness, builds consistent and memorable messages, and promotes an identity and brand for the organization. And most significant, it advances the "gentle art of teaching people the joy of giving."

For marketers in the nonprofit sector, there is no work more rewarding or more significant. As I take great pride in telling new staff members who join our marketing team at the Indiana University Foundation, "You are about to become involved in some of the most significant activity being done today in our profession and in society. Have fun, enjoy it, and bring your best energy and creativity to the tasks at hand, because this work matters."

CHAPTER THIRTY-THREE

SELECTING AND WORKING WITH FUNDRAISING CONSULTANTS

By Margaret M. Maxwell

Human talent is the lifeblood of any nonprofit organization. Board members, other types of volunteers, and staff bring a broad range of experiences to their work on behalf of the clients served by the organization. However, when venturing into new areas—whether in direct service delivery or in developing the organization's capacity to sustain itself—organizations often find that they need to bring new skills to the table. Hiring consultants can provide a valuable and cost-effective solution for the organization to gain needed skills in a timely fashion.

While many types of consultants work with nonprofit organizations, fundraising consultants in particular offer a wide range of services connected with building organizational capacity to deliver the mission in effective ways. From planning and coaching services focused on helping boards and executive leadership envision the organization's future (including the structure and leadership required to carry it out), to more focused fundraising planning for annual or capital campaigns or planned giving programs, to tactical services, to implement specific pieces of the fundraising effort, consultants are deeply involved in helping nonprofit organizations fulfill their missions. They are often valued for bringing an outside perspective that helps an organization see its options more clearly, making recommendations (based on research, best practices, or both) that can help establish future direction, developing board or staff competencies through training or coaching, and bringing needed technical expertise to the organization.

Because of the variety of ways fundraising consultants interact with nonprofit organizations, it makes sense to examine the areas individually to understand the issues related to each in greater depth.

Institutional Readiness

Fundamental to an organization's ability to achieve fundraising success is its ability to plan effectively for its future. Donors—especially those willing to invest significantly in an organization by making a major gift—want to understand how the organization will adapt and change its programs in order to remain relevant to shifting circumstances in the local community and broader society. They want to understand how the organization identifies critical needs and develops programs that have a significant impact. They want to understand the challenges the organization faces in remaining relevant. They want to know that the people involved in carrying out the organization's work—both board and staff—are skilled and that they are organized in effective ways.

Current research indicates that some donors also want very specific information about the organization's finances. They may also be looking for new ways to engage with the organization as a volunteer as well as a donor, which may present some new challenges to an organization as it envisions how to develop its program for the future.

Although nonprofit organizations usually are highly effective at developing and delivering programs, they sometimes are not so good at developing strategic plans that inspire donors and volunteers by describing a preferred future, one based on research and planning. And though board members may bring the required skill set to lead a strategic planning process, they oftentimes prefer to be fully engaged in the process as a participant rather than as a neutral facilitator.

This confluence of circumstances can be the impetus for an organization to bring in a consultant to facilitate the planning process. Although there are some consultants who specialize in strategic planning, fundraising consultants also often provide this service because of the strong tie between strategic planning and the case for support. The consultant may conduct qualitative or quantitative research, or both, as a backdrop to the planning process and lead the board and staff leadership through a series of conversations focused on reexamining the organization's mission, laying out the vision for the future, and describing the programs that will help carry out the vision. The consultant may also help put together the business plan to identify projected revenues and costs. Finally, the consultant may be the one to draft the plan for board and staff to discuss further and adopt.

Many nonprofit organizations conduct strategic planning on a regular basis—every three to five years, for example—although some instead use an event such as the arrival of new executive leadership as the impetus. Some organizations also use the planning process as a way of educating the board about the mission of the organization and their unique role as board members in safeguarding and stewarding its work. Fundraising consultants may be engaged to assist the organization in either of these activities (finding new executive leadership, such as the chief executive officer or chief development officer, or conducting board training).

Campaign Planning

An organization's strategic plan is generally used to develop its annual fundraising plans, but it may also be used as the basis for a capital or planned giving program, particularly if the strategic plan suggests that the organization should pursue significantly different directions for its future. Consultants are widely associated with planning for these types of fundraising initiatives, particularly capital campaigns.

Fundraising planning (whether for annual, capital, or planned giving programs) can involve a variety of services; these are the most common:

- Auditing the organization's current staffing and fundraising results
- Developing the case for support (drawn from the strategic plan)
- Testing the case with current and potential major gift donors
- Screening the organization's donor list to identify prospective major gift donors
- Assessing the strength of the organization's communications methods for informing potential donors
- Identifying and training volunteer leadership
- Recommending the preferred strategies for the fundraising plan
- Managing the overall effort

Even if consultants are engaged to play some or all of these roles, however, it is essential to remember that staff (including the CEO) and board members also play key roles in any campaign's success. The consultant and the organization's executive leadership and board leadership must be in agreement about the overall fundraising plan and must also have a clear delineation of each person's responsibilities for carrying out the work.

Program Implementation

Organizations may have the capability to develop well-thought-out fundraising plans, but lack the in-house skill set (or time) to carry out a particular piece of the plan. In an annual fund, for example, boosting the results from a moribund direct mail solicitation effort may require outside expertise from a specialist in this area. Similarly, launching a new special event—even if volunteers are involved in planning and staffing it—may require the services of an event planner. Special event planners are sometimes expected to generate event sponsorships and create invitations as well as handle all of the details of setting up, tearing down, and cleaning up after the event itself. At other times, they may be engaged to carry out just one part of the overall event (linen and décor selection and rentals for a dinner, for example).

For both annual funds and capital campaigns, many organizations use consultants to research potential funding sources and write proposals to institutional funders or government agencies. Although the proposals may also be written by the in-house staff responsible for developing and carrying out the program to be funded, experienced consultants can add great value by helping the organization craft a proposal that stands out because of its clear language.

Communicating with donors—through newsletters or other means—is another area in which consultants frequently assist nonprofit organizations. The consultant may be engaged to develop the communications strategy to connect with donors as well as to create the design and messages for specific communications pieces.

For any of these and other types of specific services, organizations have options for how to engage consultants. Some consultants bring a particular skill (such as direct mail design) and may be engaged to work with staff, other consultants, or both to carry out that specific aspect of the fundraising program. Another option for organizations that need a range of services is to engage a full-service fundraising firm that can provide both planning and implementation services. For these types of longer-term or more comprehensive services, board members may be involved with staff in the consultant selection process as well as in the implementation of the planning process or the work that flows from it.

Finding and Engaging Consultants

Clearly, there is a wide range of ways in which fundraising consultants are involved with nonprofit organizations—which means that engaging the right consultant to match the organization's needs is essential if the organization is to use its time and money wisely. The single most important thing an organization can do to ensure a successful consulting engagement is to be very clear up front about why a consultant is needed. Both board and staff need to discuss and agree on the scope of work, the expected outcomes, and the timetable for the work.

Ideally, an internal team should be established to oversee the consultant engagement process, especially if the consultant will be leading a study or planning process. Both board and staff members may serve in this capacity, depending on the scope of work. This committee should establish the selection criteria for potential consultants. In the process, the group should discuss the importance of geographic proximity (local versus regional or national consultants) and size of firm (solo practitioner or full-service firm). (It should be noted that some of the smaller activities described in the Program Implementation section may not warrant a committee, but can instead be supervised by appropriate staff members.)

After reaching internal agreement about the type of services needed, the type of consultant firm that can best provide those services, and the consultant selection process, the organization should identify potential consultants or consulting firms that have the expertise to do the required work. Sources for finding consultant names include the Giving Institute (formerly the American Association of Fundraising Counsel or AAFRC) and the Association of Fundraising Professionals (AFP). Depending on the type of organization, other professional organizations, such as the Association for Healthcare Philanthropy (AHP), the Association of Professional Researchers for Advancement (APRA), the Partnership for Philanthropic Planning (PPP), the Council for the Advancement and Support of Education (CASE), or other professional colleagues in the organization's particular field or community may be helpful in identifying potential names. Once a list is generated, however, it behooves the organization to narrow it somewhat by talking with professional colleagues about their experiences in working with the identified consultants and talking with the potential consultants themselves about their potential interest and ability to commit to the established timetable.

The next step in the process is to generate a Request for Proposal (RFP) that outlines the scope of work and timetable as well as pertinent background information about the organization. Examples of pertinent information include the major directions articulated in the strategic plan, a brief description of the current fundraising program (including staffing), any challenges that the organization is facing in expanding its donor base or its overall program, positive or negative perceptions of the organization among the media or with specific donor segments, and a brief description of the governing board and its role in fundraising.

In addition, the RFP should also outline the types of information the organization expects to receive in a proposal from the consultant and the format it is to be presented in. It is entirely reasonable to expect consultants to outline the process they will use to conduct the requested work, a description of previous relevant engagements (ones that presented similar challenges) and references (including contact information) of organizations for which the consultant has recently conducted similar work. Other specific information, such as the amount of funds raised compared to the goal in campaigns the consultant has worked with previously, may also be requested. In addition, the organization should ask for the consultant to outline the timetable and fee, plus any incidental expenses not covered by the fee (such as travel, duplicating, design work, or other special services), as well as the billing timetable. Ideally, the consultant will provide an estimate of the total reimbursable expenses the organization should expect to pay. The consultant also should identify how the fee will be billed and potentially tie the payment schedule to deliverable work products throughout the engagement. Finally, the RFP should include the proposal deadline and an organizational contact person, in case the consultant has additional questions.

Before determining how broadly to disseminate the RFP, the organization should keep in mind the relative scope of work. Choosing the consultants to handle an infrequent endeavor, such as a capital campaign that may go on over several years at a significant fee, may warrant casting the net for potential consultants more broadly than would the effort to find someone to write a single proposal. Both the consultants (who put together the RFPs) and the volunteers and staff (who must read through and evaluate them) appreciate having their time respected, which suggests that the goal of the RFP process is not to generate a large quantity of proposals. Rather, the process should generate proposals only from qualified candidates that the organization might actually want to work with.

Once the proposals are submitted, the internal committee should read through them and, after checking references on the candidates that seem to be a good fit, determine which consultants will be interviewed in person. In addition, the group should determine the questions to ask during the interviews and the process for "scoring" responses. Through the RFP process, ideally proposals have been requested from only those consultants who possess the skills and attributes being sought by the selection committee, and the organization has provided enough information about itself that consultants feel comfortable with the starting point for the potential engagement. Thus the in-person interviews may be focused on the fit with the potential consultants. Are their work styles compatible with the organizational culture? How flexible are they in adapting their preferred systems and tools to the needs of the organization? Is the person being interviewed the actual person the organization will be working with? Do the consultants have a strong commitment to the ethical practice of fundraising? How will the process they propose produce the results the organization needs? Do the timetables mesh?

Good Working Relationships

Any time a new individual is introduced into an organization—whether as a staff member, board member, volunteer, or consultant—the dynamics of the team within the organization will change. Even the best team relationships some-times are complicated, and it behooves a nonprofit organization to do everything possible to ensure that hiring a consultant becomes a positive decision for the organization and its relationships with constituents. To ensure the best possible outcome, there are several issues that should be addressed in the contract between the organization and the consultant.

Either party can draft the contract, but both must ensure that it spells out in as much detail as possible the scope of work, timetable, fees, and billing schedule that will guide the consultant's work. Inherent in any contract is the assumption that both parties—organization and consultant—are engaged in a true partnership and that both are thus obligated to perform work that advances the overall engagement. The organization must in a timely fashion supply the consultant with any background information the consultant requests about the organization. (Depending on the type of engagement, this could include the strategic plan, fundraising plan, donation reports, fundraising and organizational budgets, bylaws, architectural renderings, board meeting minutes, and develop-ment committee meeting minutes.) The organization also must commit to a decision-making process and timetable that advances the overall timetable for the scheduled work. (Even though committees are often involved in reviewing their work, consultants usually expect to have a single point of decision-making contact established in the contract so that there can be clear direction coming out of group discussions where sometimes-conflicting opinions are expressed.)

Similarly, the contract should outline the consultant's deliverables and the deadlines for delivering them. The contract also should contain a "back door"—a way for either party to end the agreement with appropriate notice and compensation for completed work.

Another issue to be addressed in the contract is ownership of the "work product." Oftentimes consultants bring to the engagement certain terminology, formats, templates, or other tools that they believe are proprietary. In some cases, these same types of work products might be developed in the course of the consulting engagement with the organization. The contract should spell out clearly who has the rights to use this work in the future.

In addition to a strong contract, it is important for an organization to have realistic expectations about the type of work that a fundraising consultant can actually do. For example, if the organization does not have a strong, compelling case for support, no fundraising consultant can magically create one. Although the consultant can suggest the types of things that should be done to enhance the case, there must be a commitment from the board and staff to implement these changes if the case is to be strengthened.

Similarly, a consultant cannot manage a campaign without board and organizational leadership involvement. In effective engagements, the consultant is considered a vital member of the team, not someone for the organization to outsource its work to. Consultants also should not be expected to solicit gifts, although they may accompany volunteers or staff on solicitation calls. (It is very important that the relationships developed through any fundraising campaign remain between the organization and the donor, rather than between the consultant and the donor.) Finally, codes of ethics from every professional fundraising association dictate that a consultant should never work on a commission or percentage basis.

Conclusion

Fundraising consultants bring valuable expertise to nonprofit organizations, especially when the skills needed by the organization are not readily available on the staff or board. They also bring an outsider's perspective and can confirm and validate current programs and ideas, challenge the organization's leadership to build on what already exists, and share new ideas for how to improve fundraising success. By bringing a structure and rigor to the fundraising process, they can keep the organization on schedule to achieve the results it seeks. Finally, they can help build the organization's staff and volunteer skills through training followed immediately by the opportunity to practice under their mentorship.

Consultants can be valuable members of the organization's fundraising team. Managing consultant relationships with some of the ideas presented here can help an organization grow its capacity to be successful in both raising more money and engaging constituents more deeply in its mission and work.

CHAPTER THIRTY-FOUR

FUNDRAISING FOR GRASSROOTS NONPROFITS

By Kim Klein

A grassroots organization starts like this: Some people have an idea. Perhaps they see a pressing social need and want to respond. Or they have an artistic vision and wish to create a cultural vehicle to express it. They believe a change must be made in law or public policy, or they want to protest a structural injustice. They get together in a living room or a school cafeteria and plan how to create the change they wish to see. They realize that their plan needs to include raising some money.

They start their fundraising with a garage sale or a bake sale; they canvass their neighborhood; they seek donations from local merchants, churches, and synagogues, from their friends and colleagues. They send a few appeal letters; they even identify some of their acquaintances whom they can ask for $250 or $500. This is grassroots fundraising. It does not require much research or technical knowledge, and it allows people to use the skills they have—friendliness, sincerity, and a genuine desire to see something get done—to raise money.

What Defines Grassroots Fundraising?

Grassroots organizations are characterized by ordinary people banding together to make change happen. In the process, they often change the course of history, as in the case of the grassroots efforts that provided the genesis for gaining women's suffrage and the triumphs of the civil rights movement. It is therefore a mistake to equate *grassroots* with *small*, because grassroots organizations often achieve tremendous results, both in fulfilling their missions and in their fundraising. However, for fundraising purposes, an operational definition of a grassroots is an organization with an annual budget of under $500,000. (In fact, many grassroots organizations have budgets of under $25,000, which means they do not have to file an IRS Form 990 every year.) Such organizations make up the majority of nonprofits in the United States, accounting for more than half of the organizations incorporated as a nonprofit 501(c)(3) as well as the majority of the more than eight million groups that operate in the United States without any tax designation.

Typically, these organizations are run by a team of board members or volunteers. They may have a paid staff, who are often part-time; rarely do such organizations have more than two full-time staff. Grassroots organizations also usually work in a specific geographic area, though they may be part of larger grassroots movements and their work spans the gamut of political and social issues. Because of these factors, grassroots fundraising normally focuses on strategies for fundraising from individuals rather than from foundations, corporations, or government sources.

Grassroots Fundraising Strategies

In the wide world of fundraising strategies, there are some that are fairly easily adapted to the grassroots environment and others that will not work at all. The most easily adapted are special events, mail appeals, public speaking, use of the Internet, and personal face-to-face solicitation.

Special Events

Everyone is familiar with the very large golf tournaments, award luncheons, and black tie dinner dances that raise $100,000 or even $1,000,000. They cost thousands of dollars to put on and require months of work from paid staff and dozens of volunteers.

However, special events need not be elaborate to succeed in raising funds. A grassroots organization can raise anywhere from $5,000 to $25,000 with three or four months of lead time and a handful of volunteers. Take, for example, a dinner dance. Rather than a hotel ballroom, the dance can be in the community center or the school gymnasium, which can generally be reserved for a nominal fee. Teenagers in the group can be in charge of decorations. Lots of paper streamers and balloons make it festive.

Food can be provided by members, or, to make it more fun, food can be a competition. People might pay a small fee to "enter" the food competition in different categories, such as main course, salad, or dessert. Each contestant must bring enough food to feed fifteen people. People coming to the event get a small sample of each entry and get to vote on which is the best. They then pay a small fee for a larger portion of the courses that they liked. In reality, most will be full after the sampling, so the group will not run out of food. A cash bar can provide extra income. (If this option is chosen, liability and liquor licensing issues must be carefully investigated and complied with.) Dancing can be provided by a local band that is willing to perform for a low fee or for free because it wants to become more well-known. Or dance music can be provided by a DJ who is a friend of one of the members.

Marketing and advertising the event is done largely by word of mouth, e-mail, announcements on individual members' Facebook pages and on the website of the organization, and possibly with posters put up in the neighborhood of the event. Public interest radio and television often have community calendars, so it is not hard to get the event publicized.

Each board member sells ten tickets at $15 or $20 each. This is generally not too hard either. With a hundred people attending, at $15 per person, plus each person paying on average $15 more for additional food or drink, plus the entry fee of the food competitors who each pay $15, an organization can easily gross $5,000. Expenses will include buying drinks to sell, printing up tickets and nice-looking certificates for the winners of the food contests, and possibly mailing thank-you notes to volunteers after the event. Expenses could be as high as $1,000, giving the group a net of $4,000—plus newly involved constituents. If volunteers can get a local supermarket to donate the food and a graphic design business to donate the certificates, the net will be higher. As the years pass, more and more people will want to enter the food contest, and more people will attend.

A Chocolate Lovers' Festival, put on by an organization with a total annual budget of $75,000, was organized along the lines just outlined and by the fifth year netted $40,000. It attracted top chefs from every restaurant in town, in addition to ordinary folks entering their favorite brownies or best hot chocolate. A few years later, it regularly netted $100,000. The organization is now considering spinning off some chocolate products and selling them online.

The dinner dance is just one example of how malleable fundraising events are. Each aspect of the event should be conceived as a separate component, and components can be added or deleted according to the number of volunteers and amount of time available. A silent auction can be added to the dinner dance, or a live auction could replace the dance or be added to it. An afternoon barbecue at the beach could replace the dinner; games could replace the dance. That kind of event would focus much more on families with young children. Tea and dessert followed by a lecture would appeal to a more academic or older crowd.

The secret to all of this is to do as much as possible for free or very low cost, and to charge for as many things as you can without having people feel that they are being "nickel and dimed" to death. Advertising must be effective, so that the maximum number of the right people is attracted to the event at minimum cost. Grassroots organizations need to know how to take advantage of free services, such as public service announcements, community bulletin boards, and viral marketing. Word-of-mouth remains the cheapest and most effective advertising vehicle.

Raising Money by Mail

Mail provides another avenue for grassroots groups. Of course, the kind of sophisticated testing of packages and premiums that require five thousand to ten thousand names just for the test is usually not an option for grassroots nonprofits, but very focused list acquisition can bring in impressive returns. For example, a large organization tests a mailing to two thousand people and gets a 1-percent response (considered good in direct mail terms). They have twenty new donors, who give an average of $40 each, for a gross of $800. The organization will probably spend $0.75 each on the mailing, which means they will spend $1,500 to raise $800, or $35 to acquire one donor ($700 divided by twenty new donors). They will make this money back over the next couple of years, as these donors renew and give extra gifts and the volume of people they are able to reach causes their donor list to grow very quickly. They also augment their direct mail program with e-mail and other online strategies.

A grassroots organization will not have this kind of money to spend up front, so they will need to scale back and revise the strategy. Each board member is asked to bring in ten to fifteen prospect names, and the organization sends out two hundred first-class letters, with a personal note from the board members on each letter. They spend more on postage, but nothing on list acquisition. They hand address the carrier envelope. With the cost of the letters, return envelope, reply card, and first-class stamps, they may spend $1.00 each on these letters for a total expense of $200. This highly personalized approach generates a higher response—generally around 5 percent, or ten new donors, who each give $40, for a gross of $400. This organization nets $200 in income from the first mailing.

Of course, the organization has to have board members willing to write to their friends and spend the time getting the mailing out. For ongoing success, the organization will have to find other sources of prospects. Board members' friends and colleagues can make a good but very finite list. Other prospects can be found among the people who benefit from the work of the organization or who regularly attend their events. These two sources may give them dozens or even hundreds of potential prospects. A word of caution is in order here: as is true with big direct mail appeals, not every appeal will be successful, and the organization will need to figure out how much money it can afford to invest in acquisition mailings without seeing a return for two or three years.

Also, the long-term success of a mail program is in the quality and consistency of renewals and extra appeals. Because small organizations rely a great deal on volunteers and overworked staff (if they are lucky enough even to have staff), it is critical that every step in any fundraising strategy be written down, so that a new person can easily figure out what to do. Everything should be as systematized as possible. For example, the newsletter committee plans exactly what is going in the newsletter, when copy is due, who is doing the design and layout, how it will be proofed, who is taking it to the printer, who is picking it up, and how it is getting mailed. They must stay on deadline or the membership committee's spring appeal may land the same day as the newsletter.

For a mail appeal program to be effective over time, the organization must invest in a good fundraising database and keep it up to date. As soon as possible, organizations need to move away from using spreadsheets and generic database programs that are not designed specifically for recording, retrieving, and analyzing donor information and gifts. There are some free fundraising databases—and many inexpensive ones—that are easy to use. An up-to-date and very thorough review of current databases, pricing, and capability can be found at www .techsoup.org.

Organizations also must be cautious never to promise something they cannot deliver. For example, an organization shouldn't tell people they will get a newsletter three times a year unless the organization is reasonably certain it can produce one three times a year. Many organizations advertise their e-newsletter on their website, and people visiting the site sign up. But the organization may have used up all its energy setting up their site and have no plans in place for actually sending a regular e-newsletter. Above all, organizations should not offer premiums like a book or a T-shirt unless staff or volunteers are standing by to send those out right away.

Finally, it is important to remember that acknowledging the first gift is the key to getting the second. Research conducted by The Center on Philanthropy confirms this truism: one of the most common reasons donors do not repeat a gift is that they are not thanked for their first one.

Internet Fundraising

By now almost all nonprofit organizations have a website. The website has to be changed frequently to encourage people to return to it. The homepage must feature a "GIVE NOW" icon that must lead to a page on which, at the least, people can download a form to send in with a check, or preferably, they can make a gift online. Every page of the website should encourage visitors to consider donating, and certainly all visitors should be encouraged to sign up for a free e-newsletter (if the organization can deliver on the promise of one). All e-mail signatures of staff (and volunteers who are willing) should include a reference to your organization's website.

In addition to a decent website, organizations should use e-mail to solicit gifts. There are dozens of articles and books, many of them online and free, that discuss e-mail fundraising campaigns. The psychology of using e-mail to solicit gifts is similar to that of direct mail: use a story, be specific about how much to give and where the money will go, and set a tone of urgency by asking people to act immediately. However, e-mail fundraising is not direct mail. E-mail is much shorter, and a version of the appeal will be sent at least three times over the course of a week or ten days. Organizations need to set up a "trigger" response that lets the donor know the donation was received, as well as a thank-you response, which can go out as the trigger or later.

Grassroots organizations will also want to have a Facebook page and will want to keep up with the latest thinking on whether or not to have a blog or to Tweet. Some of these decisions will depend on what else you are doing, the age of your donor base or the people you are trying to reach, and your capacity to follow through on requests and questions. The Internet is a two-way medium: donors will ask questions and expect responses.

Public Speaking

Public speaking is a wonderful way for grassroots groups to get their message out. There are typically a dozen local organizations that need speakers on a monthly or quarterly basis, such as service clubs, church and synagogue groups, college classes, and trade associations. If an organization develops a reputation for having good speakers, it will have more invitations than it can accept. Each speech will end with a low-key request for a gift, unless the speaker has permission to make a more assertive one. Some organizations will allow speakers to pass a basket at the end of the talk. Also, some organizations actually pay an honorarium, so a speaker is paid to describe the important work of his or her group. Organizations should inquire whether an honorarium is possible.

For the biggest impact, it is also important for speakers to provide listeners with some materials they can take with them. The materials need not be elaborate—a small brochure or postcard with the organization's contact information and information on how to make a gift is all that is required. Also, it is helpful for a speaker to pass around a sheet on which listeners can provide their e-mail addresses so that they can be added to the organization's e-newsletter list. If you do collect e-mail addresses, you need to send something out within a week to welcome these people to your e-newsletter list. Make sure it is easy to unsubscribe in case someone changes her mind.

Organizations that use public speaking as a serious income stream as well as a way to get their message out need to develop a speakers bureau. People who are familiar with the issues the organization addresses and who are comfortable in front of a crowd form the core group of this bureau. They create written materials for speakers to use, such as answers to difficult questions, narrative descriptions of programs and budgets, quotes from famous people in support of their work, and tips on how to handle disruptive audience members or how to structure a speech for a particular audience. Copies of notes and speeches are kept for each speakers bureau member to use, and, whenever possible, speakers are recorded so that everyone can learn and improve.

A domestic violence program that had a speakers bureau generated $10,000 a year from honoraria and thousands more from donations. Their speakers bureau also led to the creation of a full-time training program when they received a contract from a statewide law enforcement agency to train police officers in how to respond to domestic violence calls.

Personal Solicitation of Major Gifts

Major gift solicitation is built around trust between the donor and the organization. A grassroots group may not have a long track record or a nice office or well-known board members. The volunteers doing the asking rely a lot on their own reputation for integrity and thoughtfulness to raise money. Donors give $1,000 or $5,000 not because they have heard of the organization and not because they are going to get a lot of recognition, but because their friend Terry says that the group does good work, and they trust Terry.

Personal solicitation is both the easiest and the hardest strategy for almost anyone. It can be used to solicit gifts of $25 as well as $250,000 but is generally reserved for soliciting larger gifts. It is the easiest because volunteers have only to talk to their friends, who are easy to find and with whom it is comfortable to talk. There is no real cost involved, except for the time of the volunteer and perhaps the cost of taking a friend out for coffee or lunch, and the meeting can be set at the convenience of the volunteer and his or her friend. It is the hardest because it requires asking for money and running the risk of rejection. It is important for the grassroots volunteer to keep two things in mind when asking for a gift: the volunteer has the right to ask, and the prospective donor has the right to say no. It is important to recognize that many people will say no, and there is no disgrace in having your request declined. But recognize, too, that many people will say yes and be grateful that they were asked. A request for money is an invitation and an opportunity being given to the prospective donor. For those who have a fear of asking for money, the best advice is to kick yourself out of the way and let the cause do the talking.

Most organizations often find that their major donor program is their most lucrative and that the relationships they build with long-time major donors lead those donors to introduce the organization to other donors. To be successful in fundraising requires being comfortable asking for money, and grassroots organizations need to devote time and training to get as many volunteers as possible as comfortable as possible with this strategy.

The Cost of Fundraising

The most formidable issue for any organization is the cost of fundraising—and for grassroots groups, it is very difficult even to find money to spend in advance that can then be repaid from the proceeds of the strategy. Without money up front, grassroots organizations settle for cramped offices, no clerical help, computers that don't have enough memory or power, old photocopy machines, and so on. They spend a lot of time trying to get things donated and doing things as cheaply as possible. For example, if a large institution needs a new computer, it buys one. A grassroots group will spend hours trying to get someone to donate one, often winding up with a computer that can't run the newest versions of software on its archaic operating system. They can't use the computer, but they feel bad telling the donor that, so they keep it in their office and put a plant on it. Meanwhile, they send out a special appeal to their membership or hold a garage sale to raise the money to buy a decent computer. This whole process puts the organization six months behind the larger institution, which was able to fill its computer need immediately.

In spite of (or more likely because of) the problems they have with money, grassroots organizations often operate at a high level of productivity. Fired by enthusiasm for their work and belief in their cause, a few people will do a huge amount of work and do it well, accomplishing a lot each day. The director may not only write the direct mail appeal but work along with volunteers to fold the letters, put the labels on the envelopes, and sort the bulk mailing while answering the phone (there is no administrative assistant), sweating through a hot summer day (there is no air conditioning), and coordinating the efforts of the volunteers who are there to help. Often the director is paid significantly less than her counterpart at a larger institution. Ironically, she may have more skills than her peers at bigger organizations because she has to develop a wide range of skills to run the grassroots organization (bookkeeping, budgeting, administration, public relations, program development and evaluation) that other agencies are able to divide among more specialized personnel.

Staff and volunteer productivity is sometimes undermined by inefficient and outdated systems that the organization will not spend the money to replace. Grassroots organizations must learn a fundamental premise of business: you have to spend money to make money. Further, some problems can be solved only with money. High-quality equipment will usually have to be purchased. Staff must be paid living wages and need some benefits so they can focus on their work. Dreary, poorly lit, badly insulated offices will save money in rent, which will then be spent on increased numbers of sick days and high staff turnover. Investing in basic infrastructure can improve working conditions and efficiency significantly, thus allowing smaller organizations to eliminate distractions and raise much more money.

Grassroots Fundraising = Power of People

Grassroots fundraising can galvanize people to act, and this is its greatest strength. If an organization is working to change a law or to save wilderness or to end discrimination, it will need thousands of people to agree with its position. Faced with the choice of one person giving $100,000 or a thousand people giving $100 each, the organization is far better off to choose the latter, because now it has a thousand informal ambassadors discussing their issue with their friends and colleagues, which leads to more money, and which may also eventually lead to a gift of $100,000. Getting a large number of donations from a lot of people is also key to helping a cause become more visible. By definition, grassroots groups are too new, too controversial, or too small to have become publicly accepted or widely known. Many lack the skills to attract media attention or to be taken seriously. As a result, they have little name recognition. This means that much of their fundraising involves explaining their case to people, which makes their fundraising efforts much more time consuming for the amount of money raised.

Conclusion

When all is said and done, the essence of grassroots fundraising is the essence of all fundraising: building relationships. People give to people with causes, and these organizations are full of nothing if not people with causes. Successful fundraising of any kind requires ingenuity, commitment to the cause, love of people, common sense, a willingness to ask for money, and an understanding and deep appreciation of human nature. Many grassroots groups raise money with only these in place. They lack technical skills and are often weak in areas like keeping donor records, understanding prospect research, knowing how to write foundation or corporate proposals, getting money from the government, or setting up planned giving programs.

Ultimately, any successful fundraising program will probably have a grassroots component. When the public (or some subset thereof) wants to establish a charity and wants to be able to avail themselves of the many financial advantages of being a nonprofit, they can best reach that goal through grassroots fundraising techniques. Does the organization have a group of volunteers who are willing to devote a large number of hours, without any reward besides a free pizza at their meetings and possibly a round of applause at their annual convention, to get a much larger number of ordinary people to give small and large donations? These donors themselves will receive little material reward for their gift beyond a heartfelt thank-you note and a newsletter. The work of the group is the reward—for the donor, for the volunteer, for the staff, and for the greater good. At its heart and at its best, this is how all fundraising works.

PART SEVEN

ETHICS AND ACCOUNTABILITY

This part takes an in-depth look at ethics and accountability as the foundation of achieving excellence in fundraising, taking into account both the spirit and the letter of the law. This part opens with Chapter Thirty-Five, dedicated to values and ethics as they apply to fundraising, and closes with Chapter Thirty-Six, in which the law and fundraising are considered. Both are intended to prepare fundraisers to conduct themselves in a professional way, founded on both ethical and legal information as standards.

According to Independent Sector, "Those who serve the public good must assume the public trust" (2002, p. 11). Those who assume the public trust must hold themselves to a higher standard. Part Seven is about holding ourselves as fundraisers to the highest standard possible.

CHAPTER THIRTY-FIVE

ETHICAL FRAMEWORKS FOR FUNDRAISING

By Eugene R. Tempel

W hy do the actions of a few affect so many? This is one of the key questions that resulted from the study of United States fundraisers (Duronio and Tempel, 1996). Fundraisers are concerned about the ethics of their colleagues. The answer to this question lies in public expectations of the nonprofit sector. We, in the nonprofit sector, are held to a higher level of trust than our colleagues in the for-profit sector. And the Association for Fundraising Professionals (AFP) code of ethics (see Exhibit 35.1) challenges its members to accept responsibility, not only for their own behavior, but the behavior of their institutions as well, in areas such as stewardship, accountability, and confidentiality.

As fundraising practitioners work toward professional status, both technical and ethical standards are essential. Most of this volume deals with the rationale for, and technical aspects of, fundraising. This chapter deals with the ethical aspects. The ethical practice of philanthropic fundraising is essential to both the continued development of philanthropy, through increased public confidence and trust, and the professionalization of fundraising as a field of practice.

EXHIBIT 35.1. AFP CODE OF ETHICAL PRINCIPLES AND STANDARDS OF PROFESSIONAL PRACTICE.

Adopted 1964; Amended Sept. 2007

The Association of Fundraising Professionals (AFP) exists to foster the development and growth of fundraising professionals and the profession, to promote high ethical behavior in the fundraising profession and to preserve and enhance philanthropy and volunteerism.

Members of AFP are motivated by an inner drive to improve the quality of life through the causes they serve. They serve the ideal of philanthropy, are committed to the preservation and enhancement of volunteerism; and hold stewardship of these concepts as the overriding direction of their professional life. They recognize their responsibility to ensure that needed resources are vigorously and ethically sought and that the intent of the donor is honestly fulfilled.

To these ends, AFP members, both individual and business, embrace certain values that they strive to uphold in performing their responsibilities for generating philanthropic support. AFP business members strive to promote and protect the work and mission of their client organizations.

AFP members both individual and business aspire to:

- practice their profession with integrity, honesty, truthfulness and adherence to the absolute obligation to safeguard the public trust
- act according to the highest goals and visions of their organizations, professions, clients and consciences
- put philanthropic mission above personal gain;
- inspire others through their own sense of dedication and high purpose
- improve their professional knowledge and skills, so that their performance will better serve others
- demonstrate concern for the interests and well-being of individuals affected by their actions
- value the privacy, freedom of choice and interests of all those affected by their actions
- foster cultural diversity and pluralistic values and treat all people with dignity and respect
- affirm, through personal giving, a commitment to philanthropy and its role in society
- adhere to the spirit as well as the letter of all applicable laws and regulations
- advocate within their organizations adherence to all applicable laws and regulations
- avoid even the appearance of any criminal offense or professional misconduct
- bring credit to the fundraising profession by their public demeanor
- encourage colleagues to embrace and practice these ethical principles and standards
- be aware of the codes of ethics promulgated by other professional organizations that serve philanthropy

Ethical Standards

Furthermore, while striving to act according to the above values, AFP members, both individual and business, agree to abide (and to ensure, to the best of their ability, that all members of their staff abide) by the AFP standards. Violation of the standards may subject the member to disciplinary sanctions, including expulsion, as provided in the AFP Ethics Enforcement Procedures.

Member Obligations

1. Members shall not engage in activities that harm the members' organizations, clients or profession.
2. Members shall not engage in activities that conflict with their fiduciary, ethical and legal obligations to their organizations, clients or profession.
3. Members shall effectively disclose all potential and actual conflicts of interest; such disclosure does not preclude or imply ethical impropriety.
4. Members shall not exploit any relationship with a donor, prospect, volunteer, client or employee for the benefit of the members or the members' organizations.
5. Members shall comply with all applicable local, state, provincial and federal civil and criminal laws.
6. Members recognize their individual boundaries of competence and are forthcoming and truthful about their professional experience and qualifications and will represent their achievements accurately and without exaggeration.
7. Members shall present and supply products and/or services honestly and without misrepresentation and will clearly identify the details of those products, such as availability of the products and/or services and other factors that may affect the suitability of the products and/or services for donors, clients or nonprofit organizations.
8. Members shall establish the nature and purpose of any contractual relationship at the outset and will be responsive and available to organizations and their employing organizations before, during and after any sale of materials and/or services. Members will comply with all fair and reasonable obligations created by the contract.
9. Members shall refrain from knowingly infringing the intellectual property rights of other parties at all times. Members shall address and rectify any inadvertent infringement that may occur.
10. Members shall protect the confidentiality of all privileged information relating to the provider/client relationships.
11. Members shall refrain from any activity designed to disparage competitors untruthfully.

(Continued)

EXHIBIT 35.1. (Continued).

Solicitation and Use of Philanthropic Funds

12. Members shall take care to ensure that all solicitation and communication materials are accurate and correctly reflect their organizations' mission and use of solicited funds.
13. Members shall take care to ensure that donors receive informed, accurate and ethical advice about the value and tax implications of contributions.
14. Members shall take care to ensure that contributions are used in accordance with donors' intentions.
15. Members shall take care to ensure proper stewardship of all revenue sources, including timely reports on the use and management of such funds.
16. Members shall obtain explicit consent by donors before altering the conditions of financial transactions.

Presentation of Information

17. Members shall not disclose privileged or confidential information to unauthorized parties.
18. Members shall adhere to the principle that all donor and prospect information created by, or on behalf of, an organization or a client is the property of that organization or client and shall not be transferred or utilized except on behalf of that organization or client.
19. Members shall give donors and clients the opportunity to have their names removed from lists that are sold to, rented to or exchanged with other organizations.
20. Members shall, when stating fundraising results, use accurate and consistent accounting methods that conform to the appropriate guidelines adopted by the American Institute of Certified Public Accountants (AICPA)* for the type of organization involved. (* In countries outside of the United States, comparable authority should be utilized.)

Compensation and Contracts

21. Members shall not accept compensation or enter into a contract that is based on a percentage of contributions; nor shall members accept finder's fees or contingent fees. Business members must refrain from receiving compensation from third parties derived from products or services for a client without disclosing that third-party compensation to the client (for example, volume rebates from vendors to business members).
22. Members may accept performance-based compensation, such as bonuses, provided such bonuses are in accord with prevailing practices within the members' own organizations and are not based on a percentage of contributions.

23. Members shall neither offer nor accept payments or special considerations for the purpose of influencing the selection of products or services.
24. Members shall not pay finder's fees, commissions or percentage compensation based on contributions, and shall take care to discourage their organizations from making such payments.
25. Any member receiving funds on behalf of a donor or client must meet the legal requirements for the disbursement of those funds. Any interest or income earned on the funds should be fully disclosed.

Issues of Trust

America was in a crisis of trust during the end of the twentieth century. Only 57 percent of those surveyed in a national study indicated they trusted or highly trusted private higher education, and that was the highest level of trust in any American institution. The numbers for health care were 39 percent, while for private and community foundations they were 31.6 percent. Only 15.8 percent indicated they trusted or trusted highly Congress (Independent Sector, 1996). Since then, public confidence in nonprofit organizations remains low. According to a March 2008 study, 34 percent of Americans said they had "not too much" confidence in charities or "none at all." This lack of confidence seriously challenges "the sector's distinctiveness as a destination for giving and volunteering" (Light, 2008).

Scandals—stories of abuse, mismanagement, and waste—are sometimes sensationalized by the media, but they nevertheless affect people's confidence in the nonprofit sector as a whole. The events that catch our attention today are similar to those outlined in the first edition of *Achieving Excellence in Fund Raising* (Fogal, 1991):

1. Fundraising can be accomplished less and less on a "business as usual" basis.
2. The challenge to many fundraising habits comes from changes in nonprofit organizations themselves, from changes in the public's assumptions about nonprofits, and from technological shifts in how fundraising is done.
3. Being responsive to changing circumstances and conditions leads nonprofit leaders and managers to consider moral issues that pertain to their organizations (p. 265).

Ethics and Professionalism

Ethics is one of the key elements in making a group of practitioners a profession. Carbone (1989) evaluated fundraising according to six criteria commonly accepted as essential to a profession:

1. Autonomy
2. Systematic knowledge
3. Self-regulation
4. Commitment and identification
5. Altruism and dedication to service
6. Ethics and sanctions

As fundraisers have made significant progress on establishing and meeting these six criteria, fundraising is becoming a profession. The majority of fundraisers are committed both to their organizations and to their careers. Fundraisers are more generous with their resources and time than other citizens. Fundraisers are concerned about the ethical behavior of other fundraisers. And AFP has in place a process for sanctioning members who violate the code of ethics (Duronio and Tempel, 1996).

A profession is built on the notion of service to others and the trust that comes from a commitment to place the interest of clients above self-interest. Pribbenow (1999a) argues that as a profession, fundraising must focus on serving the public good rather than attempt to define itself in terms related to other professions. Service to the public good ensures trust. Trust is built on the practitioner's performance with both technical and ethical proficiency.

There is a larger knowledge base to help us develop proficiency in both arenas. Scholars have attempted to assist fundraisers faced with ethical problems and ethical dilemmas. Such efforts include those of David Smith, in his edited volume *Good Intentions: Moral Obstacles and Opportunities* (2005), and Janice Gow Pettey's *Ethical Fundraising: A Guide for Nonprofit Boards and Fundraisers* (2008). Taken together, these resources provide a framework for dealing with the ethical questions faced by fundraisers and their nonprofit organizations.

As fundraising executives, leaders, and managers, each of us has a responsibility to be informed and to think carefully and critically about the ethical standards and ethical issues that are essential to the health of the nonprofit sector and philanthropy. We also must be able to teach colleagues and donors about ethical issues. These issues are critical to the nonprofit organizations that carry out the work of the sector, and to the fundraisers who help those organizations acquire their resources.

There are standards covered later in the chapter that can help guide us in ethical practice. But most ethical issues are not as simple as a series of "do's and don'ts" that can be memorized and uniformly applied. Ethical issues require us to develop broad frameworks, principles on which we can base best choices. Robert Payton, former director of the Center on Philanthropy at Indiana University, has said, "There are no ethical answers; there are only ethical questions." Therefore, as practicing fundraisers aspiring to be professional in our work to enhance the public trust, we need to educate ourselves about the ethical questions in our profession so we can make the best choices when confronted with them.

Ethical standards can help us initially decide on a number of issues that are clearly unethical. The Code of Ethics of the Association of Fundraising Professionals (see Exhibit 35.1) provides such guidance. So do the codes of the Association of Healthcare Philanthropy, CASE (see Exhibit 35.2) and others. They provide excellent foundations for ethical practice. But they will not provide all the answers. Most decisions are not as simple as following rules. Therefore we must prepare ourselves to function in an ethical context, where our primary focus is always concern for meeting public and professional expectations as fully as possible.

Some years ago, when Robert Payton was still an executive with the Exxon Education Foundation, he posed this question to fundraisers: "Do we live for philanthropy or do we live off philanthropy?" Professional fundraising executives must keep this question before them constantly. Personal gain is the first vulnerable point of public trust. Section 501(3)(c) of the Internal Revenue Code, which provides for the establishment of nonprofit organizations, defines criteria for those eligible for charitable contributions:

> Corporations, and any community chest, fund or foundation, organized and operated exclusively for religious, charitable, scientific, testing for public safety, literary, or educational purposes, or for the prevention of cruelty to children or animals, no part of the net earnings of which inures to the benefit of any private shareholder or individual, no substantial part of the activities of which is carrying on propaganda, or otherwise attempting, to influence legislation, and which does not participate in, or intervene in (including the publishing or distributing of statements), any political campaign on behalf of any candidate for public office.

As fundraising executives, we must be cognizant especially of the "nondistribution" clause: "no part of the net earnings of which inures to the benefit of any private shareholder or individual."

EXHIBIT 35.2. AHP STATEMENT OF PROFESSIONAL STANDARDS AND CONDUCT.

All members shall comply with the Association's Statement of Professional Standards and Conduct:

Association for Healthcare Philanthropy members represent to the public, by personal example and conduct, both their employer and their profession. They have, therefore, a duty to faithfully adhere to the highest standards and conduct in:

I. Their promotion of the merits of their institutions and of excellence in health care generally, providing community leadership in cooperation with health, educational, cultural, and other organizations;

II. Their words and actions, embodying respect for truth, honesty, fairness, free inquiry, and the opinions of others, treating all with equality and dignity;

III. Their respect for all individuals without regard to race, color, sex, religion, national origin, disability, age or any other characteristic protected by applicable law;

IV. Their commitment to strive to increase professional and personal skills for improved service to their donors and institutions, to encourage and actively participate in career development for themselves and others whose roles include support for resource development functions, and to share freely their knowledge and experience with others as appropriate;

V. Their continuing effort and energy to pursue new ideas and modifications to improve conditions for, and benefits to, donors and their institution;

VI. Their avoidance of activities that might damage the reputation of any donor, their institution, any other resource development professional or the profession as a whole, or themselves, and to give full credit for the ideas, words, or images originated by others;

VII. Their respect for the rights of privacy of others and the confidentiality of information gained in the pursuit of their professional duties;

VIII. Their acceptance of a compensation method freely agreed upon and based on their institution's usual and customary compensation guidelines which have been established and approved for general institutional use while always remembering that:

1. any compensation agreement should fully reflect the standards of professional conduct; and,

2. antitrust laws in the United States prohibit limitation on compensation methods.

IX. Their respect for the law and professional ethics as a standard of personal conduct, with full adherence to the policies and procedures of their institution;

X. Their pledge to adhere to this Statement of Professional Standards and Conduct, and to encourage others to join them in observance of its guidelines.

Source: Copyright © 2002 Association of Healthcare Philanthropy. Reprinted with permission. For more information on AHP, visit www.ahp.org.

The nondistribution clause requires nonprofit organizations and those associated with them to commit themselves to the public good. It is the foundation for the establishment of trust between donors and organizations. As professional fundraising executives, we have a legal and ethical responsibility to make certain that we, and all others associated with our organizations, do not benefit personally from the funds that are contributed to the organization.

This does not mean we should not be paid fairly and equitably for our work. It does mean that we do not accept commissions on gifts. It does mean that we do not accept personal gifts from donors. It does mean that salaries must be commensurate with public expectations. It does mean that board members should not have competitive advantage in bidding for business with the organization. So important is the nondistribution clause to the issue of trust that associations representing professionals and organizations in the nonprofit sector worked together to pass legislation known as "intermediate sanctions" to aid the sector in the self regulation and to provide the IRS with penalties it can impose for excessive benefit and inside dealing (Independent Sector, 1998).

What distinguishes the professional from the technician may be trustworthiness. The professional is conscientious about putting the interests of the client first. Because we work on behalf of nonprofit organizations, we must have fidelity to their missions. We must earn the trust of the organizations that employ us. Finally, we have an obligation to understand the larger mission of the nonprofit sector—to understand the role of philanthropy generally, not just in our own organization—because the donor and the organization function in the larger environment of the nonprofit or philanthropic sector. Understanding the mission of the sector helps us view philanthropy from the donor's perspective. Increasingly fundraisers will be called on to assist donors with philanthropy in ways other than to their own organizations (Tempel and Beem, 2002).

These issues of professionalism raise such broad questions as the following (The Fund Raising School, 2009b):

- What is the role of trust in our development as fundraising professionals?
- What are the burdens placed on us as fundraising practitioners by the "nondistribution clause" in Section 501(c)(3) of the code?
- As fundraising practitioners, who is our client: the donor or the organization?
- In every transaction, what are the intents of the donor and what are the intents of the organization?
- How can we, as fundraising professionals, protect and maintain our integrity as "boundary spanners" between donors and organizations?
- How do we manage the tensions that arise as fundraisers working for organizations assist donors to expand their philanthropy?

Approaches to Ethics

In some circumstances, these and other questions are easy to answer because there is a clear-cut best choice. But when there is conflict between two goods or the appearance of conflict between two goods, the questions become more difficult to answer, as in the typical "tainted money" questions: If money obtained under less than honorable circumstances is offered for your worthy cause, should it be accepted? Does accepting it compromise your organization's integrity while it provides some public good? Does accepting it add legitimacy to the source of the money? Does denying it enhance your organization's integrity while denying fulfillment of some public need?

Payton's statement that there are only ethical questions echoes a number of other writers—Josephson (2002), Anderson (1996), Fischer (2000)—who agree that ethics in fundraising is complex. Philosophers like Kant suggested there were, in fact, right answers. But Kant's categorical imperative suggests that ethical theories and dilemmas are often difficult to assess at the level of practice.

Anderson (1996) refers to this approach as formalism. And formalism will take us a certain distance. In fact, some ethical matters can be decided based on minimum standards such as codes of ethics. But those situations in which there are competing goods require a more complex decision-making process. Both Josephson (2002) and Anderson (1996) refer to this as *consequentialism*. The question for fundraisers is "What will be best for the greatest number of constituents in the long run?" The ethical conflicts we face as fundraisers can be reconciled through sets of values, beliefs, and commitments against which we can judge our actions.

What lies behind ethics? A set of values and beliefs that lead us to trust the decisions that are made, that lead us to form expectations about the actions of others. The Josephson Institute has surveyed more than ten thousand individuals to define the values that are important to an ethical or virtuous person. *Making Ethical Decisions* (Josephson, 2002) is grounded in the advocacy of ten major ethical values that form the basis for ethical decision making. Josephson's ten values are

1. Honesty
2. Integrity
3. Promise-keeping
4. Loyalty/fidelity

5. Fairness
6. Concern for others
7. Respect for others
8. Law-abidingness/civic duty
9. Pursuit of excellence
10. Personal accountability

Anderson (1996) developed a similar list:

1. Respect
   • Individual autonomy
   • Personal privacy
   • Nonmaleficence
2. Beneficence
   • Public good
   • Charitable intent
3. Trust
   • Truth-telling
   • Promise-keeping
   • Accountability
   • Fairness
   • Fidelity of purpose

Independent Sector outlined nine commitments that mirror the ethical values listed by Anderson and Josephson. These commitments are proposed as essential to those who are associated with the nonprofit and philanthropic sectors.

   • *Commitment beyond* self is at the core of a civil society;
   • *Obedience to the laws*, including those governing tax-exempt philan-thropic and voluntary organizations, is a fundamental responsibility of stewardship.
   • *Commitment beyond the law*, to obedience to the unenforceable, is the higher obligation of leaders of philanthropic and voluntary organizations.
   • *Commitment to the public good* requires those who presume to serve the public good to assume a public trust.
   • *Respect for the worth and dignity of individuals* is a special leadership responsibility of philanthropic and voluntary organizations.

- *Tolerance, diversity, and social justice* reflect the independent sector's rich heritage and the essential protections afforded it.
- *Accountability to the public* is a fundamental responsibility of public benefit organizations.
- *Openness and honesty* in reporting, fundraising, and relationships with all constituencies are essential behaviors for organizations which seek and use public or private funds and which purport to serve public purposes.
- *Prudent application of resources* is a concomitant of public trust (2002, p. 18).

Independent Sector (2002) proposes that all of us working in nonprofit, public benefit organizations must integrate these nine commitments directly into our work. This certainly holds true for fundraising. Strengthening transparency, governance and ethical standards are so important to the health of the nonprofit sector that Independent Sector developed the *Principles of Good Governance and Ethical Practice* (2007). The report is freely available online and is an excellent resource both for new organizations just getting started and for well-established organizations who want to evaluate and improve their current practices.

These values and commitments apply to our behavior as fundraisers and to the various codes of ethics included in the exhibits in this chapter. In fact, when Peg Duronio asked participants in her study of fundraisers what they admired most about their ideal colleague, the overwhelming response was "integrity" (Tempel and Duronio, 1997).

We must be honest in our dealings with donors and organizations. Our behavior must be dependable. And we must be true to our word. And to earn integrity, we must carry out our work in ways that best represent our organizations and our colleagues. We must keep the promises we make to donors when we accept gifts. We must be loyal to both the organization and the donor. Our negotiations must be fair to both the organization and the donor. We must demonstrate concern for the donor as an individual or entity and have genuine respect for donors rather than envy them their resources or view them as objects to be manipulated for our gain.

We must not only abide by the laws but demonstrate our own civic and philanthropic responsibility as well. We have a responsibility to be the best that we can be as professionals in carrying out our work. And we must be personally accountable for our actions and the actions of our clients. Although we can agree to the set of obligations that Josephson's values promote, it is conflict among these values that requires complex decision making.

Ethical Dilemmas

What does the professional fundraiser do (personal accountability) when the organization (loyalty-fidelity) decides to use funds given for one purpose by a donor (promise keeping, integrity, honesty) for another purpose? Josephson recommends three steps for considering ethical conflicts:

I. All decisions must take into account and reflect a concern for the interests and well-being of all shareholders.
II. Ethical values and principles ALWAYS take precedence over nonethical ones.
III. It is ethically proper to violate an ethical principle only when it is CLEARLY NECESSARY TO ADVANCE ANOTHER TRUE ETHICAL PRINCIPLE, WHICH ACCORDING TO THE DECISION MAKER'S CONSCIENCE, WILL PRODUCE THE GREATEST BALANCE OF GOOD IN THE LONG RUN (2002, p. 18).

Fischer (2000) has outlined a similar approach. She poses questions around three broad themes: organizational mission, relationships, and personal integrity.

Independent Sector (2002) outlines three tiers of actions. First, some actions are clearly illegal. Our decisions about these are very clear. Second, some actions are clearly unethical. Decisions about these actions are also fairly easy to make using codes of ethics. Third, there are what Independent Sector calls ethical dilemmas. Decisions about ethical dilemmas resemble the Josephson Institute's model and Anderson's discussion of situations in which there are competing goods or conflicting values.

Independent Sector recommends evaluating these choices in terms of the commitments beyond self. It provides examples of actions involving all three levels:

- Example of an illegal act: The organization's copying and fax machines are used routinely by a friendly candidate for public office. Why is this illegal?
- Example of an unethical behavior: In lieu of salary, the staff director prefers receiving a percentage of all funds raised. Why is this unethical?
- Example of an ethical dilemma: The all-volunteer organization recognizes that hiring its first executive director will absorb all the money on hand and in sight. Half of the board argues that all the time and money will go to support the position with nothing left for programs, and the other half says it's a necessary investment in future growth. What should they do? (2002, pp. 23–24)

Josephson's model gives us a framework for getting to a best answer. The problem posed is not unlike a choice that fundraising executives confront on an annual basis. A new investment in fundraising leaves less money for programs. On the other hand, new investments in fundraising eventually produce additional dollars for programs. Under what circumstances does the future potential outweigh the current loss? What other ethical values come into play when this decision is made? Who are the key stakeholders?

Applying Ethics in Fundraising

Robert Payton designed an ethics cube to outline the categories of ethical dilemmas fundraisers face. The top and bottom of the ethics cube display the words "Individual" (here meaning the fundraiser) and "Organization," respectively. The four sides of the cube display the words "Competence," "Language," "Relations," and "Mission." These components are timeless.

The Individual and the Organization

The first ethical tension that fundraising executives must mediate is the potential conflict between themselves as individuals and the organization. Fundraising executives must examine their motives constantly to make certain that they are not acting in their own self-interest but rather in the interests of the organization.

At the same time, fundraising executives have a right to expect the organization to treat them as professionals. Issues of compensation, for example, arise from this tension. Fundraising executives have a right to expect fair and adequate compensation, in line with what others are paid in this organization and similar ones. But fundraising executives should not accept percentage compensation because it focuses their work on personal gain rather than organizational benefit.

Another tension arises when fundraisers face the question, "Who is the client?" Is the organization our client, or is the donor our client? We must protect the interests of both. This heightens the tension between the fundraiser as individual and the organization that employs her or him—a tension that, as indicated earlier, is likely to increase in the twenty-first century.

The client question is a serious one. Mediating between the donor and the organization is the most difficult role the fundraising executive must play. Grounding ourselves in ethical values and understanding the tensions that accompany this relationship are important steps in becoming fundraising professionals. We can best prepare ourselves by understanding that both the donor and the organization have rights and interests. We must first understand the boundaries, the parameters of the organization. We must also understand the boundaries of donors in general and the particular boundaries and interests of particular donors. Being honest with both the organization and the donor is the first step in mediating the interest of our organizations and our donors. Maintaining integrity, keeping promises—these are not possible without honesty about what is possible.

Competence

The concept of competence also applies to fundraising executives. If we are to be professionals, we must dedicate ourselves to being as competent as we can possibly be. What are the ethical and technical standards that we must learn and implement to become competent professionals? Training to develop technical standards and academic study to help us develop technical expertise are important. However, we must also understand ethical standards, develop ethical values, and apply those standards and values to decision making about ethical dilemmas in fundraising. The concept of competence relates to both Josephson's values and Independent Sector's commitments. Josephson's values of law abidingness/ civic duty, pursuit of excellence, and personal accountability apply here. The Independent Sector values of obedience of the law, commitment beyond the law, accountability to the public, commitment to the public good, and prudent application of resources apply here.

Language

Language is an important aspect of fundraising. The way we talk about our profession and the way we discuss the process of fundraising and philanthropy from individuals, corporations, foundations, and others are important to the dignity of our career processes. We do not refer to donors as "targets." We do not refer to the dignified process of inviting someone to make a gift as "hitting them up." The materials we develop about our organization must also reflect the mission, intentions, and purposes of the organization. We do not use case materials to respond to donor interest with no intention of fulfilling donor interest once the gift is received. The Josephson Institute values of honesty and integrity are appropriate to the concept of language. The Independent Sector commitment to openness and honesty applies to ethics in language.

Relationships

The fundraising process is about building relationships. One of the key questions for a fundraiser is "Who owns the relationship?" We must remember that the relationship we have with the donor exists only because of the organization. The organization owns the relationship. We must ask ourselves constantly who benefits from the relationship. The benefits should accrue only to the organization. The role of trust also is important here. The donor must be able to trust that the fund-raising executive will not benefit personally from the relationship. The organization must also be able to trust that the relationship will remain with the organization if the executive leaves.

The Josephson Institute values of promise keeping, loyalty-fidelity, fairness, concern for others, and respect for others help us create an ethics of relationships. The Independent Sector commitments of respect for the worth and dignity of individuals, a commitment to tolerance and diversity and social justice, help us understand the ethics of relationships. The Rosso phrase often cited in this book, "Fundraising is the servant of philanthropy," applies here.

Mission

Fundraising begins with mission. Every organization has a responsibility to understand its rationale for existence as a nonprofit organization. We as fund-raising executives must understand that mission and use mission as the means for bringing individuals, corporations, foundations, and others together with the organization based on mutual values and interests. Mission is directed to client needs. Mission is based on the public good. We have a responsibility to help organizations be true to their missions. All fundraising must be based on mis-sion. The Josephson Institute values of honesty and integrity are applicable here. Independent Sector's commitment beyond self is an excellent measure for mis-sion. Mission must be directed externally beyond those who are employed by the organization. Independent Sector's commitment to the public good is the basis for the concept of mission and provides a basis for forming an ethical understanding of our actions related to mission.

These six concepts provide a framework for bringing together the various aspects of ethical values introduced earlier in this chapter and applying them to the area of greatest tension for fundraisers.

This chapter opened with the observation that there are no ethical answers, only ethical questions. As fundraising professionals, we must develop an ability to make ethical decisions to solve ethical dilemmas. However, there are some starting points. Every profession must have a set of ethical standards about which there are no questions. As fundraising executives we may belong to several professional associations that provide us with guidance‥ A starting point for all fundraising executives is the Code of Ethics and Standards of Practice developed by the AFP. All members of AFP are asked to subscribe to both.

Another useful perspective for fundraising executives is the Donor Bill of Rights (see Exhibit 35.3). We must remember that the relationships between donors and organizations create certain expectations. If we are to develop the public trust necessary to function as professionals, we must have a minimum set of standards that protect donor rights. To remind ourselves of the importance of respecting donors and our responsibilities to them, AFP, CASE, AHP, AAFRC, and a number of other organizations have signed a commitment to a Donor Bill

EXHIBIT 35.3. THE DONOR BILL OF RIGHTS.

Philanthropy is based on voluntary action for the common good. It is a tradition of giving and sharing that is primary to the quality of life. To ensure that philanthropy merits the respect and trust of the general public, and that donors and prospective donors can have full confidence in the nonprofit organizations and causes they are asked to support, we declare that all donors have these rights:

  I. To be informed of the organization's mission, of the way the organization intends to use donated resources, and of its capacity to use donations effectively for their intended purposes.
 II. To be informed of the identity of those serving on the organization's governing board, and to expect the board to exercise prudent judgment in its stewardship responsibilities.
III. To have access to the organization's most recent financial statements.
 IV. To be assured their gifts will be used for the purposes for which they were given.
  V. To receive appropriate acknowledgement and recognition.
 VI. To be assured that information about their donation is handled with respect and with confidentiality to the extent provided by law.
VII. To expect that all relationships with individuals representing organizations of interest to the donor will be professional in nature.
VIII. To be informed whether those seeking donations are volunteers, employees of the organization or hired solicitors.
 IX. To have the opportunity for their names to be deleted from mailing lists that an organization may intend to share.
  X. To feel free to ask questions when making a donation and to receive prompt, truthful and forthright answers.

Note: The Donor Bill of Rights was created by the Association of Fundraising Professionals (AFP), the Association for Healthcare Philanthropy (AHP), the Council for Advancement and Support of Education (CASE), and the Giving Institute: Leading Consultants to Non-Profits. It has been endorsed by numerous organizations.

of Rights. The sponsoring organizations encourage you to copy the Donor Bill of Rights or to order additional copies from AFP to distribute to others in your organization.

Conclusion

A *U.S. News and World Report* article described fundraising as a "dance of deceit," in which fundraisers and donors are less than honest with each other (Streisand, 2001). Elliot (1991) gave us guidance on the concept of deception as applied to fundraising. Avoiding deception means telling the whole truth and not allowing either party to reach a conclusion because of something that has not been said. The image of a "dance of deceit" calls for an ethical response by fundraisers and their organizations. It also calls for fundraisers to educate others about the values that motivate philanthropy.

Transparency is the beginning of ethical behavior. Transparency means that organizations open their private organizational processes to public view because they serve the public good and as such they must accept responsibility for the public trust. Transparency will create larger public involvement, public understanding, and enhanced public trust.

CHAPTER THIRTY-SIX

THE LAW AND FUNDRAISING

By Philip M. Purcell

Fundraising excellence requires adherence to both the letter and the spirit of legal and ethical standards. The importance of the law in fundraising is evident in the attention given to charitable organizations and their fundraising practices by the United States Congress, Internal Revenue Service (IRS), state attorneys general, nonprofit boards of directors, and donors. For example, the IRS commonly includes documented fundraising abuses and other abuses by tax-exempt organizations or donors in its annual "Dirty Dozen" list of tax scams.

The law that governs fundraising is a complex partnership of federal and state statutes, administrative regulations, and judicial decisions. Of course, this law is dynamic and subject to change. Sources of current and accurate legal information include qualified legal counsel, independent auditors, updated reference works, consultants, and state or federal government offices (for example, state attorney general or secretary of state, IRS). This chapter will highlight the most significant aspects of this complex legal landscape to assure excellence in fundraising.

Many issues in the law of fundraising are not "black and white"; rather they present legal and ethical dilemmas that are not easily resolved by an examination of applicable standards. Resolution of a dilemma requires considerable discernment and prudent decision making. First, all facts and circumstances must be accurately clarified and understood in detail. Next, the current laws and ethical standards that may apply to the situation must be identified and examined. Discussion must take place with all appropriate parties; these may include staff, counsel, and volunteers (for example, fundraisers, staff leadership, board of directors, legal counsel, auditors) as well as donors and their professional advisors (for example, legal counsel, accountant, financial advisor). Finally, a decision must be made, implemented, and monitored or modified for similar circumstances in the future.

Governance

The beginning point for prudent decision making in fundraising is effective *governance*, which in turn depends in part on the organizational structure. Pursuant to state law, charitable organizations may generally be an unincorporated association, nonprofit corporation, charitable trust, or other options such as a limited liability corporation. The governance structure of each is determined under state law by applicable articles of association, constitution or bylaws (for unincorporated associations), trust instruments, and governing statutes (for charitable trusts) or articles of incorporation and bylaws (for nonprofit corporations) (Fishman and Schwarz, 2006). Nonprofit corporations offer a valuable balance of limitation of liability for directors and an effective governance structure. Once organized pursuant to state law, a charitable organization may seek qualification for tax exemption from the IRS as a public charity (for public or mutual benefit) or as a private foundation. Several publications freely available from www.irs.gov provide guidance: Form 1023, Application for Recognition of Exemption under 501(c)(3); Form 1024, Application for Recognition of Exemption under 501(a); and Form 557, Tax Exempt Status for Your Organization.

Duty of Prudent Care

The board of directors is ultimately responsible for the oversight of a nonprofit corporation, including the assurance of fundraising excellence. State law imposes three primary legal duties on nonprofit corporation boards of directors: prudent care, loyalty, and obedience (Fishman and Schwarz, 2006). The *duty of prudent care* requires directors to exercise their responsibilities in good faith and with the diligence and skill that a prudent person would under the same circumstances. This prudent care requires carefully made decisions relative to both expenses and revenues, including generation of revenue by fundraising. When the nonprofit is exercising this prudent care, state law may allow directors to delegate some responsibility to board designated and controlled committees that may include nondirectors. Use of development, fundraising, campaign, and other committees to oversee fundraising is an excellent means to satisfy the duty of care.

Conflicts of Interest

The *duty of obedience* requires a nonprofit corporation to carry out its legally stated charitable mission. The *duty of loyalty* requires directors to avoid acting in any manner that may harm the nonprofit corporation or that may result in the directors' personal financial gain. The duty of loyalty is imposed by state law; federal oversight is involved when charitable organizations apply for tax-exempt status pursuant to Internal Revenue Code (IRC) section 501(c)(3), requiring submission of a copy of the corporate bylaws and attestation that a conflict of interest policy has been approved by the board of directors. For example, conflicts of interest can arise in the context of fundraising if charitable gifts are used to leverage financial contracts by the charitable organization with directors or with those who may have certain relationships with directors (such as family or business).

IRS Form 990 and Governance

The IRS recently revised its annual 990 information return to ask substantive questions relative to charitable organization governance. Information concerning the board of directors, conflict of interest policies, charitable gifts, and other data is now collected and subject to IRS review. Oversight of prudent governance and fundraising practices will increasingly be a shared responsibility of federal and state authorities.

State Law Considerations

Oversight of charitable organizations at the state level often rests with the state attorney general. Other state offices with oversight may include the secretary of state (nonprofit incorporation and annual certification) and department of revenue (application for property, sales and other tax exemptions, regulation of charity gaming). The attorney general typically has the legal standing on behalf of the general public to bring a lawsuit in court or to impose other relief (for example, injunctions, asset receiverships, replacement of directors or trustees) in cases in which claims of mismanagement, theft, or other abuse have been made by donors, whistleblowers, or the general public.

Definition of a Gift and Donor Restrictions

State and federal courts have required both a subjective and objective test to determine the existence of a charitable gift. The subjective test requires that the donor's intent must be "disinterested generosity" to support a charitable mission. The objective test requires that the gift does not include any financial benefit or *quid pro quo* returned to the donor in exchange for the gift (Toce, 2010). In addition, a donor cannot impose restrictions on a gift that inappropriately constrain the duty of care owed by the board of directors over the use of the gift such as a disposition of donated assets. Although charitable designations by donors are permissible (for example, specific charitable program support), there are limits to designations, especially when uses of the gift become impossible, impractical, or illegal to fulfill. For example, in cases in which a donor is deceased, most states provide statutory procedures (such as *cy pres*, the doctrine of equitable deviation) for modifying the designations of a gift.

Charitable Pledges

Fundraising programs often encourage multiyear pledge commitments. Although lawsuits to enforce charitable pledges are understandably rare, these commitments may be deemed enforceable contracts pursuant to state law, particularly in cases in which the charitable organization has acted in reliance on the pledge (for example, building construction begins in reliance on a major gift pledge). In addition, the Financial Accounting Standards Board (FASB) requires charitable pledges to be booked as a receivable on the audited financial statement of the charitable organization. Donors with active pledges may be requested by an independent auditor to confirm their commitment. Furthermore, donors to donor-advised funds and private foundations cannot have their personal pledges paid from the donor-advised fund or private foundation.

Charitable Endowments

A fundraising goal of many charitable organizations is to establish charitable endowments for long-term financial support. Most states have adopted the Uniform Prudent Management of Institutional Funds Act (UPMIFA) as the law governing endowments. A model UPMIFA statute with comments and a current list of enacting states is available from the Uniform Law Commissioners at www.nccusl.org. Pursuant to UPMIFA and FASB accounting standards, an endowment is defined as a gift designated as permanently endowed by a donor, either in a communication from the donor (for example, transmittal letter, signed endowment fund agreement) or in response to the marketing materials of the charitable organization (endowment campaign letters and brochures). Alternatively, a gift that is not restricted by the donor for endowment but is treated as endowment by action of the board of directors is deemed to be *quasi-endowment* pursuant to FASB standards.

A board of directors must approve policies for the prudent investment, spending, and fees applicable to its endowments. Although private foundations are legally required to spend at least 5 percent of assets each year (with some exceptions), a public charity endowment does not have a required spending rate. Pursuant to UPMIFA, it is the duty of the board of directors to spend or accumulate assets as it deems prudent, balancing the short-term need for funds with the long-term perpetual support from the endowment—often with a goal of generational equity.

State Fundraising Registration

Fundraising registration requirements differ from state to state. The National Association of State Charity Officials (NASCO) is an association of state offices charged with oversight of charitable organizations and solicitation. NASCO (www .nasconet.org) offers a model charitable solicitation law, including a unified registration form that has been used or modified by some states. Some states exempt from registration those charitable organizations that are domiciled in the state and use their own staff or volunteers to fundraise. However, charitable organizations located in other states are usually required to register at least once or to provide an annual registration.

Internet Fundraising

Use of the Internet for fundraising has raised new issues and challenges for states that regulate fundraising. As a result, NASCO has promulgated recommended guidelines for Internet fundraising, the Charleston Principles. A basic premise of the Charleston Principles is that although existing state laws govern charitable solicitations on the Internet, states typically have jurisdiction to regulate fraud and other deceptive practices even if an organization is not required to register to fundraise in the state.

Fundraising Consultants and Solicitors

Instead of using full- or part-time staff, many charities hire consultants, solicitors, or both to assist fundraising activities. The regulations for consultants and solicitors vary from state to state. In many states, a fundraising consultant is defined as an independently contracted person or organization hired to advise and train the charitable organization on fundraising strategies—but not to directly solicit gifts. A fundraising solicitor is an independently contracted person or organization hired to solicit gifts directly. Many states require (1) annual registration with the attorney general or other office by fundraising consultants and solicitors before conducting business, (2) a copy of their contracts, (3) disclosure of the fees paid, and (4) verification of whether the consultant or solicitor will have custody of donations.

Percentage Requirements

Percentage limitations imposed by state law on fundraising costs are impermissible. Further, fundraising solicitors are not required to disclose affirmatively fundraising costs while making the solicitation. However, states may prosecute fraudulent practices in cases in which donors and prospects are not accurately informed of how much of their gifts will be paid to the fundraising solicitors (Fishman and Schwarz, 2006).

Telemarketing

Many states, through the attorney general or other office, maintain "do not call" lists to prevent unwanted soliciting telephone calls. However, many states exempt charitable organizations from the "do not call" list so long as the charitable organization uses its own full- or part-time staff or volunteers to make the soliciting calls.

Federal Law Considerations

The Internal Revenue Code (IRC) permits two types of charitable organizations pursuant to IRC Section 501(c)(3): public benefit charities and private foundations. Generally speaking, a charitable organization is presumed to be a private foundation unless it proves on its annual IRS 990 information return that it is a public benefit charity instead. The distinction is very important, because gifts to public charities provide greater tax benefits to donors. In addition, private foundations must comply with a number of very restrictive rules (Toce, 2010). These restrictions exist because the private foundation allows a single donor (an individual, family, or corporation) to have significant control over the investments, grant-making, or operating programs of the private foundation.

Donor-Advised Funds

A donor-advised fund (DAF) can be an attractive alternative to a private foundation. Although DAFs have been popular for many years, the Pension Protection

Act of 2006 provided the first legal definition and other requirements for DAFs. DAFs are held only by public charities such as community foundations that have a charitable mission allowing grants to other qualified charitable organizations. Gifts to DAFs qualify for the enhanced tax benefits of gifts to a public charity rather than a private foundation. Pursuant to a signed agreement, the donor retains a right to recommend grants from the DAF. However, the DAF donor does not have the legal right to control the distribution of the grants or the investment of the donated assets as he does with a private foundation. Rather, the board of directors of the charity hosting the DAF retains this ultimate legal control. Pledges of donors may not be paid from DAFs, nor may the DAF make a grant for the value of a *quid pro quo* received for a gift, such as the cost of the meal included with a fundraising dinner ticket purchase.

Types of Public Benefit Charities

The Internal Revenue Code allows for two general types of public charities, distinguished by whether the organization must pass a "public support test" or not. The public support test is a complicated formula that must be completed annually on the IRS 990 information return. In general, the public support test requires that one-third of the total support of the organization must be derived from the public and not from one person or a small number of persons. An essential component of this public support is fundraising revenue from a broad number of donors. The types of organizations that qualify as public benefit charities without the necessity of the public support test include churches, schools, hospitals, medical research organizations, state university foundations, and governmental units (Fishman and Schwarz, 2006).

Supporting Organizations

Another type of public benefit charity that is not required to satisfy the public support test is the *supporting organization*. By design, supporting organizations are created to support the charitable mission of another public benefit charity; that is, the supported organization. There are three types of supporting organizations, depending on the nature of the organizational relationship and control by the supported organization of the supporting organization (Fishman and Schwarz, 2006). From a fundraising perspective, supporting organizations can be very helpful in a number of special circumstances, such as accepting specific assets that may carry potential liability (such as real estate) or as an incubator for a charitable program that may evolve into a public benefit charity.

Member Benefit Charities

Income of a qualified member benefit organization is not taxed, but gifts to these tax-exempt organizations do not qualify the donor for an income tax charitable deduction. Member benefit charities include civic leagues, business leagues, chambers of commerce, real estate boards, social and recreational clubs, fraternal benefit societies or associations, credit unions, and veterans organizations. The income tax deduction is available for gifts to veterans organizations, fraternal societies for charitable purposes, and cemetery companies (Toce, 2010). Some member benefit charities partner with separately incorporated public benefit charities that serve as a charitable "foundation" to accept tax-deductible gifts for qualified charitable purposes (such as a fraternal organization using a foundation to accept gifts for scholarships).

Unrelated Business Taxable Income

Tax-exempt organizations do not normally pay income tax on its fundraising or other revenue. However, revenue generated by the organization from a trade or business that is regularly carried on and not substantially related to the charitable mission will be taxed as unrelated business taxable income (UBTI). Exceptions to UBTI include revenue generated from qualified sponsorship payments, so long as the recognition provided to the sponsor does not include an inducement to purchase (that is, does not serve as paid advertising). Many charitable organizations use sponsorships to meet resource development goals. Other exceptions to UBTI include passive investment income on a charitable endowment, rental on real estate, and bingo game revenue. IRS Publication 598, "Tax on Unrelated Business Income of Exempt Organizations," provides additional guidance.

Income Tax Benefits for Charitable Giving

The income tax charitable deduction was introduced in 1917 and the estate tax charitable deduction in 1921. The dollar amount of the charitable deduction depends on the asset or assets donated as well as the type of charitable organization recipient (Toce, 2010). Gifts of cash to public benefit charities (and private operating foundations) qualify for an income tax deduction up to 50 percent of the donor's adjusted gross income (AGI). Any excess deduction may be carried over for up to the five following tax years, claiming as much deduction as possible each year. Gifts of cash to private nonoperating foundations qualify for a deduction up to 30 percent of the donor's AGI with five years of carryover.

Nonoperating foundations do not directly manage charitable programs, whereas operating foundations receive enhanced tax benefits for gifts that support the charitable programs they operate.

Gifts to public benefit charities and operating foundations of long-term (held for more than one year) appreciated property such as stock and real estate qualify for a deduction for the fair market value of the property up to 30 percent of the donor's AGI with five years of carryover. Gifts of any asset other than qualified appreciated stock to private nonoperating foundations qualify for a deduction for the value of the donor's cost basis in the asset up to 20 percent of the donor's AGI with five years of carryover. The donor and charitable organization owe no capital gains tax if the appreciated property is later sold, regardless of whether the recipient is a public charity or private foundation.

Gifts of short-term appreciated property and ordinary income property such as inventory and artwork by its creator to a public benefit charity (and operating foundation) qualify for a deduction for the cost basis in the property up to 50 percent of the donor's AGI; the same gift to a private nonoperating foundation allows a deduction for the cost basis up to 30 percent of AGI, with five years of carryover for each.

Gifts of tangible personal property, artwork, equipment, books, and so on to a public charity or as private operating or nonoperating foundation, in cases in which the donee does not use the donated property for a purpose related to its charitable mission, qualify for a deduction value for the cost basis of the property up to 50 percent of the donor's AGI if given to a public benefit charity or operating foundation and 20 percent of AGI if given to a nonoperating foundation, with five years of carryover for each.

Gift and Estate Tax Benefits for Charitable Giving

There are significant differences among the income, gift, and estate tax benefits for charitable giving. First, the gift and estate tax charitable deduction does not have percentage limits. Second, the income tax charitable deduction is available only for gifts to domestic organizations, whereas the estate tax deduction is available to domestic and foreign organizations. Third, for estate tax purposes the donee must be a corporation, association, trust, or fraternal society, whereas for income tax purposes the donee may also be a community chest, fund, or foundation. For gift tax purposes, the donees are the same as for the estate tax except that gift tax law also recognizes a community chest, fund, or foundation as a qualified donee without any requirement that it be in corporate form (Toce, 2010).

Gift Substantiation and Disclosure

A donor cannot claim a tax deduction for any single contribution of $250 or more unless she obtains a contemporaneous, written acknowledgment of the contribution from the recipient organization. An organization that does not acknowledge a contribution incurs no penalty; but the donor cannot claim the tax deduction without a written acknowledgment. Although it is a donor's responsibility to obtain a written acknowledgment, an organization can assist a donor by providing a timely, written statement containing all of the following information:

1. Name of organization
2. Amount of cash contribution
3. Description (*but not the value*) of noncash contribution
4. Statement that no goods or services were provided by the organization in return for the contribution, if that was the case
5. Description and good faith estimate of the value of goods or services, if any, that an organization provided in return for the contribution
6. Statement that goods or services, if any, that an organization provided in return for the contribution consisted entirely of intangible religious benefits, if that was the case

There are no IRS forms for the acknowledgment. A donor should not attach the acknowledgment to his or her individual income tax return, but must retain it to substantiate the contribution. Recipient organizations typically send written acknowledgments to donors no later than January 31 of the year following the donation. For the written acknowledgment to be considered contemporaneous with the contribution, a donor must receive the acknowledgment by the earlier of (1) the date on which the donor actually files his or her individual federal income tax return for the year of the contribution or (2) the due date (including extensions) of the return.

The acknowledgment must describe goods or services an organization provides in exchange for a contribution of $75 or more. It must also provide a good faith estimate of the value of such goods or services, because a donor must generally reduce the amount of the contribution deduction by the fair market value of the goods and services provided by the organization. Goods or services include cash, property, services, benefits, or privileges. However, there are important exceptions for benefits considered to be tokens (insubstantial value), membership benefits, and intangible religious benefits. For a summary of the gift receipt rules, see IRS Publication 1771, "Charitable Contributions—Substantiation and Disclosure Requirements."

Noncash Gifts

To claim an income tax charitable deduction for a noncash gift—stock, real estate, artwork, equipment, software—requires the donor to complete IRS form 8283 (with an exception for gifts of small value), and to file this form with the income tax return. If the donor claims a deduction over $5,000, then a qualified and independent appraisal is required. If the donee charitable organization sells the donated noncash property within three years of the gift, it must file IRS Form 8282 reporting the sale price, with some exceptions, such as for gifts of publicly traded stock. The IRS compares the sale price with the deduction value to determine whether there may be an inappropriately inflated deduction. There are many special rules that prohibit or limit the amount of the charitable income tax deduction for certain gifts (for example, no deduction is allowed for volunteer time or services or for the loan of property). Two excellent resources available from the IRS are Publication 561, "Determining the Value of Donated Property," and Publication 526, "Charitable Contributions."

International Philanthropy

Philanthropy is increasingly global. Not surprisingly, the legal aspects of international fundraising—and the tax benefits for donors—can be quite complex. As a result of the September 11, 2001 attacks, a number of regulations (including lists of organizations linked to terrorism) were promulgated to ensure that philanthropy was not assisting terrorist activities. The U.S. Department of Treasury offers the latest information on these regulations for donors and grantmakers. In general, only gifts to charitable organizations created under the laws of the United States—or gifts subject to tax treaties between the United States and select countries (for example, Canada, Mexico, and Israel)—are income tax–deductible. This rule does not apply to the estate tax charitable deduction. Of course, U.S. charities may use tax-deductible donations for work related to the mission that may be fulfilled in other countries—church missions, Red Cross, "friends of" organizations. In addition, private foundations may make qualified grants (nontaxable expenditures) to foreign organizations so long as the private foundation satisfies an equivalency determination test or an expenditure responsibility test (Toce, 2010).

Donor Privacy and Confidentiality

All codes of ethical conduct in fundraising, as well as federal and state privacy laws, require the protection of donor privacy and confidentiality. State laws that allow access to public records may apply to donor records of organizations that receive tax revenue. Some public university foundation records have been deemed accessible by the public pursuant to state law. Other laws that may affect donor records include the Family Educational Rights and Privacy Act (FERPA) and the Health Insurance Portability and Accountability Act (HIPAA). Legal counsel should be consulted to determine the applicability of all laws and procedures for best practices to ensure donor privacy and confidentiality.

Conclusion

Fundraising excellence requires adherence to both the letter and the spirit of legal and ethical standards. Prudent management of charitable organizations requires careful attention to the "black and white" legal and ethical requirements for fundraising as well as making good decisions in cases in which a dilemma is presented and a difficult decision must be made. Good decision making requires us to clarify the facts, understand the applicable legal and ethical standards, and make a reasonable decision. Evaluating and modifying our decisions helps to continually improve our practices. Achieving excellence in fundraising demands nothing less.

PART EIGHT

YOUR CAREER IN FUNDRAISING

The profession of fundraising is relatively new as professions go, and many would say it is still an emerging profession. This part of the book takes a look at topics of interest to fundraisers who wish to know more about the history of the field, to increase their professional knowledge, and also to prepare themselves to understand fundraising as a global phenomenon with increasingly identifiable global standards.

Chapter Thirty-Seven provides a brief history of the fundraising profession, with a particular focus on emerging issues and trends relevant to fundraisers today. Chapter Thirty-Eight offers a brief overview of the difference between certification and certificate programs; Chapter Thirty-Nine provides concise advice on preparing for exam for the CFRE certification, a milestone of professional accomplishment that is recognized internationally.

The international theme continues in Chapter Forty, which examines what fundraising looks like globally based on results of CFRE International's 2009 *CFRE Job Analysis*. This part concludes with Chapter Forty-One, which offers a compendium of resources for fundraisers seeking to improve their professional and technical knowledge of philanthropy and fundraising.

CHAPTER THIRTY-SEVEN

FUNDRAISING AS A PROFESSION

By Eva E. Aldrich

While fundraising has long been a part of charitable endeavors, the professionalization of fundraising is a phenomenon of the twentieth century. Scholarly consensus is that fundraising is still an emerging profession, with the further development of research and theory being vital to the profession's future. A review of key milestones in fundraising and key issues of the emerging professional can help illuminate how far fundraising as a profession has come—and how far it still needs to go.

Milestones in the Professionalization of Fundraising

In 1641, clergymen Hugh Peter, Thomas Weld, and William Hibbens left the Massachusetts Bay Colony to travel to England to seek funds to support Harvard College, thus earning a place in history as members of the "first systematic effort to raise money on this continent" (Cutlip, 1965, p. 3). Although systematic, this effort was nonetheless ancillary to the participants' acknowledged professions as clergy. Fundraising would remain an ancillary activity rather than a professional pursuit until the middle of the nineteenth century, when the growing needs of the poor during the Industrial Revolution outstripped the ability of philanthropy to meet these needs face-to-face. Only then did fundraising begin to emerge as a distinctive discipline (Pribbenow, 1993).

Achieving Excellence in Fundraising

By the end of the nineteenth century, major campaigns at institutions such as Johns Hopkins University and the University of Chicago (where Baptist clergy Frederick T. Gates and Thomas W. Goodspeed were instrumental to the effort's success) demonstrated the way in which major fundraising efforts were increasingly professional endeavors rather than volunteer-driven efforts (Pribbenow, 1993). The work of Lyman Pierce and Charles S. Ward for the YMCA is another instance of how professional organization had begun to transform fundraising practice. Their pioneering of "the mass campaign for small donations" revolutionized fundraising, effectively "democratizing philanthropy" (p. 397) and paving the way for other successful fundraising efforts based on a high volume of small contributions, such as the National Christmas Seals and March of Dimes (Hodgkinson, 2002a). By the time of World War I, the mass campaign was an established vehicle—one that allowed the Red Cross to launch the country's first nationwide fundraising campaign, which succeeded in raising a remarkable $114 million in eight days in 1917 (Cutlip, 1965).

The end of the war saw the birth of the professional fundraising consultant. Several firms were created in that era, including Ward and Hill (Charles S. Ward was one of its founders) in 1919, Ketchum Inc. (then known as Ketchum Publicity in 1919), and Marts and Lundy (a breakaway firm from Ward and Hill) in 1926 (Cutlip, 1965). The last two firms are still in existence today.

One of the most successful firms of the era was John Price Jones, founded in 1919. Whereas previous generations of fundraisers had generally relied on personal qualities such as those recommended by Frederick T. Gates, who "exhorted himself and his followers to appeal only to the highest motives, to not flag when frustrated, and to canvas all day, everyday, rain or shine" (Pribbenow, 1993, p. 206), the firm of John Price Jones added "'scientific' and comprehensive" methods (p. 208). As Cutlip (1965) notes in discussing the methodology behind John Price Jones' fundraising efforts to help Harvard raise $14 million in 1918–1919, John Price Jones was the first to use a strategic public relations program and contemporary campaign committee structure. The discipline imposed by such a structure was a far cry from prior fundraising methodology, which relied on good fortune as much as good planning.

By the time of the Great Depression in the early 1930s, "fundraising had evolved into a legitimate profession" (Hodgkinson, 2002a, p. 397). Partly in response to this, and partly as Cutlip (1965) attributes to mounting competition and criticism of funding drives during the era's hard times, the American Association of Fund-Raising Counsel was formed in 1935. As Hodgkinson (2002a) notes, since that time many more professional organizations for fundraisers have formed, including the Association of Fundraising Professionals (then the National Society of Fund Raising Executives) in 1960, the Association for Healthcare Philanthropy

(1967), the Council for the Advancement and Support of Education (1974), and the Partnership for Philanthropic Planning (then the National Committee for Planned Giving) (1988).

The Fund Raising School, which has been noted as the "first formalized training program for fundraising professionals," was founded in 1974 by Hank Rosso, Joe Mixer, and Lyle Cook (Wagner, 2002, p. 34).

Today, no fewer than twenty membership organizations for professional fundraisers are acknowledged by CFRE International (www.cfre.org), and the Association of Fundraising Professionals estimates its membership at 30,000 fundraising professionals in 213 chapters worldwide (www.afpnet.org), all of whom ascribe to the AFP's *Code of Ethics and Standards of Professional Practice* as a condition of their membership. This code constituted "an important effort to bridge the gap between fundraising as a business (represented by the professional fundraising firms of earlier generations) and fundraising as a mission (in service of particular charitable organizations)" (Pribbenow, 1993, p. 214). This *Code of Ethics* was recently expanded to include articles aimed specifically at fundraising consultants and other businesses serving the fundraising profession (Hall, 2007a).

In addition, there are three certification designations for fundraising professionals. The Certified Fund Raising Executive (CFRE) credential, which is administered by CFRE International, has been acknowledged as "a universal baseline credential" since 1996 (Chobot, 2004, p. 32). Other credentials are the Advanced Certified Fund Raising Executive (ACFRE), administered by the Association of Fundraising Professionals, and the Fellow of the Association for Healthcare Philanthropy (FAHP) administered by the Association for Healthcare Philanthropy. At the time of his article, Chobot (2004) noted that more than 4,500 fundraisers were certified, with over 4,000 holding the CFRE designation; as of this writing, more than 5,400 fundraisers are certified as CFREs (CFRE, 2010). As Tempel and Duronio (1997) note, it is impossible to get an accurate count of the total number of fundraising professionals, but they suggest that there are an equal number of fundraisers who are not members of established membership organizations for the profession.

Issues of Fundraising as an Emerging Profession

Despite the rapid growth of fundraising as a profession, a survey of literature suggests that fundraising continues to be widely regarded as an emerging rather than an established profession (Carbone, 1989; Bloland and Bornstein, 1990; Pribbenow, 1993; Tempel and Duronio, 1997; Bloland and Tempel, 2004; Levy, 2004; Chobot, 2004; Wagner, 2007). As Bloland and Bornstein (1990) observe, "fund raisers aspire to what professions and occupations generally seek: effectiveness and efficiency in the work, control over work and work jurisdiction, and recognition of the legitimacy of the work and those who perform it" (p. 69). Carbone (1997) goes further, asserting that there are three distinct approaches with discernible steps. First is the process approach, in which the profession is first designated as a full-time endeavor, followed by the establishment of specialized educational and training programs and an acknowledged professional association. Next is the power approach, in which the profession establishes market control through convincing the public that the services it performs are vital and not readily learned by a large number of people. Last is the structural-functional approach, which demands a base of theoretical and applied knowledge, professional autonomy in decision making, service to others, the acknowledgment of professional authority, the development of a distinctive professional culture, and societal recognition of the legitimacy of the profession.

Bloland and Tempel (2004) echo Carbone (1997) while offering a shorter list of commonly accepted characteristics of professions, including "a body of applicable expert knowledge with a theoretical base, acquired through a lengthy period of training (preferably in a university), a demonstrated devotion to service, an active professional association, a code of ethics, and a high level of control over credentialing and application of the work" (p. 6). However, they note that measuring the degree to which fundraising fulfills these traits as a profession can be challenging, as an examination of each of these areas demonstrates.

Expert knowledge with a theoretical base. Bloland and Tempel (2004) note that "For a busy and successful fundraising professional, theory may seem obscure and hard to connect with practice. Yet theory that is generated through research is so significant that it is a major means for marking the difference between professions and nonprofessions" (pp. 11–12). Despite this, the fundraising profession and fundraisers in general seem to value the development of skills over the development and use of theoretical or research-based knowledge (Bloland and Bornstein, 1990). In part, this is due to the way in which fundraisers have traditionally been trained. In one study, 74 percent of respondents cited learning on the job as they way in which they learned fundraising; 43 percent cited nondegree professional development training; and less than 10 percent listed formal education (Tempel and Duronio, 2004). Although formal education programs are on the rise—and in fact are seen as currently trailing demand (Cohen, 2007)—many experienced fundraisers continue to maintain that the primary qualifications for the profession are personal qualities such as those cited by Wood (1997), which include good skills in listening, negotiation, and communication. However, by having a solely skills-based conception of the profession, these individuals overlook the consideration that "Although the work of fundraising is shared with amateurs, with a theory and research base in the hands of professionals, the distinctions between professional and amateur can be more sharply drawn, and fund raising could have a greater ability to define and defend its work boundaries" (Bloland and Bornstein, p. 82).

A demonstrated devotion to service. Pribbenow (1999a) agrees with Bloland and Bornstein (1990) that the claim of technical competence is insufficient as a claim to professionalism. According to Pribbenow (1993), fundraising as a profession "suffers for its attempts to ground its knowledge-base in a contractual understanding of human relationships" and instead must be grounded in an ethic of service (p. 221). The typical fundraiser's understanding of the profession as a set of techniques and skills to be mastered "is important only if it is understood as part of the promotion of healthy relationships between institutions and their various friends and constituencies" (Pribbenow, 1993, p. 222). Pribbenow (1999a) sees this "disconnection between knowledge and service" as a key problem and says that this disconnection explains why current efforts to professionalize fundraising further are "wrong-headed" (p. 34). He proposes that the next step in the evolution of fundraising as a profession is not to oppose the impulses of the amateur, whose pursuits are driven by love, and the professional, whose pursuits are driven by work, but rather to adopt a model whereby "love transforms work." In this way, the fundraiser's love of humankind and ethic of service to the community transforms the work of fundraising from a set of techniques into a powerful calling. This, says Pribbenow (1999a), will rightly "define the profession of philanthropic fundraising in terms of its philanthropic dimension" (p. 42).

An active professional association and a code of ethics. The area in which fundraising has perhaps gained the most maturity as a profession is the development of active professional associations and a code of ethics. As noted earlier in the history section of this chapter, there are many professional fundraising associations, the largest being the Association of Fundraising Professionals, whose members are all bound by the AFP's *Code of Ethics and Standards of Professional Practice.* Although having a code of ethics is one trait of professionalism, Bloland and Tempel (2004) point out that even this is problematic because "codes of ethics can be badly or well written. They may be too general or too specific, too stringent or too lax. They may miss the most significant measures of ethical behavior" (pp. 10–11). More important in terms of enforcement, the profession has not made it clear how to monitor ethics and standards, or what sanctions might be applied or how they might be enforced (Tempel and Duronio, 1997).

Control over credentialing. Chobot (2004) notes that "an initial stimulus for the creation of fundraising certification programs was a justification of fundraising as a profession" (p. 31). Although credentialing is not necessary to practice the profession, and fundraisers have been known to debate among themselves the value of credentialing, they nonetheless have become a standard part of the fundraising profession. In his discussion of the comparative virtues of licensing, certification, certificates, and accreditation, he points out that credentialing programs make the case that credentials such as the CFRE have a distinct "return on investment" by providing the certificant with the benefits of professional acknowledgment, donor confidence, employment advantages, higher compensation, and a profession that is stronger overall (Chobot 2004).

However, such benefits can sometimes be as perceptual as actual, if not more so. As Chobot (2004) points out, research supporting such claims is minimal to nonexistent, and although it would appear that certification suggests a certain level of competence, what it documents in actuality is a baseline level of knowledge—two conditions that may be allied but are not equivalent. In fact, he reports that the most documentable correlation between the CFRE and professionalization is the fact that reported salaries for holders of the CFRE are consistently higher than those of noncredentialed professionals. This assertion is supported by results of the AFP Compensation and Benefits Survey (2009), which reports that individuals holding the CFRE certification earn around $15,000 more annually than their noncertified peers, and those holding either the ACFRE or FAHP certification earn around $36,000 more than noncertified fundraisers annually. Overall, however, Chobot concludes that what is most important about credentialing programs for fundraisers and the fundraising profession is the way such credentials have evolved to be "exemplars of good fundraising practice" that have gained acceptance across the globe (2004, p. 47).

This voluntary adoption of credentialing is particularly important when considering the issue of professional autonomy. As Carbone (1997) points out, "Licensure is in some ways the enemy of autonomy since it is a mandate promulgated by civil authority, normally state governments" (p. 89). Not only is licensure of fundraisers by government an enemy of autonomy, but there are other serious issues attached to it. Because fundraisers must have the public's trust, they must go beyond licensing, which is based on "meeting a minimal standard of competence" (Chobot, 2004). As Pribbenow (1993) points out, the "mutual relationship between the public and the voluntary sector is on a higher level of expectation; the public good requires public trust, and trust is a mutual relationship" (p. 229).

The Future of Fundraising as a Profession

The issues that Tempel and Duronio (1997) identified over a decade ago as key to the profession's future remain relevant today: turnover, attitudes toward asking for money, the feminization of the profession, and compensation. Turnover remains a challenge in the field, as the numbered of seasoned professionals lags behind demand, particularly in the arena of major gifts (Hall, 2007a). Asking for money continues to be an act that some fundraisers are loath to acknowledge for what it is, seeing it as the "dirty work" of an otherwise respectable career as a nonprofit professional (Bloland and Tempel, 2004; Tempel and Duronio, 1997). Women now constitute the majority of individuals in the profession, though they continue to occupy fewer positions of leadership and make less money in terms of compensation than their male counterparts (Tempel and Duronio, 1997); in fact, results of the *AFP Compensation & Benefits Survey* (2009) suggest that if the AFP sample is relatively representative of the profession as a whole, fundraisers are disproportionately white (90 percent) and female (67 percent), with women earning approximately $20,000 less per year than male fundraisers. Compensation itself continues to be an issue for the profession, with parties having trouble determining appropriate levels for fundraisers, who clearly are in demand but who operate within the cultural constraints of the nonprofit sector, where it is assumed that the satisfaction of mission-driven work helps make up for lower financial compensation levels (Tempel and Duronio, 1997).

Wagner (2005) identifies another continuing challenge of the profession— that of "leading up," described as the need to "exercise leadership from whatever rank or position they [fundraisers] hold in order to motivate others" (p. 1). She goes on to assert that fundraisers are classic examples of Greenleaf's conception of the servant-leader, who are driven not by personal ambition but by a commitment to organizational mission and service (p. 97).

Conclusion

All in all, the profession of fundraising walks a tightrope. On one side is professionalization, with all its accompanying benefits, including the acknowledgment of expertise and respect from the wider society. On the other side is the ethic of service, which as Pribbenow (1999a) notes harks back to the best aspects of amateurism, the love that drives mission. Ultimately, to flourish as a profession, fundraising must grow the professional knowledge needed to elevate it from a set of techniques to a discipline possessing science to balance its traditional art. As it does this, it must continue to tell its story as one of public service and public trust. It is only in this way that, as The Fund Raising School phrases it, apology will be replaced with pride in fundraising, and fundraising will truly earn its place as a vital, appreciated aspect of the philanthropic enterprise.

CHAPTER THIRTY-EIGHT

FUNDRAISING CREDENTIALING

By Eva E. Aldrich

As mentioned in the preceding chapter, credentialing for fundraising is a subject of much discussion in the profession. It is clear that being a successful fundraiser does not require certification, as the history of fundraising is filled with many effective fundraisers who, though not credentialed, do credit to the profession. Indeed, because the nonprofit sector is so important to a thriving civil society, any sort of mandatory certification would run counter to the firm belief that citizen groups should not only be able to rally around a cause but also be empowered to raise money to fulfill their vision of change.

Voluntary credentialing, on the other hand, serves both the fundraising profession and individual fundraising professionals well. The willingness of the profession to encourage voluntary certification not only helps make sure that the profession holds itself to high standards but also helps preempt the need for mandatory certification and regulation administered by government, thus making sure that the profession of fundraising stays firmly in the hands of fundraising professionals. For individual fundraisers, certification allows not only for a sense of professional pride but also perhaps for professional reward, as increasingly employers are looking for certified fundraising professionals and rewarding them at higher levels than their noncertified counterparts, according to the *AFP Compensation & Benefits Survey* (2009).

However, many fundraising professionals can become confused about the difference between certification and certificate programs. There is a distinct difference between becoming certified and earning a certificate. This is not to say that one is better than the other; rather, certification and certificate programs have different aims. In fact, the two processes should be seen as complementary, as continuing education certificate programs (as well as credit-bearing academic certificates and degrees in fundraising, philanthropy, and nonprofit management) offered by colleges and universities can be an excellent way to prepare for certification or to enhance professional knowledge on an ongoing basis after certification has been achieved.

As is evident in Table 38.1, CFRE International offers an excellent comparison between certification and certificates that clarifies the differences between the two and also explains what each has to offer to the fundraising professional seeking to advance his or her career. One key fact that this explanation highlights is that certification is an *assessment* process. In the case of the Certified Fund Raising Executive (CFRE) certification, what this means is that the CFRE credential is practiced-based, measuring the knowledge needed in order to be able to apply best practices principles to real-life, work-related tasks and challenges faced by fundraising professionals at the five-year experience level. Certificate programs,

TABLE 38.1. CERTIFICATION VERSUS CERTIFICATE.

Certification	Certificate
Results from an assessment process	Results from an educational process
For individuals	For individuals
Typically requires some amount of professional experience	For both newcomers and experienced professionals
Awarded by a third-party, standard-setting organization	Awarded by educational programs or institutions
Indicates mastery/competency as measured against a defensible set of standards, usually by application or exam	Indicates completion of a course or series of courses with specific focus; is different than a degree granting program
Standards set through a defensible, industry-wide process (job analysis/role delineation) that results in an outline of required knowledge and skills	Course content set a variety of ways (faculty committee; dean; instructor; occasionally through defensible analysis of topic area)
Typically results in a designation to use after one's name (CFRE, ACFRE, FAHP, CPF, APRA, CAE); may result in a document to hang on the wall or keep in a wallet	Usually listed on a resume detailing education; may issue a document to hang on the wall
Has ongoing requirements in order to maintain; holder must demonstrate he/she continues to meet requirements	Is the end result; demonstrates knowledge of course content at the end of a set period in time

Source: CFRE International, 2001.

as CFRE International goes on to explain, are *educational* processes whose aim is primarily to expand the participant's base of knowledge.

Another key difference is that certification is based on industry-wide standards formulated through a rigorous evaluation and testing process, whereas certificate programs (which can also be demanding) are more likely to have their standards of performance determined by the institution or instructor of record.

Certification, continuing education certificate programs, and academic programs and degrees all have a role to play in the ongoing growth of the fundraising professional. However, to make the most of the many opportunities in support of continued professional advancement, it is important for fundraisers to know and understand the differences among these complementary but distinctive activities. Certificate and academic programs advance knowledge within the profession and among fundraising professionals; certification builds the profession through setting industry-wide standards that help build trust in the profession and ensure a fundamental level of knowledge and accomplishment among those who voluntarily certify. These complementary activities are vital for the ongoing strength of the fundraising profession, its practitioners, and the many nonprofit organizations they so ably serve.

CHAPTER THIRTY-NINE

PREPARING FOR THE CFRE EXAM

By Eva E. Aldrich

The Certified Fund Raising Executive (CFRE) exam is a career milestone that marks a baseline knowledge of best practices in fundraising at the five-year career level. Because attaining the CFRE credential is a mark of distinction that demonstrates the fundraiser's commitment to ethical and effective fundraising, professionalism, and ongoing education, many candidates choose to devote time to studying for the exam beforehand. Although there is not a single best way to prepare for the exam, a few pieces of practical advice can make things easier for the candidate.

The first and most important step when preparing to take the CFRE exam is to visit the website of CFRE International (www.cfre.org) and apply for the CFRE. To be eligible to sit for the exam, candidates must demonstrate the equivalent of five years of full-time employment in fundraising plus fulfill education, professional practice, and volunteer service requirements.

With their application complete, candidates will find a wealth of information on the CFRE International website under the "Exam Information" tab. This includes CFRE's own guide, "Preparing for the CFRE Exam," which conveniently describes and makes available all the resources on the site related to exam preparation. At the time of this writing, these resources include the following:

- The Test Content Outline, which informs the candidate of the Domain and Task areas appearing on the exam, as well as the number of questions on the exam by Domain area.

- The Study Wizard, which allows candidates to self-assess their familiarity with fundraising knowledge areas. This self-assessment helps candidates determine where their knowledge is strong (so they may not need to study as much in these areas) as well as where their knowledge is weak (so they may want to devote additional study time to these topics).
- The Resource Reading List, which provides some suggested resources candidates may want to use in their studies. It is important to note that candidates should not feel they have to read each and every book on the list. The list is provided simply as a help to candidates who would like some guidance regarding resources they may find useful as part of their individualized study plan.
- Resources for having a successful exam experience, including information on review courses, a place to connect with study groups, and tips for the day of the exam.
- General information regarding testing center locations, fees, and times when the exam is offered.

The second step to a successful exam is to take what you've learned from the resources on the CFRE International website and create your own individualized study plan. There are three main factors to take into account when you're creating your study plan:

- Based on the Domains and Tasks listed on the Test Content Outline and/or your results from taking the Study Wizard, decide the knowledge areas about which you're confident and those in which you feel you need additional work. This will help you decide the best way to allocate your available time for study.
- Review your schedule to determine how much time you will devote to studying. Generally speaking, a slow but steady pace will be more beneficial not only for exam purposes but also for long-term knowledge retention.
- Determine how you best like to learn. Do you like the intensity of concentrated periods of study in a classroom setting? In that case, a review course may be best for you. Do you prefer to learn at a steady pace in a small group setting? A formal or informal study group may be for you. Are you self-motivated and enjoy figuring things out on your own? Then studying solo may be the best learning option for you.

The third step is to make sure you're mentally and physically prepared for the exam. It's simple common sense, but anything you can do to make sure you're well-rested, undistracted, and free of stress on the day of exam will do a lot to make sure you're well positioned to do your best.

To help you prepare for the CFRE exam, Table 39.1 lists the CFRE Domain and chapters from this book that may be helpful in reviewing the knowledge represented by the Domain/Task. Table 39.1 was prepared by the author and has not been reviewed or endorsed by CFRE International. It is not meant to be comprehensive; it simply provides a starting point for using this book as part of your individual study plan.

TABLE 39.1. CFRE DOMAINS AND CORRESPONDING CHAPTERS.

CFRE Domains	Corresponding Chapters (CFRE Domain/Task: Corresponding Chapter Number)
I. Current and Prospective Donor Research	I.1: 3, 11, 30 I.2: 11, 30, 35 I.3: 3, 11, 12, 13, 14, 15, 16, 17, 30 I.4: 11, 30 I.5: 11, 24, 28,30
II. Securing the Gift	II.1: 4 II.2: 3, 11, 12, 13, 14, 15, 16, 17, 30 II.3: 2, 3, 4, 5, 6, 7, 8, 9, 18, 19, 20, 21, 22, 34 II.4: 4, 18, 19, 20, 21, 22, 32 II.5: 6, 7, 8, 9, 11, 18, 19, 20, 21, 22, 34 II.1: 11, 30, 31
III. Relationship Building	III.1: 3, 4, 5, 6, 7, 8, 9, 12, 13, 14, 15, 16, 17 III.2: 3, 4, 6, 7, 8, 9, 32 III.3: 1, 10, 27, 35 III.4: 5, 6, 7, 8, 9, 12, 13, 14, 15, 16, 17, 23, 35
IV. Volunteer Involvement	IV.1: 24, 25, 26 IV.2: 24, 25 IV.3: 6, 7, 8, 22, 24, 25, 26 IV:4: 14, 16, 17, 24, 25
V. Leadership and Management	V.1: 1, 10, 27, 28, 37, 40 V.2: 2, 5, 27, 28, 29, 30, 31 V.3: 2, 5, 27, 28, 29 V.4: 2, 5, 27, 28, 29, 30, 31, 32, 33 V.5: 4, 32 V.6: 11, 29, 30, 31 V.7: 27, 28, 29 V.8: 8, 33
VI. Ethics and Accountability	VI.1: 11, 30, 35, 36 VI.2: 35, 36 VI.3: 11, 30, 35, 36 VI.4: 35, 36 VI.5: 35, 36

If you would like to convene a local study group, The Fund Raising School has prepared a short group study guide that uses this book as its text. The study guide includes suggested readings, discussion questions, and tips for successful group facilitation. You can download this guide from The Fund Raising School's website (www.philanthropy.iupui.edu/TheFundRaisingSchool). This study guide has not been reviewed or endorsed by CFRE International.

CHAPTER FORTY

INTERNATIONAL PERSPECTIVES ON FUNDRAISING

By Sharilyn Hale

Philanthropic fundraisers are part of a worldwide profession and community. This is confirmed by a growing body of identified knowledge; demand for and proliferation of professional development, training, and academic programs; growth in transnational internships and job opportunities; and the emergence and expansion of professional associations. In 2006, practitioners from more than forty countries endorsed the International Statement of Ethical Principles in Fundraising. This demonstrates the recognition in the fundraising profession of universal guiding principles for ethical and accountable fundraising practice.

A key leader of the worldwide professional fundraising community is CFRE International (CFRE), the independent global provider of certification in fundraising practice. Unlike certificate or diploma programs offered by colleges and universities, CFRE certification is practice-based. It is not intended to teach individuals how to raise funds effectively but rather measures an individual's understanding of acknowledged best practices in fundraising.

Because professional certification programs require regular analysis of what professionals in the field are doing and supposed to know, in 2009 CFRE conducted its most recent detailed and rigorous multicountry *CFRE Job Analysis* among practicing fundraisers. This research identifies and then articulates what members of the profession indicate is important to their work and the knowledge they must master to conduct their work effectively. A job analysis uses special language to describe how it is structured and organized. For example, domains are key subject or topic areas. Task statements are specific fundraising actions or functions within each domain or topic area. And knowledge areas are the kinds of knowledge that a practitioner needs to effectively perform the tasks noted in the statements. Recognizing that nothing ever remains static (due to social, academic, and technological advances, for example), each new *CFRE Job Analysis* captures evolution and development in professional practice and the body of knowledge.

The 2009 *CFRE Job Analysis* was an independently validated identification and articulation of current fundraising practice across eight countries and three languages. Engaging close to nine hundred practitioners, the research was conducted among certified and noncertified practicing fundraisers in Australia, Canada, New Zealand, the United Kingdom, and the United States—countries in which the fundraising profession is well established and where CFRE currently offers country-specific examinations. To expand the international sample, CFRE extended the job analysis for the first time to Italy, Kenya, and Brazil, three countries where fundraising is an emerging profession. The professional fundraising communities in these countries are diverse, enthusiastic, committed, and flourishing. Their participation in the job analysis has helped to broaden the global view of documented practice, recognizing that there are many countries in the world where the profession is coming into its own.

The results of the *CFRE Job Analysis* provide us with a fascinating research-based glimpse into the work and experiences of practitioners on five continents, demonstrating that an increasingly universal body of knowledge is emerging from global practice. This research is incredibly valuable to the advancement of the profession internationally. It is currently the only research of its kind and a relevant and credible validation of contemporary fundraising practice.

In a global context, the job analysis sets practice standards, informs the content of training and professional development curricula, and hones in on areas requiring further research. With data from job analyses completed in 1997, 2003, and 2009, this research also identifies points of evolution in the profession and body of knowledge over time.

CFRE Job Analysis Methodology and Respondents

Methodology

The *CFRE Job Analysis* was conducted by Professional Examination Services and advised by CFRE's Job Analysis Task Force (JATF), which comprised ten volunteer subject-matter experts in the field of fundraising. Volunteers have an important role in CFRE, and the composition of the JATF was carefully balanced to represent fundraisers working in different types and sizes of organizations, as well as regions and countries. The JATF created a contemporary description of the work of fundraising professionals, consisting of the major subject areas (or domains) of fundraising practice, the fundraising tasks performed in each of the domains, and the knowledge needed to perform these tasks. The JATF's work was then shared for review by thirty-one independent subject-matter experts, who were also selected to represent a range of geographic areas and diverse employment settings. The reviewers assessed the delineation for completeness, redundancy, clarity, consistency, and sequencing, and their feedback was reflected in the draft validation survey for fundraising professionals.

Forty-five practitioners tested the survey. The survey included four sections, and at the end of each section survey respondents were asked to specify any items they felt were missing from the survey.

- Section 1 contained the thirty-two identified task statements with rating scales for frequency ("How frequently did you perform this task in your work during the past twelve months?") and importance ("How important is this task to effective fundraising practice?").
- Section 2 contained the six main domains of fundraising practice, asking respondents to rate the importance of each and the percentage of their time spent performing the tasks associated in each domain during the past year.
- Section 3 contained the 108 knowledge statements, with a rating scale asking, "At what level do you use the knowledge in your work?" The Level of Usage scale was designed to capture the cognitive level at which survey participants used the knowledge in their work as fundraising professionals.
- Section 4 of the survey contained a demographic and professional questionnaire, questions about opinions regarding certification, and a final open-ended question asking about major changes in the profession anticipated in the next five years.

CFREI distributed the survey to close to three thousand fundraisers. In North America, Australia, New Zealand, the United Kingdom, and Kenya the survey was distributed in English. To encourage participation, the survey was translated by practicing fundraisers into Portuguese for Brazil and Italian for Italy. The overall response rate was approximately 25 percent, which is well within the industry standard for reliability of results.

In North America, the United Kingdom, Australia, and New Zealand, the certified sample was drawn randomly from the population of current CFRE certificants. The noncertified sample was obtained in the five countries just noted as well as in Brazil, Italy, and Kenya, with support from the following organizations: Association for Healthcare Philanthropy, Association of Fundraising Professionals, Association of Lutheran Development Executives, Council for Resource Development, North American YMCA Development Organization, National Catholic Development Conference, Canadian Association of Gift Planners, Association of Fundraising Consultants—UK, Association of Development and Alumni Professionals in Education—Australasia, Fundraising Institute of Australia, Associação Brasileira de Captadores de Recursos, Kenya Association of Fundraising Professionals, and Philanthropy Centro Studi (a research center of the University of Bologna).

The JATF reviewed the results of the survey to assist with the reflection of the data in CFRE's new Test Content Outline, which reflects the key subject areas (or domains) of practice, task statements, and knowledge areas. The six key subject areas (or domains) of the Test Content Outline include Current and Prospective Donor Research, Securing the Gift, Relationship Building, Volunteer Involvement, Leadership and Management, and Ethics and Accountability. In the six domains there are thirty-two fundraising task statements, supported by 108 knowledge areas that fundraisers need to know to perform the tasks. Table 40.1 presents the CFREI Test Content Outline, which provides the complete list of the domains and task statements.

TABLE 40.1. 2011 CFRE INTERNATIONAL TEST CONTENT OUTLINE (DOMAIN AND TASK STATEMENTS).

	Task	# of Items
I.	**Current and Prospective Donor Research**	**32**
1.1	Develop a list of prospective donors by identifying individuals and groups (foundations, corporations, government agencies, etc.) who have the capacity and propensity to give, in order to qualify prospective donors for further research and cultivation efforts.	8
1.2	Implement and utilize a secure data management system that stores information about current and prospective donors to enable segmented retrieval and analysis.	8
1.3	Analyse the list of current and prospective donors using characteristics such as demographics, interests, values, giving history, relationships, and linkages to the organisation, in order to select potential donors for particular projects and fundraising programmes.	6
1.4	Rate current and prospective donors in categories of giving potential in order to prioritise and plan cultivation and solicitation.	6
1.5	Present the list of current and prospective donors and relevant information to organisational leaders in order to establish consensus for action.	4

	Task	# of Items
II.	**Securing the Gift**	**38**
2.1	Develop a compelling case for support by involving stakeholders (such as volunteers, staff, and members of the Board) in order to communicate the rationale for supporting the organisation's fundraising programme.	6
2.2	Apply prospect research data to develop a solicitation plan for involvement of individual donors and/or donor groups.	5
2.3	Plan a comprehensive solicitation programme in order to generate financial support for the organisation's purpose.	6
2.4	Prepare donor-focused and segmented solicitation communications in order to influence and facilitate informed gift decisions.	6
2.5	Ask for and secure gifts from prospects in order to generate financial support for the organisation's purpose.	10
2.6	Evaluate the solicitation programme using appropriate criteria and methodology in order to produce accurate analytic reports for effective decision making.	5
III.	**Relationship Building**	**54**
3.1	Initiate and strengthen relationships with all constituents through a systematic cultivation plan designed to build trust in, and long term commitment to, the organisation.	16
3.2	Develop and implement a comprehensive communications plan in order to inform constituents and identified markets about the mission, vision, and values of the organisation, its funding priorities, and gift opportunities.	14
3.3	Promote a culture of philanthropy by broadening constituents' understanding of the value of giving.	8
3.4	Acknowledge and recognise gifts in ways that are meaningful to donors and appropriate to the mission and values of the organisation.	16
IV.	**Volunteer Involvement**	**18**
4.1	Create a structured process for the identification, recruitment, evaluation, recognition, and replacement of volunteers, in order to strengthen the organisation's effectiveness.	4
4.2	Empower and support volunteers by providing orientation, training, and specific job descriptions in order to enhance the volunteers' effectiveness.	5
4.3	Engage volunteers in the fundraising process and related activities in order to expand organisational capacity.	5
4.4	Participate in recruiting experienced and diverse leadership on boards and/or committees in order to ensure that these groups are representative of, and responsive to, the communities served.	4

(Continued)

TABLE 40.1. (Continued).

Task	# of Items
V. Leadership and Management	**36**
5.1 Foster and support a culture of philanthropy across the organisation and its constituencies.	4
5.2 Ensure sound administrative and management policies and procedures to support fundraising functions.	6
5.3 Participate in the organisation's strategic planning process in order to ensure the integration of fundraising and philanthropy.	5
5.4 Design and implement short- and long-term fundraising plans and budgets in order to support the organisation's strategic goals.	6
5.5 Apply key principles of marketing and public relations to fundraising planning and programmes.	4
5.6 Conduct ongoing performance analysis of the fundraising programme using accepted and appropriate standards in order to identify opportunities, resolve problems, and inform future planning.	5
5.7 Recruit, train, and support staff by applying human resource principles in order to foster professionalism and a productive team-oriented work environment.	4
5.8 Contract for services in order to optimise the efforts of the fundraising function.	2
VI. Ethics and Accountability	**22**
6.1 Ensure that all fundraising activities are conducted in accordance with ethical principles and standards.	5
6.2 Create gift acceptance policies that reflect the values of the organisation and satisfy legal and ethical standards.	4
6.3 Clarify, implement, monitor, and honour donors' intent and instructions, and ensure that allocations are accurately documented in the organisation's records.	4
6.4 Report to constituents the sources, uses, impact, and management of donated funds in order to preserve and enhance confidence and public trust in the organisation.	4
6.5 Comply with all reporting requirements and regulations in order to fulfill commitment to accountability and demonstrate transparency.	5

A Snapshot of Job Analysis Survey Respondents

The survey sample provides an interesting glimpse of the global community of fundraisers. Overall, the survey respondents were mostly female and highly educated, and tended to hold middle management or senior level positions of responsibility in education, health, and public/society benefit organizations. Some were consultants. Fifty-five percent held the CFRE credential.

Health and health research organizations were the most frequently reported employers for respondents in three countries: the United States (26.5 percent), Canada (32 percent), and Australia and New Zealand (35 percent). Consultancy was the most frequent employer for the UK respondents (43.5 percent). For Brazil, it was public/society benefit (26 percent). In Kenya it was faith-based organizations (23 percent).

There were some marked differences between the countries where fundraising is an established profession and those where the profession is emerging, in particular in relation to years of experience, age, and gender. For example, respondents in the United States, Canada, the United Kingdom, Australia, and New Zealand reported more individuals with thirteen to seventeen years of experience in the profession; respondents in Brazil, Italy, and Kenya, tended to report four to five years of experience. Across participating countries, 57 percent of respondents were forty-five years of age or older. The United States sample was oldest, with 73 percent of respondents forty-five or older, and the Italian sample was youngest, with 27 percent age forty-five or older. While 62 percent of the survey participants were female (in Canada this was 74 percent), in Brazil and Kenya the majority of participants were male.

Kenyans were also the most highly educated, with 69 percent holding a master's or doctoral degree. This compares to 41 percent of all respondents who held a bachelor's degree, and 31 percent who held a master's degree as their highest level of education. Respondents in Italy (50 percent), Kenya (68 percent), and Brazil (65 percent) were less likely to work in middle or senior management compared to those in the United Kingdom (85 percent), Canada (82 percent), and the United States (91 percent).

Findings from the *CFRE Job Analysis*

The broadest message from the *CFRE Job Analysis* is the remarkable stability of fundraising knowledge and practice across the eight countries surveyed. As a collective global profession, there is much that fundraisers share in common as well as ways in which fundraising practices are different, opportunities for fundraisers to learn from each other, and a great deal to which to look forward.

Commonalities Across Countries

Overall, although there were differences among countries, the variations were statistically modest. As Table 40.2 shows, each of the six domains was noted as important to effective fundraising, all fundraising task statements and knowledge

TABLE 40.2. CFRE DOMAINS RANKED BY IMPORTANCE AND TIME SPENT ON TASKS.

Importance (Ranked from Highest to Lowest)	Time Spent on Tasks Within Domain (Ranked from Highest to Lowest)
III. Relationship Building	III. Relationship Building
II. Securing the Gift	V. Leadership & Management
VI. Ethics & Accountability	II. Securing the Gift
V. Leadership & Management	I. Current & Prospective Donor Research
I. Current & Prospective Donor Research	VI. Ethics & Accountability
IV. Volunteer Involvement	IV. Volunteer Involvement

areas were agreed to be relevant to effective practice, and the framework for the *CFRE Job Analysis* was deemed to be complete. This stability was also evident across CFRE certified and noncertified respondents, affirming that the CFRE is a practice-based credential, reflecting profession-identified best practices.

International respondents said that relationship building was the most important aspect of their work and the one on which they spent the greatest percentage of their time. In fact, compared to the 2003 *CFRE Job Analysis*, the importance and frequency ratings for Relationship Building significantly increased. In this domain are donor cultivation and communication strategies, recognition and constituency development, and promoting a culture of philanthropy. Could this increase in importance and time spent be in response to heightened donor expectations of organizations or the need to strengthen relationships during a time of economic downturn? This remains an intriguing point for further exploration.

Ethics and Accountability was the domain most commonly known across all countries surveyed. This means a high percentage of the fundraisers surveyed have the requisite knowledge in areas such as country-specific legal and regulatory requirements, appropriate gift acceptance and accounting standards, information protection, and ethical practice. The majority reported they use and apply this knowledge in their fundraising practice. This commitment to ethical and accountable fundraising across the profession is both heartening and a meaningful nexus of shared values and aspiration.

What do fundraisers across all countries do most in their work? Respondents reported that they performed the following tasks most frequently:

1.1 Develop a list of prospective donors by identifying individuals and groups (foundations, corporations, government agencies, etc.)

who have the capacity and propensity to give, in order to qualify prospective donors for further research and cultivation efforts.

2.5 Ask for and secure gifts from prospects in order to generate financial support for the organisation's purpose.

3.4 Acknowledge and recognise gifts in ways that are meaningful to donors and appropriate to the mission and values of the organisation.

6.1 Ensure that all fundraising activities are conducted in accordance with ethical principles and standards.

6.3 Clarify, implement, monitor, and honour donors' intent and instructions, and ensure that allocations are accurately documented in the organisation's records.

6.5 Comply with all reporting requirements and regulations in order to fulfill commitment to accountability and demonstrate transparency.

While respondents said all the thirty-two task statements were important to fundraising practice, there was variation about the frequency with which the respondents performed the tasks. This suggests respondents consistently judged the tasks as important to professional effectiveness, even if they did not personally perform them frequently due to job function or specialization, level of responsibility, or organizational program mix.

Differences Among Countries

Extending from this consonance of knowledge and practice emerged some subtle differences among countries. In particular, there were some notable differences between the countries with established professions and those where the profession is emerging. The development of fundraising into a formal practice and profession is a much newer reality that continues to expand and mature. Today, in the United States, Canada, the United Kingdom, New Zealand, and Australia, fundraising as a profession tends to be more established, and this was evident in the results of the *CFRE Job Analysis*. Respondents from these countries, in addition to having more experience in the profession, consistently gave higher importance ratings for the thirty-two task statements than those from the other countries. When asked to review the 108 knowledge areas and indicate whether they had the knowledge and, if they did, the degree to which they used the knowledge, they reported more often having the knowledge and applying this knowledge in their work in fundraising.

This was particularly notable in the Securing the Gift domain, where there was broad knowledge and practice across the fundraising techniques and strategies, including major gift and capital campaign fundraising and in gift planning. The broad inclusion of these fundraising techniques in countries where fundraising is a more established profession (with the exception of Australia) could in part account for the reported higher levels of the use of volunteers in fundraising and performance of the associated tasks under the Volunteer Involvement domain.

From respondents in Brazil, Italy, and Kenya, where fundraising is an emerging profession, responses demonstrated no difference or only modest differences compared to the other countries in their ratings of frequency, importance, and knowledge usage in the areas of Leadership and Management, Ethics and Accountability, and Relationship Building. This indicates a broad grounding in professional fundraising knowledge and practice. However, the level of development of the profession in countries where it is an emerging profession is reflected in slightly lower ratings for overall knowledge usage. Comparatively higher percentages of respondents did not have certain knowledge and therefore did not apply it. This was particularly true for respondents from Italy.

In other cases in countries where fundraising is an emerging profession, the respondents had the knowledge, rated it as being important to fundraising practice, but did not apply it in their work, suggesting it was not applicable, not part of current practice, or was outside the realm of their role or responsibility.

Comparable differences between Brazil, Italy, and Kenya and those countries where the profession of fundraising is more established were most evident in the domains of Current and Prospective Donor Research, Securing the Gift, and Volunteer Involvement. For example, respondents had lower frequency ratings for tasks related to the use, analysis, and application of donor research to develop cultivation and solicitation strategies. This was also true for tasks associated with evaluation of the solicitation program and ongoing program performance measurement.

Major gift and capital campaign fundraising rated significantly lower in countries where fundraising is an emerging profession, as did the respondents' indicated knowledge of the components of a comprehensive solicitation program. The most common fundraising techniques in countries where fundraising is an emerging profession included grant proposals, direct marketing, special events, and corporate partnerships, and respondents in these countries indicated greater use of for-profit activities such as product sales and charity/thrift shops. Interestingly, respondents from Brazil led the way among all countries in the knowledge and use of electronic media in solicitation and relationship building.

The responses relative to volunteer involvement in fundraising were somewhat lower among fundraisers in Brazil, Italy, and Kenya. This includes knowledge and application of strategies for volunteer engagement, recruitment, and ongoing training and management, and for governance principles. This could be due in part to the emerging development of the profession in these countries, the predominant mix of fundraising techniques that rely less on volunteers, and different governance and organizational structures and models.

The comparative results of the *CFRE Job Analysis* demonstrate clusters of evolution in the fundraising profession and identify areas for exploration, training, education, and development as the profession deepens across all the participating countries.

In countries where the profession of fundraising is more established, there is evidence fundraisers benefit from and build upon a legacy of practice and resulting capacity, resources, and organizational and social readiness. In countries where the profession is emerging, this ground work continues to be laid, through the diligence and active engagement of practitioners.

Evolution of the Fundraising Profession

The final part of the survey invited respondents to share their opinions about CFRE certification and to describe the changes they anticipated would occur in the fundraising profession over the next five years. Despite differences of country and language, established profession or emerging, a number of shared themes arose.

Regardless of CFRE certification status, respondents were in agreement (agreed or strongly agreed) that professional certification enhances the credibility of fundraising as a distinct profession. They indicated that the CFRE credential is important and beneficial to the profession.

Further, respondents from all countries believed the profession would continue to grow and that more educational and training opportunities would be available in the future.

In the United States and the United Kingdom, respondents voiced concern about the availability of talented fundraisers and succession planning, anticipating the retirement of large numbers of senior-level fundraisers in the coming years. Respondents from Canada, Australia, New Zealand, Brazil, and Kenya echoed this concern about the availability of trained and experienced fundraisers.

In Brazil, Italy, and Kenya, comments emerged about the need for enhanced professionalization in fundraising and the profession's need to deepen in capacity and practice to support burgeoning nonprofit sectors. This articulated need reflects the research results, which indicated a slight deficit in fundraising knowledge and use of knowledge in these countries. However, the responses were positive and optimistic that the profession would grow in numbers, recognition, and credibility.

Significantly, the challenge of raising funds during a time of global economic downturn was noted by many respondents, with a sense that the impact on fundraising would be felt for the long term. Increasing expectations of accountability and transparency among donors and the public were highlighted, along with an expectation that government oversight and regulation of fundraising would grow.

Respondents anticipated even more use and integration of technology, new media and social networking in fundraising activities and in building relationships with donors. It was noted that fundraisers need to increase their expertise in these areas.

Conclusion

As fundraising around the world is considered, topics such as the global community of practice, current challenges and opportunities, insights from the *CFRE Job Analysis*, and indeed CFRE certification itself, provide fundraisers around the globe with a meaningful framework of commonality and shared purpose. Regardless of geography, language, or cause, fundraisers have much to learn from each other, even as the fundraising profession shares a common body of knowledge and a certification that unifies practitioners as they work individually and collectively to make the world a safer, healthier, more just, and more beautiful place in which to live.

What is most clear from the *CFRE Job Analysis* is that the commonalities shared by fundraisers are greater than the differences. CFRE certification plays an important role in the global profession through the articulation and dissemination of a cohesive and evolving body of knowledge and shared standards of effective and accountable practice. These resonate internationally and are applied ethically and innovatively in consideration of cultural and organizational factors, economics, and technology.

CHAPTER FORTY-ONE

RESOURCES FOR STRENGTHENING FUNDRAISING

By Frances Huehls

As the fundraising profession has grown over the last thirty years, so too have resources—both academic and practical in nature—become increasingly available to fundraisers. This chapter is not an exhaustive treatment of organizations and publications that inform the nonprofit sector or even of fundraising, but a compilation of the resources that have consistently proved to be the most reliable—particularly in terms of quality. They tend to be mature, resources that will continue to persist and inform us in some format—whether print, digital, or something that we cannot yet imagine—for some time to come.

What strengthens fundraising? Strong fundraisers, armed with the best available practices and research, are the foundation of strong fundraising. Some of the resources I discuss are clearly in the realm of professional development. Others more directly strengthen informed practice. In order of appearance are descriptions of the major associations and the services they provide, formal education opportunities, published resources, and major Internet resources. The descriptive section is followed by an annotated list of all of the resources presented in this chapter.

Association Resources

Four major associations—the Association of Fundraising Professionals (AFP), the Council for Advancement and Support of Education (CASE), the Association for Healthcare Philanthropy (AHP), and the Association of Professional Researchers for Advancement (APRA)—all provide a multitude of services. As membership organizations, additional resources are available to those who join. All four sponsor conferences—U.S., international, and web-based. In addition, they offer classroom training and workshops, including CFRE certification preparation. Special offerings include academies such as the AFP Leadership Academy and the CASE summer institute for new development professionals. Each publishes a journal designed to promote best practices, in addition to having their own lines of specialized publications, such as the AHP Salary Report and the AFP Fund Development Series. Although their resource centers are restricted to members, the websites of all of these organizations are rich with information that can be accessed by anyone interested in self-study. Finally, CASE, AFP, and APRA have moved beyond their own websites, providing social networking opportunities through sites such as Facebook, LinkedIn, Ning, YouTube, and Twitter.

Two additional membership organizations of note are the Giving Institute and the Partnership for Philanthropic Practice (formerly the National Committee on Planned Giving). The Giving Institute's membership numbers thirty-five fundraising consultants. The website contains a resource library of papers and presentations. Its sister organization, the Giving Institute Foundation, publishes *Giving USA*, the annual compendium on sources and uses of philanthropic gifts. The Partnership for Philanthropic Practice has as its mission to assist donors and organizations in developing meaningful gift opportunities.

Options for Formal Education

For professionals who want the depth and breadth provided by formal education, a multitude of options are available. By far the best source for locating educational opportunities that are offered through colleges and universities is the database developed and maintained by Roseanne Mirabella at Seton Hall University. This resource lists degree and nondegree programs, including opportunities to take classes online. The most current tabulation lists continuing education (nondegree) opportunities at seventy-three institutions. Many of these courses are offered through departments of continuing studies. The number of schools offering undergraduate coursework has grown to around 130, with around 50 percent of those having American Humanics affiliation. American Humanics is a nonprofit organization that has developed an experience-based undergraduate curriculum designed to prepare students for entry into nonprofit management positions. The curriculum is largely administered through affiliate academic institutions. Post-baccalaureate certificates and master's degrees are offered at more than 168 institutions. Thirty-five institutions offer doctoral programs. The academic home of these programs varies, ranging from schools of public affairs and business to liberal arts and social work. Close to fifty institutions offer some coursework online, either as a component of a degree or certificate program or as a noncredit offering. Some also offer "executive format" programs that are more accommodating to the schedule of working professionals.

The scope of academic programs is typically broader than fundraising alone, including coursework such as law, economics, marketing, and ethics. The Nonprofit Academic Centers Council (NACC) is a membership organization of colleges and universities (currently forty-six) that offer coursework in nonprofit management. As part of its commitment to developing and maintaining high-quality academic programs, NACC has developed curricular guidelines for both undergraduate and graduate programs. Coursework in fundraising is recommended at both levels.

There are also nonacademic options for formal coursework. Two such programs are The Fund Raising School (TFRS) and the Grantsmanship Center. The Fund Raising School website lists the following offerings:

- Principles and Techniques of Fundraising (available online)
- Online Fundraising and Social Media
- Fundraising for Small Nonprofits
- Planned Giving
- Preparing Successful Grant Proposals (available online)
- Developing Annual Sustainability
- Managing the Capital Campaign
- Developing Major Gifts
- Interpersonal Communication for Fundraising
- Purposeful Boards, Powerful Fundraising
- Faith and Fundraising
- Dynamics of Women's Giving

Although many are currently listed as being offered only at the home location in Indianapolis, some courses are also held in Chicago, Denver, Orlando, and San Francisco. TFRS can also provide customized workshops. The Grantsmanship Center in Los Angeles also offers customized training in addition to these four regular courses:

- Grantsmanship Training
- Earned Income Strategies
- Research Proposal Workshop
- Competing for Federal Grants

Courses—particularly Grantsmanship training—are taught at a variety of locations in the United States. The Grantsmanship Center also offers a membership option, which provides training cost discounts.

Published Resources

Academic Research

Fueling the wide range of academic programs is a rapidly growing body of research on fundraising and nonprofit marketing. Studies published in academic journals cover a wide range of topics including donor retention and attrition, the psychology behind why people choose not to give, the role of social information in donation decisions, message framing in cause-related marketing, giving circles, relationship management, factors determining alumni generosity, and the impact of charity branding on fundraising. This literature is rapidly filling a gap in theory that has prevented fundraising from claiming full status as a profession.

The journals publishing fundraising research fall primarily into the fields of business, economics, marketing, and nonprofit studies. Access can be found through private individual subscription or through academic libraries. Because privileges at academic libraries vary from institution to institution, fundraisers interested in this research should establish a relationship with a library in their area. Indexing services that provide the best access to this content include business sources such as *Business Source Premier* and *ABI/Inform*, as well *as Philanthropic Studies Index* (Indiana University) and *Google Scholar*. The latter two are available online to all users without charge. The four journals consistently publishing academic research on fundraising are the *International Journal of Educational Advancement*, the *International Journal of Nonprofit and Voluntary Sector Marketing*, *Nonprofit and Voluntary Sector Quarterly*, and *Nonprofit Management and Leadership*.

Focus on Practice

Books on fundraising continue to be based on practice rather than research. As there is no shortage of titles to choose from, some discrimination is advised. Recommended reading lists can be found on many websites including AFP, The Fund Raising School at Indiana University, CFRE International, and the Foundation Center. The best-known experts in the field can be found as authors in the fundraising series published by Jossey-Bass, Wiley, and Jones & Bartlett.

Numerous trade journals and newsletters are available. Many have a regional or local focus. On the national level, six in particular can be recommended for keeping abreast of news and best practices:

AHP Journal. The Journal of the Association of Healthcare Philanthropy focuses on resources for the health care industry, including development programs, analysis of the philanthropic health care environment, and trends in the field.

Advancing Philanthropy. The Journal of the Association of Fundraising Professionals emphasizes practice based information and tools for fundraising practitioners.

Chronicle of Philanthropy. Biweekly news of the nonprofit sector as well as listings of conferences, continuing education opportunities, available positions, and new publications.

Currents. The Journal of the Council for Advancement and Support of Education covers aspects of educational development, including fundraising, marketing, and alumni relations.

Grassroots Fundraising Journal. The target audience is small to medium-sized organizations; articles focus on legal issues, grassroots fundraising, case studies, and major donors.

NonProfit Times. News and special reports include an annual salary survey and the NPT Top 100 Nonprofit Organizations.

Internet Resources

Without question, the Internet makes a plethora of information available, whether it is accessible for free or for a subscription price. Three resources in particular are invaluable for informing practice and are tools that no fundraiser should be without.

The GuideStar database is the single largest source of information on individual nonprofit organizations. Participating nonprofits and subscribers have access to the information of 1.8 million organizations, including extensive financial information and the Form 990. Using their advanced search engine, it is possible to create lists of comparable organizations using criteria such as NTEE code, location, and assets. Premium subscribers can download data for analysis using programs such as Excel. GuideStar also provides a basic version for the public at no charge and special versions for academic classroom use and libraries.

The Foundation Center (FC) is the top resource for information about foundations and grantmaking. To fulfill their mission of promoting transparency in foundation activity, FC engages in three major activities. The first is to report on foundation activity, which they accomplish through analyzing the information returns of private foundations (Form 990PF) and generating both special topic and statistical reports on grants and grantmakers. Much of this information is made publicly available through the FC website. Their second activity is the compilation of grant directories, both print and electronic. The *Foundation Directory* is by far the most comprehensive compilation of grant opportunities available. The third FC activity is public outreach and education. In addition to the massive amount of information on the website, FC sponsors a national network of cooperating collections that provide access to print and online grant information. An array of workshops is available, primarily related to foundation fundraising, ranging from free online tutorials to full-day classroom training.

The Nonprofit Good Practice Guide is a product of the Dorothy A. Johnson Center for Philanthropy and Nonprofit Leadership at Grand Valley State University. The resource boasts an exceptional online glossary as well as a section of resources on fundraising in the nonprofit category. This is further broken down into business activities, donor management, fund development, funding sources, fundraising activities, fundraising operations, and proposal writing. In most cases, the articles and tip sheets referenced link directly to the text. Many fundraising professionals will find other topics to be of value for personal and professional development. Other nonprofit subtopics include advocacy, evaluation, financial management, governance, human resources, information management, legal and regulatory, marketing, nonprofit change, data and statistics, news, organizational planning, and management. This resource is available to all users without charge.

Conclusion

Knowledge moves the fundraising profession forward, and the information to craft that knowledge is available in many places and forms. If I have been successful, I have demonstrated that opportunities to strengthen the field have never been greater. Associations are strong, and they offer more formal and informal venues for education and professional networking than ever before. Opportunities for formal academic education are robust and continue to expand into new areas. At the same time, viable training options exist outside of the academy. Publication is vigorous, and academic research in the field is lending a welcome level of credibility to professional practice. Strong organizations like the Foundation Center are using technology to provide high-quality information to inform practice. It is impossible to know what the state of information resources will be when the next edition of this volume is published, but—for now—the state of resources to strengthen fundraising is sound.

Organizations and Resources Referenced

American Humanics: nonprofit organization that partners with academic institutions to offer an undergraduate curriculum that prepares students to enter management positions in nonprofit organizations; program focuses on curriculum that includes experiential education; www.humanics.org; 1100 Walnut Street, Suite 1900, Kansas City, MO, 64106, 816-561-6415

APRA: Association of Professional Researchers for Advancement: international membership organization for professionals interested in research and relationship management; www.aprahome.org; 401 N. Michigan St., suite 2200, Chicago, IL 60611, 312-321-5196

Association for Healthcare Philanthropy (AHP): international membership organization representing development professionals in the health care field; www.ahp.org; 313 Park Ave., Suite 400, Falls Church, VA 22046, 703-532-6243

Association of Fundraising Professionals (AFP): international membership organization dedicated to advocacy, education, certification, and fundraising research; www.afpnet.org; 4300 Wilson Blvd, Suite 300, Arlington, VA 22203

Council for Advancement and Support of Education (CASE): international membership organization for educational institutions and their affiliated advancement professionals; www.case.org; 1307 New York Ave. N.W., Suite 1000; Washington, DC 20005-4701

CFRE International: international provider of professional certification for fundraisers; www.cfre.org/contact.html; 4900 Seminary Road, Suite 670, Alexandria, VA 22311, 703-820-5555

Foundation Center: produces the Foundation Directory (print and electronic), the most comprehensive source for grant opportunities; wide range of educational programs; compiles and publishes information about foundation giving trends; supports a network of cooperating library collections in US and abroad; foundationcenter.org; 79 Fifth Avenue/16th Street, New York, NY 10003-3076, 212-620-4230

Giving Institute: membership organization for fundraising counsel; website includes resource library of papers and presentations; Giving Institute Foundation published *Giving USA*, an annual compendium of sources and uses of philanthropic gifts; www.givinginstitute.org; 4700 W. Lake Ave., Glenview, IL 60025; 847-375-4709

Grantsmanship Center: quasi-membership organization offering training workshops; www.tgci.com; 1125 W. Sixth Street, Fifth Floor, Los Angeles, CA 90017, 213-482-9860

Partnership for Philanthropic Practice (formerly the National Committee on Planned Giving): membership organization dedicated to assisting individuals and organizations in developing meaningful gift opportunities for both donors and recipients; www.pppnet.org; 233 McCrea Street, Suite 400, Indianapolis, IN 46225, 317-269-6274

Nonprofit Academic Centers Council (NACC): coalition of university-based academic programs offering formal coursework and degrees in nonprofit and philanthropic education; www.naccouncil.org; 10900 Euclid Avenue, Cleveland, OH 44106-7167, 216-368-0969

Nonprofit Good Practice Guide: an online index of resources pertaining to nonprofit practice, including fundraising; www.npgoodpractice.org; Dorothy A. Johnson Center for Philanthropy and Nonprofit Leadership, Grand Valley State University, 201 Front Ave SW, 2nd Floor, Grand Rapids, MI 49504, 616-331-7585

Nonprofit Management Education: Current offerings in university-based programs (Seton Hall University): most comprehensive listing of continuing education, online, undergraduate, and graduate (master's and doctoral) opportunities available through formal academic institutions; academic.shu.edu/npo/

The Fund Raising School: affiliated with the Center on Philanthropy at Indiana University; offers coursework in many areas of fundraising practice; www.philanthropy.iupui.edu/TheFundRaisingSchool; 550 W. North St., Suite 301, Indianapolis, IN 46202, 317-274-7063

Indexing Sources

Due to the constantly changing nature of coverage of these products, a visit to the vendor or database site will provide more accurate information than reporting current statistics

ABI/Inform. ProQuest LLC, Ann Arbor, MI

Business Source Premier. Ebsco; www.ebsco.com

Philanthropic Studies Index. Indiana University. cheever.ulib.iupui.edu/psipublicsearch/

Google Scholar, www.scholar.google.com

Publications

Advancing Philanthropy. Arlington, VA: Association of Fundraising Professionals; bimonthly; practice-based information and tools for fundraising practitioners; ISSN 1077-2545

AHP Journal. Falls Church, VA: Association of Healthcare Professionals; biennial; ISSN 1551-840x

Chronicle of Philanthropy. Washington, DC; biweekly news of the nonprofit sector as well as listings of conferences, continuing education opportunities, available positions, and new publications; ISSN 1040-676x

Currents. Washington, DC: Council for Advancement and Support of Education; monthly; articles cover aspects of educational development including fundraising, marketing, and alumni relations; ISSN 0748-478x

Grassroots Fundraising Journal. Kim Klein; target audience is small to medium-sized organizations; articles focus on legal issues, grassroots fundraising, case studies, and major donors; ISSN 0740-4832

NonProfit Times. Davis Information Group; monthly; news and special reports including an annual salary survey and the NPT Top 100 Nonprofit Organizations; ISSN 0896-5048

International Journal of Educational Advancement. Palgrave Macmillan; quarterly; ISSN 1744-6503

International Journal of Nonprofit and Voluntary Sector Marketing. John Wiley & Sons; quarterly; ISSN 1465-4520

Nonprofit and Voluntary Sector Quarterly. Sage Publications; quarterly; journal of the Association for Research on Nonprofit Organizations and Voluntary Action (ARNOVA); ISSN 0899-7640

Nonprofit Management and Leadership. Jossey-Bass, Inc.; quarterly; ISSN 1048-6682

GLOSSARY OF FUNDRAISING TERMS

accountability The responsibility of the donee organization to keep a donor informed about the use that is made of the donor's gift as well as the cost of raising it.

acknowledgment Written expression of gratitude for gift or service.

acknowledgment letter A letter sent by a donee, or on behalf of a donee, to the donor, expressing appreciation for a gift and identifying the use that will be make of the gift. An acknowledgment letter may be a form letter, but it is usually personalized.

acquisition mailing (or prospect mailing) A mailing to prospects to acquire new members or donors.

advance gifts Gifts given or pledged in advance of a public announcement of a campaign. Advance gifts are solicited before a campaign is announced because the success or failure of a campaign may depend on the size of the advance gifts.

advisory board A group of influential and prominent individuals whose association with a development program is calculated to lend luster and implied endorsement of the program's goals and objectives.

Source: Principles and Techniques of Fund Raising (Indianapolis: The Fund Raising School, 2009b). *Glossary of Fund Raising Terms* (Alexandria, VA: Association of Fundraising Professionals, 2003). Copyright © 2010, Association of Fundraising Professionals (AFP), all rights reserved. Reprinted with permission from AFP.

analysis That section of a study that deals with the factors essential to success in a fundraising program; principally the case for support, leadership potential, and fields of support.

annual giving Annually repeating gift programs; seeking funds on annual or recurring basis from the same constituency; income is generally used for operating budget support.

annual report A yearly report of financial and organizational conditions prepared by the management of an organization.

anonymous gift A gift whose announcement, by specific wish of the donor, can include only the amount; the name of the donor is withheld.

appreciated real property and securities gift Gifts of real estate or securities, which when held long term are deductible for federal income tax purposes at the full fair market value with no capital gain on the appreciation. However, the appreciation is a tax preference item, and proper counsel should be obtained to evaluate whether this would have alternative minimum tax consequences.

associates A term used variously to describe a group of individuals who may be supporting an institution through contributions at a prescribed level, serving in a special advisory capacity, or serving as a sponsoring body for special institutional events.

audit An internal evaluation of development procedures as practiced by a nonprofit institution or agency; normally conducted by professional fundraising counsel.

bargain sale The sale of property at less than its fair market value. Frequently, a person will sell property to a 501(c)(3) organization or institution at a "bargain" price (for example, the individual's cost as opposed to its market value). The transaction is partly a gift and partly a sale.

benefactor One who makes a major gift to an institution or agency; also, an arbitrary classification of contributors whose gifts are above a certain level, which is calculated to single them out as a group and to stimulate similar giving by others.

benefit event A form of fundraising that involves the organization and staging of a special event for charitable purposes; all proceeds above expenses are designated as a contribution to the charitable institution concerned.

benevolence A disposition to do good; an act of kindness; a generous gift.

bequest A transfer, by will, of personal property such as cash, securities, or other tangible property.

big gifts A general term used to signify gifts in upper ranges, the precise limits varying from institution to institution. Their importance is emphasized in all fundraising campaigns.

board of directors Individuals selected (for example, by other directors or members) in accordance with law (usually reflected in bylaws) to establish policy and oversee the management of an organization or institution.

book value The amount of an asset stated in a company's records, not necessarily the amount it could bring on the open market.

bricks and mortar Common manner of alluding to the physical plant needs of an institution and to the campaigns designed to secure the necessary funds. A "bricks and mortar campaign" is a campaign to raise building funds.

budget A detailed breakdown of estimated income and expenses for a development program, prepared in advance. Budgets show various cost categories, including personnel, printed materials, purchase and rental of equipment, office expense, headquarters, mailing charges, costs of events, and so on.

campaign An organized effort to raise funds for a nonprofit organization.

campaign costs Expenditures that are deemed essential to the planning and operation of a campaign and that are directly related to campaign budget projections.

campaign leadership Top volunteers who are an essential ingredient of any campaign organization and one of the three major pedestals on which fundraising success must rest, the others being the case and sources of support. Campaign leaders provide and maintain the momentum and enthusiasm essential to the motivation of the entire organization of volunteers.

campaign materials General term used to denote campaign forms of all kinds; materials required for campaign workers, fact sheets, prospect lists, and numerous other items essential to the effective functioning of a campaign; printed materials such as brochures used to advance a campaign.

capital campaign A carefully organized, highly structured fundraising program using volunteers supported by staff and consultants to raise funds for specific needs, to be met in a specific time frame, with a specific dollar goal. Allows donors to pledge gifts to be paid over a period of years.

case Carefully prepared reasons why a charitable institution merits support (in the context of the "case bigger than the institution"), including its resources, its potential for greater service, its needs, and its future plans.

cash flow Predictable cash income to sustain operations; in capital campaigns or whenever pledges are secured, anticipation of annual cash receipts resulting from payments on pledges.

cash gift The simple transfer of cash, check, or currency (other than special collections) to a gift-supported organization or institution.

cause related marketing An arrangement that links a product or service with a social cause to provide the cause with a portion of the profits received by the corporation.

certified fundraising executive (CFRE) A credential granted to a fundraiser by the Association of Fundraising Professionals, which is based on performance as a fundraising executive, knowledge of the fundraising field, tenure as a fundraiser (minimum of five years), education, and service to the profession.

challenge gift A substantial gift made on condition that other gifts must be secured, either on a matching basis or some other prescribed formula, usually within a specified period, with the objective of stimulating fundraising activity generally.

charitable contribution A donation of something of value to a gift-supported charitable organization, usually tax-deductible.

charitable deduction The value of money or property transferred to a 501(c)(3) organization, deductible for income, gift, and estate tax purposes. In most cases, the term *charitable deduction* refers to the portion of a gift that can be deducted from the donor's income subject to federal income tax. A donor's charitable deduction should not be confused or equated with the value of a gift; that is, gifts for the purpose of life income agreements are not federally deductible at their full value.

charitable deferred gifts A gift made using any one of the following methods:

1. Wills: A charity may be named as beneficiary under a will in many ways. These include (a) gifts of specific property, whether it is real property or personal property; (b) a gift of a stated amount of money; and (c) a percentage of the remaining estate after specific gifts are made.
2. Revocable Trusts: A revocable trust allows the grantor to withdraw any or all assets during his or her lifetime, as well as having full enjoyment of the property during his or her life. At death the assets can flow efficiently to the beneficiaries, saving probate and administrative costs. A charity can be named as one of the beneficiaries.
3. Irrevocable Trusts: Charitable Remainder Unitrusts and Charitable Remainder Annuity Trusts. Although the principal of these trusts cannot be withdrawn,

there are additional benefits to the donor through immediate income tax deductions and fund management. The donor will receive yearly income from the trust as well as an immediate partial federal income tax deduction for the interest that ultimately passes to the charity.

4. Charitable Gift Annuities: Involves a transfer of cash or other property to the organization. In return, payment of a specified amount determined by age is made to the donor during his or her lifetime. The rates paid are the most recent ones adopted by the Committee on Gift Annuities as agreed to by most major charities. There is an immediate income deduction for the present value of the amount ultimately to pass to the charity; part of the income received by the donor is also tax free.

5. Gift of Home or Farm Retaining a Life Estate: Through this gift the donor retains use of the property for his or her lifetime. The federal income tax deduction will be based on the present value, figured on the prospective years of using the property before it goes to the charity.

6. Totten Trusts or Accounts P.O.D. (payable on death): The charity can be named beneficiary of a bank account, bond, or other security, provided state laws allow.

community foundation A philanthropic foundation that is specifically committed to the support of institutions in its own community, often receiving bequests from persons whose legacy is modest.

company-sponsored foundation A private foundation whose corpus is derived from a profit-making corporation or company and whose primary purpose is the making of grants. The company-sponsored foundation may maintain close ties with the donor company, but it is an independent organization, most often with its own rules and regulations (like those of other private foundations). Companies form foundations to enable them to invest in philanthropy with funds that otherwise would be subject to capital gains tax or income tax, and to make maximum use of the corporate charitable deduction.

constituency All people who have in some fashion been involved with the institution seeking support; consists of members, contributors, participants (past or present), clients, and relatives of clients.

consultant A specialist in one or more areas of fundraising who is hired by an organization for the purpose of recommending solutions to problems and generally providing advice and guidance related to fundraising efforts.

corporate foundation The philanthropic arm created by a corporation to deal with requests for contributions from various agencies—locally, regionally, or nationally.

corporate giving program A grantmaking program established and controlled by a profit-making corporation or company. The program does not necessarily include a separate endowment, and the annual grant total may be directly related to the previous year's profits. Giving directly from corporate profits is not subject to the same reporting restrictions as giving from private foundations. Some companies may make charitable contributions from corporate profits, operating budgets, or company-sponsored foundations.

corporate philanthropy Support through gifts, equipment, supplies, or other contributions by business firms to charitable institutions, sometimes through organized programs that may include corporate foundations.

cultivation The process of promoting or encouraging interest and/or involvement on the part of a potential donor or volunteer leader; an educative process to inform about an institution and the reasons why it merits support.

deferred gift See *planned gift.*

designated gift A restricted or commemorative gift made for a specific purpose and designated for a specific use.

development Refers to all dynamics of a continuing fundraising program (annual giving, special gifts, planned gifts, public relations).

direct mail Solicitation of gifts or volunteer services and distribution of information pieces by mass mailing.

director of development The individual who heads an organization's development program, with either this title or another, such as vice president for development or vice president for external affairs and development.

donor The individual, organization, or institution that makes a gift.

donor acquisition The process of identifying and obtaining donors.

donor-directed gift A gift or bequest to a foundation, organization, or institution whose donor specifies to whom the money should be distributed.

donor list A list of contributors prepared for a particular purpose or in conjunction with list building.

donor recognition The policy and practice of recognizing gifts, first through immediate acknowledgment by card or letter and subsequently through personalized notes, personal expressions of appreciation directly to donors, published lists of contributors, and other appropriate ways.

donor relations Planned program of maintaining donor interest through acknowledgments, information, personal involvement, and the like.

drop date Date on which direct mail letters must be delivered to a post office for mailing.

electronic funds transfer (EFT) A method whereby donors instruct their banks to make monthly deductions from their accounts, designated for the charitable organization of their choice.

employee matching gift A contribution made by an employee to a 501(c)(3) organization, matched by a similar contribution from the employer.

endowment (pure) Principal or corpus maintained in a permanent fund to provide income for general or restricted use of an agency, institution, or program.

endowment (quasi) A fund, the principal of which can be and often is invaded by a board in order to meet its operating costs. Such endowments include gifts for which donors specify their use; they may also include gifts that are given for no specific purpose, which a board treats as an endowment.

enlistment Involvement and agreement by an individual to serve an agency, organization, or institution in some voluntary capacity.

estate The total assets of a deceased person; also, the legal status or position of an owner with respect to property and other assets.

ethics The moral considerations of the activities of a philanthropic organization. Also, standards of conduct and methods of doing business by organizations of fundraising counsel that provide assurances of professionalism in client relationships.

face-to-face solicitation Soliciting a prospective contributor at the prospect's home or office or other location.

family foundation A foundation whose funds are derived from members of a single family. Generally, family members serve as officers or board members of the foundation and play an influential role in grantmaking decisions.

feasibility study An in-depth examination and assessment of the fundraising potential of an institution or agency, conducted by fundraising counsel and presented in the form of a written report setting forth various conclusions, recommendations, and proposed plans.

foundation See *philanthropic foundation*.

fundraiser One who makes his or her living from working as a member of an organization's or institution's development department, as an independent fundraising consultant or as a member of a fundraising counseling firm; a volunteer who raises funds for a cause is also referred to as a fundraiser; a fundraising event has come to be called a fundraiser.

fundraising counsel An individual operating as an independent, or a firm organized specifically for the purpose of counseling charitable institutions in all aspects of fundraising.

fundraising executive An individual employed by an institution or organization to provide direction, counsel, and management of its fundraising operations.

fundraising plan All of those elements comprised by an organization's procedure for attaining a campaign goal: a fundraising program, including objectives, case, leadership requirements, timetable, personnel requirements, and budget; and the overall strategy or grand design for successful implementation of a campaign.

fundraising program An organization's or institution's strategy, tactics, objectives, case, and needs in their entirety; a campaign that is loosely defined in terms of time frame and specific funding opportunities; a campaign; a timetable for a campaign.

GAAP An acronym for "generally accepted accounting principles."

gift A voluntary, irrevocable transfer of something of value without consideration at the time of transfer or any time in the future. If the individual making the gift entertains any ideas of reclaiming it, the transfer is not a gift.

gift annuity A contract between the donor and the charity wherein the donor transfers property to the charity in exchange for the charity's promise to pay the donor a fixed annual income for life or some other mutually agreed-upon period. The donor's right to income may be deferred for a period of years. The annuity may be in joint and survivor form.

gift-in-kind A contribution of equipment or other property on which the donor may place a monetary value and claim a deduction for income tax purposes.

gift range chart A chart of gifts that enables campaign leaders to know, in advance of a campaign, the size and number of gifts likely to be needed at each level of giving in order to achieve the campaign goal. The chart focuses the attention of campaign leaders on the sequence of gifts that will be needed.

gift receipt A form that is send to donors (with copies to appropriate officials of the campaign and organization or institution), either separately or as an enclosure with acknowledgement, officially recognizing their contributions.

gifts Any of the following types of charitable donations:

1. Advance: Strategically important gifts solicited in advance of the formal public beginning of an intensive campaign to ensure a level of giving equal to the requirements of the campaign dollar objective.

2. Big, leadership, key, strategic gift: Terms used interchangeably to indicate substantial or largest gifts—generally of six or seven figures—required to provide the stimulus for a major campaign.
3. Major gifts: In an intensive campaign, *major* refers to gifts below the level of *big* or *leadership* gifts and above the level of *general* gifts.
4. General gifts: Final 5 to 20 percent of funds raised through a multitude of gifts from constituencies or through a wrap-up mail campaign.

giving clubs Categories of donors who are grouped and recognized by the recipient organization or institution on the basis of similar gift level.

goal A concerted focus for an effort supported by specific objectives that an organization determines to achieve; the amount of money to be achieved by a fundraising campaign—that is, the dollar objective.

governance Oversight by those persons who constitute the governing authority of an organization or institution.

grant Generally an allocation from a foundation, corporation, or government agency.

grassroots fundraising Raising modest amounts of money from individuals or groups from the local community on a broad basis. Usually done within a specific constituency or among people who live in the neighborhood served or who are clients. Common grassroots fundraising activities include membership drives, raffles, bake sales, auctions, benefits, and dances.

house file The names and addresses of active and recently lapsed donors and members of an organization.

identification The process of ascertaining, through investigation, research, and analysis, which of various candidates appear to be most promising as prospective leaders, workers, and donors.

independent sector A term used to describe all nonprofit organizations, as distinct from government and corporations formed to make a profit, also called the *third sector*; not to be confused with the organization Independent Sector.

indicia Mark on an envelope indicating a nonprofit mailing permit for reduced rate bulk mailing; used in place of stamps or meters.

involvement The calculated effort, perennially undertaken by development offices, to stimulate interest and enthusiasm on the part of prospective donors and candidates for volunteer leadership through active participation in institutional affairs; an extension of cultivation.

intestate Without a will.

LAI principle The fundraising axiom of qualifying prospects on the basis of Linkages, Ability, and Interest.

leadership The force within an institution, agency, program, or fundraising campaign that stimulates others to act or give.

leadership gift Normally, the second tier of gifts to a campaign that will inspire extraordinary giving by subsequent donors.

legacy A disposition in a will of personal property. A *demonstrative legacy* is a legacy payable primarily out of a specific fund. A *specific legacy* is a legacy of a particular article or specified part of the estate.

letter of inquiry A letter sent by an organization to a foundation or corporation presenting a project for which funding is being sought and asking the foundation or corporation if they will consider funding the project or receiving a full proposal.

letter of intent A pledge form stated in less formal, nonlegalistic terms for use by potential donors who view the pledge card as a contract and refuse to commit themselves to multiple-year gift payments because of this contractual aspect.

LIA principle The fundraising axiom of separating advocates and askers from donors on the basis of Linkage, Involvement, and Advocacy.

life income gift An irrevocable gift of cash, securities, or real estate to a gift-supported organization, with the donor receiving income from the donated assets for a period of time through an annuity or trust arrangement for him- or herself or other beneficiaries.

life income pooled trusts A charitable remainder trust that holds the commingled irrevocable gifts of donors who receive income annually based on the earnings of the trust and their individual entitlement as participants. On termination of an income interest, the underlying property is transferred to a charitable organization or institution.

life insurance gifts The irrevocable assignment of a life insurance policy for charitable disposition for which the present value is fully tax-deductible, as are the premiums paid by the donor.

life interest An interest or claim that does not amount to ownership and that is held only for the duration of the life of the person to whom the interest is given or for the duration of the life of another person; an interest in property for life.

LYBUNTS Acronym for donors who gave "last year but not this" year.

major gifts A gift of significant amount (size of gift may vary according to organization's needs and goals); may be repeated periodically. Also a program designation.

market Potential source of funds, members, or clients (individuals and organizations).

matching gift A gift that is made on condition that it be matched within a certain period, either on a one-to-one basis or in accordance with some other formula; also a gift by a corporation matching a gift by one of its employees.

memorial Gift made to perpetuate the memory of an individual. *Memorial* should not be confused with a gift to honor a living person.

mission A philosophical or value statement that seeks to respond to the "why" of the organization's existence, its basic reason for being. Mission statement is not defined in expressions of goals or objectives.

needs In fundraising terms, refers specifically to the institution's dollar requirements that can constitute objectives for an intensive campaign or for a continuing fund development program, as follows:

1. Capital: Building or property needs, in the form of new construction, additions, expansion, or remodeling or acquisition of property. Sometimes related to equipment purchase or to raising funds for an addition to endowment capital.
2. Endowment: Funds required to add to the invested principal or corpus with only income used for sustaining funds, special project support, and so on.
3. Program: Annual support for the operational budget; funds required to supplement income through revenues to sustain operation of the agency or institution.
4. Project: Refers to program activity or small equipment acquisition.
5. Validated: Needs that have been identified, analyzed, and approved by management and by the governing body and other volunteers as being valid and appropriate to the functioning of the institution.

nonprofit (or not-for-profit) organization Organizations of members or volunteers, classified by the Internal Revenue Service as providing a public benefit without purpose of profit for members of the corporation.

NSFRE (now AFP) National Society of Fund Raising Executives (formerly; now Association of Fundraising Professionals).

operating foundation A fund or endowment designated by the Internal Revenue Service as a private foundation, yet which differs from a typical private foundation in that its primary purpose is to conduct research, promote social welfare, or engage in other programs determined by its governing body or establishment charter. It may make some grants, but the sum is generally small relative to the funds used for the foundation's own programs.

outright gift The simple transfer of gift property to the donee without any conditions or terms of trust.

philanthropic foundation A corporation or trust that has been created through contributed funds, whether by an individual, family, corporation, or community, for support of nonprofit organizations, and to which such organizations may appeal for grants in support of their programs and projects.

philanthropist Broadly speaking, anyone who makes a gift, but usually used to describe a wealthy individual known for his or her exceptional generosity in support of charitable causes.

philanthropy As used at the Center on Philanthropy, voluntary action for the public good, including voluntary service, voluntary association, and voluntary giving.

planned gift A gift provided for legally during the donor's lifetime, but whose principal benefits do not accrue to the institution until some future time, usually at the death of the donor or his or her income beneficiary.

planned giving The application of sound personal, financial, and estate planning concepts to the individual donor's plans for lifetime and testamentary giving.

pledge A signed and dated commitment to make a gift over a specified period, generally two or more years, payable according to terms set by the donor, with scheduled monthly, quarterly, semi-annual, or annual payments.

private foundation Although there is a technical definition of *private foundation* in the federal income tax law, the generic definition of the term is as follows: A private foundation is a 501(c)(3) organization that is originally funded from one source, that derives revenue from earnings on its investments, and that makes grants to other charitable organizations as opposed to administering its own programs. Gifts to private foundations are not normally as advantageous to the donors as gifts to a public charity.

proposal A written request or application for a gift or grant that includes why the project or program is needed, who will carry it out, and how much it will cost.

prospective donor Any logical source of support, whether individual, corporation, organization, government at all levels, or foundation; emphasis is on the logic of support.

public charity A 501(c)(3) organization that is not a private foundation, because it either is "publicly supported" (that is, it normally derives at least one-third of its support from gifts and other qualified sources) or functions as a "supporting organization" to other public charities. Some public charities engage in grantmaking activities, but most engage in direct service activities. Public charities are eligible for maximum tax-deductible contributions from the public and are not subject to the same rules and regulations as private foundations. They are also referred to as *public foundations*.

rating An evaluation or "guesstimate" of a prospective contributor's ability to contribute. The rating becomes an asking figure for the solicitor to suggest in requesting a contribution or pledge.

real estate gifts The transfer of property to a 501 (c)(3) organization or institution, the value of which is determined by the fair market value of the property.

recognition Formal or informal acknowledgment of a gift or contributed services; an event, communication, or significant item honoring a gift or a service.

renewal mailing A mailing to donors or members requesting renewed support.

restricted fund A fund in which the principal and earnings are bound by donor guidelines as they relate to investment or expenditure or both.

restricted gift A gift for a specified purpose clearly stated by the donor.

screening The process of assigning prospects to broad categories of potential giving ranges, preliminary to conducting more refined evaluations through the process of prospect rating.

seed money A substantial gift, generally by a foundation or an affluent individual, to launch a program or project.

sequential giving A cardinal principle of fundraising counsel: gifts in a campaign should be sought "from the top down"; that is, the largest gifts in a gift range chart should be sought at the outset of a campaign, followed sequentially by the search for lesser gifts.

social media The widely available electronic tools that generate interaction, participation, and collaboration, including blogs, videos, podcasts, photo sharing, and the use of social networks.

solicitor(s) Volunteers and institutional staff who ask for contributions to a campaign or development program; professional solicitors are paid to solicit for programs or causes.

special event A fundraising function designed to attract and involve large numbers of people for the purpose of raising money or cultivating donors.

special gifts Gifts that fall within the fourth tier of giving to a campaign; gifts that require special attention by the recipient organization in order to attract donor participation.

standard of giving Arbitrary but generally realistic assignment of giving potential to groups or categories of prospects, based on past performances and other criteria.

stewardship The guiding principle in philanthropic fundraising. Stewardship is defined as the philosophy and means by which an institution exercises ethical accountability in the use of contributed resources and the philosophy and means by which a donor exercises responsibility in the voluntary use of resources.

strategic plan A program incorporating a strategy for achieving organizational goals and objectives within a specific time frame and with substantive support in the form of methods, priorities, and resources.

support services Full range of activity required to support a fundraising effort: office management; word processing; gift receiving, posting, and acknowledging; budget management and control; and so on.

tax benefits Savings in income, gift, and estate taxes brought about by giving to charitable institutions.

telemarketing Raising funds or selling products or services by telephone.

telephone-mail campaign A fundraising technique, often referred to as *phone mail*, that combines mail and telephone solicitation in a sophisticated manner through the use of paid solicitors and management of the program; a telephone solicitation supported by a mail component for confirmation of verbal pledges.

third sector Used to describe all nonprofit organizations and institutions. Also known as the *independent sector*, not to be confused with the organization called Independent Sector.

timing Determination of the most favorable times to complete certain fundraising objectives in order to achieve maximum results.

trust A fiduciary relationship with respect to property, subjecting the person who holds the title to property to equitable duties to deal with the property for the benefit of another person. For example: A gives property in trust, with A as trustee, to pay income to B for life and then to give property over to C, free and clear.

trust funds Money, securities, property held in trust by an agent of wealth (bank, estate manager, attorney) or managed by an institution under trust agreement to produce income for the beneficiary.

trustee A person or agent of a trust, such as a bank, holding legal title to property in order to administer it for a beneficiary; a member of a governing board; in a corporate trust, the "directors."

unrestricted gift A gift to an institution or agency for whatever purposes officers or trustees choose.

vehicle The particular form in which a fundraising program is organized and executed; for example, annual giving, capital campaign, or direct mail.

volunteerism The willingness of private citizens to serve voluntarily a great variety of programs and causes, both in fundraising programs and in other capacities.

wills Normally a legally executed written instrument by which a person makes disposition of his or her property to take effect after death. *Holographic will*: A will entirely written and signed by the testator or maker in his or her own hand. *Nuncupative will*: An oral will made by a person in his or her last illness or extremity before a witness, often not honored in a court of law. *Pour-over will*: A will whereby assets controlled by the will are directed to be poured over into a trust. *Reciprocal wills*: Wills made by two persons in which each leaves everything to the other.

REFERENCES

AFP Compensation & Benefits Survey. Arlington, Va.: Association of Fundraising Professionals, 2009.

AFP Fundraising Dictionary. Alexandria, Va.: Association of Fundraising Professionals, 2003.

American Marketing Association. "Definition of Marketing." [http://www.marketingpower.com/AboutAMA/Pages/DefinitionofMarketing.aspx]. 2009.

Anderson, A. *Ethics for Fundraisers.* Indianapolis, Ind.: Indiana University Press, 1996.

Andreasen, A. R. "Cross-Sector Marketing Alliances: Partnerships, Sponsorships, and Cause-Related Marketing." In J. J. Cordes and C. E. Steuerle (eds.), *Nonprofits and Business.* Washington, D.C.: Urbana Institute Press, 2009.

Andreasen, A. R., and Kotler, P. *Strategic Marketing for Nonprofit Organizations* (7th ed.). Edgewood Cliffs, N.J.: Prentice Hall, 2007.

Anft, M. "Tapping Ethnic Wealth." *Chronicle of Philanthropy,* Jan. 10, 2002.

Antigua, M. "Turning the Tide: Successfully Preparing Millennials and the Organizations They Serve to Lead." Paper presented at the AmeriCorps Best Practices Conference, Arlington, Va., May 2009.

Appert, E., and Erickson, D. "Millennials and Micropayments: Social Giving and ePhilanthropy." Paper presented at the Minnesota Council on Nonprofits Conference, St. Paul, Minn., Oct. 2008.

Aristotle. *Nicomachean Ethics.* (T. Irwin, trans.). Indianapolis, Ind.: Hackett Publishing, 1999.

Arndt, W. F., and Gingrich, F. W. *A Greek-English Lexicon of the New Testament and Other Early Christian Literature.* Chicago: University of Chicago Press, 1957.

Arsenault, P. M. "Validating Generational Differences: A Legitimate Diversity and Leadership Issue." *Leadership & Organization Development Journal,* 2004, *25*(2), 124–141.

Austin, J. E. *The Collaboration Challenge.* San Francisco: Jossey-Bass, 2000.

Barton, N., and Wasley, P. "Online Giving Slows." *Chronicle of Philanthropy*, May 7, 2008.

Basile, F. Personal interview. Nov. 11, 2009.

Baumeister, R. F. *The Meaning of Life*. New York: Guilford, 1991.

Bennis, W. "Lessons in Leadership from Superconsultant Warren Bennis." *Bottom Line Personal*, July 1, 1996.

Bethel, S. M. *Beyond Management to Leadership: Designing the 21st Century Association*. Washington, D.C.: Foundation of the American Society of Association Executives, 1993.

Better Business Bureau Wise Giving Alliance. *Standard for Charity Accountability*. [http://www .bbb.org/us/Charity-Standards/]. 2003.

Beyel, J. "Ethics and Major Gifts." *New Directions for Philanthropic Fundraising*, no. 16, 50–57. San Francisco: Jossey-Bass, 1997.

Bick, J. "Write a Check? The New Philanthropist Goes Further." *New York Times*, Mar. 17, 2007.

Bishop, M., and Green, M. *Philanthrocapitalism*. New York: Bloomsbury Press, 2008.

Black, S. S. "Native American Philanthropy." In P. C. Rogers (ed.), *Philanthropy in Communities of Color*, ARNOVA Occasional Paper Series, 2001, *1*(1).

Blackwood, A., Wing, K. T., and Pollak, T. H. *The Nonprofit Sector in Brief: Facts and Figures from the Nonprofit Almanac 2008: Public Charities, Giving and Volunteering*. Washington, D.C.: National Center for Charitable Statistics at the Urban Institute, 2008.

Bloland, H. G., and Bornstein, R. "Fundraising in Transition: The Professionalization of an Administrative Occupation." In *Taking Fund Raising Seriously: Papers Prepared for the Third Annual Symposium, Indiana University Center on Philanthropy, University Place Conference Center, Indiana University-Purdue University at Indianapolis, June 6–8, 1990*. Indianapolis, Ind., 1990.

Bloland, H. G., and Tempel, E. R. "Measuring Professionalism." *New Directions for Philanthropic Fundraising*, no. 43, 5–20. San Francisco: Jossey-Bass, 2004.

Blum, D. E. "Making a Place for Arab-Americans." *Chronicle of Philanthropy*, Jan. 10, 2002.

Brest, P., and Harvey, H. *Money Well Spent: A Strategic Plan for Smart Philanthropy*. New York: Bloomberg, 2008.

Brinckerhoff, P. C. *Generations: The Challenge of a Lifetime for Your Nonprofit*. St. Paul, Minn.: Fieldstone Alliance, 2007.

Brogan, C. *Social Media 101*. Hoboken, N.J.: Wiley, 2010.

Brown, E. "Married Couples' Charitable Giving: Who and Why." In M. A. Taylor and S. Shaw-Hardy (eds.), *The Transformative Power of Women's Philanthropy*. San Francisco: Wiley Periodicals, 2006.

Brown, M. S., and Rooney, P. "Men, Women, X and Y: Gender and Generational Differences in Motivations for Giving." Paper presented at the symposium "Moving Women's Philanthropy Forward: Influences, Intent, Impact." Center on Philanthropy at Indiana University, Indianapolis, Ind., 2008.

Buber, M. *I and Thou* (2nd ed.). (R. G. Smith, trans.). New York: Scribner, 1958.

Bureau of Labor Statistics. *Highlights of Women's Earnings in 2007*. [http://www.bls.gove/cps/ cpswom2007.pdf/]. 2008.

Burk, P. *Donor-Centered Fundraising*. Chicago: Cygnus Applied Research, 2003.

Burlingame, D. F. "Corporate Giving and Fund Raising." In E. R. Tempel (ed.), *Hank Rosso's Achieving Excellence in Fund Raising* (2nd ed.). San Francisco: Jossey-Bass, 2003.

Burlingame, D. F., and Young, D. R. *Corporate Philanthropy at the Crossroads*. Bloomington, Ind.: Indiana University Press, 1996.

Business Civic Leadership Center. *Corporate Community Investment Study*. Washington, D.C.: U.S. Chamber of Commerce, 2008.

Campobasso, L., and Davis, D. *Reflections on Capacity-Building*. Woodland Hills, CA: California Wellness Foundation, 2001.

Carbone, R. F. *Fundraising as a Profession*. College Park, Md.: Clearing House for Research on Fund Raising, 1989.

————. "Licensure and Credentialing as Professionalizing Elements." *New Directions for Philanthropic Fundraising*, no. 15, 83–96. San Francisco: Jossey-Bass, 1997.

Carson, E. D. "On Race, Gender, Culture and Research on the Voluntary Sector." *Nonprofit Management & Leadership*. San Francisco: Jossey-Bass, 1993.

Carson, E. D. "The New Rules for Engaging Donors of Color: Giving in the Twenty-First Century." In E. R. Tempel and D. F. Burlingame (eds.), *Understanding the Needs of Donors: The Supply Side of Charitable Giving*. New Directions for Philanthropic Fundraising, no. 29. San Francisco: Jossey-Bass, 2000.

The Center on Philanthropy. *Bank of America Study of High Net-Worth Individuals: Initial Report*. Indianapolis, Ind.: The Trustees of Indiana University. 2006.

————. *Corporate Philanthropy: The Age of Integration*. Indianapolis, Ind.: The Trustees of Indiana University. [http://www.philanthropy.iupui.edu/Research/giving_fundraising_research.aspx#CorporateGiving]. 2007a.

————. *Philanthropic Giving Index: Summer 2007*. Indianapolis, Ind.: The Trustees of Indiana University, 2007b.

————. *Portraits of Donors: Bank of America Study of High Net-Worth Philanthropy*. Indianapolis, Ind.: The Trustees of Indiana University, 2007c.

————. *Giving USA 2008*. Indianapolis, Ind.: Giving USA Foundation, 2008b.

————. *The 2008 Study of High Net Worth Philanthropy*. Indianapolis, Ind.: The Trustees of Indiana University, 2009a.

————. *Giving USA 2009*. Indianapolis, Ind.: Giving USA Foundation, 2009b.

————. *National Donor Survey*. The Center on Philanthropy, Indiana University, 2009c.

————. *Philanthropic Giving Index: Summer 2009*. Indianapolis, Ind.: The Trustees of Indiana University, 2009d.

————. *Generational Difference in Charitable Giving and Motivations for Giving: A Study for Campbell & Company*. [http://www.campbellcompany.com/articles.html]. Jan. 2010.

————. *Giving USA 2010*. Indianapolis, Ind.: Giving USA Foundation, 2010.

Certified Fund Raising Executive (CFRE) International. "Certification vs. Certificate" [http://www.cfre.org/pdf/Certificate-vs-%20Certification.pdf]. Dec. 2001.

————. CFRE certification form. [http://app.cfre.org/Memberships.php]. Nov. 2007.

————. *CFRE Job Analysis*. Washington, D.C.: CFRE International, 2009.

Chobot, R. B. "Fundraising Credentialing." *New Directions for Philanthropic Fundraising*, no. 43, 31–50. San Francisco: Jossey-Bass, 2004.

Chrislip, D. D., and Larson, C. E. *Collaborative Leadership: How Citizens and Civic Leaders Make a Difference*. San Francisco: Jossey-Bass, 1994.

Cohen, T. "Nonprofit Training Seen Trailing Demand." *Philanthropy Journal*, May 2007.

Collin, N. "5 Reasons Creatives Hate Working for You." [http://ezinearticles.com/?5-Reasons-Creatives-Hate-Working-For-You-(And-What-to-Do-About-It)&id=3279820]. 2009.

Collins, J. "Level 5 Leadership: The Triumph of Humility and Fierce Resolve." *Harvard Business Review*, January 2001.

Committee Encouraging Corporate Philanthropy. *Giving in Numbers*. Washington, D.C.: Committee Encouraging Corporate Philanthropy, 2008.

Cone, Inc. *Cone/Roper Trends Report: The Evolution of Cause Branding Executive Summary*. Boston: Cone LLC, 2000. [http://www.coneinc.com/content1084].

Connell, J. E. "Budgeting for Fund Raising." In J. M. Greenfield (ed.), *The Nonprofit Handbook: Fund Raising* (3rd ed.). New York: Wiley, 2001.

Conway, D. "Practicing Stewardship." In E. R. Tempel (ed.), *Hank Rosso's Achieving Excellence in Fund Raising* (2nd ed.). San Francisco: Jossey-Bass, 2003.

Corbo, S. A. "The X-er Files." *Hospitals & Health Networks*, 1997, *71*(7), 58–60.

Cordeniz, J. A. "Recruitment, Retention, and Management of Generation X: A Focus on Nursing Professionals." *Journal of Healthcare Management*, 2002, *47*(4), 237–249.

Corporation for National and Community Service. *Volunteering in America Research Highlights*. [http://www.volunteeringinamerica.gov/]. Jan. 2010.

Cortes, M. "Fostering Philanthropy and Service in U.S. Latino Communities." In P. C. Rogers (ed.), *Philanthropy in Communities of Color*, ARNOVA Occasional Paper Series, 2001, *1*(1).

Court, D., Farrell, D., and Forsyth, J. E. "Serving Aging Baby Boomers." *McKinsey Quarterly*, Nov. 2007.

Covey, S.M.R. *The Speed of Trust*. New York: Free Press, 2006.

Crampton, S. M., and Hodge, J. W. *Managing Generation Y*. Presented at the ABR & TLC Conference, Orlando, Fla., 2008.

Craver, Mathews, Smith & Company and The Prime Group. "Boomers! Navigating the Generational Divide in Fundraising & Advocacy." [http://cravermathewssmith.com/wp-content/uploads/2008/07/boomer_study.pdf]. Aug. 2005.

Cutlip, S. M. *Fund Raising in the United States: Its Role in America's Philanthropy*. New Brunswick, N.J.: Rutgers University Press, 1965.

Demographics Now. Table of the United States' Population, Age by Sex Summary Report. [http://www.demographicsnow.com]. Jan. 2010.

Donor Pulse. Valencia, Va.: Campbell Rinker, 2008.

Drucker, P. F. *Managing the Nonprofit Organization*. New York: HarperCollins, 1990.

Dunlop, D. R. "Fundraising for the Largest Gift of a Lifetime: From Inspiring the Commitment to Receiving the Gift." Presented at the Council for Advancement and Support of Education (CASE) Conference, Charleston, S.C., May, 2000.

Duronio, M. A., and Tempel, E. R. *Fund Raisers: Their Careers, Stories, Concerns, and Accomplishments*. San Francisco: Jossey-Bass, 1996.

Edwards, P., and Wood, E. "The 'Inner-Game' Attitude of Major-Gift Solicitation." *Nonprofit World*, Mar.–Apr. 1992, pp. 11–14.

Elliot, D. "What Counts as Deception in Higher Education Development." In D. F. Burlingame and L. J. Hulse (eds.), *Taking Fund Raising Seriously*. San Francisco: Jossey-Bass, 1991.

Ellis, S. J., and Noyes, K. H. *By the People: A History of Americans as Volunteers*. San Francisco: Jossey-Bass, 1990.

Email Marketers Association, "Four Tips on How to Use Email Marketing During a Down Economy," Network for Good Learning Center. [http://www.fundraising123.org/article/four-tips-how-use-email-marketing-during-a-down-economy-0]. February 25, 2009.

Estes, J., and Nielsen, J. *Donor Usability: Increasing Online Giving to Non-Profits and Charities*. Fremont, Calif.: Nielsen Norman Group, 2009.

Fabrikant, G. "Charities Seek Donors to Replace Wall Street." *New York Times*, Apr. 12, 2008.

Facebook Press Room. [http://www.facebook.com/press/info.php?statistics]. 2010.

Feldmann, D. "Get Specific to Engage Next-Generation Donors." [http://www.achieveguidance.com/page/mar2010]. Mar. 2010.

Fischer, M. *Ethical Decision Making in Fund Raising*. New York: Wiley, 2000.

Fishman, J. J., and Schwarz, S. *Nonprofit Organizations*. New York: Thomson West, 2006.

Fogal, R. "Standards and Ethics in Fund Raising." In H. A. Rosso and Associates (eds.), *Achieving Excellence in Fund Raising* (1st ed.). San Francisco: Jossey-Bass, 1991.

"For the Record." Boston Globe. [http://www.boston.com/news/nation/articles/2009/10/27/for_the_record/]. Oct. 27, 2009.

Forum of Regional Association of Grantmakers. "Donors of the Future: Scanning Project Report." [http://www.givingforum.org/s_forum/bin.asp?CID=157&DID=5385&DOC=FILE.PDF]. Mar. 2006.

Foundation Center. *Foundation Growth and Giving Estimates*. New York, 2001.

———. *Foundation Growth and Giving Estimates*. New York, 2007.

———. *Key Facts on Family Foundations*. New York, 2009.

———. *Foundations Address the Impact of the Economic Crisis*. [http://foundationcenter.org/gainknowledge/research/pdf/researchadvisory_economy_200904.pdf]. Apr. 2009.

Frank, A. W. *The Renewal of Generosity: Illness, Medicine, and How to Live*. Chicago: The University of Chicago Press, 2004.

Frantzreb, A. C. "Seeking the Big Gift." In H. A. Rosso and Associates (eds.), *Achieving Excellence in Fund Raising* (1st ed.). San Francisco: Jossey-Bass, 1991.

Fredericks, L. *Developing Major Gifts: Turning Small Donors into Big Contributors*. Sudbury, Mass.: Jones and Bartlett, 2006.

Friedman, M. "The Social Responsibility of Business Is to Increase Its Profits." *New York Times Magazine*, Sept. 13, 1970, pp. 122–126.

The Fund Raising School. *Developing Major Gifts*. Indianapolis, Ind.: The Fund Raising School, 2009a.

———. *Principles and Techniques of Fund Raising*. Indianapolis, Ind.: The Fund Raising School, 2009b.

Galaskiewicz, J., and Colman, M. S. "Collaboration Between Corporations and Nonprofit Organizations." In W. W. Powel and R. Steinberg (eds.), *The Nonprofit Sector: A Research Handbook* (2nd ed.). New Haven, Conn.: Yale University Press, 2006.

Gardner, J. *On Leadership*. New York: The Free Press, 1990.

Garber, S. "The Fund Raising Professional: An Agent for Change." Paper presented at the International Conference for the Association of Healthcare Philanthropy, Chicago, Oct. 1993.

Gelb, M. J. *How to Think Like Leonardo da Vinci: Seven Steps to Genius Every Day*. New York: Dell, 1998.

Gilmore, J. H., and Pine, B. J., II. *Authenticity*. Boston: Harvard Business School Press, 2007.

Gladwell, M. *The Tipping Point: How Little Things Can Make a Big Difference*. New York: Little, Brown, 2000.

Godin, S. *Big Red Fez: How to Make Any Web Site Better*. New York: Fireside, 2002.

Gourville, J. T., and Rangan, V. K. "Valuing the Cause Marketing Relationship." *California Management Review*, 2004, *47*(1), 38–56.

Greenberg, J. M. "Forms of Bias." In *Building Bridges with Reliable Information: A Guide to Our Community's People*. Washington, D.C.: National Conference for Community and Justice of the National Capital Area Region, 2002.

Hager, M. A. *Exploring Measurement and Evaluation Efforts in Fundraising: New Directions for Philanthropic Fundraising*, no. 41. San Francisco: Jossey-Bass, 2004.

Hall, D. J. *The Steward: A Biblical Symbol Come of Age*. Grand Rapids, Mich.: Eerdmans, 1990.

Hall, H. "Evaluating How Well a Fund Raiser Does in Luring Big Gifts." *Chronicle of Philanthropy*, Oct. 1, 2007a.

———. "New Guidelines Clarify Companies' Responsibilities to Charity Clients." *Chronicle of Philanthropy*, Nov. 1, 2007b.

———. "Red Cross Retools Its Fund Raising to Overcome a Troubled Financial Picture." *Chronicle of Philanthropy*, Oct. 29, 2009, p. 23.

Hall-Russell, C., and Kasberg, R. H. *African American Traditions of Giving and Serving: A Midwest Perspective*. Indianapolis, Ind.: The Center on Philanthropy at Indiana University, 1997.

Hammarskjöld, D. *Markings*. New York: Ballantine Books, 1983.

Hodgkinson, V. "Individual Volunteering and Giving." In L. Salamon (ed.), *The State of Nonprofit America*. Washington, D.C.: Brookings Institution Press, 2002a.

———. *The Law of Fundraising*. New York: Wiley, 2002b.

Hopkins, B. R., "Standards Enforcements by Watchdog Agencies," *The Law of Fundraising*, Hoboken, N.J.: John Wiley and Sons, Inc., 2002.

Hornblower, M. "Great Xpectations." *Time*, 1997, *149*(23), 58–68.

IEG Sponsorship Report. IEG, LLC. [http://www.sponsorship.com/iegsr/]. May 2009.

Independent Sector. *Giving and Volunteering in the United States*. Washington, D.C., 1996.

———. "Public Policy Update: Special Report." [http://www.independentsector.org/programs/OldPPU/ppu_specialsanctions.pdf.]. July 1998.

———. Ethics and the Nation's Voluntary and Philanthropic Community: Obedience to the Unenforceable. Washington, D.C., 2002.

———. *Principles of Good Governance and Ethical Practice*. Washington, D.C., 2007.

Internal Revenue Service. *Personal Wealth Tables 2004*. Washington, D.C.: Internal Revenue Service, 2008.

Jackson, W. J. *The Wisdom of Generosity: A Reader in American Philanthropy*. Waco, Tex.: Baylor University Press, 2008.

Jaschik, S. "Price Check." *CASE CURRENTS*, Jan. 3, 2005.

Josephson, M. *Making Ethical Decisions*. Marina Del Ray, Calif.: Joseph and Edna Josephson Institute on Ethics, 2002.

Joslyn, H. "Foundations Report Increase in Number of Paid Staff Members." *Chronicle of Philanthropy*, Oct. 4, 2001, p. 68.

Kahn, R. L., and Katz, D. *The Social Psychology of Organizations*. New York: Wiley, 1978.

Kalata, P. "Generational Clash in the Academy: Whose Culture Is It Anyway?" In *Issues of Education at Community Colleges: Essays by Fellows in the Mid-Career Fellowship Program at Princeton University*. Princeton, N.J.: Princeton University, 1996.

Kearns, K. P. *Managing for Accountability: Preserving the Public Trust in Public and Nonprofit Organizations*. San Francisco: Jossey-Bass, 1996.

Kelly, K. S. *Effective Fund-Raising Management*. Mahway, N.J.: Erlbaum, 1998.

Kotler, P., and Andreasen, A. R. *Strategic Marketing for Nonprofit Organizations* (5th ed.). Englewood Cliffs, N.J.: Prentice Hall, 1996.

Kotler, P., and Fox, K.F.A. *Strategic Marketing for Educational Institutions* (2nd ed.). Englewood Cliffs, N.J.: Prentice Hall, 1995.

Kübler-Ross, E. *On Death and Dying*. New York: Simon and Schuster, 1997. (Originally published 1969.)

Kunreuther, F. "The Changing of the Guard: What Generational Differences Tell Us About Social-Change Organizations." *Nonprofit and Voluntary Sector Quarterly*, 2003, *32*(3), 450–457.

Larose, M. D. "Assets of Donor Advised Funds Totaled $12.36 Billion Last Year, Survey Finds." *Chronicle of Philanthropy*, May 30, 2002, p. 11.

Levy, J. "The Growth of Fundraising: Framing the Impact of Research and Literature on Education and Training." *New Directions for Philanthropic Fundraising*, no. 43, 21–30. San Francisco: Jossey-Bass, 2004.

Li, C., and Bernoff, J. *Groundswell: Winning in a World Transformed by Social Technologies.* Boston: Harvard Business Press, 2008.

Light, P. *How Americans View Charities: A Report on Charitable Confidence, 2008.* Washington, D.C.: Brookings Institution, 2008.

Lysakowski, L. *Nonprofit Essentials: Recruiting and Training Fundraising Volunteers.* Hoboken, N.J.: Wiley, 2005.

Matheny, R. *Major Gifts Solicitation Strategies* (2nd ed.). Washington, D.C.: CASE Books, 1999.

McCarthy, K. D. *American Creed: Philanthropy and the Rise of Civil Society 1700–1865.* Chicago: University of Chicago Press, 2003.

MacIntyre, A. *After Virtue.* Notre Dame, Ind.: University of Notre Dame Press, 1984.

Mesch, D., Rooney, P.M., Steinberg, K., & Denton, B. "The Effects of Race, Gender, and Marital Status on Giving and Volunteering in Indiana." *Nonprofit and Voluntary Sector Quarterly*, 2006, 35, 565–587.

Mesch, D., Moore, Z., and Brown, M. "The Effects of Gender and Generation on Donor Motives and Philanthropic Giving." Paper presented at the Association for Research on Nonprofit Organization and Volunteer Action, Cleveland, Ohio, 2009.

Minter, M. *Black Women and Philanthropy: Best Practices.* Paper presented at the symposium "Moving Women's Philanthropy Forward: Influences, Intent, Impact." Center on Philanthropy at Indiana University, Indianapolis, Ind., 2008.

Morris, T. *If Aristotle Ran General Motors.* New York: Henry Holt, 1997.

Musick, M. A., and Wilson, J. *Volunteers: A Social Profile.* Bloomington, Ind.: Indiana University Press, 2008.

Nanus, B., and Dobbs, S. M. *Leaders Who Make a Difference: Essential Strategies for Meeting the Nonprofit Challenge.* San Francisco: Jossey-Bass, 1999.

Newman, D. *Opening Doors: Pathways to Diverse Donors.* Washington, D.C.: Council on Foundations, 2002.

O'Neill, M. "Fund Raising as an Ethical Act." *Advancing Philanthropy*, 1993.

Parsons, P. H. "Women's Philanthropy: Motivations for Giving." (AAT 3155889) ProQuest Digital Dissertations, 2004.

Partnership for Philanthropic Planning. *Planned Giving in the United States: 2000: A Survey of Donors.* Indianapolis, Ind.: Partnership for Philanthropic Planning, 2001.

Payton, R. *Philanthropy: Voluntary Action for the Public Good.* New York: Macmillan, 1988.

Payton, R., and Moody, M. P. *Understanding Philanthropy: Its Meaning and Mission.* Bloomington, Ind.: Indiana University Press, 2008.

Pettey, J. G. *Cultivating Diversity in Fund-Raising.* The AFP/Wiley Fund Development Series. San Francisco: Jossey-Bass, 2002.

———. *Ethical Fundraising: A Guide for Nonprofit Boards and Fundraisers.* Hoboken, N.J.: Wiley, 2008.

Pew Research Center for The People & The Press. *How Young People View Their Lives, Futures, and Politics: A Portrait of "Generation Next."* Washington, D.C.: Pew Research Center for The People & The Press, 2007.

"The Philanthropy 50: America's Biggest Donors of 2008." *Chronicle of Philanthropy*, Jan. 29, 2009.

Pine, B. J., II, and Gilmore, J. H. *The Experience Economy.* Boston: Harvard Business School Press, 1999.

Pink, D. H. *Drive: The Moral Foundations of Trust.* Cambridge, Mass.: Cambridge University Press, 2009.

Pribbenow, P. P. "Public Service: Renewing the Moral Meaning of Professions in America." Unpublished doctoral dissertation, University of Chicago, Divinity School, Chicago, 1993.

———. "Love and Work: Rethinking Our Models of Professions." *New Directions for Philanthropic Fundraising*, no. 26, 29–50. San Francisco: Jossey-Bass, 1999a.

Reis, T. K., and Clohesy, S. J. "Unleashing New Resources and Entrepreneurship for the Common Good: A Philanthropic Renaissance." *Foundations in Europe.* Bertelsmann Foundation, 2001.

Ritzenhein, D. N. 2000. "One More Time: How Do You Motivate Donors?" In E. R. Tempel and D. W. Burlingame (eds.), *New Directions for Philanthropic Fundraising*, no. 29, 51–68. San Francisco: Jossey-Bass, Fall 2000.

Rodriguez, R. O., Green, M. T., and Ree, M. J.. "Leading Generation X: Do the Old Rules Apply?" *Journal of Leadership and Organizational Studies*, 2003, *9*(4): 67–75.

Rooney, P., Brown, E., and Mesch, D.. "Who Decides in Giving to Education? A Study of Charitable Giving by Married Couples." *International Journal of Educational Advancement*, 2007, *7*(3): 229–242.

Rosso, H. A. *Achieving Excellence in Fund Raising.* San Francisco: Jossey-Bass, 1991.

Sargeant, A., and Jay, E. *Building Donor Loyalty: The Fundraiser's Guide to Increasing Lifetime Value.* San Francisco: Jossey-Bass, 2004.

Saxton, J., Madden, M., and Greenwood, C. *The 21st Century Donor.* London: nfpSynergy, 2007.

Schervish, P. G. "The Material Horizons of Philanthropy: New Directions for Money and Motives." In E. R. Tempel and D. F. Burlingame (eds.), *New Directions for Philanthropic Fundraising*, no. 29. New York: Wiley, 2000a.

Schervish, P. G. "The Spiritual Horizons of Philanthropy: New Directions for Money and Motives." In E. R. Tempel and D. F. Burlingame (eds.), *New Directions for Philanthropic Fundraising*, no. 29. New York: Wiley, 2000b.

Schervish, P. G., O'Herlihy, M. A., and Havens, J. J. "The Spiritual Secret of Wealth: The Inner Dynamics by Which Fortune Engenders Care." Workshop presented at the Welfare Research Institute Conference, Boston, Mass., Sept. 2001.

Schervish, P. G., and Whitaker, K. *Wealth and the Will of God: Discerning the Use of Riches in the Service of Ultimate Purpose.* Bloomington, Ind.: Indiana University Press, 2010.

Schewe, C. D., and Meredith, G. E. "Segmenting Global Markets by Generational Cohorts: Determining Motivations by Age." *Journal of Consumer Behavior*, 2004, *4*(1), 51–63.

Schwinn, E., and Sommerfield, M. "Revolving-Door Dilemma." *Chronicle of Philanthropy*, Apr. 18, 2002.

Seiler, T. L. *Developing Your Case for Support.* San Francisco: Wiley, 2001.

Shaw-Hardy, S. *Women's Giving Circles: Reflections from the Founders.* Indianapolis, Ind.: Women's Philanthropy Institute at the Center on Philanthropy at Indiana University, 2009.

Skoe, E.E.A., and others. "The Influences of Sex and Gender-Role Identity on Moral Cognition and Prosocial Personality Traits." *Sex Roles: A Journal of Research*, 2002, *46*(9–10), 295–309.

Smith, B. S., Shue, S., Vest, J. L., and Villarreal, J. *Philanthropy in Communities of Color.* Bloomington, Ind.: Indiana University Press, 1999.

Smith, D. H. *Entrusted: The Moral Responsibilities of Trusteeship.* Bloomington, Ind.: Indiana University Press, 1995.

———. *Good Intentions: Moral Obstacles and Opportunities.* Bloomington, Ind.: Indiana University Press, 2005.

Smith, H. W. "If Not Corporate Philanthropy, Then What?" *New York Law School Law Review,* 1997, *31*(3–4).

Sterling, M. *Working with Creative People in 12 Steps.* Southampton, Ont.: Chantry Island Publishing, 2005.

Steinberg, R., and Morris, D. "Ratio Discrimination in Charity Fundraising: The Inappropriate Use of Cost Ratios Has Harmful Side-Effects." *Voluntary Sector Review,* 2010.

Streisand, B. "The New Philanthropy: The Tech Economy May Have Collapsed, But Tech Millionaires Are Still Giving." *U.S. News & World Report,* June 11, 2001, pp. 40–42.

Sturtevant, W. T. *The Artful Journey; Cultivating and Soliciting the Major Gift.* Chicago: Bonus Books, 1997.

Sulek, M. "On the Classical Meaning of *Philanthropia.*" *Nonprofit and Voluntary Sector Quarterly,* 2010, *39*(2), 193–212.

Tempel, E. R. "Bigger Isn't Always Better: The Importance of Small Gifts and Small Nonprofits." *NonProfit Times,* June 15, 2008, pp. 12–13.

Tempel, E. R., and Beem, M. J. "The State of the Profession." In M. Worth (ed.), *New Strategies for Educational Fund Raising.* Washington, D.C.: American Council on Education/ Greenwood Publications, 2002.

Tempel, E. R., and Duronio, M. A. "The Demographics and Experience of Fundraisers." *New Directions for Philanthropic Fundraising,* no. 15, 49–68. San Francisco: Jossey-Bass, 1997.

Thielfoldt, D., and Scheef, D. "Generation X and the Millennials: What You Need to Know About Mentoring the Next Generations." *Law Practice Today,* Aug. 2004.

Toce, J. P., and others. *Tax Economics of Charitable Giving.* New York City: Thomson Reuters, 2010.

Tulgan, B. *Managing Generation X: How to Bring Out the Best in Young Talent* (rev. ed.). New York: Norton, 2000.

U.S. Department of Labor. *Employment Statistics.* [http://www.bls.gov/data/#wages]. 2008.

Uslaner, E. M. *The Moral Foundations of Trust.* Cambridge, Mass.: Cambridge University Press, 2002.

Vesela, V. "Center's New 2009 State of Corporate Citizenship Report Shows Corporate Responsibility Weathering the Economic Storm." Boston College Center for Corporate Citizenship. [http://blogs.bcccc.net/2009/09/center%E2%80%99s-new-2009-state-of-corporate-citizenship-report-shows-corporate-responsibility-weathering-the-economic-storm/]. Nov. 2009.

Wagner, L. *Careers in Fundraising.* New York: Wiley, 2002.

———. *Leading Up: Transformational Leadership for Fundraisers.* New York: Wiley, 2005.

———. "A Crossroads on the Path of Professionalism in Fundraising." *On Philanthropy,* Sept. 17, 2007.

Wagner, L., and Hall-Russell, C. "The Effectiveness of Fundraising Training in Hispanic Religious Organizations." In L. Wagner and A. F. Deck (eds.), *Hispanic Philanthropy: Exploring the Factors That Influence Giving and Asking. New Directions for Philanthropic Fundraising,* no. 24. San Francisco: Jossey-Bass, 1999.

Wallace, N. "Big Jump in 2009 for Network for Good." *Chronicle of Philanthropy*, Jan. 7, 2010.

Waters, R. "Measuring Stewardship in Public Relations." *Public Relations Review Journal*, 2009, *354*, 113–119.

Wilhelm, M. O., and Bekkers, R. "Helping Behavior, Dispositional Empathic Concern, and the Principle of Care." *Social Psychology Quarterly*, 2010, *73*(1), 11–32.

Wilson, M. S., Hoppe, M. H., and Sayles, L. R. *Managing Across Cultures: A Learning Framework.* Greensboro, N.C.: Center for Creative Leadership, 1996.

Witter, L. *The She Spot: Why Women Are the Market for Changing the World and How to Reach Them.* Paper presented at the symposium "Moving Women's Philanthropy Forward: Influences, Intent, Impact." Center on Philanthropy at Indiana University, Indianapolis, Ind., 2008.

Wolff, E. N. "The Rich Get Richer: And Why the Poor Don't." *American Prospect.* Feb. 12, 2001. http://www.prospect.org/cs/articles?article=the_rich_get_richer.

Wood, E. W., "Profiling Major Gifts Fundraisers: What Qualifies Them for Success." *New Directions in Philanthropic Fundraising*, no. 16, 5-15. San Francisco: Jossey-Bass, 1997.

———. *Poor Richard's Principle.* Princeton, N.J.: Princeton University Press, 1996.

Wuthnow, R. *After the Baby Boomers: How Twenty- and Thirty-Somethings Are Shaping the Future of American Religion.* Princeton, N.J.: Princeton University Press, 2002.

Yang, S., and Guy, M. E. "GenXers versus Boomers: Work Motivators and Management Implications." *Public Performance & Management Review*, 2006, *29*(3), 267–284.

Yearout, S., Miles, G., and Koonce, R. "Wanted: Leader-Builders." *Training and Development*, Mar. 2000.

INDEX

Page references followed by *fig* indicate an illustrated figure; followed by *t* indicate a table; followed by *e* indicate an exhibit.

A

Accountability, 339

AFP compensation & Benefits Survey, 433, 434

AFP Fundraising Dictionary, 150, 247, 248, 249, 250

African American philanthropy: advice for working with African American causes, 192; causes and characteristics of, 191; church as primary institution for helping others, 191; increasingly higher rates of giving of, 190; and their tendency of informal help within families, 191

African American Women's Giving Circle, exploring philanthropy in, 167

Aldrich, E. E., 27, 427, 434, 437

American Marketing Association (AMA), and ethical norms for marketers, 372–373

American Red Cross, Tiffany Circle program as pilot initiative, 170

Anderson, A., 404, 405, 407

Andreasen, A. R., 139, 146, 148, 331, 332, 363

Anft, M., 185, 188

Annual appeals, 108

Annual donor list, 127

Annual fund: as base for occasional capital campaign, 50; benefits and objectives of, 53; decisions on strategies to be pursued, 55; development process in, 54*t*; and donor bonding through recurring gifts, 43; donors committed to the organization, 112; and donors who fall below certain annual giving levels, 112; establishment of base of donors for, 51; as foundation of all successful fundraising, 43; and giving through websites or social media outlets, 62; goal of setting and achieving, 55–58; good teamwork as essential to success of, 53; methods used to solicit gifts in, 59; nurturing of contributor's interest, 52; primary function to execute, 55; principles of the arithmetic of fundraising in, 55; and procedures requiring personal contact and follow-up with each donor, 60; range of gifts dictated by gift range chart, 56; smaller gifts as less actively solicited, 56; solicitation methods in, 59–62; staff support relationship of, 53–55; and success through advertising campaigns, 62; and